Religion as Knowledge — The Hindu Concept

By the same author:

Tales and Teachings of the Mahabharat, 1998
(Bharatiya Vidya Bhavan, Mumbai)

Religion as Knowledge
The Hindu Concept

Janaki Abhisheki

AKSHAYA PRAKASHAN
NEW DELHI

First published, Bombay 1988
Second rev. ed., 2003

ISBN 81-88643-03-3

Published by Harish Chandra for Akshaya Prakashan, 208, M.G. House,
2 Community Centre, Wazirpur Industrial Area, Delhi – 110 052.
Printed at D.K. Fine Arts Press (Pvt.) Ltd., A-6, Nimri Community Centre,
Ashok Vihar Phase IV, Delhi – 110 052.

DEDICATED TO
MY PARENTS

Contents

Abbreviations

A.Br. = Aitareya Brahmana

Ap. or Ap.Dh.S. = Apastamba Dharmasutra

Ap.Gr.S. = Apastambagrhyasutra

Baud. or Bau.Dh.S. = Baudhayana-dharmasutra (Mysore edition)

Bau.Gr.S. = Baudhayanagrhysutra (Mysore edition by Dr. Shama Sastry)

Br. Upanishad or Br. Up. = Brhadaranyaka Upanishad

Dh.S. = Dharmasutra

Gau. or Gaut. = Gautama-dharmasutra

Gr.S. = Grhya-sutra

Tai. = Taittiriya

Tai.S. = Taittiriya Samhita

Vas. or Vas.Dh.S. = Vasisthadharmasutra (ed. by Dr. Jolly)

V.S. = Vedanta Sutra

Yaj. = Yajnavalkyasmrti

Chan.Up. = Chandogya Upanishad

Kaut. = Kautilya's Arthasastra

Mit. = The commentary of Mitaksara on Yajnavalkyasmriti

Pan. = Panini's Astadhyayi

Vishnu Dh.S. = Vishnu Dharma Sutra

Nar. = Naradasmrti (ed. by Dr. Jolly)

Rg. = Rig Veda

Vis. = Visvarupa

Br. = Smrti of Brhaspati
Jai. = Jaimini's Purvamimamsasutra
Kat. = Smrti of Katyayana
Medh. = Medhatithi the oldest commentator of Manusmrti
Sat.Br. = Satapatha Brahmana
Sukra = Sukranitisara
Tai.Ar. = Taittiriya Aranyaka
Tai.Br. = Taittiriya Brahmana
Tai.Up. = Taittiriya Upanisad
H.D. or H.DS. = History of Dharmasastra
Mark. = Markandeyapurana

Preface

This book is a serious attempt at informing the average Indian, and particularly the Hindu, of his philosophy, culture and heritage.

Although India's is the oldest continuous civilization, for various reasons the Hindu today is largely ignorant of his heritage. While some of the reasons for this ignorance are historical, viz., the loss of freedom, etc., some of it is due to our own neglect.

India has been free for about forty years but even today the average Hindu is largely unaware of his identity and heritage — a heritage that any people would be proud to possess. Surprisingly, this most important aspect of a people, their cultural identity, is not taught in our schools and colleges. We see ignorant attitudes, misconceptions and foolish denigration, which do little credit to a civilization that respected Knowledge above all else. It is this living heritage of knowledge that is preserved in Sanskrit literature and the many Prakrit languages.

Religion is not meant for the next world but this world itself. Hindu philosophy was concerned with knowledge, which meant a study of all material 'image,' to search for its relevance and meaning. On the basis of this philosophy the ancient Hindu thinkers worked out a practical and dynamic pattern of living based on a Law, Order and a Work Ethic.

The Hindu philosophy relating knowledge to action will be seen to have helped Hindus adapt to each age and place. It has given Hinduism its demonstrable staying power. It provided the essential needs of a civilization.

The silver lining in this otherwise bleak scene is that there are many Indians and Hindus eager to know. Unfortunately they do not know where to seek.

This writer was similarly placed some ten years ago when she started her study. She found that while there were many large volumes dealing with one or the other aspect of Hindu thought and culture, their size as well as their language made it impossible for those without the necessary leisure to study them. Their language quite often was both abstract as well as obtuse. Another kind of book was more keen on effect than information and served to misinform rather than inform. There are also the books written without proper understanding based on superficial reading and ill-digested study. These only serve to perpetuate misconceptions.

Hindu thought concerns the whole. *Dharma, artha* and *kama* with the final goal of *moksa* are the four aims of man's existence. The chapters cover the most prominent of the *Dharmasastra* works and the literature that influenced the *Dharmasastras*. Separate chapters deal with *Arthasastra* and *Kamasastra*. A chapter each on *Karma, chaturvarna* and Women in Hinduism was considered necessary for a more detailed treatment. Some of the better-known and commonly used symbols are also explained, as symbols have no meaning unless we understand their relevance. There is a chapter, even if very brief, on the contributions of ancient Hindus to world knowledge. It does no credit to a people to forget the great achievements of ancient times, and more so of their own ancestors, in adding to the knowledge of mankind. 'Some problems of Indology' was also considered necessary by the writer, as it helps to trace some of the many misconceptions that prevail today.

Philosophy by itself is not enough. Good intentions must be put into practice and that too, with skill. The rules and laws in pursuance of the philosophy were laid down by the *Dharmasastras*. M.M. Kane's monumental *History of Dharmasastra* is perhaps the best-known authority. The writer has relied on it as her authority and frequently quoted it as reference.

This book consists of twenty chapters apart from the Introduction. The chapters are, *A Brief Historical Background*, *Sanatana Dharma*, *Veda*, *Upanishad*, *Smriti*, *Purana*, *Ramayana*, *Mahabharata*, *Bhagavad Gita*, *Arthasastra*, *Kamasastra*, *Karma*, *Chaturvarna*, *The Six Philosophical Systems*, *Saints*, *Women in Hinduism*, *Meanings and Symbols in Hinduism*, *Hindu Contribution to World Knowledge*, *Some Problems of Indology* and *Conclusion*.

The writer has deviated from the accepted method by quoting from the various works of literature so that the reader may get the 'feel' of the subject and also exercises his or her own judgements.

This book is not meant as anything more than an introduction for those who want a firm foundation to facilitate their own further study. Any shortcomings in the book the writer acknowledges as entirely hers. The writer has tried to do her best and hopes that others will do better.

If this book inculcates in the reader the desire to know more, the need for purity in thought, word and deed, the need for honesty and discrimination in the pursuit of knowledge, the necessity of unselfish conduct, generosity, courage, devotion and hard work which is the message of religion, then the book will have more than served its purpose.

This book's primary aim is to serve the needs of those who wish to know, and because in life it often happens that those who wish to know do not have the means to know and those who have the means do not have the wish to know!

Acknowledgement

This book could not have been written were it not for the countless men and women who have, throughout the ages, left us a most precious heritage of literature. My gratitude goes to all those who have contributed in adding to our knowledge.

A philosophy, to be of relevance, has to be translated into action. This has been done by the Dharmasastras. For information on the Dharmasastras, I turned to M.M. Kane's monumental and meticulous *History of Dharmasastra*, which took him many years of patient labour. I found the History of Dharmasastra invaluable as reference; and it only goes to prove the truth of the Gita saying that no effort is ever wasted!

My dear friend Sarala Mukhi made her significant contribution and was ever encouraging and willing to help, for which I thank her most sincerely.

My grateful thanks are also due to Prof. S.A. Upadhyaya, Dir., Post-graduate and Research Institute of the Bharatiya Vidya Bhavan, Bombay, for sparing the time to read through this work, give helpful suggestions and also the necessary encouragement that has helped me in seeing this book through into print.

I owe much to Sujata Godbole for reading and correcting the manuscript, with constructive suggestions.

My gratitude also to those of my friends and relations who patiently heard me and gave their criticisms and advice.

I am mindful of my many lapses which my husband silently over-looked and which has been the one single factor that helped me unfailingly in this pleasant task I set for myself.

Janaki Abhisheki

Introduction

If we look into the history of the world from the most ancient times, we see the urge for knowledge. Civilizations too have risen and disappeared. It is important for us to know why this happened. A civilization is built up by those with the spirit of enquiry and the fearless pursuit of knowledge. This knowledge provides them with a plan which meets the needs of civilized life and gives them the ability to exploit this knowledge to enrich the quality of life.

Very few of us would disagree with man's need for science, art and skills, because we can see before us the material good it brings. Not many, I fear, would be equally clear about the desirability of religion. This view is not to be condemned but understood when we see that the objection is to 'visible' religion consisting of rites, rituals and customs in the mistaken and self-righteous belief that it is in such performance that merit lies. But this is partly our own fault for neglecting to recognize that just as knowledge is the basis of a civilization so also philosophy is the basis of religion. Just as scientific knowledge fulfills the need of man, so religion too fulfills a deeper need which goes beyond the material values (and which science is not equipped to fulfill) to man's search for the meaning of his own life.

Religion or philosophy therefore satisfies man's need for a more permanent value on which alone he may depend. History shows that just as man has felt the urge for science he has also felt the urge to delve deeper and evolved his philosophy. Philosophy is the search for the ultimate truth of all creation, and since truth is the aim, honesty is essential for the seeker. We thus see that the understanding of truth also brings about a moral change in man.

The very fact that man feels the urge for knowledge, both scientific and philosophical, is an indication of his need for understanding not just the material world but also the moral aspect of life.

Not all feel the need for knowledge and we see man in the various stages. Those imbibed with the spirit of enquiry, are more evolved than those without activity and alertness. And those possessed of a deeper yearning to know and understand are more highly evolved than those possessed of only scientific knowledge, because ultimately the good that man does, depends not only on industry and hard work and the use of his knowledge and intelligence, but also his honest and unselfish devotion and commitment.

What we find then, is that religion is not for the next world, but this world itself. It is not a substitute for scientific thought but seeks, by asking man to understand the true value of the universe, to use his talents wisely and well for the good of all.

The really civilized society therefore is one where honesty is recognised as a moral necessity and where the right tools are used for the right purpose. It means being hard of head, which makes for clarity of thought. It means being soft of heart with the quality of compassion. And it means a hard-working body, unfailing in duty.

Knowledge, both ethical and scientific, must be translated into effective activity.

As we can see, knowledge disappears from a civilization when the spirit of quest stops. When man becomes lazy and is no longer alert and aware, when he is self-centred and starts thinking narrowly and short-sightedly, is neither objective nor impartial, is prejudiced, then he engages in immoral acts and this immorality not only affects his scientific knowledge but also destroys his material welfare. Narrow parochial views, laziness, callousness and indifference, the inability to recognize merit, and dishonesty, bring about the death of any civilization.

While knowledge enlarges the mind, ignorance narrows it. An honest and generous mind alone can be receptive to knowledge, while the narrow and selfish mind will remain ignorant as well as intolerant. It requires both faith and courage to remain honest and also stand up against dishonesty.

Thus truth and knowledge are synonymous, just as untruth is synonymous with ignorance.

Knowledge cannot be fixed to a particular time or place. It is eternal. 'Ancient knowledge' can be as relevant to modern times as any new knowledge that is acquired. We have an example of this from recent history.

Modern Europe progressed in science and technology when it threw out the constrictive mental shackles of the Middle Ages. It was the Renaissance which helped to bring about this change. The ancient Greek civilization had long since disappeared, but the works of some of the ancient pagan Greek philosophers like Socrates, Plato and Aristotle came to the notice of European thinkers, profoundly influencing them. It was due to their contribution that Europe saw a new scientific era, a new spirit of rationalism and objectivity and a new spirit of liberalism, imparted from the learning of the Greek humanities. The new awareness in Europe for the freedom of thought and expression led to the great achievements in science and technology which is there for the world to see. It is pertinent to note that this was achieved not a little by the courage of those who had the spirit of quest and were not to be discouraged in their attempts by any 'authority', religious or secular. Many suffered for it. But the modern Europe we know is largely the result of their study and will to learn and understand. Thus modern Europe owes much to ancient Greece. As Acton observes in his *Lectures on Modern History*: "Next to the Discovery of the New World, the Recovery of the Ancient World is the second landmark that divides us from the Middle Ages, and marks transition to modern life."

Those therefore who scoff at any study of the ancient, believing that there is nothing to learn, are only exhibiting their ignorance. The questing mind scoffs at nothing but instead seeks to understand.

While we are aware of great and glorious civilizations of ancient times disappearing without a trace, it is as well to know of the two ancient civilizations which did not allow themselves to disappear. These two countries, India and China, are the only two among the ancient civilizations with a continuous civilization from the ancient to present times. Of the two, India's is the older. But while acknowledging this it must also be admitted that there have been high and low points in both. There can be no doubt that when a larger number of people are alive to the need for morality, a country and people prosper. A country suffers when more are concerned with the material than the moral. At such times there is greater ignorance and less character, leading to material suffering.

Credit must go to those who even in the most difficult

days the country faced, managed to keep knowledge alive. The *Vedas* for example, did not have to be dug up from some archaeological pit. It was a living heritage kept alive by those who looked upon their profession as not merely a profession, but a sacred trust. Similarly, we send our craftsmen and artists in the various fields to take part in exhibitions both at home and abroad. In each case we find that they are a part of an ancient and continuing tradition. What made them keep these traditions? It could only be due to some power other than a merely material cause, because if it were only the latter they would have abandoned their professions long ago. It could only be because they looked upon their heritage as a sacred trust to be preserved and cherished against all odds. This necessarily requires a degree of sensitivity and commitment that are the essential requirements of civilization. The real requirement of a civilization is not to multiply its wants but to refine them.

It would do us a world of good to understand what the Hindu civilization was based on, if for no other reason then at least to further our understanding.

There are many misconceptions about Hinduism which can only be cleared when we study its philosophy. Hinduism is neither 'arts and crafts' nor just the rituals, nor 'tolerance'. It is much more than that.

The search for truth is to know the meaning and relevance of each and every thing in the world. This philosophy employed scientific thinking in the course of which was developed logical thought, the theory of atomism in the structure of matter and the theory of the evolutionary stages of nature from the most subtle to the gross.

The most important aspect of this philosophy was not only that it recognized the importance of scientific thinking but also the absolute honesty which brought home the fact that real truth is in understanding, not to be theorized but lived. The ultimate paradox of Truth cannot be studied scientifically or logically. It cannot be described in any way known to man. Yet it exists on faith alone. This philosophy thus, while recognizing the need for science, did not commit the folly of thinking that science was all. The spirit was the base of all matter and it was this spirit that gave value and meaning to all objects, institutions and actions.

The realization of this ultimate spiritual truth is aptly brought out in the Sanskrit root 'सृज्' (srij). It means both to abandon as well as to create. It expresses the concept of the great power that renunciation has in the process of creation. Renunciation is basically unselfishness and generosity. It is this concept that is sought to be demonstrated in the rite of sacrifice. It can hardly be a co-incidence that sacrifice is the basis of every religious culture. It essentially implies that only generous self-surrender helps creation. It is therefore unselfish activity alone that helps all.

There have been many changes in the religious customs and rites in India from the most ancient times. These have been in answer to the prevailing needs of the age, but the essential message has always remained the same and was not allowed to be forgotten. This message is that man should act in life with unselfishness, discrimination and devotion for the benefit of creation. Those who function in this manner are those who act according to *dharma*. *Dharma* means that which sustains, preserves and nourishes. Whenever the message has been in danger of being forgotten, religion has revived in a new form and the message has been restated not only by great men of religion but also by the saints belonging to all sects and castes.

The understanding of the 'essential truth of all' as well

as the acceptance of truth not being anyone's monopoly, promoted rationalism and tolerance in India. Tolerance was not towards dishonesty and injustice but the rites and customs and religious philosophies of others which were not unjust.

Again and again religious movements have stated the same truth seeking to balance the imbalances in society. These movements were not only for reform but also for broadening man's mind to knowledge.

It has at times been suggested that Hinduism denies individuality. On the contrary, it becomes obvious that the one important reason for the continuity of Hinduism is the recognition of individuality. Their study of nature brought home to them that all achievement was possible only through form because action is synonymous with form. Knowledge therefore was essential to make the form act more efficiently and purposefully.

It goes to the credit of the great philosophers of ancient India that they did not dwell on ideas alone but sought to translate their ideas by creating institutions, because ideas cannot be carried out without the form (institution) to support them.

The society was thus based on law which was called *dharma* and an order of *varnas* where each group had certain functions which helped them to maintain themselves as well as the society. The *varnas* were originally based on quality where each had to work for all according to capacity. The society was strung together in the strong bonds of a common identity.

While the *varnas* no doubt had their drawbacks when not properly understood which furthered exclusiveness and conceits, there can be no doubt that they functioned effectively when the aim and purpose was understood. This happened when society was more knowledgeable and rational. The caste system, for all its drawbacks, gave to Hindu society its strong individuality and that is perhaps one of the reasons why Hindu civilization retained its continuity.

It should be recognized that conceits are a form of ignorance and are as much present in societies who do not have the caste system where they are present in other forms like class, colour, region, learning, wealth, professions etc.

The problem of knowledge and ignorance is a continuous one the world over. The knowledgeable person is he who is unselfish, generous, honest, discriminating, compassionate and active.

Man is his own master and the master of his own destiny. He needs no crutch when he realises the divinity within himself. He also has consideration for others for he understands that the divine self is in him as well as in all others.

The inspiring message of man's essential divinity which he has but to realize through his own efforts, is brought out even in the oldest religious literature of the Hindus, the *Vedas*.

Three brothers born of man and collectively known as the God Ribhu, were given a place by the gods among them in heaven. They became immortal. What brought them immortality? They were extremely industrious and hard-working. They worked intelligently, devotedly and with skill. The God Indra's cup for drinking the nectar was only one. They made four similar ones and put to shame Indra's own craftsman. They fashioned horses for Indra, a chariot for the Ashwins, made old parents young again, and from the skin of a dead cow made a new cow for the sake of the orphaned calf. They did many such deeds. The gods were so pleased with their work that they made them immortal and placed them among themselves.

These and many stories are allegorical, but they convey

a message for all those who wish to look beneath the surface. It needs a far greater awareness and sensitivity to see not just the letter but the spirit, but these are the essential requisites of a civilization. It is the civilized individual who makes a civilized society.

Dharma in Hindu thought, does not mean religion. It is the subtle quality which helps to balance and sustain all creation. In worldly terms it means responsible acts which are ethical and just. There are many *dharmas*.

Where the word *dharma* is used to mean religion, it is termed *moksa dharma*. But religion is not the end. It is only the means to an end. Religion shows the way. The actual effort is the individual's. In this is the implicit understanding that an individual's worth does not depend on anything other than his own intrinsic merit.

We owe a deep debt of gratitude to those ancient teachers who, recognizing the supremacy of individual conscience, refrained from telling us what to think and do, but who, recognizing man's need for guidance, taught how to think and act. They did this in various ways meant to sharpen our discrimination and understanding.

The literature of the Hindus is in Sanskrit as well as the Prakrit languages. It is vast and varied covering both religious and secular subjects. Sanskrit was the common language of communication among learned Indians from north to south and east to west. The fare in Sanskrit is hence richer.

There are many today who are in search for their identity and who wish to know their roots. This is natural, because individuality is at the root of creation. This book makes a modest attempt to provide it.

It should not be regarded as a substitute for further study but as a foundation for further study. The main purpose of this book is to provide as much information as possible from as reliable authorities as possible.

While also providing the historical background, some of the more significant works have been dealt with. These give the philosophy and also show how this philosophy was sought to be related to life and its activities. Also given, even if briefly, are the achievements of the ancient Hindus in the many fields of human endeavour. There are also some popular misconceptions that prevail about Hinduism. Some of the reasons for these have also been discussed.

1

A Brief Historical Background

Whereas today the word 'Hindu' connotes a particular faith and culture, in ancient times it was used to describe those belonging to a particular region. About 500 BC we find the Persians referring to Hapta Hindu. This referred to the region of North-West India and the Punjab (before partition). The *Rig Veda* (the most ancient literature of the Hindus) uses the word Sapta Sindhu singly or in plural at least two hundred times. Sindhu is the River Indus. Panini, the great Sanskrit grammarian also uses the word Sindhu to denote the country or region. While the Persians substituted 'h' for 's', the Greeks removed the 'h' also and pronounced the word as Indoi. 'Indian' is derived from the Greek' Indoi.[1]

Thus we find that in ancient times Hindu meant the same as Indian. Who were these Hindus? The earliest literature we have is of a people who called themselves Aryas. Their earliest literature *The Veda* goes back to about 4000 BC,[2] some parts being of an even earlier date. From this literature we get a clear idea of the people, their life and thought. The Aryans were a vital and active people of both faith and valour. From early pastoral beginnings we see them founding great cities like Hastinapur, Benares and Taxilla.

From the *Rig Veda* it appears that the Aryans were fair and tall, being different in appearance and practices from a people who are referred to as *Dasas*. The *Dasas* were dark and snub-nosed. While the Aryans were a pastoral people, the *Dasas* were urbanised and lived in cities. It is necessary to keep in mind, however, that the *Veda* was meant for spiritual instruction and not meant to be literally interpreted as modern scholars have done. Not much is known of the origins of the Aryans. There are theories that they belonged to the steppelands of Central Asia, another that they originally belonged to the Arctic regions, and also that they belonged to India itself.[3]

Indian history, however, dates back to a time much earlier. The Mohenjodaro and Harappan civilization was a thriving one as early as 5000 BC. It cuts across in a vast triangle from the western coast of India towards the eastern coast, covering the Indo-Gangetic plain as well as the Deccan. Lothal, a port on the coast of Gujarat with its lock gates is a fine example of the scientific and building skills of these people. There was a flourishing trade in ancient times between Mesopotamia, Egypt and India. Indian teak as well as Indian cotton fabric have been found in these countries. There were many sailing practices common to both Mesopotamian and Indian sailors.[4]

Some scholars believe the *Dasas* to be the descendents of this early civilization. Whatever may be the reasons for the collapse of the earlier civilization (the earlier notion of some archaeologists that the previous civilization was destroyed by invading Aryans seems to have been discounted by later findings which leads one to the conclusion that it just wore itself out) the Aryans became the inheritors of this great culture. History shows that the Aryans, a vigorous people with intellectual curiosity and powers of assimilation, a respect for knowledge and a keen sense of justice became the fitting inheritors of the earlier civilization. The script (the earliest known) of this civilization is yet to be deciphered. Prakrit was the language of the Aryans, the purified and grammarised version of which is known as Sanskrit. The earliest script was Brahmi of which the modern day Devanagari is the descendent.

The Aryans belong to the Indo-European group of races and their oldest literature the *Vedas*, are the most ancient among the Indo-European community.[5]

The Aryans not only imbibed from the earlier culture but took from religion as well. Shiva in a Yogic pose has been found in the ruins of Mohenjodaro. The Mother Goddess is also seen in the earlier culture. In the history of nations we find that even when a more, vigorous but cruder people dominate over another who are culturally superior, the former imbibes the latter culture almost as a process of osmosis.

Since the *Rig Veda* refers to only *Brahmins* and *Kshatriyas* earlier, with the Vaishya and Sudra being mentioned only later, some scholars deduce that the latter two refer to the *Dasas*. All this however, must remain in the realms of conjecture, and there seems no justification to believe that even if this ever was so, it remained so. '*Dasa*' was first used for a people, and later for slave. It was not used for the four *varnas* (the castes). The *varna* was a social structure based on occupation. What we do find is that for thousands of years inter-marriage between all four groups did take place, it being only around the AD 1st century that the first three *varnas* were prohibited from marrying a Sudra woman and only around the AD 10th century that inter-marriage between the *varnas* was not allowed.[6] The probable reasons for this will be discussed elsewhere in this book.

In the *Mahabharata* Yudhishtira despairingly says: 'It appears to me it is very difficult to ascertain the caste of human beings on account of the confusion of all *varnas*; all sorts of men are begetting offsprings from all sorts of women; speech, sexual activity, being born, of death, are common to all human beings and there is Scriptural authority (for this view) in the words, "We, whoever we are, offer the sacrifice". Hence those who have seen the truth regard character as the principal thing desired'"

An amusing episode is worth relating here as it serves to show that there is not much difference between 'scientific' or 'religious', superstition. Although it is difficult to accept any race as 'pure', there is said to be a tribe of 'pure' Aryans living in Ladakh. Some newspapers reported that some ladies from a western country had gone there in order to beget a less impure stock from the males of this tribe. This only goes to show how fallible is the human mind. This particular tribe may have remained 'pure' encased in their mountain fastness, but as a result they also remained backward. The great contributions the Indo-Aryans made to world knowledge did not come from these pure Aryans behind their mountain barrier, but from the vital, daring and open-minded Aryans who assimilated the best of all cultures and peoples, establishing a common identity and impressing the world with original and creative thought, contributing to every branch of human knowledge. Just as the Aryans and the *Dasas* had combined earlier to form a common culture and civilization, so also, much later, India absorbed the Greeks, Sakas, Huns etc. They accepted the spiritual ideologies of India and became a part of the social fabric.[7]

The earliest centre of Aryan culture was in Punjab and North-western India. It later shifted southwards to Kuru-Panchala and then eastwards to Kosala-Videha. There was even a time when due to incursions by foreigners in the north-west that area was not considered as 'fit for Aryas'. We see the gradual spread of the Aryan civilization first where *Aryavarta* is described in the *Manusmriti* as being north of the Vindhyas upto the Himalayas with the sea on either side, and later, including the whole of India. The *Vishnu* and *Markandeya Purana* both describe *Bharatavarsha* as stretching from Cape Comorin to the Himalayas with the ocean on all three sides. Another name for *Bharatavarsha* was *Jambudweep*, it being referred to as such in an Ashokan edict. By this time the term Arya was not used to define a race or people, but one belonging to a particular culture and civilization.[8]

Bharata was the son of Shakuntala and Dushyanta and *Bharatavarsha* was named after him. Although *varsha* earlier meant a region within a *dvipa*, we find from later *Puranas* that *Bharata-varsha* meant not just India but Greater India. From about AD 400 Hindu influence spread eastwards to Malaysia, Cambodia, Java, Borneo etc. and great Hindu kingdoms arose in South-east Asia. They remained so for over a thousand years. The island of Bali in Indonesia is still Hindu.

The culture and civilization of the Hindus was based on their scientific-cum-philosophical findings which find expression in the Vedanta.

Their religion was *Sanatana Dharma* which means Eternal Law. It is a religion of rationalism, humanism and activism. Based on their observations and findings they established a structure for both man and society in order to best enable them to fulfill the aims in life. Society was divided into four classes called *chaturvarna*, each with its prescribed occupation. This is commonly referred to as the caste system. A civilization is judged by its attitude to knowledge. Hindus understood the need for both law and order in society. But they realised that there was something more than just 'law and order'. The whole material world was a world of form. These forms are constantly changing and re-forming. They are impermanent. But they are dependent on the spirit which itself is formless and unchanging. It is the spirit that lends integrity to all form. The proper understanding of the relationship of the material to the spiritual leads to the understanding that all forms must function to fulfill the need. This can be done effectively only by unselfish conduct and integrated action in thought, word and deed.

Form in the shape of custom or tradition becomes irrelevant in time. We see a constant revival and renewal in the culture of the Hindus. There were many sects who denied the caste system, of these the best known were the Jains and the Buddhists. But the *Bhagwat Dharma* as well as some other sects[9] which were very much within the Vedic fold differed from the *Smartha Dharma* (the *dharma* of the Smritis) by throwing their doors open to all, irrespective of caste or sex. Smritis laid down laws and rules as guidelines for society. The understanding of Truth as being without form and thus no one's preserve was greatly responsible for all the sects being able to live in comparative harmony. What is more important is that while the Buddhists and Jains may have differed from Hindu thought on other matters, all agreed and never disputed the doctrine of *Karma* and *Punarjanma*[10]. The *Karma* doctrine of the Hindus, Jains and Buddhists and Sikkhism that was born much later, is the greatest compulsion to rationality and morality. This doctrine makes man the sole architect of his own present and future. Destiny is man's own creation by thought, word and deed. Today in terms of religion Hindu in its narrowest sense means one-who follows the *Sanatana* (Vedic) *Dharma*. In its broadest sense it includes all those Indians who believe in the doctrine of *Karma* and *Punarjanma*. The four great religions who subscribe to this doctrine were all born in India.[11]

A word needs to be said here about Buddhism in India. Some historians claim that Buddhists in India were persecuted by the Hindus which was the cause of its disappearance from India. All these allegations have been examined carefully by no less a scholar than Rhys Davis (*Journal of Pali Texts Society* for 1896, p.87-92) and he finds little proof to support them. Not only does he say that the Pali texts are throughout appreciative of the Brahmanas, but also emphasises that both the faiths lived side by side for a thousand years which resounds to the credit of the whole Indian people and that India never indulged in persecutions the way Reforming Christians were persecuted by the Orthodox Church or early Christians by the Romans. R.C. Mitra in *Decline of Buddhism in India* arrives at the same conclusion. Baeth (*Religions of India* p.131) admits that Buddhism seems to have exhausted itself and the causes for its downfall must be seen in its own inherent defects.

Historical evidence indicates that Buddhism was not totally extinct in North India till at least the first-quarter of the AD 13th century and some remnants existed in South India upto the AD 16th century.[12]

The Smriti texts of the Hindus also show a most accommodating spirit towards differing sects. The *Mahabharata* says that there is no custom or practice that can be said to be beneficial to all alike. Variations in practice were thus to be tolerated by the king.

While we find a couple of early Smritis (*Manu* IX.225) asking a king to banish from realm gamblers, dancers, vintners, heretics, etc. and (*Manu* IV.30) even suggesting leaving a country overrun by groups of heretics, nowhere is there any violence advocated against them, and later Smritis are even more lenient. An excess of materialism is invariably accompanied by a hardening of formalisation.

Rites and rituals become more important than their real meaning. When this becomes the case, the form loses the reason for its existence. It no longer caters to the needs it is meant for.

Every religious revival the world over will be seen as an attempt to free thought from the meshes of form so that the genuine needs of society may be met. This holds equally true for ideologies. The ancient sages of the *Rig Veda* pointed out that "Truth is One; the wise call it by different names". And Truth is not the form. Similarly none of the great religious teachers, neither Buddha, Christ nor The Prophet have claimed that they were teaching anything new. They all claimed to be teaching the ancient way which was the way of Truth.

Truth requires character and the willingness to die for it. Most of all it requires complete honesty in all dealings. Mahaveera who is considered the founder of modern Jainism was a contemporary of the Buddha. But Jainism goes back earlier. Mahaveera's predecessor was the 23rd Tirthankara Parshvanath, a historical personage who lived in the 9th or 10th century BC. All these faiths had great scholars who contributed to man's knowledge. There were other systems of philosophies too which are regarded as part of Smriti literature. They contributed to man's knowledge of creation, the structure of matter and the development of logical thought. The Sankhya system founded by Kapila spelt out the evolutionary nature of all creation, and was as revolutionary in its day as were Darwin and Lamarck in the 18th century. The ethical aspect of life was stressed by all. Sankhya not only means numbers but also connotes renunciation.

Nor should it be supposed that there were no materialist philosophers in ancient India. Charvaka is the best known exponent of this philosophy. Because of its own self-imposed limitations it died a natural death and not much is known of their philosophy, but these Lokayatikas, as they were called, certainly helped to stave off superstition and exploitation. This philosophy died for lack of anything constructive.

It was a tradition that debates and discussions should be held by scholars usually in the courts of kings. Kings were expected to have knowledge and understanding of both the temporal as well as the moral.[13] "Of all *dharmas Raj Dharma* i.e. the Duty of the King was of utmost importance. A king's role was that of a Royal sage.

We find this tradition of debate and discussion carried on from the earliest times. Raja Janaka was an ideal king who is revered by the Buddhists as well.[14] All the religions born in India share many common mythologies and legends.

Just as we see the Buddhist going to a Confucian shrine in China or to a Shinto shrine in Japan, so also in India none of these religious groups feel strange in one another's place of worship. In an increasingly materialistic age with only lip-service being paid to religion in the form of rite and ritual, whether in the nature of sacrifices or 'humanitarian works', (i.e. social service) the Mahaveera and the Buddha, both men of princely families who gave up all for the good of humanity must have had a profound effect and raised the moral tone of the people. The language they used to convey their thoughts was Prakrit so that all could understand.

When the great emperor Ashoka embraced Buddhism, it flourished under his patronage. The monastic institutions founded by the Buddha had produced dynamic monks possessing both head and heart. The Buddhist universities like Nalanda and Vikramasila were famous and people from far and wide came to study. In time however Buddhist monasteries began to suffer as so many monastic institutions do. The monks became parasitical and lazy. The need was for production and accepting the duties and responsibilities of the world. We see the rise of Mahayana Buddhism which seeks to fulfill these very needs, by declaring that rather than live in seclusion seeking one's own salvation, it was better to live and accept one's responsibilities in the world and live for the good of others. Buddha became Godhead.

There is hardly any difference in the philosophies of the Vedanta and Mahayana Buddhism. By the AD 7th century, the Buddha was beginning to be recognized as an incarnation of Vishnu and by AD 10th century, he was regarded by all Hindus as such.[15] Buddhism spread to China and Japan via Tibet and Siberia, and to South and South-east Asia and westwards up to the borders of Syria.[16]

In the reign of Chandragupta II, also known as Vikramaditya, Hinduism became popular again, and under the Gupta Kings there was a great intellectual and cultural revival which spilled out of the borders of India and spread to South-east Asia. After the eclipse of the Guptas, the torch of the Hindu cultural renaissance was held aloft by peninsular India south of the Vindhyas. Even when Buddhism was at its height in India, the majority remained Hindu[17] although people from all classes and castes among Hindus had become Buddhists. Later, due to the degeneration of the monasteries, large sections swung back to the ordered life and caste system of the Hindu fold. In the AD 8th century Shankaracharya, the great *Advaita* philosopher established the order of sanyasis who were as active, as devoted and as renunciatory as the early Buddhist monks. He stressed on the One Truth. The Shankaracharya has been accused by some of being a crypto-Buddhist. But Buddha took from the *Upanishads*.[18] What they both stressed was that Truth is the moral way.

It is Truth which balances all creation. Truth is One. It has to be followed in thought, word and deed.

Although monarchy was normal, the king was in no sense considered as having any divine right. He was a wage-earning executive not above the law. Apastamba states that a king who does not punish the guilty incurs sin. *Yajnavalkya* states that a king incurs half of the sins committed by his unprotected subjects since he levies the taxes. A penance is imposed by Vashishta on a king who gives an unjust decision on a suit. Sukra declares that an unrighteous king should be declared the enemy of the kingdom and people had every right to throw him out. In extreme cases even tyrannicide is considered a just solution.

The Emperor Ashoka is known for his enlightened rule. As can be learnt from the columns erected in his time, he established hospitals and dispensaries throughout his empire. He had trees planted and wells dug alongside public highways and many other acts of social benefit. But Ashoka was not an exception. He was following a great tradition. In the first chapter of the *Arthasastra* written by Kautilya, the minister of his grandfather Chandragupta Maurya, he emphasises one of the King's many duties as that of providing for orphans, the aged, the sick, the destitute, pregnant women and their new-born children.

'*Istapurta*' was the oldest form of Vedic rite. It consisted of sacrifice and public works.[19] Public works in the form of roads, wells etc. were not only undertaken by the State, but it was considered a meritorious deed for anyone to donate for the public gifts and donations came from all classes and castes.

It would be wrong to suppose that monarchy was the established rule in India. Even during the Buddha's time we know of several republics. Some of these were the

Sakyas of Kapilavastu, Mallas of Kusivara and Pana,
Videhas of Mithila and Licchavis of Vesali.[20]

Republics in India go back to even earlier times.
From the *Indika of Arrian* (2nd century BC) translated by
McCrindle we gather "From the time of Dionysus to
Sandrakottus (Chandragupta) the Indians counted 153
kings and a period of 6042 years, but among these a
republic was thrice established . . . . . . another to 300 years
and another to 120 years. The Indians also tell us that
Dionysus was earlier than Heracles by fifteen generations
and that except him, no one made a hostile invasion of
India."

According to P.V. Kane the above passage is of great
importance as it shows that "in the 4th century BC there
was a persistent Indian tradition which carried back
Indian civilization and ordered government to 6000 years
before the fourth century BC".

A word needs to be said here about democracies and
republics. We see attempts to compare ancient and
modern concepts (usually in favour of the latter) without
taking into consideration time and place. Many of us fail to
realize that many thoughts and concepts we consider
'new' today, have been debated and tried out in earlier
times as well. Garbing a concept in a new word does not
really change the concept. The ancient Greek states, for
example, were not republics as we understand the term
today since the slaves who were in a majority had no vote!
Even democracy in its present form came to Europe only
at the end of the 18th century, and even now there are
countries in Europe which do not have a representative
government.

Among the numerous cultures and civilizations of the
world, only two, those of India and China, have a
continuous tradition of over four thousand years if not
more, inspite of recurrent invasions by foreign hordes,

internal conflicts and convulsions. Of the two, India's is the older.[21]

Obviously no civilization can be retained except through constant effort and activity. A civilization does not depend on just preservation of knowledge, but also the augmentation of knowledge. There were obviously in both India and China those who took their professional duties seriously and carried out their respective tasks in the spirit in which they were meant to be performed.

As late as the AD 11th century, Said al-Andalusi a reputed Arab astronomer and historian of science, in his work *Kitab al-Umam* (The Categories of Nations) gives India the first place among the contemporary nations which had developed science by then.[22] Not only the Indian philosophies, both of Buddhism and the Brahmanas (what is now referred to as Hinduism), but also the secular knowledge in the arts and sciences travelled to other parts of the known world, both west and east.

Much of European knowledge was received through the Arabs who about the 8th century and later possessed scholars of the necessary devotion and calibre who contributed significantly to world thought.

Indian influence has not only been in the ethical sphere but also in worldly and secular knowledge. Ethical knowledge was necessary to give a moral base to ensure the proper use of all secular knowledge. Our reasoning cannot take us beyond the paradox of whether the chicken comes first or the egg. True understanding comes by rising above the chicken and the egg. They are the same, the form only being different. It is the act of giving up or renunciation that provides the moral basis for the whole of creation. Truth sees to the good of all. Selflessness is the core of all morality as all the great religious teachers everywhere observe.

Indians benefited greatly from the living examples provided by men and women saints of all classes, castes and regions, who showed the value of truth in their conduct as well as in the priceless literature they have left.

Practice is often seen to have a far greater effect than precept. 'The understanding that all cannot be of the same attainments and that each one would evolve in his own time made Hindus tolerant towards not only people of other views within Hinduism itself, but also towards other sects.

'Hinduism is a combination of many systems, cultures and religious ideologies. These include Vedic ritualism, Vedantic thought, Vaisnavism, Saivism, Saktism and primeval cults adapted to the different types of men and communities with intellectual and spiritual disparities. What binds all Hindus are the common doctrines of *Karma* and *Punarjanma*, the unifying influence of the vast and venerated Sanskrit literature that gradually enriched the regional languages, the reverence for the *Vedas* as the final authority on all religious matters, even if all did not understand, and the geographical unity of the country emphasised by the *Puranas*.'[23]

Sabara (between AD 200–500) shows in his *Bhāsya* on Jaimini (X.I.35), that the language of the cultured people from Himavat to C. Comorin was the same. The *Mahabharata*, Sabara, *Puranas* and the *Brihat-Samhita* show that the ancient Hindus (Indians) identified their culture with *Bharatavarsha* i.e. they identified country with culture and not race with culture.[24]

Although India has been an overwhelmingly Hindu country, she has people belonging to almost all the major religions of the world. India has perhaps had Christians before Europe. The Indians have provided shelter to many people of different faiths, many of whom were fleeing religious persecution in their own countries.

The earliest Christians in India (about the AD 1st century) belonged to the Syrian Christian Church which recognized not the Roman Catholic Church but the earlier Christian Church of Antioch. Another batch is said to have come later about the AD 4th century. They were not only allowed to stay in India but also to live with dignity. It is said that Thomas the Apostle of Christ was killed in the North-west of India in the reign of Gondophernes for proselytising.[25] This is unsubstantiated. To a people who were taught to think rationally, and whose tolerance derived from the knowledge that salvation is for anyone deserving of it, no matter what caste, creed or sex they may be, and due to each one's own efforts, to support proselytism would have been like supporting superstition.

What is important is that even if Thomas was killed, his followers were not.

The Inquisitions of Europe were brought to India by the Portuguese Jesuit priests. While the Syrian Christians did not suffer for their beliefs at the hands of Hindus they were sought to be coerced into acceptance of the Roman Catholic Church by the Roman Catholic Jesuits.[26]

Mistaking form for the spirit is a common enough human failing, but something that has to be guarded against if civilization is to be kept alive.

In the AD 7th and 8th centuries, the Jews and Parsis also sought and were extended hospitality. They never at any time faced religious persecution from the Hindus. Some Muslims from Iraq fleeing the persecution of Hajjaj bin Yusuf came and settled in the Konkan in the AD 8th century. Much earlier Arab traders had settled in Kerala. These Moplahs had settled in India long before the Muslim invasion. From the AD 11th century onwards, invasions and the gradual conquest of India by Muslim invaders threw a challenge to the Hindus. This was met in various ways.

The Muslim invaders were intolerant of other religions, and the cry of 'Idol-worshippers', was a very profitable one, as it justified plunder of temples and condoned the acts of cruelty and depredations in general. Many Hindus were forcibly converted. The majority of Indian Muslims are converts from Hinduism. The policy of political conquest coupled with proselytism invited resistance from the Hindus both politically and religiously.[27]

India from the most ancient times has been a rich country. Indian knowledge and expertise was recognized and appreciated in many countries including West Asia. It is commonly believed that India's contacts with Greece started with Alexander's invasion. History shows that Indian ideas and philosophies were known to Greece at least 300 years earlier.[28] The earliest Greek literature does not go beyond 9th century BC.

Indian soldier mercenaries were in Persian armies and had, before the advent of Alexander, even fought on Greek soil. Apart from the wise men of India (one of whom Kalanos was taken to Greece by Alexander) who were well known for their philosophic contribution,[29] Indian soldiers, accountants, and cooks were also in great demand in the Muslim world.[30] An ancient Roman senator had cause to complain of the drain on his country's resources by importing silks, pearls and scents from India for which Rome paid in gold![31]

Hindu temples were not only rich, but also the centres of knowledge and culture. Religious as well as secular education was imparted and some temples even had hospitals attached to them. In times of famine and pestilence the temples afforded aid and shelter.[32] The intolerance of Muslim kings is given in the *Cambridge History of India* Vol.III. Feroze Shah Tughlak burnt a Brahmin who tried to propagate his religion (p.187). Sikander Lodi did the same (p.246) and was guilty of wholesale destructions of temples. Sultan Sikander of Kashmir offered his subjects the choice between Islam and exile (p.280). Hussein Shah of Bengal sent an army to destroy Navadvipa and converted many *Brahmins* forcibly. Emperor Jehangir says in his *Memoirs* (translated by A. Rogers and edited by H. Beveridge p.72-73) that he killed Guru Arjun for his religious activities. A record left by Bakhtiar Khilji's men refers to 'thousands of men in yellow with shaven heads' being butchered. The reference here quite obviously is to Buddhist monks, though they are referred to as Brahmanas. It would be unreasonable and untrue to deny that there was any religious intolerance among Hindus. Hindus are as human as anyone else but their philosophy was more accommodating of differing views. In *Administration and Social life under the Pallavas* (University of Madras 1938), (p.170-172). Dr. Minakshi after remarking that the Pallava kings were generally tolerant towards all religious sects says that King Pallavamala indulged in some harsh methods of persecution.

There were also the sharp differences and ugly incidents between the Shaivites and Vaishnavites in the South. But generally although some incidents must have occurred they were localised exceptions which cannot be treated as a regular and systematic persecution. 'The fanatical zeal and ruthlessness of Muslim rulers demolished almost all Hindu temples at different times from AD 1194–1670. Mosques and mausoleums were created in their sites and the materials of the temples used in constructing mosques and for serving as breakwaters. etc., Kutbuddin Aibak destroyed 1000 temples in AD 1194 (vide Elliot and Dowson's *History of India* Vol.II p.222) Allauddin Khilji boasted of having destroyed 1000 temples in Benaras alone (vide Sherring p.31 Havell p.76). About AD 1585 Narayanabhatta re-established the temple of

Visvanatha at Benares with the help of Raja Todarmal.
Even this temple was desecrated.

Elliot and Dowson *History of India* (Vol.VII p.184)
quote from the following passage from the *ma-A 'sir-i-
A'lamgiri'*. "It reached the ears of His Majesty, the
protector of the Faith, that in the provinces of Thalta,
Multan and Benares, but especially in the latter, foolish
Brahmins were in the habit of expounding frivolous
books in their schools and that student and learners,
Mussulmans as well as Hindus went there even from long
distances, led by the desire to become acquainted with the
wicked sciences they taught. The Director of the Faith
consequently issued orders to all the governors of the
provinces to destroy with a willing hand the schools and
temples of the infidels; and they were strictly enjoined
to put an entire stop to the teaching and practising of
idolatrous forms of worship. It was reported to His
religious Majesty, leader of the Unitarians, that in
obedience to the order, the government officers had
destroyed the temple of Bishnath at Benares."

A mosque which still exists was built on the site of the
Visvesvara temple by Aurangzeb, who even changed the
name of Benares to Mohammedabad. It will be difficult to
find more than 20 temples in the whole of Benares of the
age of Aurangzeb (AD 1658–1707). Many were built by the
Mahrattha chiefs and Sardars and many more under the
British occupation.

The city of Benares has a hoary past. It has been a
holy city for at least 30 centuries. To the Hindu mind it
represents a great and unbroken tradition of religious
sanctity and learning.[33]

Not only has Hinduism with its numberless sects
flourished here for centuries but the principles of
Buddhism, one of the great religions of the world were first

proclaimed by Sakyamuni at Bodh Gaya under the Bodhi tree.[34]

Benares, even in 2nd century BC seems to have been famous for its cloth. *The Mahabhasya of Patanjali* gives interesting information about the superior and therefore, dearer cloth of Benares as compared to the cloth woven at Mathura![35]

The intolerance of the Muslim invaders must have come as a shock to a people accustomed to rational thought to whom tolerance was almost a religion. The *Bhagavadgita* (IX.23-25) proclaims that the devotees who worship other Gods do worship Krishna himself though in an irregular way and that those who offer worship to the 'manes' or to the elements reach the goals they desire. The Manasottara enjoins that one should give up condemnation of or hatred towards other gods, that one should show reverence on seeing an image or a temple and should not pass it over in contempt.[36]

Considering that Ghazni plundered Kathiawar and Gujarat several times, Hindus seem to have made a distinction between the Muslim marauders and peaceful Muslims residing in Gujarat for trade. Elliot's *History of India* (Vol.II p.162-163) relates an anecdote by one Mohammed Ufi of some Muslims being killed and their mosque desecrated by some Hindus and Parsis at Cambay. One of the Muslims approached King Siddharaja with a petition. The King, disguised, enquired into the matter, satisfied himself as to its genuineness punished the offenders, and gave 100000 'balotras' for rebuilding the mosque as well as four articles of dress which were preserved in the mosque. Ufi declares he never heard a story comparable to this. The Somnath-Pattan Inscription is a remarkable document (I.A.XI p.241). A Muslim sailor from Hormuz acquired a piece of land and built on it a house, mosque and some shops in Somnath-Pattan. The grant allowed him the purchase to provide income from the shops for the religious festivals of the Shia sailors, leaving the surplus, if any, for the towns of Mecca and Medina. This grant has the dates of four eras. The first is Rasul Mohammed Samvat i.e. Hijra year 662. Then, the Vikrama samvat AD 1262, Valabhi year 945 and Simha samvat 151.

There are also records of special privileges given to Syrian Christians as well as Buddhists.

However, it is necessary to note that whereas one can take exception to the cruelties inflicted by the Muslim invaders, there are several reasons which go to make invasion successful. It was to be expected that a rich country will attract marauders. That is why countries keep armies, spies and diplomats etc. No ruler, whose function is to protect his country and his people can afford to be trusting in worldly affairs. If riches attract plunder, so do ignorance and foolishness.

It is said that Ghazni kept some cows in front of his army. The opposing Hindu soldiers refused to fire, thus allowing Ghazni in without a shot.[37] Similarly it is said that Khilji went through a mock ceremony of embracing Buddhism. The Buddhists in India were happy and invited him into India.[38] He destroyed where he went including the monks at Nalanda. Although neither Buddhism nor Hinduism teaches 'image'-worship (i.e. worship of the material), yet it is an indication of the state of ignorance they had descended to when the form of a cow or the label of religion could make the Hindus and Buddhists abdicate and forget their proper functions i.e., preserving the integrity of the country and people and fighting the invader. Later, however, they regained their balance, for had the Hindus identified their temples with the material, then the demolishing of their temples would certainly have broken them. If their spirit did not break it is in no small measure due to the teachings of the saints. These saints, who came from all parts of India and all castes and classes, preached the unity of God, the need for self-purification, condemnation of pride of caste and surrender to the deity for salvation.[39] A new awakening was created among the people. The sweetness of love and devotion brought with it the love for truth, a truth that stands above needs and wants.

The saints' teachings gave strength to the Hindu. This also found expression in action. Comprehensive digests of the Smritis were composed, the *Krityakalpataru* of Lakshmidhara in the north (about AD 1110–1130) and Hemadri's in the Deccan (3rd. quarter of the AD 13th century), being the earliest extent.[40]

Armed resistance saw the creation of independent states like the kingdom of Vijainagar (AD 1330–1565), Maharashtra (under Shivaji and the Peshwas) and the Sikhs in Punjab under Ranjit Singh.[41]

Akbar, one of the greatest and the wisest of the Muslim emperors, showed both statesmanship and tolerance. He made a marriage alliance with a Rajput princess. Akbar's son Jehangir as well as his grandson Shah Jehan, both had Hindu mothers. Akbar was not a fanatic Muslim. He even tinkered with the idea of propagating a state religion to be known as *Din-i-Illahi*, which, understandably was not acceptable to any. But he was a cultured man. He was accepted because of his wisdom and statesmanship. Akbar had many Hindu religious books translated into Persian and Persian books into Sanskrit.

But the Moghuls came to stay and in due course the Hindus and Muslims learnt to live side by side in amity. The Sufi saints also played a part in teaching the true values and were a moderating influence on Muslim fanaticism.

In the countryside by virtue of the fact that most of the Muslims were converts from Hinduism, most of their customs and behaviour remained the same as their Hindu brothers.

One is apt to get the impression from some history books that the Muslim invaders were offered hardly any resistance. This is certainly not the case. This quote from Elphinstone's *History of India* (Vol.I p.547-698) given in Dadabhoy Nowroji's *Poverty and un-British rule in British India* states, "It is generally supposed that the conquest of India by the Mohammedans was an easy task, but history tells us that none of the Hindu principalities fell without a severe struggle; that some of them were never subdued, but remain substantive states at this moment; and that Shahab-ud-Deen, the first founder of the Mohammedan dynasty in India towards the end of the twelfth century was signally defeated by the Rajput sovereign of Delhi."

Interestingly, Hindu soldiers were considered by the Greeks as the best soldiers they had fought against in Asia.[42] This was as early as 300 BC. Even today there are many regiments in India proud of their fighting heritage. The celebrated Gurkhas also belong to India and Nepal, the only independent Hindu kingdom in the world which nestles to the north of India. The word Gurkha is derived from Gorakhnath, one of the great Nath saints. Although the hereditary castes of professional soldiers were preferred, the army consisted of various categories of soldiers. Kautilya cites 6: hereditary, hired guild troops, troops of ally, friendly power or feudatories, troops that once belonged to the enemy and wild tribes as troops.

In due time and a policy of moderation, the Hindu and Muslim had learnt to co-exist in comparative harmony. Both had perhaps come to realize as had Yudhishtira earlier that ultimately in life, it is character that counts and not the religion. There were many Hindu nobles and officers in Muslim kingdoms in India as there were Muslims in Hindu kingdoms. There were men of character, ability and loyalty among both, even as there were traitors.

Perhaps nothing invites resistance so much as fanaticism. All harmony is a matter of balance, and anything that disturbs the balance creates disharmony. The state of things changed when Aurangzeb, the son of Shah Jehan ascended the throne.

He enforced the outer forms of Islam, prayed so many times a day, banned music etc. He also imposed the *jazzya* tax which was levied on all "non-Believers". (This tax was also levied on Zoroastrians in Iran by the Muslim regimes there).

Although Aurangzeb ascended the throne to head a large empire, his aggressive expansionist methods and proselytizing zeal repulsed a large segment of the Indian population and invited armed resistance from Muslim and Hindu kingdoms alike. While he was able to subdue the Muslim kingdoms in the Deccan, he could not subdue the Hindu. It could be said that the more he tried the more he lost, and he died without succeeding in his wish to get the whole of Southern India under his sovereignty.

Hindu resistance strengthened, and a time was to come when the Moghul throne itself depended for its very existence on the protection given by the Hindu Marattha sardar, the Scindia of Gwalior.

Perhaps some idea can be got of the kings and warriors and statesmen of the Deccan from Elphinstone's *History of India* (Vol.I p.547-696), "Of the character of the Hindu sovereign contemporaries of the Musulman emperors of the 14th and 15th centuries, we know nothing, but we know that their territories had attained to a pitch of power and splendour which had not been surpassed by their ancestors. We also know that the principal administrators of the Mussulman dynasties, with rare exceptions, were

Hindus — that they were entrusted with the command of armies and with the regulation of finances."[43]

The 'robber' Shivaji who entered upon the scene in the latter part of the 16th century and who shook the Moghul empire to its foundations during the reign of Aurangzeb, was an able and skillful general. His civil government was regular, he was vigorous and exacting from his pradhans and his village officers' obedience to the rules he laid down for protection of the people . . . Altogether this 'robber' hero has left a character which has never since been equalled by any of his countrymen (extract of *Anquetil du Peron's* given in Grant Duff's *History of the Marathas*).[44]

'The celebrated Hyder Ali was a contemporary and antagonist of Madhavrao by whom he was more than once signally defeated, but Hyder Ali turned these failures to good account and like Czar Peter "submitted to be worsted that he might learn to be superior".[45]

Tipu the son of Hyder Ali was both a warrior and a statesman. He bequeathed a powerful and rich empire. Diwan Poorniah kept Mysore State rich and flourishing after Tipu, and Nana Phadnavis "during the long and important period of whose administration by the force and energy of his single mind, he held together his vast empire — composed of members whose interests were as opposite as the most anomalous elements and by the versatility of his genius, the wisdom, firmness and moderation of his government he excited this mass of incongruities to one mutual and common effort. With that wise and far-seeing policy, strong in it's own resources equally rejects the extremes of confidence and despair, he supplied from the fertility of enchanted genius an expedient for every possible event."[46]

Ahalyabai the ruler of Indore is described as "one of the purest and most exemplary rulers that ever existed" and "the fond object of her life was the prosperity of all around her". When she saw bankers, merchants, farmers and cultivators rising to affluence, far from deeming it a ground for exaction she considered it a legitimate claim of increased favour and protection . . . Among the princes of her own nation it would have been looked on as sacrilege to have become her enemy or indeed not to have defended her against any hostile attempt. She was considered by all in the same light. The Nizam of the Deccan and Tipu Sultan held her in the same respect as the Peshwa, and the Mohammedans joined the Hindus in prayer for her long life and prosperity."[47]

There are records, both Hindu and Muslim, which show the rich country that India was at the time of the Muslim invasions. They dwell with admiration on the extent and magnificence of the capital Kanauj.[48]

But India was a rich country even till the arrival of the British. It was the riches of India that attracted the Europeans for trade. We see the Portuguese, the Dutch, the French and the English. They were rivals, but later it was the English who established an empire in India, with the Portuguese and the French in small pockets off the east and west coasts.

In 1687 the East India Company had already "decided to establish a large well-grounded sure English dominion in India for all time to come."[49]

After the Battle of Plassey, the civil governments of Bengal, Bihar and Orissa went under British rule from 1765. The last Peshwa Bajirao II was defeated in 1818 and the British came to control the whole of India except Punjab which was subdued in 1845. The British lost their Indian empire in AD 1947. They were thus rulers over a large part of India for 180 years, over the whole of India except Punjab for about 130 years and the whole of India for about a hundred years.[50]

Time-wise the British empire in India was of a very

short duration. But it is equally true that no conquest had the impact on India as the British. They changed the system of government and established courts of justice on the western model. They brought ideas of individualistic liberty and western modes of living and an educational system devised to suit their needs rather than India's; also newspapers, better transport, modern sciences, English literature and arts.[51] They hoped to strengthen their hold over the country not only through westernization but also Christianization. A large sum of Indian government money was funneled for proselytism.

In the words of Macauley the educational institutions devised for the subject people was to "form a class of persons, Indian in blood and colour, but English in taste and opinion, in morals and intellect".

The missionary was looked upon by the British administrator as one who helped them in this task. "As their object is not profit they can afford to reside at places till they become profitable. They strengthen our hold over the country. They spread the use of the English language; they induct the natives into the best kind of civilization and in fact each mission station is an essay in colonisation."[52]

The European missionary's part in the temporal interests of their respective countries rather than the spiritual message has been acknowledged not only in books written by western scholars but also by Christians of the subject countries. Jomo Kenyatta who fought for the freedom of Kenya observed that the "white man came with the Bible in his hand, taught us to kneel, close our eyes and to pray. When we opened our eyes their Bible was in our hands and our land in theirs." Lin Yutang also records that in China it soon became obvious that both "the missionary and the bales of opium were under the protective shadow of the gunboat."[53]

Christianity was not the first missionary religion. The first great missionary religion several centuries before Christianity was Buddhism. But it must be said to the latter's everlasting credit that they 'gave to God what belonged to God and to Caesar what belonged to Caesar.' In other words, they did not conspire to subjugate other countries and increase the empire of their respective countries. They concentrated on the message of *dharma*, which is the single message of morality for all.

While it must be said for the British that they did not indulge in forced proselytising as did the Portuguese, they certainly tried to attain their objectives in a more subtle manner. While the government gave itself a secular image engaged in providing law and order and the 'protection' of the people, 'religion' in the shape of missionaries was assigned the task of dispensing charity and education. According to Spear the British concentrated on hospitals as they thought that would have the most effect on the "Hindu mind."[54]

Although the world is aware of the Inquisitions that took place in Europe it is largely unaware of the Inquisitions outside, e.g. in Goa where established in AD 1560 it continued it's intolerant and inhuman work for 250 years. The following brief passage from J.H. de Cunha's paper "Historical Essay on the Konkani Language", is illuminating. "We shall now endeavour to investigate the causes, which under the Portuguese regime, were either favourable or contrary to the culture of the Konkani language. In the ardour of conquest, temples were demolished, all the emblems of the Hindu cult were destroyed and books written in the vernacular tongue, containing or suspected of containing idolatrous doctrines were burnt. There was even a desire to exterminate all that part of the population which could not be quickly converted; this was the desire not only during that period, but there was at least one person who, after a lapse of two centuries, advised the government with magisterial gravity, to make use of such a policy."

The long distance of Goa from Portugal, the invincible resistance offered by a numerous population amongst whom the principal castes had a high degree of civilization, obliged the conquerors to abstain from open violence and to prefer indirect, though not gentle means to achieve the same![55]

One hopes that some day the saga of Hindu resistance to Portuguese methods in Goa will be written.

The British were different to the Portuguese both racially and culturally. Whereas both at one time owed allegiance to the Roman Church, the Popes of this Church were mostly Latin. The Popes had been either French or Italian, mostly the latter. The history of the Papacy in Europe has not been confined to the spiritual alone but temporal as well. And perhaps at no time in it's history did the spiritual content drop so low as during the infamous Inquisitions.

Religion was being made an excuse for monetary gain, and the countries of northern Europe were already chafing under the extortion of the Pope and his clergy.

The last straw on the camel's back was the 'Sale of Indulgences' instituted by the Pope to fill his depleted coffers. This ensured that all those who bought these indulgences at a price, automatically gained a reprieve of some duration from purgatory.

The Reformation or Protestant movement got a further shot in the arm, and Martin Luther became it's chief spokesman. Had it been seen as a purely religious matter it is doubtful if Martin Luther would have survived the wrath of the Pope. Others before him had not only been killed but drawn quartered and burnt as well. It was

German nationalism that rallied behind Luther and saved him from the clutches of the Italian Pope.[56]

Faith is usually seen to suffer when there is a gap between precept and practice. The Protestants of Northern Europe broke away from the Roman Catholic Church, and became independent of the Papacy.

As in all movements there are some who genuinely understand the issues and some who are inspired by other motives. There were many thinking people in Europe who were deeply influenced by the thoughts and writings of the ancient Greeks during the period of the Renaissance. For the first time Christian Europe learnt of objectivity and humanism. This came to them from the literature of the ancient pagan Greeks. It was the attitude of mind, the scientific attitude that they developed as a result of their study of the ancient pagan works that spurred Europe in its great scientific achievements.

Erasmus and Thomas More are two well-known personalities of the Renaissance who laid the foundations of the English public school system with it's accent on the humanities. This brought in time an objectivity and a spirit of liberalism that was perhaps seen more in England and Holland than in any other country of Europe.[57]

The spirit of scientific enquiry led in time to scientific discoveries which were applied to industry and led to the Industrial Revolution. Northern Europe did better here than Southern Europe.

However, it would be incorrect to draw any generalisations. The Roman Catholic Church had come down very heavily on anyone seen or suspected of dabbling in anything remotely scientific. It was considered as the work of the devil. There were men of great courage like the scientist Giordano Bruno who suffered in a dungeon for seven years and who when finally taken to be burnt alive by the dreaded Inquisitors refused to retract saying, "I prefer a spirited death to a cowardly life."

Undoubtedly Bruno was a more liberated thinker than was Martin Luther who although against the authority of the Pope denounced Copernicus as a fool, charging him with turning upside down the science of astronomy, relying on the Bible which he said "declared that Joshua commanded the sun to stand still and not the earth." (Joshua 10-12).

Education does not always lead to liberal thought nor do priests of religion show themselves to be more understanding of Truth. The most obvious example of this are the Inquisitions. They were instituted and carried out by two Roman Catholic priestly Orders, both being teaching Orders! The Dominicans began the Inquisitions which were later carried on by the Jesuits. The latter even proscribed books and authors and in Spain one who was found to possess the books was sentenced to death.

Bigotry does not belong to any particular age. Even later, many scientists in Northern Europe too, including Darwin were condemned for flouting Biblical beliefs!

We do not find the same conflict between science and religion in the more ancient cultures. Aryabhatta (born AD 476) mentions the earth's rotation and revolution. This is contradicted by Varahamihira giving his own reasons for doing so. There is no record of either being condemned or suffering for his views. Both science and religion were regarded as having truth alone as their goal. They were both seen as serving the same end.

Yajnavalkya Smriti (I.343) provides that when a conqueror reduces a country to subjection he should preserve intact whatever customs, laws and judicial procedures and family usages handed down from generation to generation therein (provided they are not opposed to the *Vedas*). As the *Mitaksara* says, he should not cause confusion by imposing the usages of his own country on the conquered country. Empire meant suzerainty and not the imposition of the language and political institutions of the conqueror.[58]

Indian thinkers were clear in their minds about the role of *dharma* and that of *artha*. One was a moral law while the other dealt with a natural law dealing with politics and economics. *Arthasastra* rule is the accomplishment of a visible worldly purpose as goal while *Dharmasastra* rule has as its purpose the securing of unseen and spiritual results.[59]

Kautilya must be considered far more honest than those who tried to make out that their empire was an onerous duty by doing which they were only carrying on the white man's Christian duty. This 'white man's burden' was economically most advantageous for the white empires.

In order to make England rich 'India had to bled' said Lord Salsbury. India's national debt used for fighting England's wars kept on growing. Exports kept shrinking and so did production. India could not compete, was not allowed to — with England. In fact, those parts of the country under the Indian princes were better off than British India. India which was a rich country when the British first came became a poor country by the end of the first century of British rule.[60]

Kautilya in his *Arthasastra* uses the word '*vairajya*' for foreign rule. He describes it thus: "It comes into existence by being seized from another king who is living and therefore (the foreign ruler) thinking 'this country is not mine', impoverishes it and carries off its wealth or treats it as chattel (for sale) or when he finds that the country is disaffected towards him, abandons it and goes away."

Lord Macauley had observed in an entirely different context that the "heaviest yoke is the yoke of the foreigner." He was referring to the dire straits England had been reduced to by the monetary extortions of the Pope.[61]

However, there is no single act in the universe without its good as well as bad effects — the rail for example was introduced though, had India been a free country the railways would have added to the national exchequer in the shape of profits. But while the capital investment for the railways were given from Indian government funds all the profits went to private British rail companies in England who owned the railways.[62]

The cry of 'law and order' has been the justification for every imperial rule in history — not excepting the Roman rule of Britain.

But the Hindus and Indians had a very good understanding and appreciation of both law and order. Their traditions of civil government went back to thousands of years.

England was invaded in the past by the Danes, Anglos, Saxons etc. Within historical memory England was conquered by the Italians (the Roman Julius Ceaser in 55 BC) and later by the French (William of Normandy in AD 1066).

There can also be no doubt that England owes her roads, etc., to the ancient Romans who needed them for their garrisons. Similarly, many of the manors and castles go back to Norman times. Yet the English would prefer to identify their national spirit with that of Boedicia, symbol of resistance to foreign rule and so the symbol of liberty.

In India too we see that if the Muslim invaders gave something to India, they also in their turn were influenced by Hindu thought in the several fields of art, science and philosophy. Even though the Rajput house of Jodhpur was connected by marriage to the Moghul court and Jaipur in its service there were many among them of character and nobility, the symbol of Hindu and national resistance was the house of Mewar of Rana Pratap, who despite every adversity never bowed to the invaders. The indomitable spirit of liberty must always compel admiration and respect not accorded to others. One important difference also was that while civilization came to Britain through Rome India had already achieved a high state of civilization much before Islam or Christianity.

Indians did not accept British rule docilely. In 1857 the princely states of India had already seen the writing on the wall and knew it was only a matter of time before their states were annexed. Some of them got together to fight the British in 1857. The Indians regard 1857 as the first War of Independence while the British prefer to call it a Mutiny.

If one were to go by the definition of a mutiny, a rebellion of one's own troops, then the British description may have been justified. But British Indian troops who had rebelled formed only a part of the revolting armies. The rest belonged to the Indian states who were fighting the British.

This 'mutiny' had at its head the last of the Moghul emperors, Bahadur Shah Zafar (a poet by his own right), a number of Indian princes, both Hindu and Muslim, along with their respective armies and they were joined by soldiers both Hindu and Muslim, from the British Indian army. This 'mutiny' lasted for two years (AD May 1857– April 1859). It required the largest concentration of British troops who had to be specially brought out from England for dealing with it. It was not considered over until the general of the opposing army Tatya Tope, who belonged to the armies of the princely states, was caught and slain.

Hibbert in his *Great Mutiny* describes how the Hindu and Muslim soldiers caught, were blown off the canon's mouth and how they, each one, met his death with courage and dignity. He ascribes this rather vaguely as being probably due to their religion. Obviously according to Hibbert only a religious superstition and not courage and faith in their cause could be ascribed to those opposing the imperial white Christian government.

Regarding the war of 1857, just as happened with the Hindus and Buddhists earlier, there is a belief that the Sikhs sided with the British because some words Guru Tegh Bahadur said to the Muslim emperor under whose orders he was being tortured, were misrepresented to make it appear that the British were their saviours. Thirty years later Punjab went under British rule.

Much has been sought to be made of the fact that it was not the 'peoples' struggle, implying that the common man had nothing against the imperial rule and was quite content to stay under their imperial domination. It was sought to be implied (and some Indian scholars also supported this thesis) that 1857 was purely the selfish effort on the part of Indian princes to safeguard their own interests, the Indian states being not as concerned with public weal as were the British.

If that were indeed the case, the one single factor to judge the beneficent effects of any rule is the prosperity of the country and people. Even under British occupation, statistics show the people of the princely states (with perhaps a few exceptions) being far better off than British India, apart from the rich state of India when the British first came.[63]

A feudal system always has to have at its head the chief. The chief represents the people. Britain for all its democratic pretensions was still a monarchy, but even worse, it was an imperial power, which was bent on not only retaining its power but also expanding it. If the princely states were feudal, it need not be assumed that they were not nationalistic, or that an imperial power was any the less feudal or more philanthropic. The very same argument may be heard of those in the national movement that came later describing the political parties involved as representing only the 'bourgoisie.'

To try and down-grade an opposing force which threatens a vested interest by decrying their unselfish commitment and painting them as serving their own selfish interests has always been one of the methods used by opponents.

There are undoubtedly people of all kinds with their own compulsions, who join any movement and who belong to every ideology. There are some who believe in a cause and have no selfish axe to grind, while others may have their own selfish reasons. Even the Crusades had all kinds of men, from the noble to the lout, as well as criminal elements. Idealism quite often gets a rude knock when things do not turn out the way the idealist expected. We have, for example, at the height of the French revolution Madame Rolande crying out from the steps of the Guillotine, "O Liberty, what crimes are committed in thy name".

None of these movements become any the less significant inspite of this fact. If one were to properly evaluate the two wars of Independence i.e. the Indian and the American, it is the latter that would more qualify to be called a *Mutiny*. The American States were colonies of England from the start, and were racially, ethnically and culturally the same. As such the American militia were under the British government.

After the 'mutiny' the defeated Indian Emperor's sons were punished with death and the Emperor and his Begum sent to Burmah to languish till they died. England was undisputed master. But the spirit of revolt against foreign rule did not die. There was an undercurrent of ferment.

One way to contain it was to give it a voice. The Indian National Congress was founded by a British serving officer called Hume. This Congress itself underwent several transformations under the pressures of its members, who were irked at the timid resolutions passed. Aurobindo Ghosh described it as a 'mendicant policy'. The more forthright and vigorous elements took over. Tilak who supported Civil Disobedience is known as the "Father of Indian Unrest". Annie Besant, a Britisher was also a member of the Congress. She is well known for her theosophical institutions. But she fell out with Tilak on the issue of Home Rule. She did not wish that India sever her contact with Britain and was for limited independence. Tilak on the other hand was for complete independence. The resolution for complete independence was passed under the presidentship of a Parsi, Dadabhoy Nowroji.

None of the leaders from any part of India (and there were many) were able to involve the people as a whole in the way that Mahatma Gandhi did. There were many men and women of integrity, intellect and commitment before, as well as after Gandhi. But Mahatma Gandhi's stature remains, justifiably, the tallest.

M.K. Gandhi's reputation in India had travelled before him. He had come from South Africa after organizing the coloured people there to stand against the racialist policies of the South African Government. He had also suffered for it, but had continued despite odds.

Gandhi's main quality was his simplicity. This simplicity was based on the integrity he cherished above all else. If Gandhi is a household word even today, and if he has been able to fire the imagination of millions the world over, it is because the voice of conscience was stronger in him than in others. Truth to him mattered very deeply. If the final transition of power from England to India was largely free of the extreme bitterness and hate it engendered in other colonies, it was largely due to Gandhi's efforts to put the issue in the right perspective. He stressed again and again that India's fight was not against the English people but against an exploitative regime.

Although Gandhi was uncompromising regarding the methods to be used for India's fight for independence, not all his colleagues were of his views. Gandhi chose the path of non-violence. He showed how powerful a force non-violence can be. Non-violence is not the path of the coward. It is a force that can calmly face bullets and death. He was not unaware of the misuse the coward would make of it by using nonviolence as a shield for his cowardice. He said that if anyone were to follow non-violence because of cowardice then it were better to be violent and face death.

Gandhi stopped being a member of the Congress from 1934. Yet the Congress would not leave him because they knew well enough that the people had faith in Gandhi.

As Gandhi grew in stature he also attracted more criticism. A surprising accusation was that he 'communal-ised' politics by using 'Hindu symbols'. One could well ask, how else was a matter to be explained to the simplest peasant of whom the vast majority were Hindus if one did not use the language they understood? To use known symbols and a language that is understood is even now the most accepted and scientific method of teaching.

If words like *Ramrajya* which connoted an ideal state with an ideal king to the Hindu, were considered 'Communal' surely the English language in use in India contained a host of words which were intimately concerned with Christianity. If there could be no objection to those words then why the objection to Hindu words? But there was another reason for using Hindu words to the Hindu. In a proselytising and imperial climate 'Hindu' had almost become a dirty word. This restored to the Hindu his own identity and dignity.[64] By this time there were already some Indians who were trained by the English medium institutions to be 'brown englishmen'. They were in fact sometimes worse than their white brothers because their knowledge was limited. They had been taught to learn but not to think. They recited but without understanding (just as some Hindus did earlier with the *Vedas*). They accepted all criticism against the Indian or the Hindu made by foreign authors and based their own theories on them. For any study to be worthwhile comparison is essential. But in order to compare we must first know. These Indians did not know and so had no standards by which to compare.

Modern was a magical word for many, and this meant machinery, a western mode of living and thinking. It was the 'holy cow' mentality again, only in a different form! Many of these unfortunately were the products of educational institutions which concentrated on those western philosophers who represented the materialistic view. The Idealist philosophers of the west, some of whom had a highly developed ethical outlook and whose thinking went far deeper, were largely ignored. Basically the Realists believe in the reality of the material. Their highest goal is the 'greatest good of the greatest number'.

'The problem that arises is what is good? And who decides what is good? In eastern thought materialism is synonymous with ignorance. By believing in the limited material as the only Reality, we are limiting ourselves. The outcome is superficial and narrow minds. It is perhaps no coincidence that the materialist philosophy in the west gained ground when scientists like Darwin and others who gave their views on creation which seemed contrary to the Biblical views on creation, were condemned by churchmen and others for 'going against the Bible.' Others decided to play safe.

Many of the leaders in India belonging to all creeds were educated and well-read in not only their own culture and philosophy but also western thought. Gandhi himself had studied not only the Hindu religious books but also the Bible, Koran and books of other religions. He discovered that all religions preach the same thing. Truth and honesty are the only things worth abiding by in life. Each religion gives this message in its own way.

It is from this understanding that we judge, each according to his merit and not by his caste, creed or community. If there were people of integrity in the freedom movement there were also those outside it. If there were many diehard imperialists among the British as well as their missionaries there were also many who were not. No wholesale generalisation is ever possible, because to do so would not be true.

Another point made against Gandhi was by none other than M.A. Jinnah. He objected to Gandhi's encouragement to the Khilafat movement. He thought that by doing so he was 'communalising' the national movement. His views cannot be lightly dismissed, but there is no doubt that Gandhi's doing so resulted in the Muslims joining India's Freedom movement in large numbers.

Ultimately every action can only be judged by the intention of the action. If both acted with the highest motives and differed, also moved by the highest motives, neither can be faulted. It is for each one's conscience. But ironically India became a free country in 1947, only after she was divided on purely religious grounds. Jinnah, who headed the Muslim League after resigning from the Congress, insisted on a separate state for Muslims. When India became free, Pakistan also came into being.

The British policy of 'Divide and Rule', the seeds of which were sown much earlier, had finally paid off. For those who see that good cannot be confined to any one region or people, religion can hardly seem a firm basis for any nation. Proselytising cultures are responsible for nurturing many superstitions and beliefs that have nothing to do with the truths of the religion as taught by their prophets, but are rather the works of lesser men. The great teachers of religion the world over have invariably been against superficial divisions and conceits. They all denounce hypocricy.

Alberuni, one of the finest scholars the world has known, writing about the differences that divided the Hindu and Muslim communities mentions the contempt one community had for the other but goes on to say, "By the by, we must confess in order to be just, that a similar depreciation of foreigners not only prevails among us but is common to all nations towards each other."[65]

So also we find a group of Englishmen who observe "The object of these pages is to show on behalf of those who cannot answer for themselves, that they are neither so black nor we so white that we paint them and ourselves, that their governments and institutions were neither so defective nor ours so perfect as we assert them to have been, and that 'the History of Indian Progress' which we create in bulky volumes only means after all that the Christian Indian government of the 19th century is better than the Mohammedan or Hindu governments of the 15th and 16th centuries. This is the extent of our pretensions, and we can only support this claim by deprecating the character and doings of our predecessors and exaggerating our own, and after all leaving it very much in doubt whether the balance is really in our favour."[66]

Perhaps no single individual felt the severing of India by partition more than Gandhi, and certainly no single individual did more to staunch the wounds than Gandhi. The terrible loss of life that India suffered in partition is one of the bloodiest pages in her history.

Gandhi preferred to remain away from the power and pomp that now came with freedom to many of his former colleagues who were now in government. Nehru became Prime Minister and Vallabhai Patel the Home Minister and India owes much to them. There seems to be a misconception as to the reasons for Gandhi's death, although it is a part of very recent history. Some western publications (among them even school text-books) state that Gandhi was killed by a high-caste Hindu because of his stand on untouchability.[67] This is a clear case of two and two making five. It is an example of a poor standard of scholarship. The killings of partition that started in Quetta but engulfed both Indian and Pakistani refugees created great resentment. According to the terms of partition a certain amount of Indian government money was to be transferred to Pakistan. The Indian government, aware of the peoples' feelings, was reluctant to hand over these assets until Pakistan made reparations for the losses sustained. At this time and in these circumstances Gandhi said firmly that Pakistan must be handed its share as per the agreement. Gandhi was perfectly well aware that he may even be courting death and certainly unpopularity. He was however more concerned with doing what he thought was right. It is unfortunate that in so much that has been written about Gandhi this fact has not been highlighted enough. But this more than anything, shows the heights Gandhi in his quest for truth had achieved.

When one hears someone claiming that 'Gandhi died for Hindu-Muslim unity' it quite obviously emanates from a person who is more emotional than rational. Truth is concerned with principles and not personalities. Gandhi would no doubt have done the same even if Pakistan had been Timbuctoo. A word also needs to be said here about the assassin of Gandhi. He was a Hindu, a high caste Hindu, but he did not kill Gandhi because of his espousing the cause of the untouchables.[68] He shot Gandhi because he considered Gandhi's stand that Pakistan be given her assets as wrong and against Indian interests. The issue was in no sense either a communal or caste issue. It was to him a national issue. It becomes necessary to state with regard to the same truth that Gandhi stood for, that the assassin was no cloak-and-dagger man doing his foul deed under cover of darkness or for self-publicity. He respected Gandhi, but thought him wrong. He shot Gandhi in broad daylight in front of hundreds of people and gave himself up. He was prepared to give his life for the life he took.

Before we condemn him out of hand, it is worth recognizing that there are many who swear by Gandhi's name and indulge in anti-national and anti-social acts. They are perhaps more responsible for the murder of Gandhi than Gandhi's assassin. Godse killed Gandhi physically, but the others have killed all that Gandhi stood for.

Whether India would or would not have achieved independence with or without Gandhi is not the point. A number of causes, both perceived and unperceived, are responsible for events which take place with none being able to stem them. What is important is the effort that a people make to secure their objectives. For Gandhi, it may be said that non-violence to him was not just an instrument to be used for Indian independence. For him it was religion, the path of his own salvation. But at the best of times those who attain salvation are very few. The large numbers who followed him could not have had the same goals, but the more immediate and material one of securing the independence of the country. Many of them were prepared to give their lives for this cause, and did.

Nor did all agree with the path of non-violence. Subhash Bose, for instance, a member of the Congress, differed with Gandhi and had a large following among the youth. Yet they respected one another. The title of "Father of the Nation" was given to Gandhi by Bose. During the Second World War Bose had escaped from India and joined forces with the Japanese. Among the younger element many took the path of terrorism. They were caught and hanged. Among these were people of all creeds.

But let us not forget the silent millions who gave their moral support without being in the limelight. Those who dutifully discharged their normal responsibilities were also helping their country and should not be underestimated.

There were again those who were in the service of the alien government but were nevertheless patriotic Indians. The fact that their experience and expertise was used after independence by the Indian government without doubting their patriotism, is a tribute to the statesmanship and sagacity of the Home Minister, Vallabhai Patel.

In the freedom movement itself there were people of various hues. The Hindu Mahasabha, a Hindu party, had emerged as a balancing factor to the Muslim League. Savarkar, its leader was an uncompromising nationalist. He had suffered imprisonment in the Andamans for his views and activities. Apart from his political beliefs, he was also a reformist who believed that Hindus must rid themselves of outmoded beliefs and rituals. Among many other things, he was against the practice of untouchability as well as differences.[69] He wanted Indians to join the war as soldiers to have the experience of fighting, which free India would need.

Thinking Hindus have always had a high regard for education. This has been so from the earliest times. And this is also partly the reason for India's long and unbroken civilization. For knowledge both *tarka* (reasoning) as well as book-knowledge, were necessary. Thinking Hindus were impressed by western technological advances and also the need to acquire this knowledge.

That it is necessary to acquire a superior knowledge before independence could be achieved was clearly stated for the first time in Bankim Chandra's novel *Ananda Math*. The song *"Vande Mataram"* the most popular song of freedom during the struggle for Indian independence was from this book.

Some idea may be got of the quality of education under the British regime. "Almost all professors in colleges and the headmasters of even some secondary schools were Englishmen. All school books were prescribed by the Directors of Public Instruction in several provinces all of whom were Westerners. Even primary education was being given only to a small fraction of the children of school-going age even in 1947 when the British left. . . . . English education caused great wastage of effort in learning all subjects (including Sanskrit!) through English and disproportionate growth of library studies and neglect of scientific and technological subjects and created a wide gulf between the educated and uneducated masses. It glorified western culture and did not help Indians to study and appreciate their own culture. Educated Indians, particularly during the earlier period of British education in India, came to entertain an exaggerated respect for western institutions and unduly disparaged their own social and religious systems. . . . The British government's interest in Indian education (particularly higher) was luke-warm. The Universities (Bombay, Calcutta and Madras) first established in 1857 were for the whole of India and were only examining bodies. In the whole of Bombay Presidency there was no Science Institute entirely maintained by the Government till about 1920. An Indian could be an M.A. in Philosophy without knowing anything of ancient Indian Philosophy."[70]

But quite often the effect of certain actions may be quite the opposite of what should be expected.

"However English education by Government and missionaries produced the opposite result. The missionaries failed miserably in securing Indian (except a few of the lower castes and Adivasis) for Christ, and the classics of English literature and the works of Burke, Spencer, Mill and others generated among the educated, nationalism and discontent with their own abject political status. Political agitation daily increased."[71]

It is also true that the character of the English had also changed. The earlier thirst for knowledge for its own sake that had characterised the works of some Englishmen had been substituted by a much lower ideal in keeping with the policies of the empire. "The great age of western appreciation of Indian literature and philosophy, the age of Sir William Jones, Franz Bopp and Sir Edwin Arnold had passed. . . . 1860 marked the turning point . . . This was not fated to last. Sir William Jones' successors soon began to adopt the slightly hostile and superior attitude which characterizes the work of Englishmen writing on Indian subjects. . . from 1836 this tradition became firmly established. After the mutiny, a new type of Englishman went to the East, including journalists and schoolmasters; they brought their wives and were visited by tourists; within India a domicile English and European population was growing in numbers and developing a life of it's own. . . . The British were rapidly developing into a separate caste, strongly re-enforced by the new officials, planters and businessmen who came crowding out east after 1860. There was a natural tendency for writers to concentrate on this colony of their experienced countrymen." . . . producing a mass of cheap novels "nearly all of which were grossly offensive to the Hindu race. . . Indians only entered into the books as either domestics or women 'kept' by Englishmen. The few educated Indians who came into Kipling's books seem to have been introduced to satisfy the deep-seated prejudices of the English in India . . . Kipling allowed himself the most astounding generalisations about Hindu duplicity and mendacity or the physical cowardice of certain races."[72]

But it is interesting to see how the thought of one country travels to another and keeps knowledge alive. If Indians made use of their contact with the west so did the west due to the efforts of some of their scholars, particularly the earlier ones.

"The study of Sanskrit literature by Europeans at the end of the 18th century and in the 19th century "laid the foundation of several sciences, such as the science of language, of comparative religion, of thought and of mythology. India has preserved for itself and the world a vast treasure in the best part of which the principal theme is to ask men never to cease their efforts to control the senses and to reach higher and higher heights of morality and spirituality."[73]

Classical Sanskrit blossomed at least before 500 BC, Panini being the earliest known grammarian, but even Panini names at least 10 predecessors in his sutras (IV.3.87-88)[74] A glance at the end of this book will show the continuous contributions to knowledge from the earliest times. The table is by no means comprehensive, since it refers mostly to *Dharmasastra* literature. There was a great deal of literature on secular subjects as well.

If the Indians were impressed by the foremost thinkers of the west, these thinkers in their turn have also been influenced in no small way by the philosophies of Buddhism and the Vedanta.[75]

Indians were also quick to notice the difference between practice and precept. This was so not only in the case of the missionaries but also the western governments. What was being sold was not Christianity but Fundamentalist Christianity, a thing of miracle and superstition making conversion and not man's intrinsic worth the only way to salvation. The west had already lost faith in the Christian virtues preached by Christ.[76]

The Christian Logos doctrine which finds it's fulfillment in the incarnate Christ considering it a unique event is not shared by the eastern philosophies, which believe that a moral crisis is a recurring event.

Indians fought the British regime both politically and religiously. The British had already made religion a hand maid of their empire using their missionaries.

Perhaps nothing so brought home and in the most simple way the exploitative nature of foreign rule as Gandhi's Salt Satyagraha. This has been written about often enough but the reason for it is very rarely given. Western accounts paint it as 'unjustified since earlier regimes also taxed the making of salt'. But this is only an example of *supressio veri* and *suggesto falsi* that unfortunately characterises so many books on politics and other allied subjects.

While it is true that salt was taxed by earlier governments as well, during British rule what the Indians were paying for was not their own salt of which they had enough but salt which they did not need and which came to them all the way from England. Ships going to England with Indian goods returned almost half-empty. Salt would be filled as ballast.[77] The making of salt in India was strictly prohibited.

Gandhi's Salt Satyagraha brought home to every Indian of every class the exploitative nature of the regime.

Thinking Indians saw the blight of poverty spreading in the land. Worse still was the philosophy of dependance sought to be inculcated. The self-confidence of the people was being sapped. The Hindus being the single largest community were understandably in the freedom struggle in large numbers. But so were people from every other community.

The Hindus were in the political battle as well as engaged in a reformist movement to cleanse Hindu society of its evils. The movement was for social as well as religious reforms. In this were men and women from every walk of life and all professions.

That rules and customs need to be constantly changed and adapted to the needs of society are accepted in *Dharmasastras, Manu., Yaj., Visnudh.,* and *Puranas* all state that one should not observe but give up what was once *dharma* (custom in this case) if it became hurtful to the people and if it would end in unhappiness.

Fundamentalism is not a new phenomena in the world. It is basically the worship of form. The form becomes more important than meaning.[78] When a custom or ritual, etc., is preserved unthinkingly even when it has outlived it's utility or it's purpose, it is image-worship. Materialism and literalism are just two aspects of the image-worshipping mind. It is not surprising that Gandhi sternly forbade all attempts by his politician followers from making him out as a divine incarnation.[79] The easiest thing is to worship the form and then go one's own way!

Even here inspite of the kind of education received during British rule and the effect it had on some, not all succumbed to it. The more active and eager to learn certainly gained by cultivating discrimination as well as judgement in sorting grain from the chaff.

The Indian National Congress itself contained some elements, not all of whom understood the call of *Swadeshi*.

In *Art and Swadeshi*, A. Coomaraswamy observes, "India was once a great political power in Asia. When she colonized Java and inspired China was also the highest period of cultural achievement . . . It is the weakness of our national movement that we do not love India. We love suburban England, we love the comfortable bourgeoisie prosperity that is to be some day established when we have learnt enough science and forgotten enough art to successfully compete with Europe in a commercial war conducted on present lines. . . . Civilization consists not in multiplying the quality of our desires but in refinement of their quality. . . . The whole endeavour of true swadeshi should be to restore, not to destroy the organic life of the village communities, restoring the status of the skilled artisan and village craftsman. Trade guilds used to receive support and protection under Indian kings and these were withdrawn by the British government. The two reasons for the loss of craftsmanship was (1) Loss of independence and (2) Consequent loss of patronage."

"The problem is not how to abolish machinery, but how to regulate it that it should serve without enslaving man; how to stop competition between machine and handwork by defining and delimiting intelligently the proper share of each. The community cannot afford to dispense with the intellectual and imaginative forces, the educational and ethical factors in life which go with the existence of skilled craftsmanship and small workshops."

India became free in 1947. The Indian National Congress as the most representative political party came to power, with Jawaharlal Nehru as Prime Minister and Vallabhai Patel as Home Minister. Immediately on assumption of power they had to face the terrible killings of partition.

Nehru is given the credit for keeping democracy alive in India. But Patel's achievement was no less. Had it not

been for his firm handling there may have been no India.
The 600 and odd princely states of India had been given by
the British the option to secede if they liked from the Union
of India. Patel's firm handling of these princely states
made them all an integral part of India. Also, some of the
Indian princes on their own volunteered to sacrifice their
individual identities for the national good. Nehru was
accepted by all as Prime Minister. Different aspects of him
appealed to different temperaments. To the British and
the Anglosized in India he was acceptable because he
had been educated in an English public school and the
University of Cambridge. He also had western manners
and polish. To the Muslim (particularly of U.P.) his culture
belonged to the culture of the nawabs. He spoke in Urdu,
the language having the same source as Hindi, but which
with Persianized script was used mainly by the Muslim
rulers of U.P. To those who were guided by caste and
family considerations, he was a Brahmin and his father a
rich lawyer. To those who are emotional about such things
his joining the freedom movement meant sacrifice, having
the aura of renunciation. To those who talked in terms of
socialism, he was their man while others saw in him
science and modernity which alone could see the country
through. Nehru was known outside India as well, not only
because of his part in India's freedom struggle, but because
of his book *Discovery of India*. Nehru had both looks and
polish.

Patel who became Home Minister had his own stature
by virtue of his role in the freedom movement. He was
known nationally but not internationally. If to Nehru goes
the credit for preserving democracy, to Patel goes the
credit for consolidation. Of the two, Patel was the better
administrator. Had it not been for Patel's foresight the
Dalai Lama would not have been able to escape to the
safety of India when communist China annexed Tibet.

Unfortunately for India Patel did not last long enough. He was also hurt at the politically-inspired whispering campaign that had started after the assassination of Mahatma Gandhi implying that Patel was 'communal' and had deliberately failed to prevent Gandhi's death.

Among all of Gandhi's colleagues Patel had been one of the closest, not excepting Nehru.

Patel was not alive to see any of the wars India lived through. In 1962 there was a war between India and China about the border between the two countries. This was despite the *Panchsheel* pact signed with great fanfare.

Nehru complained that "China has stabbed us in the back" to which C. Rajagopalachari, an erudite Hindu elder statesman and free India's first governor-general, retorted that it is an "enemy's business to stab one in the back."

Hindu *Arthasastra* literature does not recommend blind trust in worldly affairs.

There have been three conflicts between India and Pakistan since independence. The last one led to the separation of Bangladesh from Pakistan.

There were many whose ideas of modernisation meant westernisation. What Indians saw with dismay was the aping of western institutions without taking into consideration the Indian situation. It was image-worship again with its attendant lack of clear thinking. But if there are the image-worshippers there are also the rational and balanced individuals. From the earliest times, secularism has been almost a creed in India, because it is the rational way to behave. Salvation can be only through worth and not birth or religious labels. All saints and thinkers for the same reason condemned pride of caste.

Gandhi's assassination was for some the ideal excuse for creating the image of the 'communal Hindu'.

We see here again vested interests, this time indigenous ones using religion for their material self-interest.

The Hindu philosophy, (which means the philosophies of all the four religions born in India) is that Truth alone is Eternal.

The Koran also says that God is Truth.

It is the nature of Truth that Christ tries to show through his parables. This is the message of all the world's great teachers everywhere.

Independent India also gave herself her ancient identity and name, Bharata. She declared her faith in her motto *Satyameva Jayate*. Truth alone prevails.

But in accordance with the prevailing westernized modern compartmentalized thought, India also gave herself a constitution wherein she declared herself to be a secular, socialist, democratic republic.

Neither secularism, nor socialism nor democracy is against Hindu thought. India has had republics before. The Hindus throughout their history have shown commendable tolerance despite grave provocation. The view that salvation comes not through any particular religion but by one's own efforts to live a useful and honest life, is a secular ideal as it makes merit and worth more important than the label. Even the Hindu caste structure as conceived was a form of socialism as from each man according to his capacity for the good of all.[80] It is a higher ideal than each according to his capacity, to each according to his needs or only for himself. Each served his profession for the good of society. The professions were seen as a function to fulfil the needs of a civilization.

Compartmentalized thinking does not belong to Hindu thought, which accepts the whole and not the part. The part cannot exist by itself. All forms are parts. Compartmentalized thought obstructs the clear flow of thought, resulting in stagnation and petty prejudices. Truth, the Spirit, is the highest and the only goal. All forms depend on Truth.

While western thought conceives of charity, faith, hope, etc. as separate virtues, Hindu thought recognizes only One Truth. If charity is practised in the spirit of Truth, i.e., with honesty, knowledge and understanding (on principle and not personality) then it is a virtue, when this is not so done it becomes a vice. Knowledge therefore receives great importance in Hindu thought. All knowledge is a search for Truth. No real enquiry can be worthwhile which does not have Truth alone as it's goal and no action worthwhile which does not have Truth as it's source. Other considerations are material considerations and flaw our enquiry. While forms and action are limited, knowledge is unlimited — Knowledge is neither 'good' nor 'bad', it is our actions that are, depending on the source from which they spring.

Republics are mentioned in Hindu political treatises. The qualities listed for a leader of a *Ganarajya* (republic) are sagacity, forbearance, self-control and non-acquisitiveness.

On the subject of ministers, the Sukra (1182-83) asks, "How can the kingdom be brought to prosperity by those ministers whom the king is not afraid to offend? They are no better than ladies who are to be decked with ornaments and fine clothes. What is the use of those ministers whose advice does not tend to the advancement of the kingdom, the people, the army, the treasury, good government and to the destruction of the enemies?"[81]

Hindu thought recognizes the importance of morality for every action. Morality comes from selflessness.

Hindu thought points out again and again with examples, that one's worth is not dependent on caste, creed, family, wealth, race, learning, sex etc., legitimacy cannot be derived from any of these external factors. Legitimacy has to be from within.

Individuality is inherent in all creations. Destroying

individuality is to destroy creation itself. Each and everything in creation is meant for the furtherance of creation. The physical, emotional and intellectual are meant for use. Existence is both creation and destruction. Wisdom lies in understanding.

Hard work and honesty are as important for the doctor as for the servant or housewife or patient. The more honest we are the more refined and sensitive we become in our behaviour towards others (as also ourselves). Good manners come from consideration for others. When only lip service is payed then such manners seem hollow and lose their value. The difference between sentiment and sentimentality is the difference between the true and the false. It is a relative difference.

The people were told not only of their duties but also their rights and responsibilities. Nobody, not even the king could be above the law. This message was taken to the people. This was a practical application of Hindu philosophical thoughts of the "One Essence in all."

One hears a lot about cleaning the Ganga. The Ganga is revered by every Hindu. This is so because of the scenic beauty as well as the fact that rivers provide life, food and also communication. It is our duty to keep our rivers and streams clean so that they might do their proper function. To worship Ganga is to keep the Ganga clean so that she can perform for the good of all. That is her purpose. Worship means to help preserve the functioning of each thing and not put it into a frame. It is this idea that is reflected in India because every stream and river is called the Ganga.

'Image-worship' is not only found among Hindus, it is common to all people. It prevents knowledge and understanding. It prevents us from using our mind, intellect, heart and hands as they are meant to be used. Hindu thinkers point out that Existence is divine. Existence alone is Reality and Truth. Truth is divine and in all creation. We have but to understand ourselves. When we understand ourselves we understand all. Sacredness is not in any object but in our attitude.

Hindus have achieved their greatest heights when they have treated knowledge as sacred, and sought to purify their own understanding in order to know more and more so that they could function better.

All things in life have their own inherent functions. Hindu religious treatises consider the gift of knowledge as one of the greatest gifts.[82]

Alberuni, one of the greatest scholars made a study of Hinduism and the Hindus of India. He writes, "According to the Hindu philosophers, liberation is common to all castes and to the whole human race, if their intention of attaining it is perfect. This view is based on the saying of Vyasa, 'learn to know the twenty-five things thoroughly. Then you may follow whatever religion you like; you will no doubt be liberated."

Hinduism considers all equal before God. Divinity is in all. We have but to realise it. We achieve by our own efforts, not through following any religion, prophet, saint or book. Hindu thought quite clearly rejects such irrational claims as 'God's chosen.'

It was this that made Hindus respect those of other religions and allow them to follow their religious practices. It was this again that made the Hindus rise up against those who sought to destroy their religion and philosophy itself. Sikhism which started as a peaceful religion had to take to arms for self-protection. This is personified in the last Sikh Guru Govind Singh. Saints and warriors pointed out that tolerance of iniquity and intolerance is submission. It violates Truth. Those who seek to promote their own interests at the cost of others cannot be endowed with truly philanthrophic motives. The British who called their empire a 'white man's burden' and successfully impoverished the lands they ruled, encouraged missionary activity. Missionary charity was in many cases a cover for imperialistic aims of which proselytism played a significant part. It was hardly surprising that discriminating Indians distrusted these agents of organized religion whose interpretation of Christianity seemed to have very little to do with the teachings of Christ.

The message of all the great saints and prophets and religious teachers has been the same. Worshipping the material is image-worship and comes in the way of Knowledge. Knowledge comes to the pure. In Hindu thought science and religion have never been in conflict. It is worthwhile not to forget it. But Hindu thought sees science, art and skill in all creation. The future of India and Hindus only time will tell and history. They will not fail if they remember that knowledge is eternal.

References

1. *History of Dharmasastra* by P.V. Kane, vol.V, pt.2, chap.XXXVI, sec.X, p.1613.
2. As per chronological table given in H.D., vol.V, pt.2, vol.III, introduction, p.147.
3. "The Aryans: A Re-appraisal of the Problem" by B.K. Thapar, in *India's Contribution to World Thought and Culture* (Vivekanada Rock Memorial Committee, Madras, 1970).
4. "India's Contribution to Islamic Thought and Culture" by N.N. Bhattacharya in *India's Contribution to World Thought and Culture* (V.R.M.C., 1970).
5. *A New History of Sanskrit Literature* by Krishna Chaitanya, chap.I (IV).
6. *History of Dharmasastra* by P.V. Kane, vol.III, p.930-934.
   Life and Culture of Indian People by K.A.N. Sastri and G. Srinivasachari (Allied Publishers), chap.V, p.108.
7. ibid., vol.V, pt.2, chap.XXXVI, sec.X, p.1617-1618.
   ibid., chap.III, p.29.

8. ibid., vol.V, pt.2, chap.XXXVI, sec.X, p.1613; See also chap.XXXIV, sec.IX, p.1526-1527.
9. *Life and Culture of the Indian People* by K.A.N. Sastri and G. Srinivasachari, p.60, 61.
10. *History of Dharmasastra* by P.V. Kane, vol.V, pt.2, chap.XXXV, sec.IX, p.1530, 1532.
11. ibid., vol.V, pt.2, chap.XXXV, sec.IX, p.1530, 1532.
12. ibid., vol.V, pt.2, chap.XXXV, sec.V, p.1012.
13. ibid., vol.V, pt.2, chap.XXVIII.
    The Painter in Ancient India by S. Sivarammurti.
    Pathway to God in Hindu Literature by R.D. Ranade, 1954, p.283.
14. *Gita Rahasya* by B.G. Tilak (Marathi), chap.III.
15. *History of Dharmasastra* by P.V. Kane, vol.V, pt.2, chap.XXV, sec.V, p.1025.
16. "India and Soviet Central Asia" by B.A. Litvinsky in *India's Contribution to World Thought and Culture* (V.R.M.C., 1970), p.263.
17. *History of Dharmasastra* by P.V. Kane, vol.V, pt.2, chap.XXV, sec.V, p.1006.
18. ibid., vol.V, pt.2, chap.XXV, sec.V, p.1006, 1007.
    Hinduism and Buddhism by A Coomaraswamy.
    Vivekananda's Complete works, Bk.II.
19. ibid., vol.V, pt.2, chap.XXIV, sec.V, p.947, 948.
20. ibid., vol.III, chap.III, p.89, 90.
    Life and Culture of the Indian People by K.A.N. Sastri and G. Srinivasachari (1974), p.27.
21. ibid., vol.V, pt.2, chap.XXXVI, sec.X, p.1617, 1618 (also p.1615 notes).
    A. Toynbee's *Reconsiderations*, vol.XII of his *Study of History*.
22. "India's Contribution to the History of Science" by B.V. Subbarayappa in *India's Contribution to World Thought and Culture* (V.R.M.C.), p.47.
    Life and Culture of the Indian People by K.A.N. Sastri and G. Srinivasachari (Allied Publishers, 1974), p.92, 93, 94.
23. *History of Dharmasastra* by P.V. Kane, vol.V, pt.2, chap.XXXVI, sec.X, p.1621.
24. ibid., vol.V, pt.2, chap.XXXIV, sec.IX, p.1527.
25. Unsubstantiated, with differing views, e.g. *Paper on St. Thomas' Tomb* by T.K. Joseph in Mahamahopadhyaya Prof. D.V. Potdar Commemoration Volume, 1950, p.265.
    History of India by Romilla Thapar (Pelican, 1976), p.134.
    Life and Culture of the Indian People by K.A.N. Sastri and G. Srinivasachari, p.23.
26. *History of Dharmasastra* by P.V. Kane, vol.V, pt.2, chap.XXV, sec.V, p.1019.
    Profile of Indian Culture by K. Chaitanya.

27. ibid., vol.V, pt.2, chap.XXIV, sec.V, p.969, 970.
     Life and Culture of the Indian People by K.A.N. Sastri and G.
     Srinivasachari, p.34, 35, 36.
28. *Hindu Sculptures in Ancient Afghanistan* by P. Banerjee.
     The Spice and Silk Roads by Anil de Silva, p.300.
     "Indian Religion and the West: Historical Perspectives" by B.M.
     Pande, p.615, 616; p.216, by R.C. Agrawala in *India's Contribution to
     world Thought and Culture* (V.R.M.C., 1970).
29. *History of Dharmasastra* by P.V. Kane, vol.II, pt.2, chap.XXVII, p.928.
     "India in the eyes of Muslim Scholars" by Arjun Dev, p.616 in *India's
     Contribution to World Thought and Culture* (V.R.M.C.).
30. "India's Contribution to Arab Civilization" by W.H. Siddiqi, p.582 in
     India's Contribution to World Thought and Culture (V.R.M.C.).
31. *Decline and Fall of the Roman Empire* by Edward Gibbon, chap.II, p.55.
     Life and Culture of the Indian People by K.A.N. Sastri and G.
     Srinivasachari, p.93.
32. *History of Dharmasastra* by P.V. Kane, vol.II, pt.2, chap.XXVI, p.906,
     907, 909.
33. ibid., vol.IV, chap.XIII, vol.I, p.173 (Ref. to Alberuni on Benares).
34. ibid., vol.IV, chap.XIII.
35. ibid., vol.IV, chap.XIII.
36. ibid., vol.III, chap.XXXIII, p.881.
37. *Muslim Politics in Secular India* by Hamid Dalwai (Hind Pocket Books,
     1968), p.36.
38. *Siddhanta* by Deoras.
39. *History of Dharmasastra* by P.V. Kane, vol.V, pt.2, chap.XXIV, sec.V,
     p.969, 970.
40. ibid., vol.V, pt.2, chap.XXIV, sec.V, p.969.
41. ibid., vol.V, pt.2, chap.XXIV, sec.V, p.969.
     Life and Culture of the Indian People by K.A.N. Sastri and G.
     Srinivasachari, p.3, 35, 47.
42. *Poverty and un-British Rule in British India* by Dadabhai Naoroji
     (London, 1901), p.584.
43. ibid., p.591.
44. ibid., p.591.
45. ibid., p.594.
46. ibid., p.603.
47. ibid., p.606.
48. ibid., p.585.
     Life and Culture of the Indian People by K.A.N. Sastri and G.
     Srinivasachari, chap.III.
49. *A New History of Sanskrit Literature* by Krishna Chaitanya, chap.I.
     Life and Culture of the Indian People by K.A.N. Sastri and G.
     Srinivasachari, chap.III, p.49.

50. *History of Dharmasastra* by P.V. Kane, vol.V, pt.2, chap.XXXVII, sec.X, p.1658.
51. ibid.
52. *The Christians* by Bamber Gascoigne.
53. *From Pagan to Christian* by Lin Yutang (Heinemann, 1960), p.35, 36.
54. *History of India*, vol.II, by P. Spear (Pelican).
55. *History of Dharmasastra* by P.V. Kane, vol.V, pt.2, chap.XXV, sec.V, p.1020.
56. *The Christians* by Bamber Gascoigne.
57. ibid.
58. *Life and Culture of the Indian People* by K.A.N. Sastri and G. Srinivasachari, chap.III, p.32.
    History of Dharmasastra by P.V. Kane, vol.III, chap.III, p.68.
59. *History of Dharmasastra* by P.V. Kane, vol.III, chap.XXXIII, p.868.
60. ibid., vol.V, pt.2, chap.XXXVII, sec.X, p.1659.
61. *Poverty and un-British Rule in British India* by Dadabhai Naoroji, p.624.
62. *In the Woods of God realisation* by Swami Ram Tirtha, vol.III quoted from Romesh Dutt's *Economic History of British India*.
63. *Poverty and un-British Rule in British India* by Dadabhai Naoroji.
64. *Life and Culture of the Indian People* by K.A.N. Sastri and G. Srinivasachari, chap.VI, p.110.
65. "India in the eyes of Muslim Scholars" by Arjun Dev and "Indian Religion and the West" by B.M. Pande in *India's Contribution to World Thought and Culture* (V.R.M.C., 1970).
66. *Poverty and Un-British Rule in British India* by Dadabhai Naoroji, p.614.
67. *Life and Culture of the Indian People* by K.A.N. Sastri and G. Srinivasachari, chap.VIII.
68. ibid.
69. *History of Dharmasastra* by P.V. Kane, vol.V, pt.2, chap.XXXVI, sec.X, p.1621 and 1622.
70. ibid.
71. ibid., vol.V, pt.2, chap.XXXVI, sec.X, p.1662.
72. *Wisdom of China and India* by Lin Yutang.
73. *History of Dharmasastra* by P.V. Kane, vol.V, pt.2, chap.XXXVI, sec.X, p.1650.
74. ibid., vol.V, pt.2, chap.XXXVI, sec.X, p.1651.
75. ibid., vol.V, pt.2, chap.XXXVI, sec.X, p.1625, 1650.
    ibid., vol.V, pt.2, chap.XXXV, sec.IX, p.1547.
    In the Woods of God realisation by Swami Ram Tirtha, vol.III.
    Some Problems of Indian Literature by M. Winternitz, chap.IV.

76. *History of Dharmasastra* by P.V. Kane, vol.V, pt.2, chap.XXXIII, sec.VIII, quotes from Archibald Robertson in *Rationalism in Theory and Practice*, p.41.
    C.H. Tawney in *Acquisitive Society*, p.12, 13.
77. *Gandhi His Life and Thought* by J.B. Kripalani (Publication Div., New Delhi, 1970).
78. Bamber Gascoigne in *The Christians* enumerates what some Christians considered as 'fundamental beliefs' for all Christians. It can be seen that none of these 'beliefs' have any relevance to the teachings of Christ. If Christ's teachings were meant to promote knowledge and understanding, these 'fundamental beliefs' encourage myth and superstition.
79. *M.K. Gandhi* by Romaine Rolland (Publication Div., New Delhi, 1976).
80. *History of Dharmasastra* by P.V. Kane, chap.XXXVI, sec.X, p.1634, 1635.
81. ibid., vol.III, chap.IV, p.108.
82. ibid., vol.II, pt.2, chap.XXV, p.848.

Sanatana Dharma

Among the world's oldest religions still alive and practised today is Hinduism. Almost one-fifth of the human race follows this faith, yet there is no single set of dogma, no single book of faith such as the Koran for Islam and the Bible for the Christian, which can be called the prescribed religious book of the Hindus.

To the Hindu the *Sanatana Dharma* is the Eternal Truth, the moral imperative which sustains the whole Cosmic Order. The earliest reference in regard to Hindu thought and philosophy is to be found in the monumental collection of Hymns known as the Samhitas, the earliest *Rig Veda* being probably over four to six thousand years old in point of time.

The *Sanatana Dharma* is not a religion in the sense of the revelation of a prophet, but more correctly a system of knowledge derived through patient and persistent enquiry into the existence of the Universe and the purpose of man's existence. What is awesome to the modern mind is the similarity between the methods of enquiry utilized by the Rishis — composers of the ancient hymns — and the tools of enquiry used by modern scientists today.

Utilizing observation, inference, comparison and intuition, these great Seers delved into the mysteries of the material world, i.e. the world of perceived phenomena.

In the sublime setting of India's great mountains, rivers and forests, these Seers cogitated into the nature of the Real and the Unreal. Meticulous observation of natural phenomena led them to conclude that in time all things that the senses can perceive, i.e. plants, animals, man, even mountains, change; are in a state of flux, and dissolution.

In this quest to understand the world of matter they noted that the diverse forms of nature including man, do not merely decay, but there is also a resurgence of life — the butterfly dies, but before it dies it lays eggs from which emerge the caterpillar and then the butterfly.

They further noted a pattern of opposites i.e., life and death, day and night, joy and sorrow etc. From this they concluded a pattern of Cause-and-Effect; Action-and-Reaction; underlying the principle of creation and dissolution visible in the world of phenomena. This rhythm or pattern of order underlying sensory experience they termed *Rta*, viz., the Force or Law that accounts for balance in the world of phenomena.

Thus began the search for "that which is beyond the senses, the mind and intellect". In this way did the ancient *rishis* arrive at some of the most sublime and elevating philosophical concepts known to man — a quantum jump from enquiry into the nature of physical existence, viz., physics, to the nature of the primal energy, the Ultimate Reality or Prime Consciousness viz., the realm of metaphysics.

Since Reality or the Pure Consciousness cannot be perceived by the senses, it cannot be subject to the law of time, space and causation. It is therefore permanent, incorruptible, unchanging, indestructible and therefore indescribable.

Guided constantly by their keen observation of natural phenomena, they went on to conclude that all things, insects, plants, animals, rocks, man were inter-dependant and inter-linked. Anything or anyone that disturbed the inter-dependance and inter-relationship between these diverse entities of nature would cause harm to all. How then did the Pure Consciousness or Prime Cause maintain the balance? From these cogitations they arrived at the concept of an eternal law or *dharma* which governs the universe.

The word *dharma* is derived from the Sanskrit root *Dhr* meaning, to sustain, to nourish, to uphold'. *Sanatana* means eternal. *Dharma* therefore acquires meaning in terms of "moral duty" that which will sustain, support and uphold the Eternal Truth, or *Satya*, or Pure Consciousness of which the individual consciousness is part and which, when the material body is cast off merges into the Universal Life Force or Pure Consciousness. *Dharma* thus means ethical behaviour — that which is true, good, fair in itself, and which is not affected by what the material world, i.e., the "unreal world", projects.

The material world due to its impermanance, can only be called the world of "relative truth". What then is Truth? The Eternal, unchanging, incorruptible, indestructible Pure Consciousness/Intelligence/Soul/Truth/Reality/ *Atma* — the "Truth beyond the truth". Ignorance leads man to believe in the form, ignoring the spirit. Knowledge alone can dispel ignorance and enable man to discover his true nature. To attain *Sat*, the Eternal Truth or Reality, the seeker must detach himself from the world of the senses (undertake self-purification). The perception of truth is only possible by removing the veil of ignorance. This comes through pursuit of knowledge. The philosophy of the Vedanta seeks to dispel the darkness of ignorance so as to make perceptible the light of Truth.

The man of Truth, who has knowledge and wisdom, fears none. The *Samhitopanishad Brahmana* relates how Saraswati, goddess of learning, approached the teacher saying, "Preserve me, I am verily thy treasure. Do not deliver me to one full of envy or discontent, one not of straight conduct or of uncontrolled passions, but deliver me to one you know to be pure, attentive and chaste."

But how was man to understand *dharma*? Four sources are given by the composers of *Dharmasastras*, viz., the *Vedas*, Smritis (authorities in regard to rules of law and behaviour), *sadachara* (the good examples set by the good), and fourthly doing that which is 'good for the soul', i.e. the attainment of spirituality.

What therefore is the goal of life? Smritis describe the four-fold goal of *purushartha*. *Dharma, artha, kama* and *moksa* constituted the fourfold goals. *Dharma* stands for ethical training and behaviour, *artha* for attainment of and the means of fulfilling worldly needs, *kama* for fulfilment of the creative urge (procreation/and cultural pursuits), and *moksa* meaning liberation from attachment and desire.

For the pursuit of these goals man's life was viewed as comprising four stages called *asramas*. To establish a sound moral base *brahmacharya* or the first stage was devoted to the pursuit of knowledge and wisdom under a guru. *Gryhasta* was the stage when man took a wife and sought to provide his family with material and other comforts. He also fulfilled his duty towards society by performing religious rites, offering hospitality and giving in charity. *Vanaprastha* was the third stage. When man grew older he retired from worldly affairs, handed over his house-hold responsibilities to his son and retired to the forest to seek his spiritual welfare through study and meditation. In the last stage, *sanyas*, a man cuts himself off from worldly ties, from family and friends, and wanders from place to place on pilgrimage, freeing himself from all attachments as the ultimate preparation for moksa (liberation).

The organization of social structure known as *chatur-varna* is also four-fold, social distinctions being based on occupation known as the four castes. Each imposed certain responsibilities for the common good. The *Brahmin* was the repository of knowledge — both secular and spiritual; the *Kshatriya* was the warrior whose duty was to protect others; the *Vaisya* undertook trade and commerce, agriculture and the care of livestock; and the *Sudra* served the other castes or was employed in some occupation catering to the needs of society. Woven into the concept of *chaturvarna* was the common obligation to serve society, each caste in its prescribed way, to fulfill the goal of welfare of all. This social organization based on man's *dharma* or ethical duty aimed at harmonizing the needs and requirements of the family as well as those of society as a whole.

Hindu philosophy views the entire creation as manifestation of the cosmic will. God as the Pure Consciousness/ Intelligence the *Param Atma*, is beyond the ken of mind and speech (*neti, neti*, not this, not this). The *jivatma* being the individualised manifestation of the Pure Intelligence is given to ceaseless activity. Each activity or desire is thus activated by will and manifests itself as action. The assertion of Existence is called Reality (*Sat*). The yoga of Knowledge purifies the faculty of understanding until it reaches culmination in intuitive Knowledge and Bliss, (*Chit, Ananda*). All matter or *Prakriti* is impermanent, i.e., subject to decay, it is unreal and therefore called *Maya* or Illusion.

Purusha or Soul is the Life Force, a part of Pure Consciousness that exists in all created things, hence it is permanent. It does not perish even when the body suffers decay and death. The Soul is beyond matter and therefore beyond the dualities, the opposites of pleasure and pain, good or bad etc.

Thus came the concept of *karma* and *punarjanma*. As long as man is in this world, the world of material existence, he cannot avoid action. All action or *karma* leads to some result. Actions done for the good of others lead to the evolution of the *jivatma*. Noble actions (the motive behind the action being pure and not selfish) contribute to ethical evolution of the *jivatma*. Actions that harm others cause a setback.

As per the actions undertaken man goes through a cycle of birth and rebirth, until he attains *moksa* or liberation. As one's actions, so one's evolution. The *Sanatana Dharma* emphasises the ethics of higher behaviour for each individual as part of the duty enjoined on him by occupation. The *jivatma* (the individualised consciousness) is not subject to decay. Thus it acquires another material body with its demands and desires. If this cycle of birth and rebirth is to be ended, man must work towards *moksa* or liberation by means of higher and higher ethical behaviour, i.e., detachment from desire. As noted earlier, the *chaturvarna* (four-fold social organization) and the *asramas* (four-fold-stages of life) constitute a system of ethical behaviour that serves as a lifelong training for the attainment of supreme bliss — the merging with the Pure Consciousness.

The *Sanatana Dharma* is the Eternal Law, the code of moral conduct which has through millenia given India men and women, the earliest seers and yogis, saints and great religious teachers.

In course of time the abstract philosophical concepts were transmitted to the people through a variety of means, among them being stories, myth and legend, aphorisms and sayings so that the fundamental message of the *Sanatana Dharma* could reach and be practised by society at large. The *Upanishads*, the *Brahma* (Vedanta) *Sutra*, the *Mahabharata*, the *Ramayana*, the *Bhagavad Gita*, the

Puranas and many other verses transmitted by word of mouth and recorded, constitute the treasure-house of a philosophy of life of which creativity and ethical behaviour are the key-note. India's classical traditions of dance, music, sculpture, architecture, as well as its folk art are living manifestations of this perennial philosophy.

Veda

The word *Veda* is derived from the Sanskrit root 'vid' to know. *Veda* means knowledge. *Vedas* are the most ancient literature of the Hindus. They are also the most revered.

The *Vedas* consist of four *Samhitas* and the *Brahmanas*[1]. A *Samhita* is a collection of *mantras*. The *mantras* are hymns addressed to gods and goddesses. The four *Samhitas* are *Rk*, *Sama*, *Yajur* and the *Atharva*. *Rk*, means verse, *Sama* means a song, and *Yajur* means a prose passage.

The *Rk Samhita* is the oldest and the most important. It is believed to be about six thousand to six thousand five hundred years old, some parts being of a later date while some are even earlier. Consisting of 1028 hymns and 74000 words, it was preserved intact orally for thousands of years before it was written down. This astonishing feat of memory compels admiration.

Sometimes the *Vedas* are referred to as three, omitting the *Atharva*. The first three deal largely with sacrifices and other rites, while the last was for popular education.

The *Puranas* indicate that the *Vedas* were first only one, but later divided into four parts by Vyasa who gave each disciple one part so that they be better preserved.[2]

The *Brahmanas*, of a later date (about 2500 BC) are attached to each *Veda*. They deal mostly with rules and regulations concerning rites and sacrifices. They delve into the meanings of words and their roots, and contain myths and legends, usually of contests between gods and titans. The *Brahmanas* are divided into injunctive and explanatory passages. *Brahman* means prayer, and *Brahmana* is derived from this word. The *Brahmanas* also contain the oldest known prose in the Indo-European group of languages, though prose passages of a date earlier than the *Brahmanas* are seen in the *Yajur Veda Samhita* as well.[3]

The *Mantras* and *Brahmanas* together are known as the *Karma Kanda*. *Karma* means deeds, action or performance. *Karmas* were exploits or Valiant deeds as well as religious rites and sacrifices.

Sacrifices were the earliest forms of Hindu faith and worship. They bear a close resemblance to the practices among the early Iranians. There is much in common between the Vedic Agnistoma and the Homa ceremony of the Parsis. Whole stanzas of Avestic, the language of the sacred literature of the ancient Iranians may be, by applying phonetic laws, translated into Vedic, corresponding not only to the word but also its spirit.[4]

Vedic language in its most archaic form is found in the earlier portions of the *Rig Veda*. The later hymns were the next phase, the last being the *Brahmanas*.

The *Vedas* are, by tradition, regarded as authorless. Every hymn or *mantra* of the *Rig Veda* has a *rishi* (sage) who is not considered as the author but a seer. It was the heightened and enlightened perceptions of these self-realised sages that enabled them to perceive Truth; hence they were regarded as seers.

From the most ancient times nobody could repeat or teach a *mantra* without knowing the *rishi*, the metre, the deity and its use. The *mantras* as perceived Truth are eternal, but not the *padapatha* or *krama* arrangements of the *Rig Veda*, these being the work of human authors.[5]

From the earliest times the *Vedas* were meant to be studied and imparted to others. It involved memorizing, reflecting on the meaning, keeping fresh by constant repetition, *japa* and imparting the knowledge to pupils. Knowing and understanding the meaning determined Vedic knowledge.[6]

The worship of fire earlier was both an individual as well as a congregational affair. The daily *agnihotra* was individual, needing no officiating priest, while most other *yajnas* (sacrifices) needed the services of many priests and were congregational in character. There were three fires, morning, midday and evening.

The intention or concept of sacrifice, from the earliest times was that of offering. It was an act of surrender or renunciation. The words accompanying the offering are नमम (not mine). Nor were sacrifices performed only for the attainment of heaven but for the good of all.

The later *Purusha Sukta* portion of the *Rig Veda* represents the whole creation as being created by the sacrifice of the Primordial *Purusha*. The spiritual power created by this act of self-surrender is the all-pervading *Brahma*.

The material follows the spiritual as a natural consequence. An act of sacrifice was beneficial not only spiritually but materially as well, since "the properties produced through *yajna* are carried through fire to the sun (Surya), from Surya to *Purjanya* (rain), from rain to food and from food to mankind." (*Manu*. 3.76)

Sacrifice was not an 'appeasement of the gods' but the unselfish sharing of what one has. Jaimini's *Poorva Mimamsa*, the recognized authority on the Vedic *Karma Kanda*, states that it is not the gods that are important but the act of sacrifice itself.[7]

A moral life is a life that entails some sacrifice which is really unselfish conduct. "Who has the power should give into the needy." (*Rig Veda* X.177) and, "One who feeds all by himself sins all by himself." (*Rig Veda* X.117).

It is essential to remember that non-violence was an important 'doctrine even in Vedic times, although the Vedic Aryans were meat-eaters.[8] They were perhaps more honest than those of present times who while having no compunction regarding the taking of life for their own gastronomical pleasure, nevertheless recoil with horror at the idea of a life being taken and offered to god as sacrifice. The ancient Aryans no doubt realised it would make no difference to the animal whether it was to be killed to the chanting of *mantras* or the rattle of kitchen cutlery!

Most Vedic sacrifices except a few daily ones or those performed on special or auspicious occasions, have lapsed. The *Panch Mahayajna* is a daily sacrifice involving neither animal nor priest. Food was offered to the *Devas* (gods), *Rishis* (sages), *Pitros* (ancestors), *Nri* (guests and the hungry) and *Bhutas* (lower animals). The sacrifice was offered to the gods. It was offered to the *rishis* by the recitation and teaching of the *Vedas*, by offering of water to the ancestors, and by feeding the last two. It was considered that those who ate the remnants of the offering were freed of any sin that may have incurred at the five places of animal slaughter, the pestle or mortar, grinding stone, fire-place, place where the water-pot is kept and the broom.

This indicates that food prepared to sustain and nourish all living things and in the spirit of service necessitating the destruction of living things like plants and animals, itself is an act of sacrifice and because of its purity of purpose, is free from sin.

Sacrificial offerings could consist of rice or other grain in clarified butter, or fish, flesh of hare or birds, hog, goat, deer, antelope, the gayal or sheep, or cow's milk and its products.

The *Aswamedha Yajna*, the horse sacrifice was performed but rarely as it could only be performed by a very strong and powerful king.

The *Visvajit* sacrifice could not be performed by anyone having less than 112 heads of cattle. All property had to be given away, except relations and the attendant *Sudras*, who were free and could not be regarded as 'property'.[9]

One sacrifice involved eleven human beings representing different professions, but theirs was purely a symbolic presence, as for the actual sacrifice, animals would be substituted.[10]

Many references in the *Rig Veda* give us an idea of the social conditions that existed at that time. A word of warning is necessary here. Modern scholarship tends to fall into the trap of regarding the *Vedas* being merely a source of information for social and other conditions of life existing at that age. It should not be forgotten that the *Veda* is primarily a spiritual work and meant for man's spiritual uplift. Even the two 'races' — the *Aryas* and *Dasas* are used only in the figurative sense, i.e., to express a material and selfish culture as opposed to a spiritual and unselfish culture. The terms 'dark' and 'light' are used to denote ignorance and knowledge. The fact that the *dasas* belong to cities probably only denotes that the cities are corrupt. Such ideas are present in all societies even today. The references to social conditions, it should be borne in mind, are only incidental.

We find graphic descriptions of chariots, either three-wheeled or two-wheeled drawn by two horses. Slavery existed in those times as there are references to men and women being given as gifts. We do note, however, from the later *dharmasastra* literature that there were strict rules regarding the benevolent treatment of slaves. All ancient civilizations had slaves, and India was no exception. There are at least fifty Vedic passages which shed light on the various forms of marriage, different kinds of sons, adoption, partition, inheritance, *shraddha* etc.

Women seemed to have married on maturity, and marriage was considered as an equal partnership between man and woman. They were regarded with approval. The *Atharva Veda* says: "Be thou a queen after reaching thy husband's home". And both the *Rig Veda* and the *Brahmanas* agree that the wife is verily the home.

Avenues of learning were open to women. They undertook Vedic study and underwent the *Upanayana* ceremony. There was even a rite prescribed for those wanting a learned daughter! *Stridhan* can be traced to Vedic times.[11]

There are wry references to some girls preferring the wealthy to the worthy, just as of some men having more affection for a maiden's wealth. The perceptiveness of the ancients is borne out by this observation in the *Rig Veda*, "Bounteous Indra! Endow this woman with excellent sons and fortune. Give her ten sons and make her husband the eleventh."[12] There is gentle humour in this excellent advice that she should care for her husband as though he were her youngest!

There is gentle irony and an unreproachful understanding of life when the poet (*Rig Veda* IX.112) observes, "We all have various thoughts and plans, and diverse are the ways of men. The carpenter desires a rift so that he may repair it, the doctor looks out for a fracture so that he can set it right. A bard am I, my father a doctor, my mother grinds corn with the millstone. Striving for wealth with varied plans, we follow desires like kine."

There were originally only two classes, the *Brahmin* and the *Kshatriya*. The former meant prayer and the latter valour.[13] Faith and performance are both needed in life. These two classes were not based on birth but were interchangeable. We find one brother a *Kshatriya* while the other chooses to be a *Brahmin*. *Vaisyas* and *Sudras* appear in the latter portion of the *Rig Veda*,[14] no doubt to meet the needs of a developing society. We find the chariot maker, (when perhaps there were fewer in number) taking part in Vedic sacrifices[15] before the class of *Sudra* was created.

The term 'varna' in the early *Rig Veda* is used in the sense of light or colour. The *dasas* for example were dark in colour. 'Varna' was never used in reference to *Brahmin* and *Kshatriya*.[16] Varna when used to describe the four-tiered class system, is used in the sense of quality and not colour.[17]

We find religion, rules of law, morality, health and hygiene mixed up in ancient works. *Atharva Veda* condemns urinating while standing and even goes on to give a list of places where one should not urinate![18]

It should be remembered that at a time when writing was not in vogue, all information had to be compressed into what could be put to memory. All kinds of knowledge was needed to make the best of life. *Ayur Veda* the science of medicine can also be traced to the *Atharva Veda*.

The *Vedas* set much store by courage and manliness. Although the elemental gods were hailed, there was a consciousness even in those times of the One Eternal being the One on whom all, including the elements depended. We see in them too the spirit of sacrifice, devotion, work and worship. "Gods befriend none except those who have been tired. They do not like indolent sleep." (*Rig Veda*).

"May I not have to live upon the earnings of others. (*Rig Veda* II.28)

"Let a man think on wealth and strive to acquire lawfully and through worship," (*Rig Veda*, X.31)

There is a reference to ascetics even then, they being referred to as *yogis* and *munis*.

Here also we see those who have renounced the world and those who have not. Says the *Aitareya Brahmana*: "What is the use of dirt, what of goat skin, what of long hair and what of fervour?...... A sonless person cannot attain heaven.... the delights in the earth, the delight in the fire, the delight in the waters, greater than these is that of a father in a son."[19]

In these very ancient times as well we see the pessimist and the optimist attitudes.

The Vedic sages were perfectly aware of the need to discriminate between the true and the false. It is difficult to judge by mere externals. "True speech and false speech run a race against each other. Soma protects of the two what is true and straight-forward and strikes down what is false."[20]

We see three words in the *Rig Veda*. These are *Rta* (Cosmic order), *Vrata* (laws and ordinances deemed to have been laid down by the gods) and *Dharma* (religion, rites and sacrifices or fixed principles). Gradually *Rta* receded with *Satya* (Truth) taking its place. *Dharma* became an all-embracing concept while *Vrata* was confined to sacred vows and rules of conduct.

Although animal sacrifices were the norm in the Vedic *Karma Kanda*, we see even then the realisation of the importance of the spirit. *Satapatha Brahmana* states, "He who sacrifices to the gods does not win such a place as he who does so to the *Atma*."

The *Aitareya Brahmana* (VI.9) "He who offers a cake performs a sacrifice equal to the offering of all sacrificial animals."

The *Taittiriya Brahmana* provides that the forest sacrificial animals, after a fire-brand is carried around them be let off for the sake of *Ahimsa* (non-violence). *Satapatha Brahmana* (X.4.4.9) says: "He who is to become immortal through knowledge (*Vidya*) and through sacred works (*Karmas*) shall become immortal after separating from the body" and asserts that those who do not know this come to life again and again. Says the *Satapatha Brahmana* (S.B.E. Vol.44 p.83). "Therefore let a man speak nought but truth."

P.V. Kane points out that the "deep study of Vedic sacrifices is quite essential for the proper understanding of Vedic literature, for arriving at approximately correct statements about the chronology, the development and the stratification of the different portions of that literature and for the influence that literature exerted on the four *varnas* and the caste system, on the splitting up of the *Brahmanas* themselves into several sub-castes and on the institutions of *gotras* and *pravaras*..... Most of the Vedic *Samhitas* that we now have are arranged (except the *Rig Veda* to some extent) definitely for the various aspects of the cult of the sacrifice and indicate a state of things when different priests were required for the sacrifices, who used *mantras* from the collection they had studied. For a thorough understanding of the Vedic sacrifices the several Vedic *Samhitas*, the *Brahmanas* and the *Srauta Sutras* must be carefully studied... In his *Poorvamimamsa Sutra* Jaimini submits thousands of texts to the principles of *Mimamsa* elaborated by him and arrives at definite conclusions on matters affecting the details of various sacrifices."[21]

The *Vedas* are called *Sruti* meaning 'That which is heard'. The *Mimamsicas* regard the Vedic *Karma Kanda* as *Sruti*.

References

1. *History of Dharmasastra* by P.V. Kane, vol.V, pt.2, p.1222.
2. ibid., vol.V, pt.2, chap.XXII, sec.4, p.859.
3. ibid., vol.V, pt.2, chap.XXIX, sec.VII, p.1223.
4. ibid., vol.V, pt.2, chap.XXIX, p.978.
   A New History of Sanskrit Literature by K. Chaitanya, chap.I.
5. ibid., vol.V, pt.2, chap.XXII, sec.IV, p.859, 860, 861.
6. ibid., vol.II, pt.1, chap.VII, p.356.
7. ibid., vol.V, pt.2, chap.XXIX, sec.VII, p.1202, 1212.
8. ibid., vol.V, pt.2, chap.XXXV, sec.X, p.1646.
9. ibid., vol.V, pt.2, chap.XXX, sec.VII, p.1313.
10. ibid., vol.III, p.962.
11. ibid., vol.III, chap.XXX, p.770.
12. *A New History of Sanskrit Literature* by K. Chaitanya, chap.II.
13. *History of Dharmasastra* by P.V. Kane, vol.II, pt.1, chap.II, p.32.
14. ibid., p.27, 28.
15. ibid., vol.V, pt.2, chap.XXXV, sec.X, p.1642.
16. ibid., vol.II, pt.1, chap.II, p.27, 28.
17. ibid., vol.V, pt.2, chap.XXXV, p.1634, 1635.
18. ibid., vol.II, pt.1, chap.XVII.
19. *A New History of Sanskrit Literature* by K. Chaitanya, chap.I.
20. *History of Dharmasastra* by P.V. Kane, vol.II, pt.1, p.4.
21. ibid., vol.V, pt.2, chap.XXIX, p.976, 977.

4

Upanishad

The *Upanishads* are the concluding portion of the *Vedas*. They are also regarded as the culmination of Vedantic thought. Enlightened thinkers, through successive ages, kept adding to the *Vedas*. After the four *Samhitas*, the *Brahmanas* (about 2500 BC) re-stressed the necessity of performance and explained the meanings of rites and ceremonies in order to ensure that these are done with understanding. The *Aranyakas* were a later phase. These were so called because the ideas were developed in the seclusion of the forests. The last and final phase was of the *Upanishads*. The word *Upanishad* is derived from the Sanskrit *sad* which means to sit down, to destroy, loosen, *upa* meaning nearby and *ni* meaning devotedly. The word therefore means the instructions being given by a teacher to a devoted disciple sitting near, to loosen the knot of ignorance and set him free from the bonds that tie.

As we study Vedic literature from the earliest times we see a greater stress from performance to knowledge and understanding. We see a slight shift even in the *Brahmanas*, more so in the *Aranyakas* and clearly in the *Upanishads*.

While the *Samhitas* and *Brahmanas* are the Vedic *Karma Kanda* (action) portion of the *Vedas*, the *Upanishads* are regarded as the *Jnana Kanda*, knowledge portion of the

Vedas. Some *Aranyakas* are included in the *Karma Kanda* while others are part of the *Jnana Kanda*.

The Upanishadic age is generally deemed to have ended by 1500 or 1000 BC. Some *Upanishads* are attached to the *Vedas* while others are independent works. There are altogether 108 *Upanishads*, of which the ten principal ones are the *Isa, Kena, Katha, Prasna, Munduka, Mandukya, Taittiriya, Aitreya, Chhandogya*, and *Brihadharanyaka*. The *Svetasvatara Upanishad*, although not counted among the ten principal *Upanishads*, is nevertheless held in reverence because of the profundity of its teachings, its beauty and deep fervour.

All philosophy is a search for Truth. Religion is meant to show us that Truth can only be attained through upright moral behaviour. Every age has its own compulsions. Both action as well as understanding are necessary in life. The teachings of all religions have a theoretical portion as well as practical, and general rules of behaviour. Religion is not concerned with after-life as much as with this life itself.

It is reasonable to suppose that while the age of the Vedic *Karma Kanda* demanded acts of valour and the performances of sacrifices, the later Upanishadic age was an intellectually alive and sophisticated age, with a settled and cultured civilization.

It would be unfair to say that the *Karma Kanda* was unaware of the need for knowledge and understanding. It is more than obvious that then too they were well aware of the need to know both the act and its meaning. But the acts of sacrifice became less important in a civilization with different needs. As it happens, the *Upanishads* develop the ideas expressed in the mantras of the latter portion of the *Rig Veda*, the *Atharva Veda* and the *Brahmanas*.

The problem in the world has always been of knowledge and ignorance, and hence the need has to be constantly re-stressed because man's habit is to adhere to form, without understanding the need for the form. All forms get stale while Truth is vital and eternal.

The Upanishadic age was a deeply introspective age. It was an age of culture and sensibility. It was no doubt observed by the sages that the problems of the world arise not so much from the act itself as the intention and aim of that act. If the intention is dishonest then the act is morally wrong; if the intention is honest then the performer cannot be faulted, no matter what the consequences of that act. But mere intention is not enough. A man must prepare himself with study (both secular and religious) and take all precautions in order to try and make as correct a judgement as possible. Those who are guided by material considerations are guided by passion, prejudice, parochial and other considerations, while those who are guided by Truth alone take a balanced view, free of passion, prejudice and partiality, in the interest of all.

Dishonesty comes from belief in the material and acts inspired by material considerations. Honesty derives from the eternal value of Truth. Truth being free, is uncorrupted by the material. Yet the material can only be served through Truth. Character comes only from the conviction that truth alone counts and this comes to the mind after study. This is not a superstition, but the result of study, observation, meditation and self-purification. Selflessness is the core of all morality, while selfishness is inspired by material desires.

The *Upanishads* show how the whole universe is dependent on Truth alone. Truth being a value cannot be identified with the material. This value or spirit is called *Brahma* or Soul/*Atma* of the universe.

Each *Upanishad* approaches the subject of *Brahma* being the unmanifest Soul of all the manifest universe from a different angle, and each arrives at the same conclusion.

Although Truth is unmanifest and beyond the comprehension of our senses, Truth alone exists when all the material has disappeared. The all-pervading *Brahma* or Truth is in all things and exists undivided. It is ever free, the eternal substratum of the universe.

The famous Upanishadic Mahakavyas are:

Aayamatma Brahma i.e, *Atma* (soul) is Brahma.

Tattwamasi, meaning That thou art (the same Truth resides in all).

Brahmavid Brahmiva Bhavati, The knower of Brahma himself becomes Brahma.

Vigyana Brahma, Brahma is wisdom.

The *Isavasya Upanishad* points out how man, misled by the material objects, seeks to possess them. Seeing many, he tries to possess that which belongs to another. He does not realise that Truth, the only Value worth having, is his too and that he has it the same as all others. Truth being One and indivisible there is nothing to possess. He has the whole, the same as others.

"With a golden vessel

The face of the Real is covered over,

That do thou, O Pusan, uncover

That I devoted to Truth may behold".

Pusan the celestial god, is asked to show light, so that Truth, the real value, may be appreciated.

Kena Upanishad points out that function determines the organ. But what keeps the organs functioning in our bodies is the force of the Spirit. Without it they would collapse. It points out that the Spirit is beyond our perceptions yet deserving our sincerest efforts. Truth cannot be appreciated by that mind which thinks in terms of opposites. It comes to the balanced and unselfish mind. It cannot be understood by the lazy, sluggish or the self-righteous. Only to a mind free of opposites (attraction — repulsion) in the warmth of love, does it come as a lightning flash of recognition. This flash changes one's whole life. This message is allegorically given as a fight between the gods and demons. The gods win and they are proud of themselves. Brahma, the Spirit, decides to enlighten them as to the Real Force that was responsible for their winning. He confronts them as a magnificent form. The gods send *Agni* (fire) to find out who the form may be. On being asked, *Agni* tells Brahma he can burn any and everything. Brahma then places a dry blade of grass before him to burn. Try as he might *Agni* cannot burn it. He returns downcast. They next send *Vayu* (air). Brahma places a blade of grass before the boastful *Vayu* and asks him to blow it off. *Vayu* cannot blow off that blade of grass. He also returns downcast. Indra, known as the generous, then goes. As he approaches, the apparition disappears and he sees only friendly darkness. Then he sees Usha the dawn. Usha tells him that while they all were priding themselves on their victory it was really due to Brahma that they had won.

Fire represents energy which frees the mind for honest quest. *Vayu* represents a steady flow of activity or movement in the mind to free it of all its clutter of conceit or ego. Indra denotes the quality of *Satwa*, the quality of generosity and harmony in nature. Nature possesses three characteristics, *Satwa*, *Rajas* and *Tamas*, (harmony, activity and inertia). By conquering inertia, by directing one's activity purposefully and in the spirit of open-minded generosity, one may better understand the Unknown.

Katha Upanishad deals with death. We are given the story of Nachiketa. The word Na-chiketa means 'something unperceived'. Nachiketa seeks the Inner Truth undeterred by outward appearance.

Seeing his father performing a sacrifice and giving away old and useless cows, he wonders in what way such actions can secure heaven. He asks his father to whom will he give his son Nachiketa. Pestered for an answer the father angrily says to 'Yama'. Yama is the God of death. The father regrets his words but Nachiketa goes to the gates of Yama's palace. Being the first time anyone has voluntarily come to Yama's abode, the servants of Yama did not know how to welcome Nachiketa. When Yama comes, he is apologetic that Nachiketa has not been welcomed as a guest, and offers Nachiketa three boons. After asking the first two boons, Nachiketa asks the last and final boon. He wants to know whether 'after-death' is a condition of 'being' or 'non-being'. Yama says it is too subtle a question and offers all kingdoms and the wealth of the earth to Nachiketa instead. Nachiketa answers that all these are no use to him as he will have to leave them some day anyway.

At last Yama says "that which the *Vedas* declare, which all austerities indicate, and which men accept when they lead a life of continence, is *Om.*" *Om* is both the manifest and the Unmanifest, and the secret lies in the Soul. 'In the land of the *Atma* the sun shines not, nor does the moon, nor the stars, lightning shines not here, much less the earthly fire. From it's light all these give light and its radiance illumines all creation."[2]

Yama explains to Nachiketa that there are two paths before every man. Although both are linked to man they serve different ends. One path is of good, while the other is pleasant. Yama tells Nachiketa "You have not accepted that chain of possessions wherewith men bind themselves and beneath which they sink. There is the path of wisdom and the path of unwisdom. May pleasures move you not."

Those who follow the path of pleasure keep going to their death again and again. The great secret of death does not come through reasoning but only in communion with death. Nachiketa has not been afraid. He has gone to face death while alive. Only such people know the secret of immortality.

Prasna Upanishad, a part of the *Atharva Veda*, is in the form of questions and answers between teacher and students. When the students come to the teacher to ask him to teach them the true nature of things, the teacher first asks them to prepare themselves for his teachings by practising austerity, purity and faith for one year. After that he says with humility he will teach them 'if he knows'.

The Upanishadic teachers called this knowledge *Madu Vidya* (Knowledge of Nectar) and warned that it should be given only to those worthy of it. This was to avoid the danger of wrong interpretations by narrow materialistic minds.

When they re-assemble, the teacher points out how all things are created through thought. The duality of life and matter comes into existence. All forms, solid or subtle, are matter. Matter is dependant on life. Creation is synonymous with time. Time is a movement in duality. Taking the measures of time the teacher shows how at each level there is a duality. Day and night, the dark and light fortnights of the month, the sun moving north and again to the south, etc. He explains how the problems of good and evil also are dualities. All actions belong to the one or the other. The appropriateness of an action depends upon the source from which it springs. When it springs from life, it will be an appropriate action and when from matter, it will not.

The teacher goes on to show how each outer layer of the body is related to the next inner. He leads them from the outer physical body to the vital body and then to the mind and the various states of the mind. It is only in the highest state of consciousness that the mind, free, is illuminated by intelligence. So long as the mind thinks in terms of labels and forms and symbols, it is not free. When it realises that they all really represent the same thing, then alone is it illuminated. The *Atma* can be realised only by an illuminated intelligence.

It is for each person by his own efforts to realise the *Atma*.

Munduka Upanishad is also a part of the *Atharva Veda*. It carries forward the teachings of the *Prasna Upanishad*. *Munduka* means razor. It is razor-sharp in cutting the weeds of the mind.

It explains the two types of knowledge, the lower and the higher. The lower knowledge is all academic knowledge, and this includes the *Vedas* themselves. The higher Knowledge is where the 'Wise behold Brahma everywhere'. This knowledge is the understanding of the essential Unity of all creation. "Which can neither be seen nor grasped, which has no root or attribute, no eyes, no ears, no hands or feet, which is eternal and omnipresent, all-pervading and extremely subtle, which is imperishable and the Source of all things."[3]

All creation comes as a result of an inner fullness. It is an act of love and warmth without motive. The omnipresence of *Brahma* reveals itself through this love and warmth that sustains the universe. This knowledge is Higher Knowledge or wisdom, and comes to one of pure mind. While placing Higher Knowledge as the ultimate goal for all, the teacher nevertheless also recommends the study of 'lower knowledge'. He points out that it is the end for which we perform our acts that determine whether the acts are 'good' or 'bad'. It is thus necessary to keep in mind as to why we seek the knowledge. No knowledge is an end in itself, just as acts of sacrifice or social service also cannot be an end in themselves. Sacrifices performed because of Scriptural injunctions, not for the joy of performance but the reward, are performed without any understanding of truth. The target should be Brahma. The *Vedas* should be studied as well with the help of a guru 'who is well versed in the *Vedas* and deeply rooted in *Brahma.*' The guru should know not only the letter but the spirit of the *Veda*. The guru thus, is a man of both head and heart. His role is not to make a student dependent but independent. He takes the student logically up to a point where logic itself fails. The student is then on his own. Unmanifest *Brahma* or Soul and manifest *Brahma* or creation are the "Being and the becoming" of Vedantic thought.

Mandukya Upanishad is the shortest *Upanishad*. It examines the three states of man's consciousness. Western psychology has grown by treating the abnormal conditions of man's psyche. Hindu psychology is concerned with mental health in order that man understands himself better and thus be better equipped. The *Mandukya* deals with man's three mental states, the subconscious, the unconscious and the super-conscious. It goes on to explain how these mental states affect man's behaviour. The first is the closest to the animal state, where the reaction comes as a result of fear and self-interest. It comes from the subconscious. The next state is higher and not as superficial as the first, but still within duality. It is stimulated by racial memory. It is affected as an upsurge which may be caused through religious gatherings, places of worship, historical or mythological figures. Both these two states react to anything that threatens continuity.

It also explains how man may free himself from this hypnotic state. The third stage is beyond continuity. It lives only in the present. It withholds judgement. It is free of all stimulation whether from without or within. Truth reveals itself in *Turiya* the fourth stage. This is Absolute Good, where all things are seen in their true nature.

The *Taittiriya Upanishad* is from the *Yajur Veda*. Here we see the teacher *Taittiriya's* concern for the welfare of his students, his humility and wisdom.

This *Upanishad* is divided into three sections called the *Siksa Valli, Brahmananda Valli* and *Bhrgu Valli* dealing with the social, intellectual and spiritual education of the student.

Discussing the science of language, the teacher moves on to combinations. He shows how to bring about a union of words there has to be an 'arranger'. This inducer is the *Sandhan*. The urge to unite comes from the *Sandhan*. He then goes on to explain the inter-relationship between the part and the whole. Only a real communion based on understanding is lasting.

He explains the art of human relationships. He speaks of social obligation, intellectual understanding and spiritual communion. During the house-holder's stage, the stress is on duty while during the *Vanaprastha* stage it is on intellectual understanding. The last stage of *sanyas* is solitary, loving and peaceful to all. His parting message to his students is inspiring, "Speak the Truth. Do thy duty. Do not neglect your study .... Be thy mother to thee like unto a deity, be thy father to thee like unto a god. Revere thy guest like a god. Whatever actions of ours that were blameless those you must follow, not the others. Whatever actions were good in our conduct those shalt thou respect, not the others. And those teachers who are superior to us, you should honour. Give thou must with faith, not without respect, with pleasure, with modesty, with friendliness. If you have a doubt about a duty or conduct, conduct yourself as is done by such learned men who can deliberate well, are devoted to their duties on their own and others' behalf, are not severe and are desirous of righteousness. This is the inner teaching of the *Veda*."[4]

Aitareya Upanishad is a part of the *Rig Veda*. It deals with the creation and beginning of conscious life. It discusses the visible and invisible states. It discusses the states of consciousness as well. It seeks to show how

Brahma in the body acts as the unifying force in physical as well as psychological functions.

It describes the whole mind-emotion process. "The Spirit is that which is heart and mind too. It is consciousness, perception, discrimination, intelligence, wisdom, insight, steadfastness, thought, thoughtfulness, impulse, memory, conception, purpose, life, desire and will."[5]

Chandogya Upanishad is in the *Sama Veda*. It explains the Reality of the Void. How that which incarnates into all forms, yet remains supremely formless. This Void is the Truth. This alone is everlasting.

The teacher points out the futility of mere academic or scientific knowledge without trying to realise what alone is of real worth. To the student Narada, who comes asking for instruction, the teacher asks what he has learnt earlier. Narada answers, "Sir, I have learnt the *Rig Veda*, the *Yajur Veda*, the *Atharva Veda*, history and traditional stories which together are called the fifth *Veda*, the method of remembering and repeating the *Vedas*, the technique of *Shraddha*, grammar, philosophy, mathematics, astronomy, astrology, science of augury, jugglery, logic, ethics, music, science of dance, poetry, science, science of war, and many other branches of knowledge."

The teacher Sanat Kumar then tells Narada, "Dear Narada, all you know is mere names and verbiage, mere words. By your present knowledge you can only achieve what words can achieve, nothing else."[6]

The teacher explains that all names are only symbols. The form is only the expression of the Being. It is the content of the form that is important and not the form. The discovery of one's own *Atma* is the discovery of Reality (Truth).

It is the knowledge of this formless 'Void' that gives

value to all things. The *Chandogya* mocks at rituals, comparing the sacrificial priests and sacrificer to a chain of dogs each holding the other's tail in the mouth.

We are given the story of a generous and philanthropic King Janasruti. He was known far and wide for his philanthropy. He was proud and happy at the religious merit he had achieved through his charities. One day he heard two birds flying overhead talking. One pointed him out to the other extolling his philanthrophy. The other said it was nothing compared to the cartman Raikwa. The king thereupon resolved to go to Raikwa and find out. Laden with gifts, he located Raikwa and asked him to teach him the way to peace and happiness. The cartman answered that worldly wealth could not buy spiritual knowledge and hence those presents were of no use to him. The king could take them back. Janasruti returned to his palace, but he was restless and desirous of learning. He went to Raikwa again but this time in supplication and humility. Seeing that the king was now ready for instruction Raikwa said, "Various are the gods that people worship. The sweeping wind, the flaming fire, the breathing vital force are all worshipped as god by man. But the Spirit, itself uncreated, creates all and supports them. The Spirit eats not anything (i.e., does not stand in need of anything). It is self-supporting and self-sufficient. All belongs to the Spirit. All are but instruments of its will." He tells the king to be rooted in this One, for one so rooted, behaves differently. "Go thou, O king to thy palace. Give, but not with pride. Give generously but not with egotism. Give freely but not with an eye to fame. Give, but not as something that is yours, but as something given to you by the Spirit for giving to others. He who sees this Truth becomes a seer and for him nothing is wanting. He becomes the enjoyer of all things."[7]

We see here how the cartman may have been poor, but

he had a better understanding of the real Value than the king. Charity is a state of mind. He does not ask the king to give up the palace, he instead shows him what true wealth really is.

We are told the story of Satyakama. He wanted to study and become a religious student. He asks his mother about his father. His mother replies that she was a maid working in many houses. She did not know who his father was. He should call himself Satyakama Jabala, since Jabala was her name.

Satyakama then goes to the teacher Hardrumata Gautama and when asked for particulars of his family, repeats what his mother has told him. On hearing him the teacher says, 'You are a *Brahmin* because you have not told a lie nor departed from truth, come what may." He instructs Satyakama to get him the *samidha* and inducts him as a student.[8]

We see here in Jabala, her son and the teacher a respect for truth, unmindful of social conventions or stigma. Throughout Upanishadic teachings we are told the search for Truth requires strength and courage. Quality and merit are more important than labels.

There is the story of Svetaketu and his brilliant father, the teacher Uddalaka Aruni.

When Svetaketu returns home after 24 years of education his father asks him whether he has learnt that "whereby what is not heard becomes heard, and what is not thought about becomes the subject of thinking, and what is not known becomes known." Svetaketu respectfully asks how there can be such teaching. His father replies that "just as one lump of clay can tell all there is of mud, the difference being only of name, the truth being that all is mud."

This *Upanishad* discusses the 'Being and non-being.' The Unmanifest is Being, while the non-being (the universe) is the Being with attributes which has its source in the Being. All manifestation contains the essence of Being. Says the father, "This true Being, the subtle source of the world; that is Truth, that is Self that thou art O Svetaketu." His son asks for further instructions. His father asks him to cut the fruit of the banyan tree. It is full of tiny seeds. He asks the son to cut one of these seeds. The son cuts it and finds nothing. Then says the father, 'My son, from this that you call nothing there comes into existence this vast banyan tree. Believe me my son, a subtle and intangible essence is the Spirit of the whole universe. That is Reality, that is *Atma*, that thou art."[9]

Svetaketu then asks his father how to realise the Reality? The teacher then asks him to get a glass of water and put some salt into it. He is asked to taste the top. It is salty. He then tastes the middle. This too is salty. He then tastes the bottom. Here too the water is salty. His father then tells Svetaketu 'My dear child, just as salt pervades this entire quantity of water so the Spirit pervades all existence." How then does one realise it, asks Svetaketu. The father asks him to throw the water on the ground and come the next day. Next day the water has evaporated leaving the salt deposit on the earth.

Just as the water was thrown away to recover the salt so the form has to be negated. When all the images in our minds are negated we see Reality.

The *Brihadaranyaka* is one of the oldest *Upanishads*. In this *Upanishad* we see one of the most brilliant sages — Yajnavalkya. It has the same invocation as the *Isa Upanishad*. Fear arises out of Duality because each point of duality wants to possess the other. Where there is no duality there is nothing to possess. Only the identification with the One can dispel all fear.

When Yajnavalkya wishes to retire into seclusion he wishes to divide his property between his two wives. His wife Maitreyi however asks how the property will help her for it will fetch her no immortality. Yajnavalkya is pleased with her reply. He says, 'My dear, your life will be as comfortable as wealth and material means can make it. There is no hope of immortality through wealth." He points out that there is a clear distinction between comfort and happiness. He explains how we love all things, husband, wife, sons, wealth and everything for love of the Self . "The Self (*Atma*) my dear Maitreyi should verily be realised by hearing about it, by reflecting upon it and meditating on it."[10]

The Self is the merging place of all differentiations. "As a lump of salt thrown into the water dissolves in water and none can pick it up even so this great endless Infinity is Pure Intelligence. In the formless state it has no particularised consciousness. In this lies the secret of immortality".

In this *Upanishad* we find the first clear statement on the sequence of desire, will and act. Man's deeds and their relationship to transmigration is clearly expressed.[11]

The secret of immortality lies in the understanding of the Rhythm of Existence.

We are told of Prajapati who had trained his three sons, Gods, Men and Demons. On completing their training they asked their father for a message. "My message is just one syllable DA". The gods rightly understood the meaning as *Damyata* (Restrain yourself). To the men also he gave the same two syllables DA. The men also understood it correctly as *Datta*-(Be charitable). The demons also were given DA. They understood it, correctly as *Dayadhwam*-(Be sensitive).[12] The gods, men and demons represent the three *gunas* (characteristics) in nature, *satwa*, *rajas* and *tamas*: Each of the *gunas* when used wisely and well results in good, while harm is caused by using them improperly. The three qualities when unthinkingly and foolishly used can result in self-righteousness, censoriousness and insensitivity. When used well and wisely in the spirit of Truth they serve all through humility, charity and sensitivity.

Yajnavalkya's saying that we love all things, husband, wife, sons, wealth and everything for the love of the Self has been often misinterpreted. This has been pointed out by many scholars. What Yajnavalkya was trying to explain was that it is not wrong to love. All love is divine. Nor is it wrong to love the material. The soul comes into earthly existence because of the desire for experience. The World is served, by love for one's family which makes one discharge one's responsibilities in life. Productivity is also essential in the world. There is nothing wrong with money either. What has to be realised is that all the material is dependent on the moral. Through Truth alone, all-embracing love and impartial, can the material be served. It is because of Truth that we love the material as well, because all are caused from Truth and contain Truth.

It must be remembered that Yajnavalkya was the preceptor of the great King Janaka, revered for his justice and sagacity. While a *sanyasi* might retire from life and devote himself to meditation and solitude, the universe cannot survive without those engaged in normal activity. Hindu thought makes a clear distinction in rules set for a *sanyasi* and ones set for an individual living with worldly responsibilities. A king cannot be like a *sanyasi*. While a *sanyasi* is not to get angry or engage in violence, a king, or another, must feel righteous anger and must not shirk from his responsibilities, even if it means violence. The good have to be encouraged and protected. The two ways, *Nivrutta* and *Pravrutta*, i.e., Passive and Active have been recognized from the earliest times. A man takes the path that suits his nature.

There is an amusing story of how Yajnavalkya

demonstrates that Truth is not foolishness nor false modesty. King Janaka once performed a sacrifice at which a great number of learned men and women had assembled. The king then declared that he would give a thousand cows with horns adorned with gold to the wisest among them.

Since no one came forward Yajnavalkya asked his pupil to drive home all the cows. The learned Brahmins were angry with Yajnavalkya at his conceit. Asvala asked Yajnavalkya whether he was the greatest scholar in their midst. Yajnavalkya replied humorously, "I salute the greatest Vedic scholar. I only wish to have the cows"

The debate then started with a volley of questions and answers. Understanding of truth does not come from avoiding the material, but from the realisation that all the material itself is dependent on the spiritual. Truth cannot come to those who take extreme postures. It comes to the balanced, clear thinking, and understanding mind. Nothing is 'good' or 'bad' in itself. It is the intention and aim that determines the good or bad.

Throughout religious teachings we see the constant attempt to set society on the right lines, to prevent it from going to extremes.

Different types of men may hold different views. What is important is that they are thoughtfully and honestly held. If they are dishonestly held then they are morally wrong. Needs may differ according to time and place. They are none the less true. Truth has to do with honesty and purity of mind which comes from unselfish conduct.

Below are some quotations from the *Upanishads*:

"He who knows both knowledge and action, with action overcomes death and with knowledge overcomes immortality."   (*Isavasya Upanishad*)

"What cannot be spoken with words, but whereby words are spoken, know that alone to be Brahma, the Spirit — and not what people here adore. What cannot be thought with the mind, but whereby the mind can think, know that alone to be *Brahma*, the Spirit — and not what people here adore. What cannot be seen with the eye, but whereby the eye can see, know that alone to be *Brahma*, the Spirit — and not what people — here adore. What cannot be heard with the ear, but whereby the ear can hear, know that alone to be *Brahma* the Spirit — and not what people here adore."   (*Kena Upanishad*)

"If you think 'I know *Brahma* well' then surely you know but little of its nature. You know its nature only as conditioned by man or by gods. Therefore *Brahma*, even now is worthy of your enquiry."   (*Kena Upanishad*)

"He by whom *Brahma* is not known, knows it; but by whom it is known, knows it not. It is not known by those who know it. It is known by those who do not know it."
(*Kena Upanishad*)

"*Brahma* comes to the thought of those who know it as beyond thought. *Brahma* does not come to those who imagine it can be attained by thought. *Brahma* is unknown to the learned and known to the simple."

(*Kena Upanishad*)

"*Prana* is born from the Spirit. Even as a man casts a shadow, so does the Spirit cast its shadow and it is known as *Prana. Prana* enters the body through the activities of the mind."   (*Prasna Upanishad*)

"*Brahma* cannot be seen by the eye and words cannot reveal it. It cannot be reached by the senses, or by austerity,

or by good actions. By the grace of wisdom and the purity
of mind, it can be seen, Indivisible, in the silence of non-
distraction."

"As rivers flowing into the ocean find their final place
and their name and form disappear, even so the wise
become free from name and form and enter into the
radiance of the Supreme Spirit who is greater than all
greatness."   (*Munduka Upanishad*)

"Truth is the flower and fruit of speech. And he will
become a master, a man of renown, one of excellent repute
he who speaks this flower and fruit of speech, Truth".
                                    (*Aitereya Upanishad*)

"He is *Brahman*, he is Indra, he is Prajapati, he is all
these gods, and the five gross elements, namely, the earth,
air, space, water, light, these things and those that
are mingled of the five, as it were; origins of one sort or
another, those born from an egg, and those born from
a womb, and those born from sweat and those born
from sprout; horses, cows, persons, elephants, whatever
breathing thing there is here whether moving or flying and
also what is stationary. All this is guided by Intelligence.
The world is guided by Intelligence. The basis is
Intelligence. *Brahma* is Intelligence.   (*Aitereya Upanishad*)

"Two are the phases of *Brahman* — that with form and
that without form — the mortal and the immortal, the
limited, fixed to a place, and the unlimited which is not
fixed to a place, the perceptible and the imperceptible. That
which is subtle, immortal, unlimited and imperceptible is
the Essential."   (*Brihadaranyaka Upanishad*)

"Of what use is the repeating of the sacred hymns of
the *Vedas*, if one does not know the imperishable source
from where the *Vedas* have emanated?"

"In the unbounded Imperishable Being, the pair of knowledge and ignorance, *vidya* and *avidya* are mysteriously co-existent. Ignorance is perishable, Knowledge is Immortal. He who controls both knowledge and ignorance is beyond the realm of both. 'Being' is neither male nor female".   (*Svetasvatara Upanishad*)

"I surrender to him who is the bridge of immortality, who is without parts, who is motionless, who is beyond corruption, who is above all attachment — who is like the Flaming Fire that emits no smoke'."

(*Svetasvatara Upanishad*)[13]

The Upanishadic philosophy is known as the philosophy of the Vedanta. Vedanta means the end and culmination of the *Vedas*. Here Vedic thought reaches the highest point. The *Upanishads* show us that the Soul of both man and universe are one and the same. This is the only real Value. Our understanding of this Truth illumines our understanding and gives value to all our actions in thought, word and deed.

The *Upanishads* are aware of the need for action. What they expose is the foolishness of performing meaningless rituals, quoting authority, thinking it will lead to salvation, which is superstition. They condemn not only animal sacrifices of the Vedic *Karma Kanda* but also other rituals like 'humanitarian works' all done in the belief that it will bring salvation. Those who act without understanding or with a motive of self-gain or reward or recognition, do not really possess the spirit of understanding or charity and hence cannot attain salvation.

People in the world today are no different. Prayer in temple or other place of worship and other rites as well as 'social service' can be just as hypocritical or mindless today. But all acts performed with faith, devotion, discrimination, and in the spirit of selflessness can help man towards the higher spiritual goal.

The *Upanishads*, the *Vedanta Sutra* (*Brahma Sutra*) and the *Bhagavad Gita* are considered the three most important authorities on Hindu religion and philosophy.

References

1. *History of Dharmasastra* by P.V. Kane, vol.II, pt.1, chap.III, p.107.
2. *The Call of the Upanishads* by Rohit Mehta, (Bharatiya Vidya Bhavan, Bombay, 1970), p.83.
3. ibid., p.118.
4. *A New History of Sanskrit Literature* by K. Chaitanya.
5. *The Call of the Upanishads* by Rohit Mehta, p.217.
6. ibid., p.221, 222.
7. ibid., p.227.
8. ibid., p.229.
9. ibid., p.239.
10. ibid., p.260; see also *Pathway to God* by R.D. Ranade, p.283.
11. *History of Dharmasastra* by P.V. Kane, vol.V, pt.2, chap.XXXV, sec.IX, 1547.
12. *The Call of the Upanishads* by Rohit Mehta, p.289.
13. All quotations taken from *The Call of the Upanishads* by Rohit Mehta.

5

Smriti

While the Vedas are referred to as *Sruti*, meaning that 'which is heard', *Smriti* means 'from memory'.

Hindu thinkers used both reasoning as well as traditional knowledge. While reasoning consists of observation, inference, and comparison, traditional knowledge acts as reference material and a useful guideline. This is no different from what is followed in the world today. Since it is impossible for any one person to accumulate so much knowledge in one lifetime one has to take recourse to the experience of others. Before we unthinkingly accept the opinions of others, it is necessary to discriminate. Credibility of the author, the common experience of many as well as the fact that the common experience has the advantage of being time-tested, all add to the acceptance or rejection of any 'authority'. In short, 'authority' as reference material, must also be subjected to one's discriminating faculty.

Dharma is the moral law. It means that which upholds, sustains and nourishes. Creation can be sustained and nourished through moral acts alone.

The four sources of *dharma* given in Hindu thought are the Vedas, Smritis, *Sadachara* (conduct set by the good), and doing what is good for the Soul.

To enable us to do what is good for the Soul (act in the best interest of all) we have to achieve a detached, selfless and balanced personality, physically, emotionally and mentally, with an understanding of morality.

While the Higher Knowledge is the direct spiritual realization of the individual through his own efforts, the other three sources of *dharma* can be studied and reflected on for a better understanding of *dharma*.

Although they are of 'lower knowledge' they nevertheless help us to judge better by enlarging our vision and clarifying our thoughts, to enable us to see each issue in the right perspective.

Education is meant to help us perform better in life. Since the Vedas are regarded as authorless and the *mantras* of the Vedas represent the inner vision gifted to the seers who had reached the highest state of Self-realisation, the Vedas are the highest authority.

Next to the Vedas only, come the Smritis. The Smritis are dharmasastras, i.e., science or discipline dealing with moral acts.

The *mantras* in the Vedas are flashes of insight which show the light. But it is necessary for man to have a clearer idea of when an act is moral and when it is not. The Smritis seek to give man clear guidelines of behaviour so that he may function better and for the good of all.

The Spiritual, being abstract, is difficult for most of us to understand and there are many times in life when one is in two minds as to which is the more moral act.

The Smritis spell out the highest goal for each and all to strive to achieve. They help by setting a pattern of behaviour for both individual and society. They lay down duties for the individual at different ages, as well as for each strata of society. They exhort, and also lay down punishments for harmful acts.

They make the abstract concept more intelligible

in practical and everyday terms. 'The writers of the dharmasastras meant by *dharma* not a creed or religion, but a mode of life or a code of conduct which regulated a man's work and activities as a member of society and an individual and was intended to bring about the gradual development of a man to enable him to reach what was deemed to be the goal of human existence.'[1]

Dharma was divided into the *Srautha* and the *Smartha*. The first concerned the rites and ceremonies that the *Vedic Karma Kanda* (of the *Samhita* and *Brahmanas*) were concerned with. The *Smartha* was the *dharma* that the Smritis were concerned with. This concerned the various classes of professions (*varnas*) and the stages of life (*asramas*). The Dharmasastras are mostly concerned with *Smartha Dharma*, the *Grhyasutras* mostly being the authorities on the former.

Another and more comprehensive classification of *dharma* is six-fold. These are *Varna Dharma* (injunctions on *varnas* alone), *Asrama Dharma* (rules such as begging etc.), *Varna-Asrama Dharma* (rules of conduct for a particular class at a particular stage in life), *Guna Dharma* (such as protection of subjects in the case of a crowned king), *Naimitikka Dharma* (expiation on doing what is forbidden), *Sadharana Dharma* (what is common to all humanity), *Ahimsa* and other virtues.

While Smriti in a larger sense includes all ancient orthodox non-Vedic works, including Panini's *Grammar*, the *Srautha*, *Grhya* and *Dharma sutras*, *Mahabharata*, *Manusmriti*, *Yajnavalkya Smriti* and the philosophical systems, in a narrower sense the Smritis and *Dharmasastras* are synonymous.

That *Dharmasastra* works existed before 600 BC is known. They had attained supreme importance by the 2nd century BC.[2]

The earliest were the *Dharmasutras* of which

Apastamba, Baudhayana, Gautama and *Vasishta* are often quoted.

After the Sutras came the early Smritis. Some Smriti works like those of the earlier Sutras are known only by quotations.

Following the Smritis we have the Commentaries on them and later, the Digests. All these belong to Dharmasastra literature. The two epics *Ramayana* and the *Mahabharata* and the Puranas also played a great part in the development of Dharmasastra.

The Smritis belong to different and widely separated ages and as a consequence reflect the changes in their laws and customs.[3]

Some Smritis are in prose while a large number are in verse. Some of the ancient Smritis were composed centuries before Christ, some like Yajnavalkya and Parasara in the AD 1st century and most of the others between AD 400 and 1000.[4]

All Smritis are not equal in authority. The pre-eminent Smritis are the *Manusmriti* and next to it the *Yajnavalkya Smriti*.

A general rule is that in case of a conflict between the *Sruti* and the *Smriti*, the rule of the former will prevail. Kumarilla states that, "Inference is set aside by direct perception, *Smriti* by *Sruti*, a self contradictory *Smriti* not composed by an authoritative person set aside by one composed by an authoritative person and not self contradictory, a *Smriti* that has a visible worldly purpose by one that has an unseen spiritual purpose, a *Smriti* based on inference drawn from a *Sruti* or commendatory Vedic passage is set aside by *Smriti* based on a direct *Sruti* text; a usage is set aside by a *Smriti* and one usage is set aside by another usage that is accepted by more respectable people."[5]

Kumarilla however also shows how sometimes the visible and invisible spiritual purpose may be mixed. He shows how giving respect to a teacher may have a seen result (i.e. the teacher being pleased and therefore teaching enthusiastically) and also an unseen spiritual result (i.e. completion of Vedic studies without obstacles). He argues that all Smritis are authoritative according to the purpose they serve. Whatever portion of the Smritis are concerned with *dharma* and moksa have their authority in the Vedas, while that which is concerned with *artha* and *kama* (wealth and satisfaction of desires) is based on worldly practices.[6]

Thus those *dharmas* of the Smriti that are seen to have a visible worldly purpose take their authority from that visible fact, while those having no visible purpose may be inferred to be based on the Vedas.

Explaining this, Kulluka quotes from Sabara, showing how the injunctions of *Manu* (III.7), regarding the kind of bride to be chosen is based on the known fact that certain diseases are medically considered to be hereditary and hence likely to affect the progeny. A violation of the injunction based 'on a visible worldly purpose' would not therefore involve breaking a Vedic injunction.

From this the Dharmasastras draw a very important rule, viz., any act or rite that is performed contrary to a rule with a visible purpose, does not make the act invalid or void. But if a rule based on an unseen spiritual purpose is infringed, the act itself becomes void or invalid.[7]

Kumarilla shows how all knowledge is helpful and useful to man even in his spiritual goal. He cites the didactic portion of the *Mahabharata* and the Puranas, the Angas of the Vedas, and how they are useful in the proper understanding of the Vedas. Sankhya, Vedanta and Kanada's atomism serve to explain the creation and dissolution of the world, the performance that gives rise to the subtle *apurva* that leads to heaven and how human effort and destiny have their own spheres of operation. He goes on to explain how the Buddhist philosophy of *Vijnana* form the *Arthavada* passages of the *Upanishads* and how they also help reduce man's attachments to sensual pleasures. He winds up saying that wherever the result or reward of a course laid down were to take place in the future, with no possibility of experiencing it in the present, that should be deemed to be based on the Veda, whilst where, as in the science of medicine, the result can be seen taking effect, that knowledge is authoritative only because of the visible result.[8]

In *Rig Veda*, Manu is spoken of as the father of mankind. The extant *Manusmriti* tells of how Viraj sprang from and Viraj produced Manu from whom were born the sages Bhrgu and Narada. *Brahma* taught Manu the *sastras* (sciences) who in turn imparted them to the ten sages. They asked Manu on the *dharma* of the *varnas* and intermediate castes and Manu directed them to learn these from Bhrgu.[9]

There were several Manus and it is not possible to say which Manu is responsible for the extant *Manusmriti*. It discusses both *dharma* and *artha*.

The *Yajnavalkya Smriti* is next only to the *Manusmriti* in authority. The author of this *Smriti* however is not the same as the brilliant sage of the *Brihadaranyaka Upanishad*, even if he shares the same name. Nevertheless the author of this *Smriti* has been more than equal to his task. The *Smriti* is "a master-piece of conciseness and brevity with a direct and flowing style. Dividing the work into three sections without repetition he reduces *Manu's* 2700 verses into about a thousand. It is no small tribute to this *Smriti* that it has become the guiding work for the Hindus in all parts of India. This is a recognition of its clear and concise statement of principles, breadth of vision, and comparative impartiality towards the claims of both the sexes and the different *varnas*.'[10]

Since the Vedas contained only disconnected statements on the various aspects of *dharma*, the Smritis fulfilled the need of a formal and connected treatment of topics on Dharmasastra.

Concerned with morality, they did not pander to superstition. *Katyayana Smriti* (218-219) prescribes that if one party relies on human means of proof and the other on divine proof, the judge is to accept the human means and not the divine; and that if human means are able to establish only a part of the allegation (in the plaint) then the human means should be accepted and no divine modes of proof even though they may be complete, i.e., completely cover all allegations.[11]

The *Mahabharata* also contains an interesting discussion between a king and his son on the merits or demerits of capital punishment. The arguments given by the son who is against capital punishment are similar to those given today. The king tells his son that laws are meant for the general good. Punishments are for offenders who are not afraid of transgressing the laws. There are some who are not afraid even of capital punishment. These laws are therefore to be retained for the protection of society.[12]

Nobody has been able to explain how feelings of guilt or sin arise in the human mind. The concept of a fall from grace seems to have been there in Vedic times too. This happened when *Rta* was violated.

While the Hindus accept 'sin' as a violation of the moral law, the concept of 'original sin' does not exist. Divinity is the basic essence of all created things. Sin is synonymous with ignorance. Those who falsely identify with their material selves commit acts which are 'sinful' because they go against the natural order. When Arjuna asks Sri Krishna in the *Mahabharata* as to what impels man to sin, Krishna answers, 'This is the three-fold door to hell that is ruinous to the self — lust, anger and greed. Therefore a man must shun these three."

The difference between 'good' and 'evil' is not of kind but of degree. There is knowledge at one end and ignorance at the other. Ignorance is the lower end of the ladder.

The Smritis contain a list of sins both major and minor. Divergent views with corresponding atonements are prescribed in various Smritis. Normally a parishad (council) of learned *Brahmins* decided on the atonement (*prayaschitta*). While they dealt with minor atonements, the more serious ones had to be referred to the king, who, after having satisfied himself with the help of a *purohit* (learned priest) enforced the *prayaschitta*.

Some acts violated religious laws while not going against state laws, and some acts violated state laws without going against religious laws. Some offended both and attracted punishment from both. In such cases one of the atonements would be milder, to avoid double punishment.

Atonements were prescribed taking into account whether it was a first offence or repeated, the circumstance, the time, place, caste, age, capacity, sex, learning and wealth."

While it was a most heinous crime to kill a *Brahmin* or steal from him, capital punishment was meted out to a *Brahmin* only in very rare cases and when the same crime was committed by all castes the atonement or punishment was three quarters for a *Kshatriya*, half to the *Vaisya* and a quarter to the *Sudra* to that meted out to the *Brahmin*. In cases such as incest the atonement prescribed by the

Smritis as well as the state were the same i.e. removal of the testicles and penis.

Atonements that involved death were modified and made more humane by later *Smritikars* as, according to them, the penance was to purify and not to lose a life for, 'The body that is all in all (the only source of the observance) of *dharma* must be protected with efforts; just as water oozes down from the mountain so *dharma* springs from the body."[14]

Giving false witness was one of the gravest sins. Even the unnecessary cutting of shrubs and creepers, unless for the purpose of agriculture or sacrifice, was condemned and atonement stipulated. This was also for the killing of large or small animals.

Confession formed a part of the ritual of sacrifice along with liberality and was also for self-purification and atonement since Vedic times. *Manu* (VII.227-230) provides that a sinner is relieved of the consequences of sin by proclaiming his sin to people, by repentance, by austerities, by recitation of Vedic texts, by gifts in case he is unable to undergo *tapas*. A man after committing a sin becomes free of it if he feels remorse and resolves never to do it again.[15]

While the earlier belief was in heaven and hell (above and below respectively), as thought progressively developed, this was adjusted to heaven and hell being in this world itself, as rewards and punishments for acts.

The consequences of sin were two-fold. One led to hell and the other resulted in loss of caste. This prevented the sinner's social intercourse with members of his community.

An important matter dealt with by the Smritis was re-conversion of those converted by force by invading *mlecchas*.

Manu (VIII.169), *Vishnudharmasutra* (VII.6-7), *Yajna-valkya* (II.89), all declare that what is given by force, enjoyed by force, caused to be written by force and all transactions that are brought about by force, are void.[16]

The ceremony of Shuddhi was performed on those re-entering the fold. Those not born Hindus but wishing to become Hindus were initiated by performing Vratyastoma. This would account for the indigenous Hindus of Java, Bali, Sumatra, Śiam and other South-east Asian countries.

There are inscriptions of Hindu pilgrims at a Fire Temple called Jvalaji at Suruhani near Baku, the capital of Russian Azerbaijan. These begin with an obeisance to Ganesa and belong to the 18th and 19th centuries.[17] Ex-communication was called *Ghatasphota*.

It was recognized that society could not remain static. Changing of the people had to be attended to while retaining the foundation on which all society is based. *Dharma* was law, duty, and justice.

The general rule was that the customs of countries, castes, and families which were not opposed to the Vedas, should be authoritative and binding. The *Apastamba Grhyasutra* declares that one should regulate one's course of action (in doubtful matters) according to conduct unanimously approved by all Aryas, who are disciplined, mature, with their senses restrained, and who are neither hypocritical nor covetous. It says also that the *dharmas* not laid down may be understood from women and men of all castes.[18]

There is enough historical evidence to prove that the tolerance expressed in the Smritis was actually followed. Smritis and Digests, particularly the latter ones, prescribe that even the usages of heretical sects should be enforced by the king.

It appears that about the AD 10th century. some

learned men got together as they felt that certain customs and practices, though formerly allowed, were detrimental in the Kali age. These prohibitions, about 55 in number, were called *Kalivarjya* and included *govadha, niyoga,* the giving of a larger share to the eldest son, etc.[19] Most of these seem to be due to the prevailing unsettled conditions, and were an attempt to preserve the community, make it more tightly-knit and prevent an exodus to other lands. Although only *Brahmins* were forbidden to cross the seas, other castes including *Sudras* later also abided by it. The rule for *Brahmins* must have been specially thought of to prevent 'brain-drain'. Earlier the *Brahmins* had come eastwards right up to east Borneo.

Some quotes from the Smritis are given below, which provide a window to the attitude of the Smritis and are of greater value than any amount of writing about them.

Udyogparva states: "*Dharma* is so called because of its character as sustainer of all beings."[20]

Shantiparva: "What was *dharma* (in one age) may become *adharma* in another and that *dharma* and *adharma* are both subject to the limitations of country and time."[21]

Shantiparva: "Conquerors do not secure victory so much by their armies and prowess as by truthfulness, freedom from cruelty, observance of *dharma* and energetic action."[22]

ON CHARITY:

Devala: 'That is described as *daana* (charity) when wealth is given according to sastric rules so as to reach a receiver who is a fit recipient as defined in the sastras. What is given to a worthy person without an eye to any particular object (to be achieved by such a gift), but solely with the idea of doing one's duty, that is called *dharmadaan*."[23]

Daksa (III.17-18) states, "A gift made to one's parents,

'guru, friend, to a well conducted man, to one who has laid the donor under obligation, to the poor, to the helpless, those endowed with special excellence, leads to rewards; while gifts made to rogues, bards, wrestlers, those who devote time to bad lores, gamblers and deceitful persons, to 'catas' to 'caranas' and thieves bring no merit."[24]

Veda Vyasa (IV.30-31) explains that charity begins at home.[25]

Apastamba Dharmasutra (4.9, 10-12) and Baudhayana Dharmasutra Sutra (II.3-19) ordain that one should not stint one's dependants (whom one is bound to maintain), one's servants, and one's slave for distributing food to guests and others.[26]

Yajnavalkya Smriti (II.175) prescribes that one should make gifts in such a way as not to cause detriment to one's family.[27]

Brihaspati explains this saying that one may give away wealth over and above what is required for maintaining one's family and for clothing, and that the charity of one who disregards this rule is something that is sweet like honey at first but like poison in it's effect.[28]

Anusasana Parva (37, 2-3) declares that if one makes a gift stinting one's servants one makes oneself a sinner, even though one may say that one would give whatever anyone begs for.[29]

Vishnudharmasutra directs that in gifts of food and clothing the only consideration should be the need and not caste or quality of beneficiary.[30]

Indiscriminate begging has never been allowed by the Smritis even for Brahmins, much less for others. Parasara (I. 60) calls upon kings to fine that village where persons of the higher classes wander about begging though they were not observers of any vows (like brahmacharis) and not studying the Veda.[31]

Regarding documentation and justice:

Vasisthadharmasutra (16-10), *Vishnudharmasutra* (VI.23) and *Yajnavalkya Smriti* (VI.22) mention *likhita* (written document) as the first means of proof.[32]

Narada Smriti (IV.70-71) says, "Had the Creator not created writing which is, like an excellent eye, the world would have come to grief and that a document is an indubitable means of apprehending time, the place, the object, the material, the extent and the duration of a transaction."[33]

Smriti of Brihaspati (quoted in *V.P.* p.141) says that since people begin to entertain doubt (about a transaction) the Creator created in the hoary past letters which are recorded in writing material.[34]

Lalitavistara (about AD 2nd or 3rd century) mentions 64 scripts as being known to the Buddha, the first being Brahmi. (chap.X p.143)[35]

There is an interesting reference to gunpowder in *Sukranitisara* (AD 13th or 14th, century) Gunpowder is called *agnicurna* (1193, 196, IV.7.28) guns (IV.7.209-211) and gives the formula for gunpowder in IV.7-201.[36]

It was about this time that gunpowder as we know was first used in Europe. *Atharvaveda* (I.16-4) refers to leaden balls discharged from cylinders. Dr. Opport holds that gunpowder was known in India long before the 13th century.[37]

Nitivakyamrta refers to the appointment of auditors when there is discrepency in items of income and expenditure.[38]

Mahabharata says there is no custom or practice that can be said to be beneficial to all alike (hence variations in practices were to be allowed by the king.)[39]

Yajnavalkya Smriti (II.192) calls upon the king to safeguard the special usages of guilds and heretics and their modes of livelihood.[40]

Manu, Yajnavalkya Smriti, Vishnudharmasutra and

Puranas expressly provide that one should not observe but give up what was once *dharma* (custom or law) if it became hateful to the people and would end in unhappiness.[41]

Manu (VIII.48) highly eulogizes the office of king as divinity in human form.[42] *Kautilyas' Arthashastra* (VIII.5, p.276-277) cites at great length the causes that lead to the impoverishment of the subjects, to the kings being greedy and disaffected.[43]

Among these he mentions "Not paying what ought to be paid and exacting what ought not to be exacted, not punishing the guilty and severely punishing the not guilty, not protecting the people against thieves and robbing them of their wealth."

Yajnavalkya Smriti says, "The fire springing from the wrath caused by the harrassment of the subjects does not cease without burning the family, the wealth and life of the king."[44]

Shanti (88.26-27) says the person of the *duta* (ambassador) is sacred.[45]

Smriti of Brihaspati warns that decision (in a cause) should not- be given by merely relying on sastras, for in the case of a decision devoid of reasoning loss of *dharma* results."[46]

Narada Smriti (I.40) "When there is conflict between two texts of Dharmasastras, it is declared that the method to adopt is to resort to reasoning, for the practices (of 'sistas') are of great force and the strict letter of the law are overruled by them (or properly understood through them)."[47]

ON WOMEN:

Even if Manu is credited with being hard towards women, he does have some good things to say too.

A good guide, which explains the presence of criticisms in Smriti texts, are Sabara (on Jaimini II.4-21). "The purpose of a text censuring anything is not censure pure and simple, but to enjoin the performance of the opposite of what is censured and to praise such performance."[48]

Manu (III.56) and *Anusasana* (46-5): "Where women are honoured there the gods love to reside; where they are not honoured, there all religious acts come to nought."[49]

Manu (IX.10) makes quite clear that women could not be guarded through forcible seclusion, that their minds must be occupied in family work as stated by him, that the husband must try and preserve her regard and affection, and show her honour.[50]

If there are a few slighting references to women and also men in the *Rig Veda*, women are also described as a 'haven of rest'. (III.53-54). The slighting references to women must be taken as directed at those after only pleasure and self-indulgence. "An outcaste father may be abandoned but a mother is never an outcaste to her son."[51]

ON MARRIAGE:

Manusmriti (IX.90) provides that a girl should wait for three years after puberty during which her parents or relatives may choose a bridegroom for her and if they failed to do so, then she may herself choose a partner.[52]

Manusmriti (III.51-54-55) "A father should not take even the smallest gratuity for his daughter; if he takes a gratuity through greed he becomes the seller of his child. When relations do not take for themselves wealth given by the bridegroom as gratuity (but hand it over to the girl) the wealth so taken is for honouring the maiden and is only taken from the bridegroom out of loving concern for them. Father, brother, husband and brother-in-law desiring their own welfare, should honour women and give them ornaments."

Manusmriti (IX.98): Even a *Sudra* should not take gratuity when giving his daughter since in taking gratuity he clandestinely sells his daughter." "Whoever sells his son for a price or gives a daughter for the sake of his own livelihood in return for a gratuity would fall into a most horrible hell."

Anusasana (45.18-19) "Even a stranger cannot be sold, what of one's own children."[53]

The Smritis are against making marriage a commercial transaction.

Manu (V.106) says that he who is pure as to money matters is really pure and not he who washes himself with sand or water.[54]

Shanti (189-4, 8), "That man is known as a *Brahmana* in whom are seen truthfulness, generosity, absence of hate, absence of wickedness, shame, (restraint for avoiding wrong-doing) compassion and a life of austerity. If these signs are found in a *Sudra* and not found in a *Brahmana* then the *Sudra* is not a *Sudra* (should not be considered a *Sudra*) and a *Brahmana* is not a *Brahmana*."[55]

Manu and *Vishnudharmasutra*, "Wealth, kindred, age, (performance of) religious rites and sacred knowledge confer title to respect, but each succeeding one is superior to the preceding one".[56]

Gautama Dharma Sutra (VIII.24-26) holds that compassion and love for all beings, forbearance, freedom from envy, purity of body, speech and thought, absence of painful efforts or ambition, doing what is commended, not demeaning oneself before others, not hankering after sensual pleasures or the possession of others are the qualities of the Soul and the person who has these qualities even if he does not have all the forty *samskaras* will realize *Brahma*.[57]

Says *Vasishta* (XXX-I) "Practice *dharma* (righteousness) and not *adharma*: speak the truth and not untruth; look far ahead and not near; look at what is highest; and not at what is not highest.[58]

Shantiparva asserts "Whatever deeds a man does in four ways, viz., with eye, with thought, speech and action, he receives (in return) that same kind of action; a man does not enjoy (i.e. experience the results of) the good or evil deeds of another. Man attains (a result) in consonance with actions done by himself.[59]

Udyogparva states, "*Dharma* is so called because of its character as the sustainer of all beings."[60]

Manu (IV.161), "Assiduously do that which will give satisfaction to the *antaratma* (soul)" and again, "No parents, nor wife, nor sons will be a man's friends in the next world, but only righteousness."[61]

Devala: "Sacrifice, gift and study lose their value and perish by being declared to others, by boasting about them or by repenting having done them. Therefore one should not without good reasons (such as protecting a gift, etc.) proclaim one's meritorious act."[62]

The Smritis recognize the importance of form as an instrument to fulfill the functions of life. In order to function well it is necessary to understand the need and the requirements of that need. All forms have to be kept alert and in trim to enable proper functioning'. Man and universe, the physical, emotional and mental are there to serve the Spirit. Truth is the basis of all creation. It supports all creation and is the goal of all creation. The Smritis try their best to ensure that man disciplines himself to fulfill his role in life. The spirit, the subtlest of all, is all-pervading and present in all things. Creation is served by serving the spirit. It is truthful acts, i.e., spiritual acts alone that serve all material creation.

References

1. *History of Dharmasastra* by P.V. Kane, vol.II, pt.1, p.2.
2. ibid., vol.I, p.9.

3. ibid., vol.I, p.134, vol.V, pt.2, chap.XXIX, sec.VII, p.1271.
4. ibid., vol.I, p.134.
5. ibid., vol.III, chap.XXXII, p.855, vol.V, pt.2, chap.XXIX, sec.III, p.1277, 1278.
6. ibid., vol.V, pt.2, chap.XXIX, sec.VII, p.1261.
    ibid., vol.III, chap.XXXII, p.836, 837.
7. ibid., vol.III, chap.XXXII, p.838.
8. ibid., vol.III, chap.XXXII, p.839, 840
9. ibid., vol.I, p.137.
10. ibid., vol.I, p.176.
11. ibid., vol.III, chap.XIV, p.363.
12. ibid., vol.III, chap.XV, p.399.
13. ibid., vol.IV, chap.III.
14. ibid., vol.IV, chap.III.
15. ibid., vol.IV, chap.I.
    ibid., vol.V, chap.XXXV, sec.IX, p.1593.
16. ibid., vol.IV, chap.IV.
17. ibid., vol.IV, chap.IV.
18. ibid., vol.III, chap.XXXIII, p.856.
19. ibid., vol.III, chap.XXXIV, p.930-964. vol.V, pt.2, p.1267.
20. ibid., vol.V, pt.2, chap.XXXVI, sec.X, p.1627, 1628.
21. ibid., vol.V, pt.2, chap.XXXV, sec.X, p.1630.
22. ibid., vol.III, chap.VIII, p.209, 210.
23. ibid., vol.II, pt.2, chap.XXV, p.842.
24. ibid., vol.II, pt.2, chap.XXV, p.845.
25. ibid., vol.II, pt.2, chap.XXV.
26. ibid., vol.II, pt.2.
27. ibid., vol.II, pt.2.
28. ibid., vol.II, pt.2.
29. ibid., vol.II, pt.2.
30. ibid., vol.II, pt.2, p.846.
31. ibid., vol.I, chap.III, p.133.
32. ibid., vol.III, chap.XI, p.307.
33. ibid., vol.III, chap.XI, p.308.
34. ibid., vol.III, chap.XI, p.308.
35. ibid., vol.III, chap.XI, p.308.
36. ibid., vol.III, chap.VIII, p.213, 214.
37. ibid., vol.III, chap.VIII, p.216.
38. ibid., vol.III, chap.VII, p.199.
39. ibid., vol.III, chap.XXXIII, p.860, 861.
40. ibid., vol.V, pt.2, chap.XXXIII, sec.VIII, p.1482.
41. ibid., vol.V, pt.2, chap.XXXV, sec.X, p.1630.
42. ibid., vol.V, pt.2, p.1639.
43. ibid., vol.III, chap.VII, p.198.

44. ibid., vol.III, chap.VIII, p.199
45. ibid., vol.III, chap.IV, p.127.
46. ibid., vol.V, pt.2, chap.XXVIII, sec.VII, p.1470.
47. ibid., vol.III, chap.XXXII, p.867.
48. ibid., vol.II, pt.1, chap.XII, p.581.
49. ibid., vol.II, pt.1, chap.IX.
50. ibid., vol.III, chap.XXV, p.537.
51. ibid., vol.II, pt.1, chap.XI, p.580.
52. ibid., vol.V, pt.2, chap.XXV, sec.VII, p.1338.
53. ibid., vol.II, pt.1, chap.IX, p.506.
54. ibid., vol.V, pt.2, chap.XXXV, sec.X, p.1648.
55. ibid., vol.V, pt.2, chap.XXXV, sec.X, p.1636.
56. ibid., vol.II, pt.1, chap.VII.
57. ibid., vol.II, pt.1, p.6.
58. ibid., vol.II, pt.1, chap.I, p.6.
59. ibid., vol.V, pt.2, chap.XXXV.
60. ibid., vol.V, pt.2, chap.XXXVI, sec.X, p.1627.
61. ibid., vol.II, pt.1, p.7.
62. ibid., vol.I, pt.2, chap.XXV, p.848.

6

Purana

The word *Purana* is derived from *pura* which means 'formerly' or 'from ancient times' and *na* meaning 'to breathe' or 'live'. *Purana* therefore means that which lives the past or which breathes ancient times. The Puranas are regarded as *Itihas* (history).

Puranas are referred to even as far back as the *Atharva Veda*, the *Satapatha Brahmanas*, and the ancient *Upanishads*.[1] It is clear they had attained a state of sacredness like the Vedas and were associated with Itihas even in those times, though we know nothing of their contents in those early times.

The probable dates of most of the extant Puranas are between AD 300 and 600. We know however, from the references made to them that other Puranas were in existence at the time of Bana (early 7th century) Sabara (between AD 200 and 400) Kumarilla (7th century) and Shankaracharya (between AD 650 and 800), We also know that their contents were similar to those in the extant Puranas.[2]

The eighteen extant Puranas are the *Brahma, Padma, Vishnu, Vayu, Bhagavata, Naradiya, Markandeya, Agni, Bhavisya, Brahmavaivarta, Linga, Varaha, Skanda, Vamana, Karma, Matsya, Garuda* and *Brahmanda*.[3] Both Buddhism and Tantricism had their effect on the Puranas which are graded as satwic, rajasic and tamasic. There has also been some unscrupulous tampering with the Puranas e.g. *Bhavisya Purana.*[4]

Ballasena, a King of Bengal shows a bold discriminating faculty when he records that for his work on *Daana* he studied the epics, the Smritis and thirteen principal Puranas. He does not rely on some of the Puranas for various reasons which he mentions. In some Puranas, *Daanas* are absent. Some are tainted with the doctrines of heretical sects. Some are mere compilations, while others contain wrong procedures for various acts. Some contain incoherent tales and false genealogies while others give stories of love affairs and give credence to buffoons, heretics or those who make a livelihood by mere use of external symbols.

A Purana is meant to discuss five topics. It contains legends, geography of the earth, dynastic lists, measures of time and a description of what will happen in future.

The Puranas concern themselves with historical existence. Kumarilla explains the usefulness of a Purana, by showing how the tales and anecdotes have a meaning and authoritativeness as do the commendatory passages of the Vedas. The divisions of the earth are narrated to distinguish the regions for undergoing the consequences of acts according to *dharma* and *adharma*, which are based partly on personal experience and partly on Vedas. The orderly presentation of dynasties is to facilitate knowledge of the *Brahmin* and *Kshatriya* castes and their *gotras* which are based on actual experience and traditional knowledge. Countries and measures of time are intended to help worldly transactions and astronomical needs, and these are based on actual perception, mathematics, tradition and inference. The narration of what will happen in future is based on the Veda since it deals with a variety of consequences that result from the ripening of acts of *dharma* and *adharma*, and knowledge of the characteristics of the *yugas* that have been in operation from time immemorial.[5]

Among the Puranas the *Vishnupurana* comes closest to the definition of a Purana with regard to its contents.[6]

Most Puranas devote themselves to one god in whom is personalised the concept of the One *Para Brahma*. The *Vishnu Purana* invokes the God Vishnu.

In a conversation between Satanika and Sumanta, the latter says that the Dharmasastras consisting of the eighteen Puranas, the *Ramayana* and the *Mahabharata* are meant for the education and enlightenment of the common people and are for all the four *varnas*.[7]

The Pauranic *mantras* could be recited by all. The Puranas introduced several striking changes in the religious rites, practices and ideals of the people.[8]

The Puranas gave the people a world-view, a sense of identity and a moral foundation. Though not history as we know it today, it could be argued that they teach something more than mere history. The philosophical concepts were told in a manner that the uneducated would understand. The abstract *Brahma*, pure and without attributes was made more intelligible by depicting god in personalised form with all the virtues as attributes. In Hindu thought god in personalised form with attributes, is Isvara. Isvara has different names but the same attributes. The formless takes form only for man's better understanding. The devotion given to one god is really devotion to every god as they all essentially represent the One only.

The *Vishnu Purana* has Vishnu for its deity. In it are contained all the stories connected with Vishnu in his various incarnations. Vishnu is the Preserver. His incarnations look remarkably like the process of evolution, being first fish, then tortoise and successively, boar, man-animal, dwarf, giant man, perfect man and lastly as the divine man Krishna.

Each time the principle of *Prakriti* (Nature) also accompanies him. This is Lakshmi, the consort of Vishnu. When he comes as the dwarf she is Padma or Kamala, she is Parsuram's wife *Dharini*, she is Sita the wife of the perfect man Rama, and she is the divine Krishna's Rukhmini.

Beginning with an invocation to Vishnu, the *Vishnu Purana* is in the form of questions and answers between the sage Parasara and his disciple Maitreya.

The world, we are told, is produced from Vishnu, the Creator, Preserver and Destroyer who comprehends in his nature the four, viz., *Pradhana* (primary matter), *Purusha* (spirit), *Vyakta* (visible substance) and *Kala* (time). 'Vishnu being thus discrete and indiscrete substance, spirit and time, sports like a playful boy and you shall learn by listening to his frolics.'

Supreme *Brahma* enters matter and spirit agitating the mutable and immutable principle, which is the beginning of creation. *Purshottama* is both agitator and the thing to be agitated, being present in the essence of matter both when it is contracted and expanded.

It goes on to explain the creative process along the lines of Sankhya and accepted by Vedanta.

Time is measured from 15 twinklings of an eye onwards to the four *yugas*, *Krita*, *Treta*, *Dvapara* and *Kali*. The *Krita yuga* lasts for 4000 divine years, the *Treta* lasts for 3000, the *Dvapara* for 2000 and *Kali* for a thousand divine years. There is a rest period between each *yuga*. All the *yugas* together total 43,20,000 man years.

The dissolution of all things, we are told, is of four kinds: occasional, elemental, absolute and perpetual.

Occasional dissolution takes place 'when *Brahma* sleeps', when torrential rains submerge all in water, and from whence when the water subsides life begins anew. This happens after 1000 periods of the four ages (*yugas*).

Elemental dissolution is when the mundane egg resolves back to the primary element from which it started, each of the five elements losing their properties before relapsing into the primary matter.

Absolute dissolution is that of the meditating sage for whom the world is non-existent, due to his knowledge and absorption in the Supreme Being.

Perpetual dissolution takes place continuously and involves the generation and regeneration of living things.

We are told of the two states of *Brahma*, one with form and one without. The first is perishable while the second is imperishable. This is inherent in all beings. The Imperishable is the Supreme Being while the perishable is all the world.

It should be the endeavour of the wise to attain the Supreme Being. The means for this are through knowledge and works.

Knowledge is of two kinds: that which is derived from Scriptures and that derived through reflection.

Brahma that is the word (form) is composed of Scripture. *Brahma* that is Supreme is understood through reflection, which enables discrimination between soul and matter.

Ignorance is utter darkness, and in darkness knowledge derived through the senses (i.e. hearing, seeing etc.) shines like a lamp. But the knowledge that comes through reflection bursts through the darkness of ignorance like the sun.

Thus from study to meditation and meditation to study, the perfection in both makes the Spirit manifest. He who is one with *Brahma* sees not with the eye of the flesh. (The 'eye of the flesh' enables us to see the external while the Truth can only be realised through an inner vision).

The Vedas prescribe two kinds of works, Active and Passive, (*Pravrutta* and *Nivrutta*), by both of which God is worshipped. The first deals with performances of rites while the second is through meditation and devotion to the soul of Vishnu by sages.

The Vedantic philosophy is conveyed through stories and allegories. The practice of meditation through Yoga is described.

In the story of Kesidhwaj and Khandikeya we are shown how ignorance arises from the erroneous notion that the self is really what is not self and property what is really not one's own. The mind of man is the cause of his bondage as well as his liberation. Addiction to sense objects is the cause of bondage, and separation from these brings liberation.

Another story is related of King Bharata. Handing over the reigns of the kingdom, to his son, he detaches himself from his family and retires to the forest for meditation. Here he gets attached to a deer. For this attachment he is reborn for a short while as a *Brahmin*, in which form he attains the Supreme Being. Liberation comes from non-attachment. Attachment to specific individuals or objects is discriminatory. The same divine essence is in all and hence precludes any particularised attachment.

This *Brahmin* who has now realised the Self tells King Sauria, "This end which is eternal cannot be secured through the performances of sacrifices and rites which consist of only in using perishable material things. Only the transient and the material can be accomplished through the transient and the material. Rites are only a means to an end and not the end itself. Even meditation cannot be considered an end, for, through it, we are able to distinguish between the soul and body (spirit and matter), and the great end or Truth is without distinction. Some say union of self with the Supreme Spirit is the great end; yet, even this is false, since the same substance cannot be another. The great end of all is the Soul, all-pervading, uniform, perfect, incorruptible, independent, detached, all-knowing, without beginning and without end, and the knowledge that this Spirit is essentially One, in one's own and all other bodies. This is the great end or true wisdom. Just as the one diffusive air passes through the perforations of the flute, producing different notes of the scale, so this great Spirit is single, though seen in manifold forms arising as a result of acts. When the form is destroyed there is no distinction. Thus the great end of life or Truth is not to bring about the union of two things or two parts of one thing, but to know that all is Unity."

Manu is known as the Father of mankind. The first Manu is known as Manu Swayambhu. Every age has a Manu, and each of these ages is called a Manvantara. Manus are men of devotion and righteousness who become the lawgivers of every age.

We are given the story of Dhruva, the grandson of Manu. Dhruva's father King Uttanapada had two wives Suniti and Suruchi. Suruchi was the favourite. One day five-year-old Dhruva, the son of Suniti saw his half-brother on his father's lap and wanted to be taken up too. His father, seeing Suruchi nearby, refused. Suruchi told Dhruva that only her son could be taken by the father on his lap. Little Dhruva, deeply hurt, went and complained to his mother. Suniti, hearing him, sighed and said that Suruchi was getting these favours because of the piety she had accumulated in her previous birth. If Dhruva wished for things then he must strive to get them through his own merit which he must acquire by being good to those around and to all living creatures, by being pious and friendly, for "prosperity descends upon merit as does water towards low ground." Thereupon Dhruva decided to secure merit by his own efforts and acquire a place higher than all. Going to the forest he sees seven rishis sitting on antelope hides spread with holy Kusa grass. He approaches them and on being asked what he seeks, tells them his story. His listeners marvel at how in this *Kshatriya*, even one so young, there is pride and sensitivity as well as courage and fortitude. They ask what he wants of them. He tells them that he wants neither riches nor dominion, but only a station that nobody has reached before and asks them the way. They tell him that one way is through devotion to Vishnu and they teach him the method of Yoga. Thanking the rishis Dhruva departs to a grove called Madhusudan on the banks of Mathura. There he engages himself in single-minded concentration and devotion. The gods become alarmed. They try every ruse to break his meditation. Demons and goblins are sent to frighten him as well as the sweet words of his mother asking him to stop his penance. They are of no avail. Vishnu then sends them all away, and pleased with Dhruva, appears before him. Telling Dhruva he is pleased with his devotion he grants Dhruva a boon. Dhruva tells Vishnu that now that he has seen him he has no other desire but that he should continue to worship Him.

Vishnu then tells Dhruva that in a previous birth he had been born a *Brahmin*, but being friendly with a prince, he had desired to be the son of a king. He was re-born as a prince. "But", said Vishnu, 'I am happy that being a king's son has not spoilt you, which by others would be considered a great boon. So, you will sustain the stars and planets — above the Sun, Moon, Mercury, Venus, Saturn and all other constellations, above the regions of the Seven Rishis (The Great Bear). Some essential beings endure for four ages, some for the reign of one *Manu*. But you will stay for one Kalpa. Your mother Suniti will be the bright star and will be there for the same term. All those who glorify you at dawn will acquire merit."

(Here we see how even a little child like Dhruva with the qualities of his professional class puts these qualities to good use by devotion to Truth and how he achieves self-purification through his own ceaseless and determined striving. Even our misfortunes in life can spur us on to effort which enables us to rise above them.)

The North Star is Dhruva.

Interestingly, the Purana describes the movements of the constellations as following the North Star and remarks that the constellations are suspended in space by 'ropes of air'.

We are given the story of Vena, a descendant of Dhruva. Vena was evil. He insisted that the sacrifice be not made to the gods but to him, since he represented all. The wise men told him that such an act would be unwise and would bring misery on all. When he still refused to listen, the 'rishis' flayed him with grass ropes and killed him. After his death as there was no king, there was no law and order and looting and robbery became the norm. The rishis then took out the evil from Vena's body by rubbing his thigh from which issued a dark, flat-featured dwarf. Then rubbing Vena's right arm the sages produced the resplendent Prithu.

An act of sacrifice is essentially an act of worship. It is an unselfish act and not a selfish one. Vena thought in material terms. Arrogance comes from identification with the material. Selfish acts are material acts. Vena was evil because he was ignorant of a higher ideal. Here we see that although a descendant of Dhruva, Vena does not possess the same character. A ruler though necessary for ordered government must also be enlightened. An authority is also necessary for order. Prithu was the first king. At the sacrifice performed by *Brahma* at his birth, the bards Suta and Maghada were asked to sing Prithu's praises. They resisted, saying he had yet to accomplish something. They were then told to praise him for the heroic acts he would perform and for the virtue he would display. They did so and the king listening, was pleased and resolved to do as they said. "The king", they sang, "always stood by truth, kept his promises, was bounteous, wise, benevolent, patient, fearless and a terror to the wicked. He knew his duty. He gave others their due by acknowledging and appreciating their services. He was kindly and compassionate, a performer of sacrifices, respecter of the venerable, he revered the *Brahmins*, cherished the good and was impartial in justice."

Prithu followed these qualities of a good king. When his subjects came to him complaining that the earth had withheld edible plants due to the anarchy and famine, he in anger took up his bow *Ajagana*, and went after the earth. The earth, in the shape of a cow, fled. Prithu pursued relentlessly. At last she turned around and said: "did not he know that it was a sin to kill a female?" Prithu replied that if the happiness of many depended on the death of one evil being then the act became a virtue. The earth then asked how he hoped to help his subjects by killing her. He answered he would do so by his own devotions. The earth then told him that all undertakings were successful by the employment of suitable means.

All the vegetables that were destroyed would be restored again through her milk. She asked him to level the earth and bring her calf so that her secreted milk, the seed of all vegetables could flow around. Prithu levelled thousands of mountains. Before him there were no boundaries of villages or towns. There was no cultivation, no pasture, no agriculture nor highways for merchants. All these things, all civilization originated with Prithu.

(We see here how the ideal of a good king held up by the bards influenced Prithu to good acts. In his wish to do the best for his people, Prithu did not mind breaking 'conventions' such as not killing a woman or a cow. The earth on her part helped him only when she found he was prepared to give of himself for the good of his people which is the only justification of any good ruler. The earth teaches him that mere good intentions are not enough nor just fighting. Right methods have to be used to procure the right results. She teaches him the methods of agriculture and tending livestock. This is the first step of a settled civilization. Prithu was the founder of an orderly and settled civilization).

A descendant of Prithu, Prachinaverhis, a devout man, married Suvarna, the daughter of the ocean. They had ten sons, all skilled in the art of military science. Since their father had told them that mankind had to be increased and this could only be done through devotion to Vishnu they all went under water observing their duties and religious penances for a thousand years. On surfacing however, they found that during the time they were under water, the trees had spread and overshadowed the earth blocking out wind and sky and men were dying. At this they were angry and sent forth flames from their mouths to burn away the forests. When Moon, (Soma) Lord of the vegetable kingdom saw this, he asked them to spare the remaining trees and said he would form an alliance between the trees and them by giving them in marriage Marisha, the daughter of the woods. She would be their bride and multiply the race of Dhruva. Her son, the Patriarch Daksha, would have their vigour and the moon's lustre, and like a resplendent fire would multiply the human race.

The story of Marisha is a poetic one. She was the offspring of the sage Kandu and the nymph Pramlocha. Kandu going for his penance one morning sees Pramlocha and falls in love with her. She has been sent to distract him from his penances. Living happily with her for years he suddenly one day gets himself ready for his penance. Pramlocha informs him that he has already broken his penance. He is annoyed with himself and with her. She in fear of his wrath, flees from there. She is with child. As she passes the trees, she wipes the perspiration from her body with the leaves of the trees. The leaves collect this living dew. Taken to the top of the tree this living dew is nourished by the moon's rays and grows into the lovely Marisha.

(In the story of the sons of Prachinaverhis we see here how nature allowed unchecked, can destroy, like the trees overgrowing and spreading in an uncontrolled manner. But the trees cannot be completely destroyed because by doing so man also may destroy himself. The balance in nature must be kept. Nature to be beneficial, must be used wisely and knowledgeably).

The sage Daksha, (son of Brahma in an earlier life) the son of Marisha, created progeny for the furtherance of mankind and all living beings. He created by his will both male and female. It was from then onwards that living beings came to be propagated through sexual contact. Before this they were propagated by sight, touch, and the religious austerities of saints.

(Sex has a legitimate place in nature's scheme. It is meant for the purpose of propagation and not mere self-indulgence. Sex is perfectly legitimate when engaged in for moral and not immoral reasons).

We are given the story of Prahlad. Diti, one of Daksha's daughters has two sons. Hiranyakasipu and Hiranyaksa. The former has a son called Prahlad who is a devotee of Vishnu. Prahlad's father was a rich and powerful king with even the elements (gods) under his control. He calls Prahlad and enquires of him as to what he has studied under his teachers. Prahlad answers that he has learnt to adore him who is "without beginning, middle or end, the

Imperishable, the Universal Cause". The wrathful
Hiranyakasipu demands of the teachers whether they
have taught this to Prahlad. They deny it. He then asks
Prahlad from whom he has learnt it. Prahlad replies,
"From whom else but the king of the three worlds,
Vishnu?" The father is annoyed that someone else should
be considered as king of the three worlds and asks Prahlad
whether he wants to die. Prahlad answers that Vishnu is
the protector and creator of not only him but also of his
father and the whole universe. He is again sent back to his
teachers, but again when brought before the king does not
recant on his previous words. The wrathful king orders
him to be killed. Prahlad replies that Vishnu is present in
the weapons also as he is in his body and that no harm can
befall him. Inspite of all the devices they try they cannot
kill him. Then the *Brahmin* sons of the illustrious sage
Bhargava, the reciter of the *Sama Veda*, intercede for him
and tell the king they will teach him how to destroy his
enemies. But Prahlad teaches them instead saying that the
abandonment of enmity itself is a pleasure and explains
how the whole world is itself a manifestation of Vishnu.
"Let us then try and rid ourselves of the angry passions of
our race and strive by doing so to attain pure eternal
happiness beyond the power of all elements. Wealth,
pleasure, virtue are things of little moment. Precious is the
fruit that can be gathered from the Tree of True Wisdom."

His teachers report Prahlad's behaviour to the king,
who is annoyed at such impious doctrines being preached
by him. Prahlad does not succumb to poison. The priests
who are asked to kill him with rites try and reason with
him telling him to listen to his father the king, instead of
depending on God or the Eternal. When he does not listen
they chant rites to kill him but get killed instead. Prahlad
then prays to Vishnu that they be brought back to life.
They revive and bow to Prahlad, blessing him.

Hiranyakasipu then asks Prahlad where he gets his powers. Are they from magic rites? Prahlad answers "he who meditates not of wrong to others but considers them as himself is free from the effects of sin. But he who inflicts pain on others in thoughts, speech and acts sows the seeds of future births and the fruits that await after birth is pain. When I wish no evil to others, do and speak no offence, why should any harm come for I see Vishnu in all beings as in my soul? Love for all creatures is assiduously cherished by all who are wise in the knowledge of Vishnu."

Every method is used to kill Prahlad but he stands steadfast. Vishnu appears to Prahlad and grants him three boons. Prahlad asks that his faith in Vishnu never wanes, that since he has been saved by Vishnu, Vishnu should save his father too and lastly that his faith should always remain undiminished. Vishnu grants him all his boons.

When Prahlad goes to his father and bows to him his father repents his ill-treatment to his son. Hiranyakasipu, the invincible king who cannot meet death at the hands of man or beast meets his death at the hands of Vishnu who comes in the incarnation of a man-lion.

(The story of Prahlad shows the two value systems prevalent in the world. Hiranyakasipu thinks he is invincible and all-powerful in the world, being the most powerful monarch. He thinks in material terms alone and fears none. He cannot understand his son Prahlad and is offended that he should not be impressed nor acknowledge his father's power. When Prahlad remains undaunted inspite of persecutions, with his integrity intact, he orders him killed because it is unthinkable that any should challenge a king. The king's lack of understanding of the power of Truth is further demonstrated when he asks his son whether his powers are due to magic. The materialist finds it easier to believe in magic and superstition).

We are given the story of the sage Visvamitra, a king and a *Kshatriya* by caste, whose sister Satyavati is the mother of sage Jamadagni. Visvamitra himself turns an ascetic *brahmin* in order to acquire merit through penance and meditation. One day while the sage Jamadagni is away, a King Kartavirya wanders to the hermitage. He is offered hospitality by wife Renuka. He is so impressed with the milch cow of the sacred oblation that he forcibly takes it away. This misuse of his powers as a king and his obligation as a guest infuriates Jamadagni when he hears of it on his return. Jamadagni kills Kartavirya. The king's sons in revenge kill Jamadagni. When Jamadagni's son Parsurama hears of it he vows to destroy the *Kshatriya* race and does so seven times.

The stories serve to point out the dangers of power being misused by the greedy for selfish ends. Those who forsake *dharma* are destroyed. They are really responsible for their destruction by their own acts.

Many instances are given of change of caste, of *Brahmins* being born out of *Kshatriyas*.

A long list of kings and dynasties are given.

We are also told of the kinds of systems there will be in the *Kali* age. "There will be contemporary kings, churlish, violent, addicted to falsehood and wickedness. They will seize upon the property of their subjects, inflict death on women, children and cows. With limited power, insatiable desires, lacking in piety they will rise and fall rapidly. People of other countries, intermingling with them will follow their example, will receive their patronage to the exclusion of purer tribes who, neglected, will perish. Wealth and piety will decrease to general depravity. Then property will give rank, wealth will be the reason for devotion, passion will be the uniting bond between the sexes, falsehood will bring success in litigation and women will be only objects of gratification. Earth will be valued only for her mineral products. The Brahmanical thread will signify a *Brahmin*; external accessories (like garb and staff) will differentiate between several orders of life; people will thrive on dishonesty, dependance will be promoted through weakness; menace and presumption will be the substitute for learning, liberality will mean devotion, a simple wash will be considered a purification, mutual assent will be marriage; fine clothes will confer dignity, water at a distant place will become a holy spring. He who is strongest amongst all castes will rule over a degenerate principality. The people will seek refuge from avaricious sovereigns, in the mountain valleys living off herbs, roots, flowers, fruits and wild honey. They will cover themselves with the bark of trees and be exposed to cold, heat, wind and rain. Lives will be short. Thus in the *Kali* age the human race will approach its ultimate annihilation through decay.

When the practices taught by the Vedas and Smritis have all but ceased, the end of the *Kali* age will be near and a portion of the Divine Being will be born as Kalki, a *brahmin* in the family of Vishnuyasas of Sambhala village endowed with the eight *siddhis*. By his irresistible might he will destroy the *mlecchas*, thieves and the iniquitous. He will re-establish righteousness on earth. The minds of men will be awakened and become again as clear as crystal.

While giving a summary of the sovereigns Parasara relates a chant of the Earth as related by Muni Asita to King Janaka.

"How great", said the Earth, "is the folly of princes, who having the faculty of reason, cherish ambition, when they themselves are but foam on the waves. Busy as they are, subduing their ministers, servants and subjects, overcoming their foes to conquer the earth, they do not see death which is not far off. It is however no mighty matter for a man who can subdue himself to subdue the earth.

True liberation only comes through self-control. It is foolish infatuation unmindful of history that makes them wish to possess me. They aspire for me even when they have seen others before them dead, compelled to relinquish me. When I hear a king send word to another through his ambassador, "this earth is mine, resign your pretensions to it', I am first moved to violent laughter which however, soon gives way to compassion for the infatuated fool."

Parasara shows how all the kings of the past, including the greatest, of unbounded wealth and power have all perished, being now only the subject of narration. All are subject to the same fate. A wise man will not go after individual appropriation of transient temporal possessions. He will not consider children, posterity, lands, property and whatever else is personal, to be his own.

Parasara relates what Bhishma told Yudhistira when Yudhishtira asked him what are the acts that free men from subjection to Yama, the god of death. Those who have Vishnu in their hearts do not fear Yama. The worshipper of Vishnu is one "who never deviates from the duties prescribed for his caste, who makes no distinction between friend and enemy, who does not deprive others nor injures any human being. One who seeing hidden gold looks upon the wealth of another as grass, meditating only on Vishnu. Vasudeva (Vishnu) is present in one who is pure in thought, contented, without malice, leading a holy life, with tenderness towards all creatures, speaking kindly, wise, humble and sincere. The Eternal cannot abide in the heart of one who covets another's wealth, injures living creatures, who is harsh and untruthful, proud of his own iniquity and with an evil mind. Janardana (Vishnu) does not occupy the thoughts of one who is envious of another's prosperity, calumniates the virtuous, never sacrifices nor bestows gifts on the pious, is blinded by the darkness of his ignorance. He is no devotee

of Vishnu who through avarice, is unkind to his nearest
friends and relations, to his wife, children, parents and
dependants. The brute whose evil thoughts lead him to
unrighteous acts, seeking the company of the wicked
constantly engaged in criminal acts, is no worshipper of
Vishnu."

The Supreme Vishnu is "pleased with those who
observe the institutions of caste, order and purifactory
practices. The *Brahmin*, *Kshatriya*, *Vaisya* and *Sudra* who
attend to the rules of their caste are those who worship
him best. He is most pleased with those who do good to
others, who never utter abuse, calumny or untruth, who
bear ill-will towards none, coveting not another's wife nor
wealth, who neither beats nor slays any animate or
inanimate thing, who serves diligently the gods, *brahmins*
and his spiritual guru, always desirous of the welfare of all
creatures, his children and of his soul, having a pure heart
free of love and hatred. The man who confirms to the
duties enjoined by the scripture in each order and
condition in life is he who best worships Vishnu".

The Purana goes on to describe the duties and
obligations of each order (caste) in life. This order was
based on quality, '*Brahma* appoints the robust and valiant
as *Kshatriyas*, the pure and pious as *Brahmins*, those less
powerful but assiduous in cultivation and industrious as
Vaisyas, and the weak in spirit as *Sudras*'. All are assigned
their occupations. Each belongs to a part of *Brahma's*
body. They are thus all divine and inter-dependant on
each other for the common good. Theirs is a duty without
any privileges. Apart from their duties a common
obligation is assigned to all. All the *varnas* are to work
assiduously to maintain their families, produce progeny
through wedlock, bestow tenderness on all creatures,
have patience, humility, truth, purity, contentment,
decorousness, gentleness of speech, friendliness and

freedom from envy and repining and from avarice and detraction. These are to be followed in all the four *Asramas* (stages) in life.'

[Although the *sanyasi* (ascetic) was held in high respect, the great contribution of the householder was never discounted. The Shankaracharya, although a *sanyasi* and a man of renunciation himself, refers to the three *asramas* as rivers, and the *gryhasta* (householder) as the sea. It was accepted that the three other *asramas* were dependent on the householder. This sentiment is also echoed in other religious texts.[9]]

We find advice given to the householder. This covers hygiene, etiquette and sound commonsense dashed with humour. These correspond almost word for word with the institutes of *Manu*. "The wise man is asked to contemplate on the two objects of life, wealth and virtue and advised that wealth and desire be avoided where they give uneasiness to virtue, and to abstain from virtuous and religious acts if they involved misery and censure by the world".

There is detailed description of worshipful acts and habits of personal cleanliness. Hospitality, specially for guests from out of town was incumbent. The householder was also to treat as a guest a known *Brahmin* well-versed in the Vedas or a religious mendicant student.

The householder was to eat only after the aged, the infants, the pregnant women and those married women staying in their father's house had completed their meals. He was to eat only blessed food, be cleanly dressed and in clean surroundings.

The kind of food as well as the vessels to be used are described in detail.

Detailed description is given as to the householder's morning and evening prayers, duties of hospitality, the importance of cleanliness, the wearing of clean clothes, the

time for bed as well as of co-habiting with his wife. He was
to be always happy, cheerful and attentive.

Adultery is frowned on. Man should sleep with his
wife, advice being given in these matters as well.

A respectable householder venerated the gods, kin,
brahmins, saints, the aged and teachers. He performed
Sandhya twice a day, was clean, tidy and properly dressed
in untorn clothes, neat hair agreeably perfumed and
always well turned out.

He is advised 'not to appropriate another's property,
not to speak unkindly but amiably and truthfully without
publishing another's faults'. He is advised 'not to mount a
crazy vehicle, or take shelter under the bank of a river (lest
it should fall on him). A wise man would not be friendly
with and would avoid a rake, sinner or drunkard; a man
with many enemies, a dirty man, a pimp, a pauper, a liar,
a prodigal, slanderer or knave. A wise man would not
bathe against a strong current, nor enter a house on fire,
nor' climb to the top of a tree, nor was he (in company) to
clean his teeth, blow his nose, nor emit noisy wind, nor
clear his throat, nor cough nor laugh loudly nor bite his
nails, nor, cut grass, scratch the ground, nor crumble
mud . . . .'

He was 'not to seek protection from the unworthy or
the company of the dishonest, a prudent man would avoid
even at a distance animals with tusks and horns and shun
exposure to frost wind and rain . . a wise man would avoid
engaging in dispute with either a superior or inferior.
Controversy and marriage should only be between equals.
A prudent man would avoid disputes which would only
get him unprofitable enmity. It was better to bear a small
loss than wealth that only brought hostility . . . a decent
man would not spit or eject any impurity in front of the
sun, moon, fire, water, wind or any respectable person.'
(This effectively ruled out doing so in any but the most

private place!) 'He should not urinate standing, nor on the highway. He was to avoid stepping over phlegm, ordure, urine or blood, nor was it allowed to expectorate mucus from the throat before eating, offering sacrifices, oblations or prayer or in the presence of a respectable person'.

No man should treat women with disrespect, nor place entire trust in them. He was to be neither impatient with them, nor invest them with authority over important matters. He should be liberal towards the poor who are virtuous and revere those learned in the Veda.

He who is wise, balanced and kind, goes to worlds which are eternal sources of happiness. He who is intelligent, modest, devout, who respects wisdom, his superiors and the aged goes to heaven. . .'

There is much more of commonsense advice such as carrying an umbrella against sun and rain, carrying a staff while travelling through the woods by night, wearing shoes to protect the body etc.

"The earth is upheld by the virtuous who have subdued their passions, behaved righteously, uncontaminated by desire, greed or wrath. A wise man should always seek to be pleasant and speak the truth. Where the truth is likely to be painful he should not speak. However, he must not utter that which may be pleasant and acceptable but is detrimental, because if so, then it is better to speak the truth, even if it were to give great offence. A considerate man will always cultivate in act, thought and speech that which is good for all living beings in this world and the next."

These personal and social obligations of the Hindus given as above in the *Vishnu Purana* conform with the institutes of *Manu* and many passages follow *Manu* word for word.

The Puranas give a list of sins, the first being the giving

of false witness. The cutting of trees is forbidden and also the consulting of astrologers before each and every act!

The *Vishnu Purana* gives us the story of Bhagwan Sri Krishna from his birth to death. We see the little baby with divine powers; then the little child, mischievous, playful and unafraid. The boy teasing the milk-maids generating love in all; the valiant youth, the friend in all seasons to whom rich and poor are alike, as are good times and adversity. He is the eloquent upholder of justice and fair play, the Divine Charioteer who explains to Arjuna the art of living and dying. In him is the universe and he is beyond our comprehension. With the death of Krishna from a hunter's arrow, begins the *Kali yuga*.

The Puranas also point out some advantages to be had from the *Kali* age. *Vishnu Purana* tells of sages appearing to Vyasa and asking him "in what age does a little *dharma* yield very great rewards?" and Vyasa answers that both the *Sudra* and women are blessed in the *Kali* age. Even man is better off in the *Kali* age than in the other ages as he secures in one day what men in the *Krita*, *Treta*, and *Dvapara* achieve through *tapas*, celibacy and *japa* in ten years, one year and one month respectively! He points out that while the other three *varnas* had strict rules of observances the *Sudra* did not. He can offer *pakayajnas* (without mantras) and hence is more blessed than a *dvija*. Similarly, woman by serving her husband in thought, word and deed, secures with less trouble what her husband secures with far greater effort. In the *Kali* age the acquisition of *dharma* is secured by men who wash off their sins by the quality of their souls. *Sudras* do the same by intent service and women do the same by service to their husbands.[10]

One of the rites the Puranas recommend consists of offerings to ancestors. The ancestors are the *pitras* (fathers). Offerings were made daily and regularly, and also for births or sometimes for the attainment of some desire. The first two were performed without expectations. The rite to the ancestors is called *shraddha*. This is derived from and has the same meaning as *shraddha* (faith).

From the earliest Dharmasastras (600 BC) to the most modern, all praise, give importance, and talk of the benefits of *shraddha*. Every *dvija* (twice-born, the second birth being the birth of education) is considered to have come into this world with three debts; debts to the *rishis* (sages) which are to be repaid by studying and teaching the Vedas; debts to the gods which are repaid by the offering of sacrifice; and debt to the *pitras* (ancestors) which are repaid by having progeny, thereby ensuring the continuance of the race.

The *shraddha* ceremony consisted of *homa*, the offering of *pinda* (cooked food), and gratification of *Brahmins* invited to dine.

However, it was the gratitude and remembrance that was considered most important. The *Vishnu Purana* gives directions on performance of the *shraddha* ceremony, but also says that where it is not possible to follow these then the ancestors will be pleased if a person does the following: "If he cannot give the *Brahmins* dressed food, then he must, in proportion to his ability, present them with unboiled grain, or such gifts, however trifling, as he can bestow. Should he be utterly unable even to do this, he must give to some eminent *Brahmin*, bowing at the same time before him with sesamum seeds adhering to the tips of his fingers and sprinkle water to us from the palms of his hands upon the ground; or he must gather as he may, fodder for a day, and give it to a cow, by which if firm in faith, yield us satisfaction. If nothing of this kind is practicable, he must go to a forest, and lift his arms to the sun and other regents of the spheres and say aloud, 'I have no money, no property, nor grain nor anything whatever

fit for an ancestral offering. Bowing to my ancestors,
I hope the progenitor will be satisfied with these arms
tossed up in the air in devotion."

P.V. Kane comments on the *shraddha* ceremony,
"The main underlying concept of *shraddha* is certainly
admirable, viz., a tender and affectionate regard for one's
near and dear relatives. It is good practice to set apart at
least one day in a year for the remembrance of one's near
and dear relatives who are no more, to invite friends and
learned people to a lunch in memory of the dead and
bestow monetary gifts on the poor but learned persons of
character and devoted to the practice of plain living and
high thinking. This will be in keeping with our past
traditions and will also give a new orientation and infuse
new life into practices and usages that have become lifeless
and meaningless to many people. Nothing can be more
sublime than the formula which one has to repeat at the
time of offering *pindas* and water (with sesame) at Gaya:
"may those of my ancestors that are in the form of *pretas*
be all satiated (by means of the balls made of barley flour
mixed with sesame) and may everything whether
moveable and immoveable from *Brahma* up to blades of
grass derive satisfaction from the water offered by me."[11]

The constant exhortation in the Puranas for making
gifts to *Brahmins* was due to the fact that with the growing
popularity of Buddhism the maintenance of the *Brahmins*
from princes had dried up. It was necessary for them to
propagate so that at least some would be there to keep the
Vedas alive.[12]

The *Sutras* and Smritis emphasize that gifts were to be
made only to the discerning, learned and well-conducted
Brahmins.

'Gifts made to good *Brahmins* who are free from anger,
intent on *dharma*, devoted to truth and self-control, yield
great rewards.'

The *Bhagavad Gita* and the Puranas changed the whole outlook of society, high or low, by promising spiritual rewards to all who did their work as a social duty without looking for worldly reward and as an offering to god.[13]

The Puranas substituted pilgrimages and baths for many of the Vedic sacrifices. They played a great part in educating the people not only in the spiritual, but also on moral behaviour as well as in worldly matters. The Puranas lay great store by 'Purta *Dharma*' works of public utility, charity, social service and relief to the poor and distressed.[14]

All acts were to to be performed with discrimination and understanding. We are cautioned that pilgrimages cannot be made an excuse for not carrying out one's obligations and duties.

"That person who abandons his proper duties and resorts to holy places does not reap the fruits of pilgrimage in this world or the next."   (*Kurma Purana*)

"Charity, sacrifices, austerity, cleanliness, frequenting sacred places, learning — all these are no purifying ablutions if the mind is not pure."

(*Padma Purana, Uttara Kanda*)

Bhagavad Gita and the Puranas lay great stress on the moral values, like truthfulness, absence of stealing, charity, forbearance, self-control, purity, equanimity, fearlessness, tapas etc.

The Puranas are however against carrying *ahimsa* (non-violence) to extremes. *Brahmanda* and *Vayu* both say that the sin of having killed does not attach to a person if by such an act (killing a tyrant or desperado) many will be happy.[16]

"Puranas sound modern when they put social service and removal of suffering and distress as the highest *dharma.* They at the same time also stress on the heart being more important than works."[17]

References

1. *History of Dharmasastra* by P.V. Kane, vol.V, pt.2, chap.XXII, sec.IV, p.853.
2. ibid., vol.V, pt.2, chap.XXII, sec.IV, p.821.
3. ibid., vol.V, pt.2, chap.XXII, sec.IV, p.829-831.
4. ibid., vol.V, pt.2, p.855.
5. ibid., vol.V, pt.2, chap.XXII, sec.IV, p.823.
6. ibid., vol.V, pt.2, chap.XXII, sec.IV.
7. ibid., vol.V, pt.2, chap.XXIV, sec.V.
8. ibid., vol.V, pt.2, chap.XXIV, sec.V, p.928.
9. *Gita Rahasya* by B.G. Tilak, chap.II (Sha 268.6; *Manu* 3.77).
10. *History of Dharmasastra* by P.V. Kane, vol.V, pt.2, chap.XXIV, sec.V, p.928.
11. ibid., vol.IV, chap.X.
12. ibid., vol.V, pt.2, chap.XXIV, sec.V, p.1938, 1939 and 1940.
13. ibid., vol.V, pt.2, chap. XXIV, sec.V, p.929.
14. ibid., vol.V, pt.2, chap.XXIV, sec.V, p.947, 948, 949.
15. *A New History of Sanskrit Literature* by K. Chaitanya, chap.V.
16. *History of Dharmasastra* by P.V. Kane, vol.V, pt.2, chap.XXIV, sec.V, p.947.
17. ibid., vol.V, pt.2, chap.XXIV, sec.V, p.949.

7

Ramayana

No literature has had as much influence on the Hindus as the two great epics the *Ramayana* and the *Mahabharata*.

Although the events related in the *Ramayana* occurred before the *Mahabharata* war, the *Ramayana* was written after the *Mahabharata*. The sage Valmiki was the composer of the *Ramayana*. Valmiki is not only a poet, but a man of sensitivity and sensibility. The *Ramayana* is a literary gem; but it is more than that. It is a story of love, duty, devotion, sacrifice, separation and endurance. There is virtue and tenderness. The truth and power in its depiction of human emotions strike a responsive cord in every listener, be he prince, or pauper. To the Hindu, Rama is an ideal man and Sita, the ideal woman. The story of the *Ramayana* forms the basis for the moral instruction of a nation.

The *Ramayana* is not India's alone; like a fragrant flower, the spirit of the *Ramayana* enthralls and is a prized heritage of the countries of South-east Asia as well.

The *Ramayana* consists of seven books. The first book gives a summary of the whole epic, while the last book continues with the story after Rama's return from Lanka. It also informs us that the *Ramayana* consists of 500 cantos and 2400 couplets. We are given the information that the descendants of Rama and his brothers founded some of the great cities and states known to have been in existence in the fifth and fourth centuries before Christ. These were Taksha-sila (known as Taxila) and Pushkalavati, east and west of the Indus, Kurupada and Chandrakanti in the Malva country, apart from being kings of Mathura and Vidisha.

When the modern Indian languages evolved out of the ancient Sanskrit and Prakrit around the AD 9th and 10th century, it was the *Ramayana* that inspired the poets and it was the *Ramayana* which was translated into Tamil in AD 1100 by Kamban. Tulsidas's *Ramayana* is a classic in Hindi, Krittibas' *Ramayana* a classic in Bengali and Shridhar's in Marathi.

Among the many cultured people in ancient India some of the most enlightened were the Kosalas of Oudh and the Videhas of North Bihar. Their rulers were renowned for their learning, and their philosopher-priests who taught in the forest universities were known far and wide for their teachings. Their researches and discoveries in science, and their philosophy made them outstanding among the gifted races of ancient India.

The *Ramayana* provides glimpses into the life, thoughts and traditions in that golden age. It also shows us that the real problems of man, those of vice and virtue, are the problems of every age. Rama is regarded as an incarnation of Vishnu, who came to the earth as man, subject to the laws of men. He comes to show man his own essential divinity, the awareness of which makes man act in the interest of all and be an inspiration to all mankind.

The duties of a king are different to those of an ascetic or a philosopher. The prayer of the philosopher-ascetic has to be translated into action, because all manifestation is action. The world cannot survive without action. The mental attitude of an ascetic-philosopher inspires the right action. This mental attitude is present in Rama. He does not hanker for power and pelf, and yet we see in him the obedient son, loving husband, respectful pupil, virtuous prince, friendly comrade, and valiant warrior, all subordinating to the prime duty of a king towards his people.

In Hindu thought *Raja Dharma*, the duty of a king, is given pride of place. This is so because countless lives are affected by the actions of a ruler. With a king the good of the subjects must come first before the good of him or his family.[1] Rama kept this ideal before him. When the ideal king rules we get an ideal state. In Hindu thought Ramrajya has come to mean an ideal state ruled by an ideal king.

The capital of the Kosalas was Ayodhya, ruled by King Dasharatha who had four sons, Rama, Lakshmana, Bharata and Shatrugana. Rama the eldest, is the hero of the story.

Rama wins the hand of Sita, the beautiful daughter of King Janaka, the ruler of Videha. Janaka is renowned as a wise and good ruler. The name Sita means child of earth, because she has been discovered in a furrow. The tournament in which Rama wins Sita is attended by suitors from all over India.

Rama, because of his many qualities is the beloved of all, and when his father decides to crown him King it is widely acclaimed. However, Dasharatha's third wife Kaikeyi, who had welcomed the decision initially, is instigated by her maid Manthara to insist that her own son Bharata, and not Rama, be made king. She invokes an old promise made to her by Dasharatha whose life she had once saved, granting any boon she might ask for, and which she had not availed of till then.

Dasharatha is horrified and aghast that she should make such an unreasonable and heartless demand, because along with her son being made King she also wants Rama to be banished to the forest for fourteen years. He pleads with her to reconsider her request, but she is adamant. Dasharatha is finally left with no alternative but to break the news to Rama. For Dasharatha to reject Kaikayi's request would be to break his word. A king's word must not be broken.

Rama accepts his father's decision with equanimity, harbouring no bitterness either towards his father or his step-mother Kaikeyi. Sita refuses to stay behind and insists on accompanying Rama. Lakshmana also accompanies them. Taking leave of the elders and his mother, Rama departs along with Sita and Lakshmana to the forest. Dasharatha in the meanwhile, dies of heart-break.

When Kaikeyi's son, Rama's step-brother, turns from his grandfather's place where he had gone on a visit, he is appalled at his mother's action. He up-braids her bitterly and immediately sets out along with the elders and army to bring Rama back.

Bharata pleads with Rama to return as all want him back. Other elders, including Rama's mother are there, but Rama gently refuses because he says the word of a king must be kept. Even if his father is dead he is duty-bound to keep his father's promise. Sita too supports him.

Bharata then takes Rama's sandals and returns with a heavy heart. He lives a simple life of a recluse, keeping Rama's sandals on the throne and ruling in the name of Rama till he returns.

In the meanwhile Rama's journeys take him to the forest where he visits the ashrams of various sages. He fulfills his destined role of ridding the forest of demons who harassed the sages in their austerities and harmed the inhabitants of the forests. He performs many deeds of valour.

After they have come to the forest of Panchavati, one day Sita spies a beautiful golden deer. She begs Rama to catch it for her. Rama takes his bow, and telling Lakshmana to remain with Sita, sets after the deer. The deer, however, is a demon in disguise, sent as a decoy by Ravana, King of Lanka.

On hearing a cry, Sita suspects Rama to be in danger and pleads with Lakshmana to go to his aid. Lakshmana refuses, saying he must stay with Sita according to Rama's instructions. Sita in her fear for Rama's safety, forgets herself, imputing motives to Lakshmana for his refusal to go. Lakshmana, stung by her unfounded accusation, goes to Rama.

As soon as Lakshmana leaves, Ravana, who was waiting for this moment, appears in the robes of a sanyasi and requests Sita for water. Ravana then seizes her and holding the struggling Sita, flies off with her to Lanka.

On the way they meet Jatayu, king of the birds and devotee of Vishnu. There is an aerial fight between Ravana and Jatayu, who tries to rescue Sita. Jatayu, mortally wounded, sinks to the ground. He is able to tell Rama what has befallen Sita, before he dies.

The rest of the story deals with Rama's preparations, without power and without an army, for rescuing Sita. He makes an alliance with Sugriva, the King of the monkeys, whose General Hanuman is a devotee of Rama. Rama and Lakshmana along with this monkey army, are ready to fight the powerful, rich and mighty kingdom of Lanka to recover Sita.

Sita all this time is held captive by Ravana and has refused to respond to his overtures. Hanuman is able to get across to Lanka and give Sita the heartening message that Rama is near and coming to her aid. Hanuman is caught, sets fire to Lanka and escapes. The final battle, the freeing of Sita and their return to Ayodhya is the story of the *Ramayana*. The banishment of Sita is given in the supplementary. The banishment of Sita is a natural corollary of Rama's earlier banishment which was because of his duty as king. As King he was responsive to the good of the subjects. He sent away Sita, whom he had fought for and won back, again, because he could not keep as queen one whom his subjects believed to be defiled, for "as the king does, so his subjects do".

Sita is given sanctuary by sage Valmiki where her two sons Lava and Kusha are born. Many years later, on the occasion of the great Aswamedha yajna performed by Rama, his two sons transfix the audience by chanting the story of the *Ramayana*. It took 25 days to complete the 500 cantos.

Rama recognizes his sons and yearns for Sita. Sita is called, but when she is once again asked to prove her virtue, she refuses, calling upon Earth, her mother, to take her back. The earth opens and receives her into her bosom. Sita's unfortunate story shows how the innocent suffer from injustice in the world due to no fault of their own; and how all are the play-things of destiny.

Rama's concern for the subjects and his understanding of good administration is demonstrated when he enquires of Bharata when he comes to seek Rama's return, about the measures taken for the good of the state. "Depending on tanks for their water supply, free from all fears of wild animals and unrighteous men, do not the provinces remain happy and contented?" And again he asks Bharata, "Dost thou not, at the proper time grant thy soldiers what thou should, namely, provision and pay? Remember that if the proper time for these be past, they get angry, and great is the evil that springs therefrom."

Ayodhya is a constitutional monarchy. The king is responsive to the will of the people. He consults his council of Elders and the assembly at every stage. Rama is a democratic King.

Lakshmana, deeply devoted to Rama, is against him

giving up his kingdom, although they share the same values. It is his concern for Rama and affection that makes him talk thus. He says, 'We cut at the very roots of our *dharma* (code of the warrior) when we give up the kingdom. He who possesses wealth and prosperity is surrounded by friends and relations. He is credited with learning, his prowess applauded. He has wisdom and virtue. The world is for him and not for us."

But Rama, a *Kshatriya*, well knows the code of the warrior. He was not relinquishing his kingdom to an enemy but to his good able and faithful brother Bharata. The people would be well cared for. On the other hand, by not respecting his father, the King's word, he would have been destroying the moral fibre of his people, because 'as the king does so his subjects do.'

Ravana too was a learned and energetic man with an appreciation of beauty. He had acquired powers through single-minded austerities. He was a strong and powerful king. In his arrogance he soon came to regard his kingdom as being meant for him. He allowed his self indulgence to over-ride the good of his people. As he is about to die he realises the folly of his acts and how they have brought about the ruin of all. Ravana's indefensible act in abducting Sita brings about his downfall.

Rama as the victor shows chivalry towards his dead foe, and orders that Ravana be given a befitting funeral. Says Rama, "Though unjust, this warrior was ever energetic, valiant and courageous in battle. It is said that even the gods were not able to overcome him. He was magnanimous and powerful, this oppressor of the worlds. All enmities stop at death. Let his funeral rites be performed. He is to me what he is to you."

Given below are some quotations from the *Ramayana* translated into English by Romesh Dutt,[2] which will give

an idea of the depth and beauty of expression of the
Ramayana, and may help to explain why the *Ramayana* has
stayed and will continue to stay evergreen in the hearts of
so many. It should be borne in mind that however
excellent a translation, which this one undoubtedly is, it
cannot be an improvement on the original, which is the
Valmiki *Ramayana*.

When, after being told he has to spend fourteen years
in the forest Rama informs Sita, bidding her look after the
elders and bear ill-will towards none, Sita refuses to be left
behind.

'Rama spake, and soft-eyed Sita, ever sweet
    in speech and word,
Stirred by loving woman's passion
    boldly answered thus her lord
'Do I hear my husband rightly, are
these words my Rama spake,
And her banished lord and master
will the wedded wife forsake?
Lightly I dismiss the counsel which
my lord hath lightly said,
For it.ill beseems a warrior and
my husband's princely grade
For the faithful woman follows
Where her wedded lord might lead
In the banishment of Rama Sita's
exile is decreed.
Sire nor son nor loving brother
rules the wedded woman's state
With her lord she falls and rises
with her consort courts her fate ...
For my mother often taught me,
and my father often spake,
That her home the wedded woman

doth beside her husband make,
As the shadow to the substance, to her
Lord is faithful wife,
And she parts not from her consort
Till she parts with fleeting life!"

And when Rama and Sita go to Rama's mother Queen
Kausalya to take leave of her before their departure:
'Tears of sorrow and of suffering flowed
from queen Kausalya's eye,
As she saw departing Sita for her
blessings drawing nigh,
And she clasped the gentle Sita and she
kissed her moistened head,
And her tears like summer tempest
choked the loving words she said:
"Part we, dear devoted daughter, to thy
husband ever true,
With a woman's whole affection render
love to husband's due.
False are women loved and cherished,
gentle in their speech and word,
When misfortune's shadows gather
who are faithless to their lord.
Who through years of sunny splendour
smile and pass the livelong day
When misfortune's darkness thickens
from their husbands turn away.
Who with changeful fortune changing
oft ignore the plighted word,
And forget a woman's duty, woman's
faith to wedded lord,
Who to holy love unconstant from
their wedded consort part,

Manly deed nor manly virtue wins
the changeful woman's heart
But the true and righteous woman
loving spouse and changeless wife
Faithfull to her lord and consort holds him
dearer than her life.
Ever true and righteous Sita, follow still
my godlike son,
Like a god to thee is Rama in the woods
or on the throne."
And says Rama to his mother:
"Sorrow not my loving mother, trust in
virtue's changeless beam,
Swift will fly the years of exile like a
brief and transient dream.
Girt by faithful friends and forces, blest
by righteous gods above,
Thou shalt see thy son returning to thy
bosom and thy love."

And when Bharata goes to Rama to plead with him to
return,
'Sweetly gentle Sita answered, answered
Rama fair and tall,
That a righteous father's mandate
dutious son may not recall."
Then came Jabali and a
Sophist skilled in word,
Questioned Faith and Law and Duty, spake
to young Ayodhya's lord:
"Wherefore Rama, idle maxims cloud
thy heart and warp thy mind,
Maxims which mislead the simple and
the thoughtless human kind?

Love nor friendship does a mortal to his
kith or kindred own,
Entering on this wide earth friendless,
and departing all alone.
Foolishly upon the father and the mother
dotes the son
Kinship is an idle fancy save thyself
thy kin is none!
In the wayside inn he halteth, who in distant
lands doth roam,
Thus on earth are kin and kindred, home
and country, wealth and store,
We but meet them on our journey, leave
them as we pass before.
Wherefore for a father's mandate
leave thy empire and thy throne
Pass thy days in trackless jungle
sacrificing all thy own.
Wherefore to Ayodhya's city, as to longing
wife's embrace,
Speeds't thou not to rule thy empire, lord of
Raghu's royal race?
Dasharatha claims no duty, and his will is
empty word,
View him as a foreign monarch, of thy
realm thou art the lord,
Dasharatha is departed, gone where all the
mortals go,
For a dead man's idle mandate wherefore
lead this life of woe?
Oh! I weep for erring mortals who on
erring duty bent
Sacrifice their enjoyment till their
barren life is spent,

Who to gods and fathers vainly
still their offerings make,
Waste of food! for god nor father does
our pious homage take!
And the food by one partaken can it
nourish other men,
Food bestowed upon a brahmin, can it
Serve our father then?
Crafty priests have forged these maxims
and with selfish objects say —
Make thy gift and do thy penance, leave
thy worldly wealth and pray!
There is no hereafter Rama vain the hope
and creed of men,
Seek the pleasures of the present, spurn
illusions pure and vain,
Take the course of sense and wisdom cast,
all idle faith aside,
Take the kingdom Bharata offers, rule
Ayodhya in thy pride."
Jabali tests Rama by providing him with every
practical suggestion and reason to return.
But Rama answers:
"Fair thy purpose" answered Rama 'false thy
reason leads astray,
Tortuous wisdom brings no profit, virtue
shuns the crooked way
For the deed proclaims the hero from the
man of specious lies,
Marks the true and upright Arya from
the scheming worldly-wise,!
If assuming virtue's mantle, I should seek
the sinful path,
Gods who judge our secret motives

curse me with their deepest wrath,
And thy counsel helps not rishi,
Mansions of the sky to win,
And a king his subjects follow, adding
deeper sin to sin!
Sweep aside thy crafty reasoning
truth is still our ancient way,
Truth sustains the earth and nations, and a
monarch's righteous sway,
Mighty gods and holy sages find in truth
thy haven shore
Scorning death and dark destruction Truth
survives for evermore!
Deadlier than the serpent's venom is
the venom of a lie,
From the false than from the cobra
men with deeper terror fly,
Dearer than the food to mortals, Truth as
nourishment is given,
Truth sustains the wide creation, Truth
upholds the highest heaven.
Vain were gifts and sacrifices, rigid penances
were vain,
Profitless the holy *Vedas* but for Truth
which they sustain,
Gifts and rites and rigid penance have no aim
and purpose high
Save in Truth which rules the wide earth
and the regions of the sky!
I have plighted truth and promise and my
word may not unsay,
Fourteen years in pathless forest, father's
mandate I obey,
And I seek no specious reason my

relinquished throne to win,
Gods, nor Fathers nor the *Vedas* counsel
tortuous paths of sin!
Pardon rishi, still unchanging
shall remain my promise given
To my mother Queen Kaikeyi to my
father now in heaven.
Pardon rishi, still in jungle we shall
seek the forest fare,
Worship gods who watch our action,
and pervade the earth and air!
Unto *Agni*, unto *Vayu* shall my
constant prayers run,
I shall live like happy Indra hundred
sacrifices done.
And the deep and darksome jungle
shall be Rama's royal hall,
For righteous father's mandate
dutious son may not recall."
Oh hearing that Rama is coming with an army Ravana
holds a council of war. All vociferously support Ravana
except his youngest brother Bibhishana who has the
courage to speak the truth. In doing so he incurs the
displeasure of all including Ravana. Says Bibhishana:
"What dark deed of crime or folly
hath the righteous Rama done,
That you stole his faithful consort
unprotected and alone,
What offence or nameless insult hath
the saintly Sita given,
She who chained in Lanka's prison
pleads pitious tears to heaven?
Take my counsel, king and elder, Sita
to her lord restore,

Wipe this deed of wrong and outrage,
Rama's righteous grace implore,
Take my advice Raksha monarch,
Vain, against him is thy might,
Doubly armed is the hero — he who
battles for the right!
Render Sita to her Rama ere with
vengeance swift and dire,
He despoils our peopled Lanka
with his bow and brand and fire,
Render wife unto her husband ere
in battle's dread array,
Rama swoops upon thy empire
like a falcon on it's prey,
Render to the lord his consort ere
with blood of Raksha's slain
Rama soaks the land of Lanka to his
margin in the main!
Listen to my friendly council-
though it be I stand alone,
faithful friend but fiery foeman is
this Dasharatha's son,
Listen to my voice of warning — Rama's
shafts are true and keen
Flaming like the writhing sun-beams
on the summer's parched greens.
Listen to my soft entreaty — righteousness
becomes the brave
Cherish peace and cherish virtue and thy
sons and daughters save."

We see the three different psychological levels in the advice
given to Ravana, the highest state being that of Bibhishana
devoted to truth, and the lowest being Ravana's courtiers.

The 'dream state' is seen in the second brother Kumbha-karana, who is also (suggestively) known as a great sleeper. He knows that Ravana is at fault and tells him so but nevertheless will fight for his king, right or wrong.
"Na 'theless faithful Kumbhakarna will
his loyal duty know,
He shall fight his monarch's battle
he shall face his brother's foe
True to brother and to monarch he be
right or he be wrong
Kumbhakarna fights for Lanka
'gainst his foemen fierce and strong'
The battle is fought and Lanka is devastated. Mandhodari, Ravana's devoted and pure wife weeps by his dead body. She realises that it is his own weakness that has led to his downfall.
"Sorely wept the queen of Lanka,
Rama tender, tearful, true,
Bade the funeral rites and honour to
fallen foeman due,
And they heaped the wood of chandan
and the fragrant garland laid,
On the pyre they lifted Ravana in
the richest robes arrayed . . . ."

Bibhishana is placed on the throne as the king of Lanka by Rama before leaving for Ayodhya. Bibhishana places at Rama's disposal an aerial car to take him and Sita back. The overflight back to Ayodhya describes the places they pass over.

Rama's birthday is celebrated as Ramnavami. Dasara day when effigies of Ravana and his two aides are burnt, marks the victory of the forces of good over evil. *Divali* the festival of lights is the welcome of the people to Rama, Sita and Lakshmana on their return to Ayodhya on a moonless night. The people in their joy, light up the city, turning night into day.

References

1. *History of Dharmasastra* by P.V. Kane, vol.III, chap.III, p.60.
2. *The Great Epics of Ancient India* by Romesh C. Dutt (Ess. Ess. Publications, Delhi, Indian re-print 1976, first published 1900).

Mahabharata

If the prevailing sentiment in the *Ramayana* is idealism, the approach in the *Mahabharata* is intellectual. The *Mahabharata* faces life in the raw, by showing that problems in life have to be squarely faced. Neither violence nor non-violence is an end in itself. Creation, destruction and preservation are a part and parcel of nature. The appropriate action is the correct action. What makes the action 'right' or 'wrong' depends on the purpose of the action. If the purpose is to serve one's interest, one's family, organization, or anything material or if an action is influenced by greed, fear, hate or lust, then the action is wrong and attracts the return-in-kind of the law of *karma*.

When an action, even violence, is not pursued for reasons of self-interest of any kind (either self, 'religion' or country etc.) not because of the passions of greed, hate or lust and performed in a state of equanimity for upholding the Truth (the highest *Dharma*), in the interest of all, then that action is the right action. Not to prevent unrighteous acts under the false impression that violence involves committing sin, is not to have understood life at all. Action is of thought, word and deed. Knowing an action to be wrong, and yet to allow it, despite the misery, it will ultimately cause because of the break-down of the moral fibre, is also 'action' but the wrong action.

The hypocrite is he who does not believe in the just cause he is fighting for, but pays lip service to it in order to suit his own selfish ends. Truth and falsehood are buried deep in the heart of each. It is not a coincidence that all religions revile hypocrisy.

The *Mahabharata* is the story of a war between cousins. It is the final culmination of various acts of omission and commission in which destiny also plays a part. The war does not solve the basic problems of man; on the other hand, it causes great misery; yet it has to be fought, because not to fight it out would have been a greater crime.

We see on one side those blinded by hate and arrogance of power, with greater trust in the might of the material than the moral, and on the other those who have been deprived of all and have faced it with fortitude, prepared to give up even legitimate claims for the sake of peace and harmony, but who ultimately are forced to take up arms because not to do so would be to encourage the forces of unrighteousness.

King Santanu of Hastinapur, of the line of Bharata, falls in love with a beautiful fisher-girl. She promises to marry him on the condition that her son becomes king. The king's son Bhishma from his previous wife Ganga, surrenders all claims to the throne and takes a vow of celibacy.

The fisher-girl has two sons, one of whom dies in battle and the other dissolute, dies without an issue. The sage Vyasa blesses the queens with sons. The blind Dhritarashtra is born to Queen Ambika, Pandu is the son of Queen Ambalika and Vidura is born to the maid.

Because of the blindness of Dhritarashtra, Pandu is made ruler. Pandu has two queens, Prita (Kunti) and Madri. Yudhishtira, Bhima and Arjuna are the sons of Kunti, while Nakula and Sahadeva are the sons of Madri.

Dhritarashtra and his devoted wife Gandhari have a hundred sons and a daughter Dussala. Duryodhana is the eldest son.

Kunti has also had a son born to her earlier through Surya (Sun), as a result of a boon. She wraps the little baby, puts it in a basket and leaves it in the waters. It floats down and is recovered by a childless charioteer. He and his wife bring up the little baby as their son Karna. Pandu dies and Dhritarashtra becomes ruler. All the young princes are brought up together. This is the beginning of the rivalry between the Kurus and the Pandavas (the sons of Pandu). Yudhishtira is declared heir-apparent. Duryodhana, eaten with jealousy, plots the death of his Pandava cousins. They are persuaded to go to a resort and Duryodhana arranges to set fire to their house and trap them inside it. They are tipped off in time, and manage to escape. It is during this period of wandering incognito that they win the hand of Draupadi, a Panchala princess.

On their return, Dhritarashtra divides the kingdom, the Kurus retaining Hastinapur and the Pandavas being given Indraprastha. Duryodhana is angered to see the success the Pandavas have made of their kingdom. He challenges Yudhishtira to a game of chess knowing this to be his one weakness. According to the code of honour a challenge has to be accepted. Yudhishtira loses, through trickery, and the Pandavas lose their kingdom reducing the entire family to slavery.

Dhritarashtra however releases them and restores their kingdom. The fretting Duryodhana challenges Yudhishtira again. Again the Pandavas lose. This time they are compelled to go to the forest for twelve years and live incognito for the thirteenth year, which they faithfully carry out.

While living in adversity in the forest, they are visited

by Krishna who is kin to both sides, and who visits them in their adversity as he has in their days of glory. They also hear old legends and stories from sages whom they meet. The story of Dushyanta and Shakuntala as well as of Nala and Damayanti are given in the *Mahabharata*. All these go to make the *Mahabharata* not only a treatise on ethics and politics, but also a store-house of ancient myths and legends.

At the end of their enforced banishment, Krishna agrees to act as their spokesman in the court of the Kurus. He dwells on the virtue of living together in peace and harmony and its benefit to all. He forgoes kingdom, and reduces the Pandava demand to five villages, then one village and ultimately just one house. Duryodhana refuses to agree to anything at all being given to his cousins. The elders cannot dissuade him. Krishna returns. Both sides prepare for war.

While we see the unreasonable hatred of Duryodhana towards his cousins, his particular object of hatred is Bhima whom he considers his professional rival as wielder of the mace. Another rivalry that runs throughout the *Mahabharata*, ending only with the death of one is the deadly rivalry between Arjuna and Karna, both excellent archers.

At a tournament Karna, a charioteer's son, challenges Arjuna, but he is disqualified from doing so due to the technical drawback of his not being of noble birth and without a kingdom. Duryodhana, keen to see Arjuna worsted, befriends Karna, giving him a kingdom and thus makes him eligible. For this gesture of Duryodhana, Karna is ever grateful and remains his life-long friend and loyal companion. Karna is also known as a noble and generous man, and one sympathises with him as being a victim of circumstances.

Kunti his mother discloses to Karna his identity, before the battle. He promises not to hurt any of his brothers except Arjuna whom he has vowed to kill, a vow he has to keep.

We see Yudhishtira known for his righteousness and justice. We also see his one-time lapse during the battle, when knowingly, he tells a lie even though technically the lie is not a lie. He is believed because of his reputation for truth. He later is to lose his finger for that lie.

We see Drona the proud and arrogant Brahmin guru of these *Kshatriya* princes, who is unable to forget past slights.

We see the patriarch Bhishma. As he dies he gives sound advice to Yudhishtira on politics and the duties of a king.

We see the wise and good Vidura, the half-brother of Dhritarashtra and Pandu.

Each character stands out as a flesh-and-blood character. We see their strengths and their weaknesses. And we see the events taking their inevitable course.

If, in the *Ramayana*, we have duty, simplicity, courage and endurance, the *Mahabharata* is a tale of surging passions, rivalries, jealousy, nobility and daring. We see how events lead step by step to their final culmination, the *Mahabharata* war, a war between the races of Bharata which engulfs the whole country as each augments his army with the help of friends and allies.

Sri Krishna is related to both the Pandavas and the Kurus. He takes no part in the fighting, but is the charioteer of Arjuna. How this comes to pass is interesting. Both Arjuna and Duryodhana go to Krishna for help. Krishna is asleep. Arjuna sits at his feet while Duryodhana sits besides his head. As it happens when Krishna opens his eyes, his eyes rest first on Arjuna. He asks him what he wants. Arjuna tells him. He asks Arjuna whether he wants Krishna or his army. Arjuna says he does not want his armies but only him. Krishna agrees to be Arjuna's charioteer. He turns to Duryodhana and asks him. Duryodhana is pleased that Arjuna has not asked for Krishna's armies and he asks Krishna for them, for, what is a battle without an army? Krishna gives his armies to Duryodhana.

Duryodhana loses despite a larger army. His great reliance on the material has made him blind to the power of the spiritual truth, which Krishna represents. His arrogance based on wealth, family, and power is contemptuous of everything else.

The war lasts for eighteen days, losing according to Yudhishtira one hundred and sixty million, twenty thousand and six men. The Kuru army consisted of eleven *aksauhini* and the Pandavas seven. It might be of interest to students of history to know that this is the only ancient epic in the world, where flags and standards are described as being used in battle. Amidst the dust of battle, the clash of armour and the cries of war, great deeds of valour are performed. We see the death of Abhimanyu, Arjuna's valiant son, the fall of Karna, and the death of Bhishma. All the Kurus perish.

The turn of events in the war is related to blind Dhritarashtra by his charioteer Sanjay who has been granted this special sight. Below are some of the descriptions given in the epic translated by Romesh Dutt:[1]

"Bhishma's glorious palm-tree standard over the field of battle rose, Arjuna's monkey standard glittered cleaving through the serried foes."

And earlier there is the event that leads to the culmination of the war, when Yudhishtira has lost all and they have all been reduced to being slaves. Duryodhana

sends his younger brother Dushasana to fetch Draupadi.
On hearing his taunting words Draupadi pales.

'Rose the queen in queenly anger and with woman's pride
    she spake:
"Hie thee, menial, to thy master, queen Draupadi's answer
    take,
If my lord, himself a bondsman, then hath staked his
    queen and wife,
False the stake, for owns a bondsman neither wealth nor
    other's life,
Slave can wager neither wife nor children, and such action
    is undone,
Take my word to prince Duryodhana, queen Draupadi is
    unwon."
Dushasana goes and returns and this time drags Draupadi
to the hall.

'Loose attired, with trailing tresses, came Draupadi weak
    and faint,
Stood within the council chamber, tearful made her
    piteous plaint:
"Elders! versed in holy sastra and every holy rite,
Pardon if Draupadi cometh in this sad unseemly plight,
Stay thy sinful deed Dushasana nameless wrongs and
    insults spare,
Touch me not with hands uncleanly, sacred is a woman's
    hair,
Honoured elders, righteous nobles, have on me protection
    given,
Tremble sinner, seek no mercy from the wrathful gods in
    heaven!
Here in glory, son of *Dharma*, sits my noble righteous lord,
Sin, nor shame nor human frailty stains Yudhishtira's
    deed or word
Silent all? And will no chieftain rise to save a woman's life,

Not a hand or voice is lifted to defend a virtuous wife?
Lost is Kuru's ancient glory, lost is Bharata's ancient name,
Lost is *Kshatriya's* kingly prowess, warlike worth and
   knightly fame,
Wherefore else do Kuru warriors tamely view this impious
   scene,
Wherefore gleam not righteous weapons to protect an
   outraged queen?
Bhishma, hath he lost his virtue, Drona, hath he lost his
   might,
Wherefore are ye mute and voiceless, councillors of mighty
   fame,
Vacant eye and palsied right arm, watch this deed of
   Kuru's shame?"
Spake Draupadi slender waisted, and her words were
   stern and high,
Anger flamed within her bosom, and the tear was in her
   eye,
And her sparkling glances fell on Pandu's sons like fire,
Stirred in them a mighty passion and a thirst for
   vengeance dire
Lost their empire wealth and fortune, little wrecked they
   for the fall,
But Draupadi's pleading glances like a poniard smote
   them all!
Darkly frowned the ancient Bhishma, wrathful Drona bit
   his tongue,
Pale Vidura marked with anger insults on Draupadi flung,
Fulsome word nor foul dishonour could their truthful
   utterance taint,
And they cursed Dushasana's action when they heard
   Draupadi's plaint
But brave Karna, though a warrior, — Arjuna's deadly foe
   was he,

'Gainst the humbled sons of Pandu spake his scorn in
  scornful glee:
"'Tis no fault of thine, fair princess, fallen to this servile
  state,
Wife and son rule not their actions, other's rule their
  helpless fate,
Thy Yudhishtira sold his birthright, sold thee at the
  impious play,
And the wife falls with the husband and her duty — to
  obey!"

Hearing Karna's words Bhima is red with anger and
anguish, and points out bitterly to Yudhishtira that they
would not have to hear all this but for him losing his head
in dice and staking them all.
But when Duryodhana drags Draupadi and tries to place
  her on his knee,
'Bhima penned his wrath no longer, lightening-like his
  glance he flung,
And the ancient hall of Kurus with his thunder accents
  rung:
"May I never reach those mansions where my father's live
  on high,
May I never meet ancestors in the bright and happy sky,
If that knee by which thou sinnest, Bhima breaks not in
  his ire,
In the battle's red arena with his weapon, deathful, dire!"
    The Raven's cry and jackal's wailing are heard and
there are ominous omens. Dhritarashtra asks Draupadi to
pardon the wrong done to her by Duryodhana, and grants
her a boon. She requests that the Pandavas be freed. They
leave, to seek their fortune, like true *Kshatriyas*, by their
deeds and prowess. The elders urge Kunti to stay behind.
The Pandavas with Draupadi pass the stipulated thirteen

years, which are eventful. Draupadi, smarting under the insults she has suffered, with the support of Bhima urges Yudhishtira to disregard the conditions of exile and recover the kingdom, but Yudhishtira will not budge from his plighted word.

But they prepare themselves, through penance and worship, to acquire celestial arms. Arjuna impresses Shiva with his prowess and is given the Pasupat weapon. He gets weapons from Indra as well.

Krishna acts as the messenger for the Pandavas in the court of the Kurus:

"Known to all, ye mighty monarchs! May your glory ever last,

True to plighted word Yudhishtira hath his weary exile past,

Twelve long years with fair Draupadi in the pathless jungle strayed,

And a year in menial service in Virata's palace stayed,

He hath kept his plighted promise, braved affliction woe and shame,

And he begs, assembled monarchs, ye shall now his duty name.

For he swerveth not from duty kingdom of the sky to win,

Prizeth hamlet more than empire so his course be free from sin,

Loss of realm and wealth, and glory higher virtues in him prove,

Thoughts of peace and not of anger still the good Yudhishtira move!

Mark again the sleepless anger and the unrelenting hate

Harboured by the proud Duryodhana driven by his luckless fate

From a child, by fire or poison, impious guile or trick of dice,

He hath compassed dark destruction by deceit and low
   device!
Ponder well, ye gracious monarchs, with a just and
   righteous mind,
Help Yudhishtira with your counsel, with your grace and
   blessings kind,
Should the noble son of Pandu seek his right by open war,
Seek the aid of righteous monarchs and of chieftains near
   and far?
Should he smite his ancient foeman skilled in each
   deceitful art,
Unforgiving in their vengeance, unrelenting in their heart?
Should he rather send a message to the proud unbending
   foe,
And Duryodhana's haughty purpose seek by messenger to
   know?
Should he send a noble envoy, trained in virtue true and
   wise,
With his greetings to Duryodhana in a meek and friendly
   guise?
Ask him to restore the kingdom on the sacred Jumna's
   shore,
Either king may rule his empire as in happy days of yore?"

Krishna's elder brother who is fond of Duryodhana,
asks him to accept the offer, return Yudhishtira his throne
and avoid a war. Satyaki urges the opposite. Bhishma's,
Drona's and Krishna's counsel for doing what is right falls
on deaf ears. Duryodhana rejects Yudhishtira's offer. He is
supported by Karna and the wily Shakuni. Krishna pleads
again saying:
'Trust me, mighty Dhritarashtra trust me lords who grace
   this hall,
Krishna pleads for peace and virtue, blessings unto you
   and all,

Slaughter not the armed nations slaughter not thy kith and
    kin,
Mark not, king, thy closing winters with the bloody stain
    of sin
Let thy son and Pandu's children stand beside thy ancient
    throne,
Cherish peace and cherish virtue, for thy days are almost
    done."
Duryodhana is deaf to the urgings of Bhishma, Drona,
    Vidura and his father and tells Krishna:
'Take my message to my kinsmen, for Duryodhana's
    words are plain,
Portions of the Kuru empire sons of Pandu seek in vain,
Town nor village, mart nor hamlet, help us righteous gods
    in heaven,
Spot that needle's point can cover shall not unto them be
    given!"
After this ultimatum, both sides prepare for war.
"Beat of drum and blare of trumpet and the sankha's lofty
    sound,
By the answering cloud repeated, shook the hills and
    tented ground,
And the voice of sounding weapons which the warlike
    archers drew,
And the neigh of battle chargers as the arm'd horsemen
    flew,
Mingled with the rolling thunder of each swiftly speeding
    car,
And with peeling bells proclaiming mighty elephants of
    war!
Bhishma led the Kuru forces, strong as Death resistless
    flail,
Human chiefs nor bright immortals could against his
    might prevail,

Helmet wearing gallant Arjuna came in pride and mighty
    wrath,
Held aloft his famed Gandiva, strove to cross the
    chieftain's path!
Abhimanyu, son of Arjuna, whom the fair Subhadra bore,
Drove against Kosala's monarch famed in arms and holy
    lore,
Hurling down Kosala's standard he the dubious combat
    won,
Barely escaped with life the monarch from fiery Arjuna's
    son!
With his fated foe Duryodhana, Bhima strove in deathful
    war,
And against the proud Dushasana brave Nakula drove his
    car,
Sahadeva mighty bowman, then the fierce Durmukha
    sought,

And the righteous King Yudhishtira with the car-borne
    Salya fought
Ancient fued and deathless hatred fired the brahmin
    warrior bold,
Drona with the proud Panchalas fought once more his
    feud of old!
Nations from the eastern region against the bold Virata
    pressed,
Kripa met the wild Kaikeyas hailing from the further west,
Drupada proud and peerless monarch with his cohorts
    onward bore
'gainst the warlike Jayadratha chief of Sindhu's sounding
    shore,
Chedis and the valiant Matsyas, nations gathered from
    afar,
Bhojas and the fierce Khambojas mingled in the dubious
    war!

Through the day the battle lasted, and no mortal tongue
can tell
What unnumbered chieftains perished and what countless
soldiers fell.
And the son knew not his father, and the sire knew not his
son,
Brother fought against brother, strange the deeds of valour
done!
Horses fell, shafts of chariots shivered in resistless shock,
Hurled against the foeman's chariots speeding like the
rolling rock,
Elephants by mahouts driven furiously each other tore
Trumpeting with trunks uplifted on the serried soldiers
bore! . . . .
Bhishma leader of the Kurus, as declined the dreadful day,
Through the shattered Pandava legions forced his all-
resistless way,
Onward went his palm-tree standard through the hostile
ranks of war
Matsyas, Kasis nor Panchalas faced the mighty Bhishma's
car!
But the fiery son of Arjuna, filled with shame and bitter
wrath,
Turned his car and tawney coursers to obstruct the
chieftain's path,
Vainly fought the youthful warrior though his darts were
pointed well,
And dissevered from his chariot Bhishma's palm-tree
standard fell,
Anger stirred the ancient Bhishma and he rose in all his
might.
Abhimanyu pierced with arrows fell and fainted in the
fight!
Then to save the son of Arjuna, *Matsya's* gallant princes
came,

Brave Uttara, noble, Sweta, youthful warriors known to
    fame,
Ah! too early fell the warriors in that sad and fatal strife,
Matsya's dames and dark eyed maidens wept the princes
    shortened life! .....
We see the fall of Bhishma and then of Drona, and the
    death of Abhimanyu:
"Drona on that fatal morning ranged his dreadful battle
    line
In a circle darkly spreading where the chiefs with chiefs
    combine,
And the Pandavas looked desparingly on the battle's
    dread array,
Vainly strove to force a passage, vainly sought their
    onward way!
Abhimanyu young and fiery, dashed alone into the war,
Reckless through the shattered forces all resistless drove
    his car
Elephants and crashing standards, neighing steeds and
    warriors slain
Fell before the furious hero as he made a ghastly lane!
Onward still went Abhimanyu, Kurus strove and fought
    in vain,
Backward reeled and fell Duryodhana and his bravest
    chiefs were slain! .....
Abhimanyu fells Dushasana with his arrow and continues
    his relentless course slaying as he goes.
'Then the impious Jayadratha, King of Sindhu's sounding
    shore
Came forth in unrighteous concert with six car-borne
    warriors more.
Darkly closed the fatal circle with the gulfing surge's
    moan,
Dauntless with the seven brave chieftains Abhimanyu
    fought alone!

Fell, alas, his peacock standard and his car was broke in
    twain,
Bow and sabre rent and shattered and his faithful driver
    slain,
Heedless yet of death and danger, misty with the loss of
    blood,
Abhimanyu wiped his forehead, gazed where dark his
    foeman stood!
Then with wild despairing valour, flickering flame of
    closing life
Mace in hand the heedless warrior rushed to end the
    mortal strife,
Rushed upon his startled foemen, Abhimanyu fought and
    fell
And his deeds to distant ages bards and wandering
    minstrels tell!"
And:
'Arjuna swept like sweeping whirlwind
    all resistless in his force,
Sought no foe and waged no combat held his even onward
    course,
For he sighted Jayadratha midst the circling chiefs of war,
Now the day god rolled his chariot on the western clouds
    aflame.
Karna's self and five great chieftains round brave
    Jayadratha came'
Arjuna fights and kills Jayadratha,
'Short the strife; as angry falcon swoops upon its helpless
    prey,
Arjuna sped his vengeful arrow and his foeman lifeless
    lay!
Arjuna and Karna meet on the battlefield. During their
    combat Arjuna's bowstring breaks,
'Hold!, cried Arjuna to his rival, 'mind the honoured rules
    of war.

Warriors strike not helpless foeman thus disabled in the
     car,
Hold, brave Karna, until Arjuna mends his overstrained
     bow
Arjuna then will crave for mercy not from god nor mortal
     foe.'

Karna continues to shower him with arrows. The bow
mended, Arjuna redoubles his attack on Karna. Just then
the wheel of Karna's car gets stuck in the soft earth and
Karna calls to Arjuna,
"Hold!, he cried to noble Arjuna
Wage no false and impious war,
On a foeman helpless carless-thou upon thy lofty car"
Loudly laughed the helm'd Arjuna answer nor rejoinder
     gave
Unto Karna pleading virtue Krishna answered calm and
     grave.
"Dids't thou seek the path of virtue mighty Karna archer
     bold
When Shakuni robbed Yudhishtira of his empire and his
     gold,
Dids't thou tread the path of honour, on Yudhishtira's
     fatal fall,
Heaping insults on Draupadi in Hastina's council hall?
Dids't thou then fulfil thy duty
When, Yudhishtira's exile crost.
Krishna asked in right and justice for Yudhishtira's empire
     lost.
Dids't thou fight a holy battle when
with six marauders skilled
Karna hunted Abhimanyu and the
Youthful hero killed?
Speak not then of rules of honour
blackened in your sins you die

Death is come in shape of Arjuna
Karna's fatal hour is nigh."

Karna is killed in battle. The war is over. When Kunti
informs the Pandavas that Karna is their eldest brother,
they are deeply grieved. Although the Pandavas have
won the war, there is general devastation. There is no
satisfaction.

Later, Yudhishtira performs the Aswamedha horse
sacrifice.

After hearing of the death of Krishna, Parikshit, the
son of Abhimanyu is placed on the throne and the elders
leave for the Himalayas.

An incident takes place on the way to heaven, which
gives an insight into Yudhistira's character and his innate
sense of justice. Draupadi and his brothers are all dead.
Yudhishtira trudges on alone. Only a dog follows him
keeping him company. Indra, king of the gods, passes by in
a carriage and offers Yudhishtira a lift. Yudhishtira climbs
in with the dog following. Indra then says there is no room
for the dog. Hearing this Yudhishtira gets off the car
saying "O Indra, this dog gave me company when all had
left me. How can I forsake him? If you have no place for
him, then you have no place for me either... Indra drives
on, and the dog is transformed into Dharmaraj, god of
righteousness, and he blesses Yudhishtira saying, "My
child, you did not forsake *dharma* even in these hard and
lonely days. I bless you and may your journey be fulfilled".

The Kali age begins with the end of Krishna's life on
earth.

No justice can be done to the epic in a few pages. It has
been written with compassion and understanding.
Duryodhana was not all bad. His blind hatred led him into
acts which led to his undoing. The problems confronting
each character, including Karna, are problems faced by all

individuals in one form or another. Karna is a victim of circumstance, but so are all people. Our births are not, consciously at least, in our hands. Karna is a man of many great virtues, but his gratitude and loyalty to Duryodhana and rivalry with Arjuna lead him to support even his wrong acts. Gratitude and loyalty are virtues, but they were misplaced, for he might have helped Duryodhana more by advising him to follow the right path. Loyalty to truth is higher than loyalty to a person.

The *Mahabharata* war is believed to have taken place around 1400 BC. The first composition of the poem was perhaps around 900 BC. With the passage of time, it was revised twice, the last being about 500 BC.[2] There is internal evidence to show that the revisions did not interfere with the work. The need for clarification is always a need in ancient works as the language becomes archaic and difficult to comprehend. Myths and legends also continued to be aded to make the *Mahabharata* the longest epic in world literature. It is about eight times the size of the *Ilaid* and the *Odyssey* together.

Although it first consisted of about 25,000 stanzas, ancient myths, legends and poems continued to be added till it attained it's present size of 1,00,000 stanzas.

The composition was first known as 'Jai', meaning victory. Later it was given the title of Bharata, since it related to a war between the races of Bharata and finally it became known as the *Mahabharata*.

There is also evidence to show that Lord Krishna's message to Arjuna on the field of battle has undergone no change in content but has been clarified to make its relevance obvious to the people of each age.[3]

The traditional author of the *Mahabharata* is Veda Vyasa. We are told that the *Mahabharata* was written for the benefit of all, but particularly *Sudras* and women who could not study the Vedas. 'If women and *Sudras* could not read the Vedas, the Vedas would go to them' so that they too could attain *moksa*. Of the *Mahabharata* Vyasa comments, "what is here is elsewhere and what is not here is nowhere else." It is referred to as *dharmasastra*, *arthasastra* and *moksasastra*, and known as the fifth Veda.[4]

The *Mahabharata* upholds the *Bhagavat dharma* propounded by Bhagavan Krishna himself, that each should do his duty in the spirit of sacrifice and devotion, as worship. The door of salvation is thrown open to each and all, and it stresses that *moksa* can be attained as much from active worldly duties as from sanyas. What is essential for both the sanyasi as well as others is inner purity, which all should strive to attain.

The *Mahabharata* shows that vice and virtue are not confined to any one member of the social order but depends entirely on each individual. Classes or castes are only a man-made social order for the general welfare of society, with each working in the interest of all. *Shanti* (189.4 & 8) avers that 'that man is known as a *Brahmin* in whom are seen truthfulness, generosity, absence of hate, absence of wickedness, shame (restraint for avoiding wrongdoing), compassion, and a life of austerity. If these signs are found in a *Sudra* and not found in a *Brahmin* then the *Sudra* is not a *Sudra* (should not be treated as a *Sudra*) and the *Brahmin* is not a *Brahmin*'.

It is said that Narada felt that Vyasa had in the *Mahabharata* dwelt too much on themes and incidents that people of a lower intellect and those who were literal-minded may not be able to understand. He prayed that Vyasa should compose a work breathing the spirit of pure devotion. Vyasa then created the lyrical *Bhagavata*.[5]

The *Mahabharata* is not only a fund of information on ethics, duty, politics and ancient myths and legends, but contains the shining gem of the advice by Bhagwan Shri

Krishna to Arjuna on the battlefield of Kurukshetra. This message, the message of the *Bhagavadgita*, is for all people of every age. The *Mahabharata* points out that while all form is essential for achievement in the world, form must not be allowed to violate the Spirit. When that happens, form invites destruction. The spirit is eternal and supreme. The revolutionary message of the *Mahabharata* was taken to one and all.

References

1. *The Great Epics of Ancient India* by Romesh C. Dutt (first published 1900. First Indian re-print 1976, Ess.Ess. Publications, New Delhi).
2. *Gita Rahasya* by B.G. Tilak.
3. *A New History of Sanskrit Literature* by K. Chaitanya.
4. *History of Dharmasastra* by P.V. Kane, vol.V, pt.2, p.925, 1641, 1642, 952 & 967.
5. *New History of Sanskrit Literature* by K. Chaitanya.

9

Bhagavadgita

The *Bhagavadgita* is a part of the *Mahabharata*. *Bhagavad* means the way shown by Bhagawan (God). Here Bhagawan Lord Krishna explains to the warrior Arjuna the way to act in life so that the final aim of *moksa* may be achieved. Although in the *Mahabharata* Krishna is advising Arjuna, this advice is for all mankind since the problems facing Arjuna are faced by all in life.

It is necessary to understand the teachings of the *Gita* in view of the prevailing philosophies in those days. This debate does not pertain only to ancient times but modern times as well.

Most of the philosophers were also ascetics who practised renunciation from worldly activities. They did this not because they were against creation but because they considered that renunciation helped creation. Renunciation basically is an unselfish conduct. They withdrew themselves from worldly activities and responsibilities and became *sanyasis* in order to perfect themselves to realise the ultimate goal of *moksa*.

Most of the *Upanishads* (though not all) as well as Sankhya philosophies favoured renunciation. There can be no dispute that unselfish conduct is the core of all morality. But unfortunately few understand that unselfishness is that which must guide man's actions and is not necessarily concerned with living as an ascetic or otherwise. Most ordinary people go by outer manifestations and labels. This is equally true of people today. It was true then as well. Whether a man chooses to become a *sanyasi* or keeps on with his worldly activities and responsibilities depends on his own nature. Each must choose what his nature is best suited for.

In the *Bhagavadgita*, Lord Krishna explains to Arjuna who has his place in the worldly scheme accepting worldly order and responsibilities, how he can ensure that he lives and acts morally and how by doing so man can achieve *moksa* even as a *sanyasi* can. He explains to Arjuna that it is not by becoming or not becoming a *sanyasi* that *moksa* can be achieved but unselfishness and devotion to truth. Creation is served by doing one's prescribed professional duties in the spirit of unselfishness, devotion and dedication.

The *Mahabharata* war was a result of unrighteous acts inspired by hate and jealousy. Duryodhana, the eldest son of the Kuru King Dhritarashtra is responsible for most of these acts due to his unreasoning jealousy of his Pandava cousins. The various acts of omission and commission of others also are other reasons which bring matters to a head and see the two armies poised for battle.

The redoubtable Pandava warrior Arjuna asks his charioteer Bhagawan Sri Krishna to take the chariot between the two armies so that he can survey the opposing forces. Seeing those arrayed opposite him, he is suddenly smitten with the enormity of the sin he would be committing. For the mere winning of a kingdom, a bauble, he would be sacrificing his own salvation, which surely was of far greater worth. Horror-stricken, he expresses his doubts to Sri Krishna, saying that rather than commit such a crime of killing his cousins, uncles, teacher and other elders, an unrighteous act in itself, he would rather give up claims to kingdom and retire to a life of seclusion, there to meditate and seek his own salvation.

Hindu thought accepts the two ways of the *Nivrutta* (Retiring) and the *Pravrutta* (Forging ahead). Rules for both are different. While the first opts out of the ordered life of class, professions and other duties of maintenance of oneself and family, the other has another set of rules to follow. These *dharmas* relate to the profession (*varna*) as well as to each stage of life and towards other members of the family and society. Arjuna, seeing his brothers, teachers and respected elders in the opposing army feels he will be violating his *dharma* towards his brothers, teachers and respected elders by opposing them in battle.

Arjuna was faced with conflicting loyalties. To preserve one *dharma* meant violating another. Here Arjuna feels that by sacrificing his *dharma* of profession and preserving the *dharma* towards teachers and relations he will secure his own salvation.

It is this confusion in Arjuna's mind that Sri Krishna removes. But there is also another reason why Sri Krishna advises Arjuna and not just anyone else. Arjuna asks Sri Krishna for his advice, and Arjuna also shows himself capable of self-surrender and sacrifice. He is prepared to sacrifice his material interests for the good of his soul.

Arjuna was no coward. He was a famous warrior. He was a *Kshatriya* whose *dharma* was that of a soldier. He was a man of the world who had accepted worldly duties and responsibilities.

But by demonstrating that he was prepared to surrender everything for the good of his soul, and would forego all acts that would come in the way of achieving his aim, Arjuna shows himself a fit recipient for the Lord's teachings.

Sri Krishna first reminds Arjuna of his professional duty. He gives the reasons for these duties. These duties are

functions meant to fulfil the needs of society. He tells
Arjuna that as a soldier he has only two courses open to
him. Either he dies doing his duty or he wins. If he dies
then he attains heaven (in Hindu thought all who die on
the battle-field reach heaven) and if he wins he regains
his kingdom. He thus attains something either way by
performing his prescribed functions. He also explains to
Arjuna the worldly consequences if Arjuna puts into
practice his desire of leaving the battlefield to become a
sanyasi. Even if Arjuna, because of genuine qualms of
conscience, has decided not to fight, others who cannot be
expected to appreciate his inner turmoil, will inevitably
think him to be a coward and see his action as that of one
running away from battle. Not only will Arjuna's honour
be besmirched but, even worse, he will be setting a bad
example to others.

Sri Krishna thus points out how decisions in life cannot
be taken on the spur of the moment on emotional
considerations alone, but in a considered and responsible
manner, as all who take on worldly responsibilities also
have the responsibility of setting the right example. Others,
without Arjuna's inner conviction will quote Arjuna as an
example in order to justify abandonment of their own
prescribed duties.

Thus from the worldly point of view, Arjuna's action
might do more harm than good.

Arjuna is not easy to be convinced, and he repeatedly
questions Sri Krishna on various aspects of *dharma*. Sri
Krishna, with a smile, answers all. The whole *Gita* is in the
form of questions and answers between God and man. The
whole Vedanta philosophy is explained in the *Gita* by God
(Narayana) to man (Nara). Sometimes in life, it is not
leaving all but carrying on with one's duties in life which
may be an act of sacrifice and selflessness.

Sri Krishna explains to Arjuna that he is wrong in

supposing that he would be responsible for killing those opposing him. Their acts of *Karma* have ordained that they should die. Arjuna would be only an instrument for what has to happen anyway. Those who have the Knowledge know that Existence is eternal. The mere disappearance of the physical body does not mean death, because the Soul, being eternal, never dies.

Sri Krishna explains to Arjuna how from the earliest times there have been two accepted ways to the final goal of *moksa*. There was the way of *sanyas*, renouncing from worldly activities and leading a life of self-purification, reflection and meditation, known as the *Jnana Marga*, and there was the way of *Karma Yoga* which sought to attain final liberation not by leaving life's activities but by accepting its responsibilities. Both helped the world but, only when genuinely followed with knowledge and understanding.

Knowledge and wisdom are as necessary for the *sanyasi* as for the *Karmayogi*. Those who act from this Knowledge act for the highest good. This Knowledge is that the Spirit is One and in all.

Acts inspired by this knowledge are really 'Inaction in action', because while the body might be acting, it is doing so in the interest of the Highest Truth, which is inactive. Since the Spirit is beyond the law of *Karma*, acts inspired by Truth and in the interest of Truth, are acts done with equanimity, objectivity, impartiality, dispassion, unselfishness, understanding, discrimination and fearlessness. These are all manifestations of the Spirit. All karmic acts are worldly acts inspired by worldly motives. These actions come under *Karmic* laws. A man who has freed himself from such selfish and material considerations is already a free man and acts in the interests of Truth alone. Since his motives are pure he does not invite the law of *Karma* and hence can secure *moksa* just as a *sanyasi* can.

Sri Krishna also points out to Arjuna that to think that a *sanyasi* escapes action and so finds it easier, to attain *moksa* is incorrect. All creation is synonymous with action. If there were no action there would be no creation. The *sanyasi* may be living a different life to the man of the world, but he also has his own acts to perform. No person can live in the universe without action.

It would be incorrect to assume that a person, merely because he is sitting quietly in a corner, unmoving, is not acting. Action is related to thought, word and deed. Action is not only the visible external act. A man sitting quietly might yet be full of worldly desires. His thoughts would attract the law of *Karma* as well.

It is not action that invites the law of *Karma*, but the karmic acts that invite the law of *Karma*, and which come in the way of attaining *moksa*. The *Karmic* acts are those inspired by worldly motives.

The highest acts, that are above karmic laws, are the acts of *Nishkamyakarma*. These are acts performed for the act alone, with devotion and by surrendering worldly expectations and desires. Thus these acts are pure in motive and for the act itself. These acts are performed with discrimination, renunciation, and devotion.

These acts alone can lead to *moksa* and this applies as much to the *sanyasi* as to the *Karmayogi*.

Sri Krishna explains how Bhakti, the path of devotion to the Highest Truth is necessary and also how *Raja Yoga* known as *dhyana* (meditation) helps man achieve the equanimity of mind that can take him to the highest goal. Sri Krishna thus shows Arjuna how man can achieve the highest goal through his own efforts to achieve the Self. Through *dhyana* he learns discrimination, through

Bhakti he learns devotion, through Knowledge he learns renunciation and through *Karma* he acts in the interest of all.

In the *Gita* Sri Krishna teaches Arjuna that he who acts in life with discrimination and devotion to the highest Truth in the spirit of renunciation, without expectation of any rewards, is really worshipping God. *Nishkamya-karma* is work offered as worship without self-interest.

Sri Krishna shows Arjuna how doing one's professional duty helps in the worldly sense by serving both man and society, but he also shows how doing one's professional duty in the spirit of discrimination, dedication and devotion and as the highest worship leads to the final goal of *moksa*.

Here principles are involved and not personalities.

"Janaka and others attained perfection by action only; even with a view to the protection of the masses thou shouldn't perform action."

" Whatsoever a great man does that other men also do; whatsoever he sets up as standard, that the world (people) follows."

"For the protection of the good, for the destruction of the wicked, and for the establishment of righteousness, I am born in every age."

Sri Krishna points out how a mind that is not steady and disciplined destroys itself. "When a man thinks of objects, attachment for them arises, from attachment desires are born, from desire anger arises, from anger comes delusion, from delusion loss of memory, the destruction of discrimination, from destruction of discrimination, he perishes."

"There is no knowledge (of the Self) to the unsteady, and to the unsteady no meditation, and to the unmeditative no peace and to the peaceless there can be no happiness."

"The man attains peace who abandoning all desires moves about without longing, without the sense of mine and without egoism."

"Not by non-performance of actions does man reach actionlessness, nor by mere renunciation does he achieve perfection. Thought is real action. Rag-dwesh, action-repulsion constitutes real action. Only he who is free from this can be said to have attained actionlessness."

"He, who restraining his organs, sits thinking in his mind of the sense objects, he, of deluded understanding, is called a hypocrite."

"From food comes forth beings; from rain food is produced; from sacrifice arises rain; and sacrifice is born of action."

"Therefore do thou always without attachments perform action which should be done; for by performing action without attachment man reaches the supreme."

"Sages look with equal eye on a *Brahmin* endowed with learning and humility, on a cow, on an elephant, and even on a dog or an outcaste."

"Let a man lift himself by his own Self alone, let him not lower himself; for this, Self alone is the friend of oneself, and this Self alone is the enemy of oneself."

"He, who being established in Unity, worships me, who dwells in all beings, that Yogi abides in me whatever his mode of living may be."

'I am the rapidity in the water, O son of Kunti, I am the light in the moon and the sun, I am the syllable Om in all the *Vedas*, sound in ether, virility in men.

I am the sweet fragrance in earth and brilliance in the fire, the life in all beings, and austerity in ascetics.

Know me O Partha, as the eternal seed of all beings; I am the intelligence of the intelligent; the splendour of the splendid objects am I. Of the strong I am the strength devoid of desire and attachment, and (in) all beings, I am the desire unopposed to *Dharma*, O lord of Bharatas. Whatever beings (and objects) that were pure, active and inert, these know them to proceed from Me; yet I am not in them, they are in Me. Deluded by these natures composed by these three *gunas* (of *Prakriti*) all this world knows not me as distinct from them and Immutable."

"Whoever offers with devotion a leaf, a flower, a fruit, water, that I accept, offered by the pure-minded by devotion.

Whatever thou doest, whatever thou eatest, whatever thou offerest in sacrifice, whatever thou givest, whatever thou practiceth as austerity, O Kunteya, do it as an offering to Me.[1]

Thus thou shalt be freed from the bonds of actions yielding good and evil fruits with the mind steadfast in the Yoga of renunciation and liberated, thou shalt come unto Me."

The Universal Soul is the guiding Spirit of all matter. The Spirit works through form. Nature is an instrument of God. Historical existence is a part of God's scheme.[2]

Truth never compels. It only enlightens. Sri Krishna enlightens Arjuna, and resolves his doubts. But even after Sri Krishna explains all to Arjuna, he tells him, "do as you please". The ultimate decision is Arjuna's. In this case Arjuna flings himself into battle.

God is Truth. Truth is detached. Sri Krishna himself takes no part in the battle. He is Arjuna's charioteer because Arjuna has shown his value for him and hence for Truth.

Apart from resolving Arjuna's doubts on the battlefield of Kurukshetra, the teaching of the *Gita* has relevance for all mankind. It happens in life that there is a choice and one is in doubt as to which is the moral course. Here the Lord's message is that it is the intention or inspiration for the action that decides whether the action is *Karmic* or not.

We must use our discrimination and judge and evaluate the consequences of our actions, and then the course we decide must be followed with devotion and the renunciation of expectations and gain, for the highest reason. The 'moral' way is not always the commonly accepted one.

It is not unusual for us to see even in these times people engaged in 'social service' often at the cost of their own duties and professions. It is not that 'social service' is right and 'professional duties' wrong or the other way round. It is that there are those who are neither renunciatory nor devoted, who use the one or the other as a cover for not fulfilling their responsibilities. It is not always the visible action that is the pure action.

There is an allegorical interpretation of the *Gita*. The blind Dhritarashtra represents ignorance. Arjuna is the individual soul. Sri Krishna, the charioteer, represents the Universal Soul, the Indweller of the heart. Our body is the chariot, the sense and motor organs being the horses. Mind, egoism, senses, *samskaras*, desires, cravings, anger, hatred, lust, jealousy, greed, pride and hypocrisy are our enemies. These battles within are being fought continuously in life.

The *Bhagavadgita* ranks as an *Upanishad*. It is the *Upanishad* of Sri Krishna to Arjuna.

Although Sri Krishna comes as a personalised God, the monistic principle is constantly kept in view in His utterances. The *Bhagavadgita* of Sri Krishna lights the way of the *Bhagavat dharma* which assures all, irrespective of caste, class or sex, that they can achieve liberation by continuing with their daily tasks and activities in a spirit of devotion and renunciation, that all must try and purify themselves and that all were equally dear to God. This message found instant response among all sections of the people. The worship of Krishna is open to all irrespective of caste or sex.[3] Perhaps no book has had so many commentaries written on it as the *Bhagavadgita*. The oldest and the universally acknowledged commentary on it is Sri Shankaracharya's. Shankaracharya's philosophy was based on renunciation. Other Vedantic sects also commented on the *Gita*, each claiming it as an authority for their particular persuasion. More often than not in the prevailing commentaries, the renunciatory aspect has been stressed. The devotional as well as the *dhyana* aspect also has been stressed in some. Hardly any stress the *Karma Yoga* aspects of the *Gita*. This was remedied by B.G. Tilak in his *Gita Rahasya*.

It cannot be ignored that the Lord's message was given to Arjuna on the battle-field of Kurukshetra when he was beset with doubts of whether 'to do or not to do'.

The Lord shows that the issue is not one of 'to do or not to do' at all, but doing fearlessly what we judge to be right.

Issues in life have to be confronted and faced. Problems cannot be ignored. They have to be solved, or at least an attempt has to be made to solve them. When unrighteousness raises it's ugly head, does it have to be met fearlessly and challenged or is it to be ignored under the presumption that by challenging it we will be violating a moral law?

Truth is a principle and no material considerations can be allowed to come in the way.

The *Mahabharata* war does not end any future wars and creates misery as all wars do. At the same time when certain issues confront us they have to be squarely faced. Not having the war was leading to misery too.

The *Bhagavadgita* has been translated into every major Indian language. It has also been translated from the Sanskrit into Greek, Latin, French, English, German etc. Most of the foreign translations have been made from the commentaries of those who have subscribed to

Shankaracharya's philosophy of renunciation, and so lay greater stress on that aspect.

Mahayana Buddhism which replaced Hinayana Buddhism in many countries in the east, rejected the cloistered renunciatory life of a monk and stressed that man could attain salvation equally through work and that service of others was more selfless than seeing to the salvation of one's own soul.

In the Tibetan records of Buddhist history by the Buddhist Taranath, he mentions that the architect of Mahayana Buddhism, who was the Guru of the great Nagarjuna, owed his inspiration to Lord Ganesha (God of wisdom) and Sri Krishna.[4]

Bhagawan Sri Krishna's message is the *Bhagavadgita*.

The influence of the *Bhagavadgita* spread far beyond it's national frontiers. Like the *Upanishads* much earlier, the *Gita's* Vedantic philosophy influenced some of the finest minds in the west. Many of the moral ideas of nineteenth century Europe and America can be traced to the translations of Buddhist and Vedantic philosophies. To the Hindu, the *Bhagavadgita* is in a class by itself. There are other *Gitas*, but only one *Bhagavadgita*.

Through the many centuries of its existence the *Bhagavadgita's* message remains as relevant as it ever was. Its lustre is undimmed. Justifiably, no literature of the Hindus is as dear to the Hindu as the *Bhagavadgita*.

Gita gives the most clear and convincing reason of the importance of right knowledge for action.

References

1. *The Bhagavadgita*, commentary by Swami Chidbhavananda (Sri Ramakrishna Tapovanam, Tamil Nadu, 1984) All verses from the *Gita* quoted from above.
2. *A New History of Sanskrit Literature* by K. Chaitanya.

3. *History of Dharmasastra* by P.V. Kane, vol.V, pt.2, chap.XXIV, sec.V, p.967.
   ibid., vol.V, pt.2, chap.XXXV, sec.X, p.1636, 1641, 1642.
4. *Gita Rahasya* by B.G. Tilak (Marathi).

10

Arthasastra

Arthasastra deals with the science of government. Since Hindu thought conceives *dharma, artha, kama* and *moksa* as the four *purusharthas* (goals) of man, there is literature on each of the first three activities of man.

Dharmasastra deals with the various aspects of *dharma* providing the moral base for man's activities. *Arthasastra* has to do with man's economic well-being and aims to furnish him with the knowledge and intelligence needed to pursue the aim of *artha* in life.

Man's economic well-being is closely inter-woven with the government of a state, and hence the art or science of government was closely studied and no aspect of it ignored.

The best known work on *Arthasastra* is that of Kautilya. Kautilya was also known as Chanakya and Vishnugupta. But Kautilya's was not the only work on *Arthasastra* as Kautilya refers to other schools before him. These schools were of Sukracharya, Brihaspati, Manavas and others.

Kautilya is, by tradition, known as the minister of Chandragupta Maurya. He helped Chandragupta overthrow the Nandas. He has many other literary master-pieces to his credit. No aspect of learning was left untouched by Kautilya and while his forte was politics and administration he also had sound knowledge of ethics, morality, psychology, sex, dietetics etc. Indeed he knows so much about herbs and drugs that some consider his *Materia Medica* more extensive than even *Susruta's!*[1]

Kautilya belonged to an era when the necessity was for a strong imperialist state. But empire in India meant acknowledged suzerainty and not the imposition of the language or governmental system of the conqueror.

Although a staunch imperialist there is at the same time a clear commitment to a welfare state. The functions of government did not end with peace and order but it had the duty to promote culture. The king was also called upon to support the helpless, aged, blind, cripples, lunatics, widows, orphans, diseased, those suffering from calamities, helping pregnant women with medicines, food and lodging etc.[2]

Kautilya stresses the importance of character in every profession. Without this *guna* all can come to nought.

Although hereditary monarchy was the usual norm in ancient and medieval India, there were also republics and oligarchies till about the AD 5th century. The greatest safety for *ganas* (as the republic was called) was union, because of internal dissension.[3]

The leader of a *sangha* had to have the qualities of sagacity, forbearance, self-control and non-acquisitiveness.

'Ancient writers did not rely on the natural moral impulses of man to do the right thing. The goal of king and state was to enable man to attain the four *purusharthas*.

While Dharmasastra authors held that *dharma* was the supreme power in the state and was above the king who was only the instrument to realize the goal of *dharma*, Kautilya, true to his position as a writer on *Arthasastra* finally states as his opinion that *artha* is chief among the three as the other two depend on wealth for their realisation.'[4]

Although hereditary rights of kings were normally accepted and descent traced to gods, Hindus did not accept the Divine Right of Kings as conceived in the western countries where king was responsible to god alone and non-resistance and passive obedience enjoined on all. While Americans saw Taxation and Representation as going hand in hand, Hindus saw Taxation and Protection going hand in hand.'[5]

People of all varnas have been kings in India.

Killing a bad king was sanctioned. The greatest emphasis has been placed on a king's duties and comparatively little on his rights.

List of kingly qualities were approachability, noble family, godly, spirited, consulting the elders, virtuous, truthful, not failing in his promises, grateful, taking broad views, highly enthusiastic, not given to procrastination, powerful enough to control his feudatories, firm in mind, having a council of ministers of no mean calibre, and desirous of self-discipline.

The most essential qualities for a king are truthfulness, valour, forbearance, liberality, and capacity to appreciate the worth of others. The essential elements of a state are (a) a sovereign, (b) a system of government (c) a definite territory and (d) a population of some size.

The state consisted of seven parts, the ruler, minister, the territory of the state and it's people, fortified city or capital, accumulated wealth in the ruler's treasury, army, and friends and allies. This sequence is important as some authorities expressly state that when calamities befall and deterioration sets in, in each of these seven elements, those that befall each preceding one are more serious for the state than those of each succeeding one. There is an organic unity of each of these seven elements, each element being predominant at a needed time.

The ruler was to preserve himself through his own efforts, his ministers by showing them proper respect, the people, by keeping them contented, the fortified capital by abundant wealth and grain, the army by proper expenditure, punishments by following one's *dharma*, and friends by truthfulness.

According to Kautilya 'The King is State'.

The ideal of kingship was that of a Royal Sage. The King's highest *dharma* was the protection of his subjects from internal aggression, i.e., corrupt practices, thieves, robbers, tricksters etc. and from external aggression.

The king had to study the science of government which was a purely secular view. The king had to know the philosophy of Vedas as well as *Dandaniti*. The secular science of politics was not mixed up with sacred books and metaphysics in the case of the king.

The qualities for a *mantri* (minister) are, he should be a native of the country, of high family, influential, well trained in arts, farsighted, wise, of good memory, vigilant, eloquent, bold, intelligent, endowed with enthusiasm and dignity, capable of endurance, pure (in mind and action), well-disposed, firmly devoted (to the king), endowed with character, strength, health, spiritedness, free from arrogance and fickleness, affectionate, who would not have recourse to hatred (even when offended by the king). An important qualification for a *mantri* was that he should have secured the confidence of the *puranas* and *janapadas*.

There were two kinds of ministers, those for giving advice and those for carrying it out. They were to be tested by tempting them as regards *dharma*, *artha* and *kama* as well as fear. They were to be employed if found honest in all four tests.

Kautilya states that welfare of the state arises from peace and exertion. While the latter achieves the completion of works that are undertaken, the former brings undisturbed enjoyment of the fruits.

Six means or methods result in action and peace. These are the making of agreements, taking up a hostile attitude, neutrality, attacking an enemy, taking shelter, making peace with one king and adopting a hostile attitude towards another.

The results of adopting the above measures may result in deterioration, stagnation or progress. Success depends on both human and divine causes that govern the world. The human causes can be seen and anticipated and result either from good policy resulting in welfare, or the impolitic way which results in loss and an unfavourable state. Kautilya says that the king who understands right policy, and is endowed with the *atmaguna* (character) and all the elements of a state, will conquer the whole world even if his was originally only a small kingdom.

Kautilya says that land, gold and friends are the three fruits of policy.

Kautilya was a believer in the theory of *Mandala*, inter-state relationship. The central idea of this theory is to keep the balance of power among a circle of states.

'Mantra' was a result-oriented policy. This consisted of carrying out the state business, gauging and anticipating the good or bad consequences of actions, revenue and expenditure, government (punishing those deserving of punishment), subduing enemies, taking measures against calamities like famine, and guarding the king and the kingdom.

All administrative undertakings were to be preceded by a consultation with ministers. These were to be done in seclusion.

Justice was the king's concern. The king was not to

decide by himself but with the help and guidance from others. The king was to wear no gaudy clothes or ornaments when dispensing justice. He was to be accompanied by learned Brahmins and ministers proficient in statecraft and to be free of hot temper or greed and decide according to laws laid down by the *Dharmasastras*.

Justice was to be dispensed only in open court and not secretly. Kautilya gives five reasons that lead to partiality in judges: hot temper, enmity, greed, threats and hearing disputes in private.

In the absence of *Smriti* texts, judgements were given according to the rules of the country or usages which had the approval of the people and did not go against the Vedas and *Smritis*.

In certain cases outside help was also sought. In cases of disputes among traders, artisans, and actors, since it was impossible to give a correct decision, matters were decided by experts in those fields, who understood the usages and conventions of those professions.

The king was the ultimate court of appeal. Some could claim trial by jury. The jury system is very ancient in India. In criminal cases no court fees were paid in ancient India. Those found guilty paid the Court. Civil suits also did not pay court fees at the inception of the suit. Court holidays were on 8th, and 14th *tithis, amawasyas* and fullmoon days.

Law was taken from Vedas, customs of countries, castes and families not opposed to the Vedas, usages of husbandmen, traders, herdsmen, moneylenders and artisans, reasoning (ratiocination), and opinion delivered by assemblies of men deeply learned in the Vedas.[6] Kautilya observes, "He who inflicts severe punishment becomes oppressive to all creatures. He who inflicts mild punishment is overpowered. He who inflicts just punishment is respected."

Kautilya cites at length the causes that lead to impoverishment of the people, which make them greedy and disaffected. He mentions, "disrespect shown to good people and encouragement to the unrighteous; acts of unprecedented and unrighteous violence; stoppage of righteous and appropriate customs; encouragement of vice and discouragement of virtue; not punishing the guilty and severely punishing the innocent; doing what ought not to be done and preventing what ought to be done; arresting those who should not be arrested and not arresting those deserving to be arrested; undertaking schemes which result in loss and stopping those which would result in gain, accepting donations which should not be taken and not giving donations which should be given; harming important leaders of the people and dishonouring respectable ones, estrangement of elders, nepotism, falsehood etc."

Kautilya is quite clear that moral qualities are essential for a ruler and his governing officials. Impartiality and efficiency are essential for good government.

Aware that standards of living cannot be maintained without increasing production, he does not tolerate any curtailment of production. He believed in organised labour. Guilds of labourers and day workers were encouraged and it was they who spoke on behalf of the labourers. There were no rights without responsibilities. A person leaving the guild before completion of work already started, was punished by fines. Any person neglecting his proper share of work was to be excused for the first time, but expelled from the guild if he repeated it. Certain privileges were granted to labour by the state. Seven days over and above the stipulated period was allowed for fulfilling a contract. Extra wages were given for work on holidays. An overseer delaying payment or harrassing women workers was severely fined.

Kautilya has no time for world-renouncing ascetism. Those who leave without providing for the maintenance of their dependants are heavily fined. If the king is not allowed abdication of responsibility, neither are the people. Activism is encouraged throughout not only in *Arthasastra* literature but also Dharmasastra.[7]

The cities were to be kept clean by a strict municipal administration. Anyone throwing litter on the streets was fined.

'Bela' (*dânda*) was an important element in the power of the king. Among the six tools of punishment the first is the army. Troops were of six kinds: (1) hereditary, (2) hired, (3) guild troops, (4) troops of ally friendly power or feudatories, (5) troops that once belonged to the enemy, and (6) wild tribes as troops. Kautilya considers each previous one as superior to the next. The armies obviously consisted of people from all varnas. Soldiers could even be 'mlechas' and mixed castes provided they were brave, restrained, well-built, devoted to their master and *dharma* and hated the enemy.

The army was composed of four parts, elephants, horses, chariots and foot soldiers. It was composed of six parts if policy and treasury were included.

The eight elements of the army consisted of the earlier four and labourers or porters, boats, spies and guides.

A 'sena' constituted five hundred elephants, five hundred chariots, fifteen hundred cavalry and twenty-five hundred foot soldiers. Rules laid down for fighting would do credit to any modern day Geneva Convention. That non-combatants were not molested has been attested to by foreign observers.[8]

There are copious written texts on weapons of war.

While bows and arrows, *ankusa*, 'parasu,' dagger, 'najra' made of *ayas* and poisoned arrows are mentioned, there are many significant references that suggest that the ancient Indians knew about firearms and 'leaden balls discharged from cylinders killing hundreds.[9]

Weapons were divided into four classes:

(1) Thrown or discharged
(2) Not thrown (like swords)
(3) Thrown and not thrown (like weapons which can be taken back)
(4) Mantranukta (weapons which cannot be taken back)

The king's power was of five kinds: derived from brute force (army), acquisition of ministers, derived from wealth, that derived from noble descent and the last and best being the power of wisdom.

Ambassador (*Duta*) is mentioned even in the *Rig Veda*. Among the qualities required of a *Duta* were that he should not be stiff necked, not timid, not dilatory, should be kind and amiable, not liable to be won over by others, free from diseases and endowed with a fine mode of speech.

Kautilya dilates at length on *Duta*. *Duta* is distinguished from *Cara* (spy). While one is open the other is secret. He devotes four chapters to spies.

Kautilya's *Arthasastra* consists of 15 *Adhikaranas*, 150 chapters, 180 topics and 6000 slokas (units of 32 letters). It is in prose interspersed with verse. The whole work, its careful arrangement of topics is the product of a single brilliant mind. It sheds valuable light on the social, economic, political and religious life of ancient India. The subjects dealt with in the fifteen *Adhikaranas* will give some idea of its breadth and depth. Nothing seems to have been left uncovered:

(1) *The disciplines of a King*: Sciences to be learnt by him,

the place of *anviksiki* and politics, qualifications of ministers, *purohitas* and their temptations, institutions of spies, council meetings, ambassadors, protection of princes, duties towards harem, king's personal safety.

(2) *Superintendents of various state departments*: Founding of villages, pastures and forests, forts, duties of a chamberlain, commissioner of revenue from forts, country mines, forests, roads etc.; accountant general's office; embezzlement of public funds; royal edicts; examination of precious stones for the treasury and mines; superintendent of gold (coins issued from mints); Superintendent of storehouse (agricultural products etc.); of commerce, forests, arms, weights and measures, tools, weaving, liquor houses, slaughter houses, prostitutes, shipping, cows and horses, capital and cities.

(3) *Administration of justice*: Rules of procedure, forms of marriage, duties of married couples, 'stridhan', twelve kinds of sons, other titles of law.

(4) *Removal of thorns*: Protection of artisans; merchants; remedies against natural calamities like fire etc. flood, pestilence; tanneries; demons, tigers, snakes etc.; suppression of those who live by foul means; detection of juvenile crimes; arrest of criminals on suspicion; accidental or violent deaths, torture to extort confession; protection of all kinds of state departments; fines in lieu of cutting off limbs; sentence of death with or without torture; on intercourse with maidens; punishment of fines for various wrongs.

(5) *Conduct of courtiers*: Award of punishment for treason; replenishing of treasury in emergency; salaries of state servants; qualifications of courtiers; consolidation of royal power.

(6) *Constitution of Mandala*: Seven elements of sovereignty; qualities of king; peace and arduous work as source of prosperity; six-fold royal policy; three-fold *Sakti*.

(7) *Circle of states is the field for employment of six lines of policy*: The six *gunas*: causes leading to dwindling and disloyalty of armies; combination of states; *sandhi* for the acquisition of a friend, gold or land, an enemy in the rear; recouping of lost strength, a neutral king and a circle of states.

(8) *About 'vyasanas'* (vices and misfortunes); several elements of sovereignty, troubles of the king and kingdom; problems of men and of army.

(9) *Work of an invader*: Proper time for invasion; recruitment of the army; accoutrements; internal and external trouble; disaffection, traitors, enemies and their allies.

(10) *About war*: Encamping the army, battlefields, work of infantry, cavalry, elephants etc., array of troops for battle in various formations.

(11) *Concerning corporations and guilds.*

(12) *Concerning a powerful enemy*: Sending an envoy, intrigues, spies with weapons, fire and poison, destruction of stores and granaries, capture of the enemy with stratagem. Final victory.

(13) Capture of forts, sowing dissensions, enticing of king by stratagems, spies in a seige, restoring peace in a conquered country.

(14) Secret means, stratagem for killing an enemy, producing an illusive appearance, medicines and incantations.

(15) Division of this work into sections and their illustrations.

Many of Kautilya's views coincide with the *Manu* and *Yajnavalkya Smritis*, though his are closer to the latter than the former.[10]

Smritis also dealt with *artha* from the point of view of *Dharma*. For example, *Shanti* (87-36) says that if the *Vaisyas* (who bore the brunt of taxation) were neglected, they may disappear from the country and dwell in forests.[11] *Manu* warns kings who, through folly, rashly oppress their subjects, that they may lose their own lives, their relatives and their kingdoms.

Says Yajnavalkya, "The fire springing from the wrath caused by the harrassment of the subjects does not cease without burning the family, the wealth and life of the king."

Since law was meant for justice, the "judge should be proficient in the texts on the 18 titles of law and their 8000 sub-heads; in logic, and he should be a master of the Vedas and *Smritis*. Just as a physician takes out from the body an iron dart by the employment of surgical instruments so a judge should extricate from a law-suit the deceit (underlying it)."[12]

Fabrication of royal edicts and private documents was strongly condemned. False witnesses too were severely condemned and considered very sinful. They understood the unreliability of purely circumstantial evidence and danger of defective reasoning which leads to loss of *dharma* — a thief being held not to be a thief and a good man held wicked in judicial proceedings (not arrived at by proper reasoning).[13]

'There is in all the rules a spirit of tolerance; kindness and concern for the weaknesses of mankind."[14]

Normally human proof was adduced to prove a positive proposition while a divine proof could be resorted to prove a negative proposition. Ancient criminal laws of Gautama and *Manu* were severe and drastic, but from the time of Yajnavalkya, Narada and Brihaspati, punishments were lessened and fines were the normal punishment for many crimes.

Manu mentions four methods of punishment, gentle reproof, severe reproof, fines, and corporal punishment. There was punishment for practising witchcraft and superstition.[15] Kautilya (IV.4) prescribes for the employment of spies to find out those who profess to use charms for securing illicit love, and banish them, and also adds that those engaged in witchcraft for injuring others may be similarly dealt with.

"The Hindu Law of pleading and evidence compares favourably with similar laws of many other countries and has extracted the admiration and encomiums of such eminent jurists and judges as Sir William Jones, Sir Thomas Strange and others. Sir Thomas Strange says, "The Hindu doctrine of evidence is for the most part distinguished nearly as much as our own, by the excellent sense that determines the competency and designates the choice of witness with the manner of examining and the credit to be given to them; as well as the solemn earnestness with which the obligation of truth is urged and inculcated; insomuch that less cannot be said of this part of their law than it will be read by every English lawyer with a mixture of admiration and delight, as it may be studied by them to advantage. Even the 'pious perjury' which it has been supposed to sanction (this refers to the texts of *Gautama* 23-29, *Mahabharata*, *Manu* and *Yajnavalkya* cited in p.353 of vol.III) being responsible after all into no greater liberty than what our juries (not indeed with perfect approbation) have long been allowed to take, where the life of a prisoner before them is at stake; credit is to be given for the pregnant brevity of the Hindu oath viz., "What you know ... declare at large and with truth." (*Manu* VIII:80) and also to the noble warning with which the subject as detailed by *Manu* is ushered in. 'Either the court must not be entered by judges, parties and witnesses, or law and truth must be openly declared.' (*Manu* VIII.13)."[16]

'The medieval digests made a near approach to the modern ideal of equality of all men before the law. The Hindu jurists evolved tolerably clear and sound ideas about debts, deposits, pledges, sales, mortgages, and gifts of immovable properties, developed a system of joint family rights and liabilities, and laid down a peculiar law of inheritance and succession to males and females. The Hindu system of inheritance and succession pursues a middle course. It does not distribute the estate of a deceased person simultaneously among several heirs as under Mohammedan Law, nor does it confine the descent to a single person among a group of heirs of the same degree and sex as in the English system before AD 1926 (where the eldest son succeeded to the real estate of the deceased)."[17]

The *Arthasastra* was first published by Dr. Shamashastri in AD 1909, in the Mysore Sanskrit Series and translated by him. There have been differences of opinion on Kautilya's actual date, some scholars like Keith and Winternitz questioning the traditionally accepted date and preferring to place him around AD 300. Most of their arguments however have been dealt with by P.V. Kane in his *History of Dharmasastra* (vol.I p.88-104). By those who place Kautilya later, it has been argued that it was impossible to have been in possession of so much knowledge at that time (about 300 BC). But since they can give no convincing reason to support this view, others find it unacceptable.

What is important to note is that Kautilya was a part of a tradition. There were others who had specialised in *Arthasastra* before him as well. Even if for the sake of argument, Kautilya lived in the AD 3rd or 4th century, the depth and scope of his knowledge would still evoke admiration.

What is even more remarkable is the ability of those who specialised in secular fields of knowledge not to mix religion with politics. All scholarship needs detachment. Even the scholars of today seem more confused than

Kautilya. For example, Winternitz seems rather shocked that the same Kautilya who in many places of the *Arthasastra* proves himself to be an orthodox *brahmin* and always admonishes the kings to protect *Brahmins* and often recommends the performance of religious acts, ascetics and to take due regard of their privilege — that the same Kautilya has no scruples whatever in recommending stratagems which can only be called an abuse of religious institutions, and a speculation on the credulousness and religiosity (or you may call it superstitiousness, for what is superstition for one is the religion of the other) of the people."[18]

Kautilya recommends the use of temple funds for the people in times of famine. This can hardly be considered as wrong for a king who is supposed to consider his country as God and the people his special charge. To Kautilya good administration itself was religion. Kautilya was talking of a Hindu state. It is doubtful if Kautilya would have suggested the same in 'secular' India. He would either have made all religious communities contribute or touched none at all.

Clear thinking means being free from worship of the image. Kautilya's brief was to teach worldly wisdom. He does not recommend the rule of the despot. He constantly stresses the need to control oneself first. But if a king's duty is for the good of the country and it's people, he has to survive to do so. Discrimination is necessary to distinguish between the good and the bad, and the honest and dishonest. It would be the height of foolishness for a king to submit to being killed by knaves who want to fulfill their own vile ambitions.

If one were to choose between the two scholars, Winternitz and Kautilya, it is Winternitz who seems the more naive. Kautilya's attitude was clearly not merely academic, meant for discussion in ivory towers. His was a result-oriented text-book for kings and nations who have to survive in a world where the only true morality is the survival of the fittest. It is a game of knowledge and intelligence, of moves and counter-moves, and the ability to anticipate. Kautilya makes quite clear that whereas moral rectitude is of supreme importance in a ruler personally, where affairs of the state are concerned whatever methods he employs for the good of the state, are moral.

The royal game of chess (not surprisingly) was invented in India. It is called *Buddhi Bala*, the power of intelligence.

What is right for the ascetic is not right for the king. The ascetic is seeking the Formless and has figuratively left the world of form. Activity is essential to the world of form and this activity should be productive. Order and discipline are both necessary. Even the ascetic cannot escape it in his field. The world of form means the manifest world. To believe that form is reality leads to foolishness and wickedness. Those who understand that the seen is not reality but is dependant on the unseen for it's sustenance and survival are those who have understood the balance and rhythm of life. It is not the external act that determines the morality of an act but the reason for the act.

Many people are incapable of thinking in any other terms but the visible. For a king it is important not only to be just but also be seen to be just.

The dishonest are not only the thief and the *goonda*, but also those in various professions who use their professions not for their real function but only as a means to cheat the public. This is equally true for the king. Kautilya's 4th *Adhikarana* deals with 'clearing the land of thorns' which means clearing the land of dangerous and criminal elements by means of criminal law and the police. Thorns are also the artisans of all kinds who cheat their customers, the careless doctor, dishonest merchant and others who cheat the public. In short, it was the king's duty to promote honesty and integrity in the land, which alone could secure the welfare of the people.

Kautilya also discusses the question whether one's own army or that of the enemy is the greater disaster for the people and he gives as his opinion that the enemy's army is the greater plague for the whole country for it oppresses by robbing, burning, destroying and abducting.

The importance of freedom and independence was understood both by Dharmasastra writers as well as *Arthasastra* writers. Kautilya defines foreign rule (*Vairajya*) thus: "It comes into existence by being seized from another king who is living and therefore the (foreign ruler) thinking 'this country is not mine,' impoverishes it and carries off it's wealth or treats it as chattel (for sale) or when he finds that the country is disaffected towards him, abandons it and goes away."[19]

Manu also notes (IV.160) that individual and national happiness lie in freedom.

Arthasastra did not specialize in politics alone but all aspects dealing with man's economic well-being. These included politics, economics and the scientific and technical arts.

The following are some quotations from Kautilya's works:

"If rulers are righteous, people are righteous; if they are sinners, people are also sinners; like ruler like people."

"A ruler with character can render even unendowed people happy. A characterless ruler destroys loyal and prosperous people."

"It is better not to have a ruler than a bad ruler. Where is happiness for the people in a state ruled by a bad ruler?"

Kautilya stresses the necessity for the ruler not only to

be of good character but also to be well-versed in studies and political science so that he is a fit recipient for good counsel, else, says Kautilya, he will be obstinate like a "mad elephant, mounted by an intoxicated mahout, which tramples on everything it comes across".

"A ruler should appoint as counseller one who respects him, one who is learned and who is free from fraud". (He is against classmates as ministers even though trustworthy as, being classmates, they will not respect their ruler.)

"Exercise of power and achievement of result should be properly matched by the ruler. He should adopt the same mode of life, same dress, same language and same customs as those of the people."[20]

"A ruler with contiguous territory is a rival. The ruler next to the adjoining one is to be deemed a friend."[21]

"One should fight with an inferior but sign a treaty of peace with one's equal or superior."[22]

"The ruler should attend to all matters promptly and never postpone them. A matter deferred consideration and decision becomes more difficult or impossible to tackle."

"Every morning the day's task should be planned. Tomorrow's deed should be done today. What is to be done in the afternoon should be done in the forenoon."

"One who desires speedy accomplishment of tasks does not look at the stars to know his fortune. Rational prognostics are superior to stars in guidance."[23] He advocates equal attention to righteous duty, acquisition of wealth and enjoyment of pleasure, "anyone of the three, if excessively indulged in, harms itself and the other two." What he recommends is the balanced approach.

"The mother and father are enemies who do not give education to their children". "Teaching wrong things is a great crime."[24]

"By undertaking all kinds of activity the ways to profit develop."

"One should earn wealth as though one is immortal."

"Wealth will desert the childish man who always consults the stars."[25] "Wealth earned through unlawful means lasts ten years. In the eleventh year it is completely lost."

"Wealth earned should not be stored but spent."

"Spending riches earned is like saving, like the removal of water stored in the body of a tank."

"Enjoyment adorns wealth".

"Even the fangless serpent should raise it's hood, for with or without poison a raised hood is frightening."

"The mirage looks like water, the enemy looks like a friend."

"The cloud which rains heavily is defeated by a cluster of grass."

"The enemy can be defeated by a combination of good people."

"In the fight between the dog and the pig, the ultimate victory is that of the pariah who gets the meat to eat."

"Sandalwood does not give up it's fragrance even if broken, the elephant does not give up sex even if old, sugarcane does not give up its sweetness even when thrown into a crushing machine. Great ones do not give up their good qualities even when they are weakened."

"The bee is capable of cutting wood, but is harmless in the lotus bed. There are many bonds. But the bond of love is something different."

"An entire forest gets fragrant by a single flowering tree, like a family by a good son."[26]

Scholars in ancient India, even while discussing the most serious subjects never lost touch with the normal problems and reactions of man. The above quotes would appeal to all irrespective of their intellectual level. A man finds a subject far more intelligible when he can identify it to his life and needs.

Arthasastra was not only for the intellectuals. A work we all know of, but have not thought of as an *Arthasastra*, yet describes itself as one, is the veritable mine of stories dealing with each and every aspect and experience in a man's life, the *Pancha Tantra*!

As Winternitz points out, "But no work of India belongs so truly to the literature of the world as the *Panchatantra*. It is one of the most fascinating in the history of world literature to follow up the traces by which Indian stories and motifs of stories have wandered from nation to nation, so that we meet them among all the people of Asia and Europe — nay even among Somalis and Swahilis of Africa. Not only have single Indian tales been spread to other people by travellers, merchants and itinerant monks, but even whole Indian books and fables have been the common property of many peoples. Most prominent of these is the *Panchatantra*, and when Theodos Benfry in the epoch-making introduction of his German translation of it (AD 1859), with his astounding knowledge of eastern and western languages and literature, traced the history of the *Panchatantra* and it's wanderings through world literatures he laid the foundation of what has since been termed "Comparative History of Literature," "and has become a new branch of historical and literary research. Already in the AD 6th century it's fame had reached Persia. Physician Burxoe under orders of King Khosran Anosherwan ordered translation of a north-western Indian recension of the work. Then came the Syrian and Arabic translations."

"In AD 570 Syrian Christian Bud translated it into Pehlevi titled *Kalilag and Damnag*. Later in AD 750 it was translated into Arabic as *Kalila wa Dimna*. These are corruptions of the names of the two jackals in the first book of the *Panchatantra*. It had inspired "whole nations to which kings and princes paid attention and honour."[27]

Pehlevi works drew not only from the *Panchatantra* stories but also from *Mahabharata* and Buddhist tales. The Arabic version was translated into Greek in the AD 11th century and then into Italian, Latin, German and Slavonic languages. It has travelled by numerous channels both east and west.

The *Arthasastra* is meant to teach worldly wisdom. It is not meant to make us fools and knaves but to teach us how to deal with fools and knaves. No tears need be shed for those who wish to remain fools. *Arthasastras* show how even the so-called 'learned' can still be fools! The *Arthasastras* try and cultivate in us the discrimination that discerns the genuine from the spurious, the knave and hypocrite from the good. They teach self-dependance. *Arthasastras* are strong on commonsense, a sense alas, altogether rare.

References

1. *History of Dharmasastra* by P.V. Kane, vol.I, p.103.
2. ibid., vol.III, chap.III, p.59, 60.
3. ibid., vol.III, p.87, 89.
4. ibid., vol.III, chap.X, p.241.
5. ibid., vol.III, chap.II, p.36.
6. ibid., vol.III, p.100.
7. ibid., vol.III, chap.V, p.169.
8. ibid., vol.III, chap.VIII, p.209, 210.
9. ibid., vol.III, chap.VIII, p.213, 214.
10. ibid., vol.I, p.94.
11. ibid., vol.III, chap.VII, p.199.
12. ibid., vol.III, chap.XI, p.271.
13. ibid., vol.III, chap.XIII, p.355, 357.
14. ibid., vol.III, chap.XV, p.389.
15. ibid., vol.III, chap.XV, p.405.
16. ibid., vol.III, chap.XXXI, p.818, 819.

17. ibid., vol.III, chap.XXXI, p.819, 820.
18. *Some Problems of Indian Literature* by M. Winternitz (Cal.1923) on Kautilya's *Arthasastra.*
19. *History of Dharmasastra* by P.V. Kane, vol.III, p.102.
20. *Fine Arts in Ancient India* by Anil Baran Ganguly, p.9.
21. ibid., p.11.
22. ibid., p.11.
23. ibid., p.12.
24. ibid., p.13.
25. ibid., p.13.
26. ibid., p.15, 16.
27. *Some Problems of Indian Literature* by M. Winternitz (Calcutta 1923).

11

Kamasastra

Hindu thought considers the balanced personality as the rational personality. The four goals of man (soul) are *dharma, artha, kama* and *moksa*. Both *artha* (economic well-being) and *kama* (progenation as well as the acquiring of culture) are legitimate and even necessary aims as these are needed to make the best of life, provided that these are pursued on the basis of morality. The selfish pursuit of aims is against morality and hence neither recommended nor condoned.

Higher knowledge is the direct realisation and understanding of Truth which leads to value-based actions.

Lower knowledge is the knowledge that comes from a study of arts and sciences. This is needed to enable us to function well in life. Functions are there to meet needs. Knowledge of need and function help in efficient utilization of all the resources available.

To meet the needs of man, there is literature concerning *dharma, artha* as well as *kama*. Along with each specialization there were allied arts and sciences to be acquired. The number sixty-four is a favourite number. Each area of specialisation, i.e. *dharma, artha* and *kama*, had sixty-four allied skills thought of as being worthy of acquiring. Some of these skills are common to all while others pertain to that particular field of specialisation alone.

Just as specialists in the other fields show that theirs is a continuation of thought in that particular field, so *Kamasastra* also has an ancient tradition.

Self-indulgence and prudery are the two extremes we see often enough in life. Neither is a balanced approach. Knowledge leads to a proper understanding. Understanding and discrimination enable us to take the right action. Hindu thought does not label knowledge as 'good' or bad'. It is not knowledge that is good or bad but the use the knowledge is put to.

It is only an open, discriminating, balanced, impartial, objective, understanding, fearless and unbiased approach that can lead to the acquiring of any worthwhile knowledge. We see this admirable objective attitude in these ancient Hindus. They were also aware of the tendency of the human mind to be governed by fixed images rather than a free enquiry into the need and function, which alone would make an act suitable or unsuitable.

The greatest value of study of any subject is to dispel, through knowledge and understanding, fears and prejudices promoted by lack of information in those fields. There is as much ignorance of sex as there is in any other field of knowledge. It is today conceded by many scientific minds that a proper understanding of sex is needed to ensure a harmonious married life as well as a balanced and understanding personality. Sex education is felt to be a necessity for many reasons. It was felt so in ancient times as well. Ancient societies also sought to put sex in the right perspective to show that sex was natural and necessary to life. This attitude may be seen in the Chinese classic *Ching Ping Mei* and the Arab classic *The Perfumed Garden*.

In India the best known work on *kama* is the *Kamasutra* of Vatsyayana. Just as the *Arthasastra* of Kautilya is the recognized authority on *artha*, the *Kamasutra* of Vatsyayana is the recognized authority on *kama*. It is believed to have been written some time between the AD 1st and 4th centuries. The authoritative extant commentary on it is the Jayamangala of around AD 11th century. Just as the *Dharmasastras* and *Arthasastras* quote earlier authors, so does the *Kamasutra* of Vatsyayana. The influence of the *Kamasutra* spread not only to all parts of India but also abroad. It influenced Java, and in Cambodia, Vatsyayana is referred to as an authority on love.

In India the *Kamasutra* influenced the poetry of Kalidas and also Jain and Buddhist literature. It influenced religious poetry like Jayadeva's *Gita Govinda*. We see it's influence on the sculpture of Konarak and Khajuraho symbolising the divine union where all dualism is merged.

The *Kamasutra* provides an insight into the life and times as prevailed then. It was mainly for the urban elite, or the educated. Both men and women of these classes seem to have been highly educated. There was social freedom. Women generally married at a later age. There is no reference to child marriage. Widows were allowed to remarry. Life was regulated and economically prosperous. The society was gay and cultured. It was generally a high state of civilization.

It appears that the *Kamasutra* was also studied by women. Vatsyayana recommends it to young maidens before marriage and also after marriage with the permission of their husbands, along with the other sixty-four arts listed by him. There is advice to courtesans as well. In ancient India the courtesan had a privileged place in society. She was normally intelligent, talented, cultured and respected for her attainments. She was not the ordinary prostitute. At one time young noblemen and even princesses were taught manners and deportment by them.

Vatsyayana's *Kamasutra* amply filled the needs of Kama. It provided sex education for men and women. It encouraged the acquisition as well as appreciation of art and culture and advocated a high standard of excellence in all things.

Vatsyayana is referred to as a Maharishi. India's learned men and women excelled in the art of teaching and this is what enabled India to reach the highest peaks of civilization. There is no pompous admonishing or moral lectures. The message was put across in the easiest, most painless, and yet the most telling way possible, mostly in the form of stories! Written in sutra form the *Kamasutra* has the same format as the *Arthasastra* of Kautilya. We are told that the original author on *kama* was Nandi. This *Kamasutra* was later abbreviated by Svetaketu, and again abbreviated further by Bhabravya of the Panchala country, to whom Vatsyayana acknowledges his debt.

Vatsyayana approaches his task in a manner remarkable for its scientific objectivity and clinical detachment. He begins by raising three possible objections to his subject and rebuts these charges. The objections illustrate the different attitudes that people have towards sex. To the objection that no literature on sex is necessary since sex comes naturally to all, being a part of brute creation, unlike *dharma* which needs comment, he replies that it is specifically for avoiding the thoughtless and unrestrained manner of brute creation that it is necessary to show the proper means so that an ideal man-woman relationship can be achieved.

To those who declare that it is useless to waste time on such matters when fate rules all, he points out that all achievements are the result of effort and exertion. Proper means are necessary to achieve ends.

To those who argue that it is wrong to seek pleasure as it leads to grief, he replies that pleasure is as necessary as *dharma* and *artha*. *Kama* should be followed intelligently.

The author describes *kama* as the enjoyment of appropriate objects by the five senses of hearing, seeing, feeling, tasting and smelling, assisted by the mind and the soul.

Vatsyayana gives his object, as, "He who is acquainted with the true principle of this science (of *kama*) pays regard to *dharma* (religious duty), *artha* (world welfare), *kama* (the life of the senses) and to his own experiences as well as to the teachings of others, and not act simply at the dictates of his own desire . . . an art is never looked upon with indulgence for the simple reason that it is authorised by science, because it ought to be remembered that it is the intention of the science that the rules which it contains should only be acted upon in particular cases. . . . This work is not intended to be used merely as an instrument for satisfying one's desires. A person acquainted with the true principles of this science and who preserves his *dharma*, *artha* and *kama* and has regard for the practices of the people is sure to attain the mastery of his senses. In short, an intelligent person attending to *dharma* and *artha* and attending to *kama* also without becoming the slave of his passions, obtains success in everything he may undertake."

With scientific detachment, Vatsyayana records all practices even if he is careful to point out as a moralist that certain practices are condemned. But he also observes that morality has to do with time, place and attitudes. What may be regarded as moral in one country may be regarded as immoral in another.

Vatsyayana particularly recommends the learning of the arts and sciences to the daughters of kings and ministers for, 'if a wife becomes separated from her husband and falls into distress, she can support herself easily even in a foreign country by the knowledge of these arts; even the knowledge of them gives attractiveness to a woman." There are sixty-four arts in all.

The *Kamasutra* concerns itself with the whole range of man-woman relationships, education, courtship, marriage and conjugal rights. The *Kamasutra* of Vatsyayana is in seven parts. The first deals with general topics, the second deals with sexual union, the third deals with the acquisition of a wife, the fourth is about a wife, the fifth deals with the wives of other people, the sixth is about courtesans while the seventh and last is about attracting others to oneself.

Vatsyayana recommends the study of the sixty-four arts and sciences along with the *Kamasutra* in addition to those arts and sciences that are studied along with the *dharma* and *artha* works. The sixty-four arts and sciences to be studied with the *Kamasutra* were: Singing, instrumental music, dancing, the combination of these three; inlaying walls and floors with glass or precious stones; drawing and painting tattooing, decoration of idols, painting, dyeing, staining and colouring of hair, lips, teeth, nails, body and garments, the art of making beds; spreading and laying out carpets and cushions for reclining; playing musical notes on bowls filled with water; storing water in tanks, aqueducts cisterns and reservoirs; making necklaces, garlands etc.; chaplets and other headgear of flowers; scenic representations and dramatic performances; the art of making earrings and other ornaments; perfumery; the correct way to use jewels and other ornaments in dress; magic, sleight of hand and skill; culinary arts; making all types of (alcoholic and nonalcoholic) drinks; sewing and tailoring; making tassles, flowers, braids knobs etc. of yarn and thread; word and speech puzzles and games; relay games dealing with sentences; art of imitation and mimicry; reading, chanting and intoning; games of words and sentences difficult to pronounce; practice of sword, bow and arrow stick and quarter-staff; logical exercises on inference, carpentry and carpenter's work; architecture and art of building; knowledge of gold and silver, coins, jewels and gems; chemistry and mineralogy, colouring jewels gems and 'beads'; knowledge of mines and quarries, gardening, layout, plant-care and diseases; art of cock, quail and ram fighting; art of perfuming the hair and, body as well as braiding etc., the art of writing in code and cipher; different forms of speech such as scrambling, adding extra syllables, changing word endings, interposing syllables etc., knowledge of languages and vernacular dialects; art of making flower carriages; art of drawing mystical diagrams, spells and charms; mental exercises concerning poetry and literature; composing poems; knowledge of dictionaries and vocabularies; the art of disguise; the art of making coarse things look good; different forms of gambling, possession of another's property by means of incantations and mantras; skill in sports; manners and deportment; the martial arts; of war and armies etc.; gymnastics; reading a person's character by the features; knowledge of scanning and constructing verses; arithmetical recreation; making artificial flowers and making clay figures and images.

Of the arts, music has prime place, having its divine origin in 'Aum' (Om) the primary sound of creation. Compared to dance, painting or sculpture, music is relatively momentary. It is thus considered as being closest to the spirit. Melody is the soul of music.

Indian music has its roots in the *Sama Veda*. The two

main branches of Indian classical music are the South Indian known as Karnatik music and the North Indian known as Hindustani music. They both have the same source, share the same Srutis and fundamental principles. The basic principles are based on a scientific and mathematical calculation. The Indian musical system is one of the few important musical systems in the world.

Hindustani music has been influenced to some extent by Persian, Arab and Moghul influences. Karnatik music has retained most of its original character.[1]

Instrumental music was divided into four groups: string instruments, blowing instruments, leather-covered percussion instruments, and instruments on which notes were produced through striking. There are well-known exponents of both sexes in vocal and instrumental music.

Dancing was divided into *natya nritya* which included dramatic arts and *anatya nritya* consisting of performances by professional artists. (Some 2200 year old caves have been discovered in Chota Nagpur where the stage consists of two floors, one above the other, along with green rooms. Stages had eighteen different shapes. Scenes would be painted on the walls and then covered with a fine white cloth.)[2]

The Sutradhar is an important part of a play as he introduces to the audience in an interesting way the subject matter, the author and the actors in the play. Unity of action is the basis of Indian dramatic theories and the most important element is sentiment.

The great dramatists Kalidas, Bhasa and Bhavabhuti were masters of sentiment. Kavya was also a subsidiary of the dramatic arts. All stage performances begin with the worship of the *Jarjara*. The story connected with this worship will no doubt be appreciated by dramatic troupes all over the world!

Apparently since Sudras could not study the *Vedas*, the gods asked Brahma to compose a fifth *Veda* irrespective of caste and creed. The *Nata Veda* was composed. It contained the dialogue of the *Rig Veda*, music of the *Sama Veda*, acting of the *Yajur Veda* and the rasa of the *Atharva Veda*. It was on this that Bharata Muni composed his *Natya Sastra*. His hundred sons became actors while the 'apsaras' became actresses. A full dramatic troupe was formed with the Sage Narada and the Gandharvas doing the musical compositions. Its very first performance was to celebrate the victory of the gods over the *asuras*. Both the gods and *asuras* attended. The *asuras* however were annoyed to see that the subject matter of the play depicted their defeat by the gods. They became unruly. To quell the disturbance Indra hurled his *Indra-dhwaja* (thunderbolt) upon the *asuras*.[3] Since then it has become the custom to hoist a *Jarjara* staff in front of the stage before commence-ment of a play — to ensure no disturbance!

There is also an amusing legend about music which makes the point that not only is melody vital in music and the performer but also an appreciative and knowledgeable audience.

The gods wished to give a musical performance in honour of Siva and Parvati. Narada offered to sing. While he was singing, however, the Ragas and Raginis started to loose their hands, feet and even heads. Only a correct and melodious musical recital could restore them to their original forms. The gods implored Siva the master musician, to sing. Siva agreed on the condition that Vishnu be the listener. The gods went to Vishnu, who agreed. Siva sang and Vishnu listened. Slowly the Ragas and Raginis returned to their original forms. Vishnu was enraptured and lost in the music. So affected was he that he started to melt. Brahma collected the melted water in his water jug. This water is the River Ganga flowing from the feet of Vishnu![4]

Painting is called *Alekhya* in Sanskrit. It was considered auspicious to have a painting in a house. Painting was a highly developed art. The *Vishnudharmottara* gives in detail all the information that is required for drawing and painting. Chiaroscuro or three-dimensional effects are mentioned even in the *Mahabharata*. There are many references to painting by playwrites and poets. Many kings and queens were good artists and painters. Like all else paintings and sculptures were the expression of an urge to depict religious themes. Pictures on silk or canvas would be rolled and preserved in silk cloth. Wood also was used for painting. It was the wall painting though, which was the most popular. The present day Rajasthani or Pahari paintings are the miniature descendents of the wall paintings of ancient India.

The arts connected with body decoration were well-known. There are 1,74,720 methods for manufacturing perfumery articles given in the 77th, chapter of *Vrhat Samhita* by Varaha Mihira.[5] In the fourth chapter of the first *Adhikarana*, Vatsyayana gives all aspects of *Angaraga* (toiletry) in detail. The aim was beauty, cleanliness and health.

The six canons of Indian painting are *rupa-bheda* (form), *pramanam* (proportion), *bhavam* (External depiction of inner mood), *lavanya* (depiction of lustre), *sadrisya* (registering given appearance), and *vasnika bhanga* (Correct application and disposition of colour). These six canons migrated to foreign lands and are the basis of the six canons of paintings outlined by Hsien Ho, the famed Chinese painter of the AD 6th century.[6]

One minor art dealt with dress. The dress should be worn so well as not to slip off; to wear it in such a way as to hide it's blemishes and tears and also to wear it so that a coarse and unfitting dress might look fine and fitting.

(It is claimed that this is why Draupadi could keep her sari from being unravelled by Dushasana — in other words, God helps those who help themselves!)

Toiletry known as *angaraja* dealt with cleansing the body and make-up. *Phenaka*, an oily substance which produces foam when mixed with water was used to clean the body. *Lodhra-renu* was used as a face-powder. Light Alaktaka colour was used to colour the lips which would then be lightly rubbed over with *Sikhthaka gutika* (candle balls) to make the lips brighter and shiner. Hindu thought has always been appreciative of a wife always appearing well-dressed and attractive to her husband. There is an account in the *Ramayana* (*Aranyakanda*, 3rd Sarga) of sage Atri's wife Anusuya presenting Sita with an everlasting paint. *Udvartana* was the name of these fragrant unguents meant for cleansing the body as well as making it fairer and brighter.

Ornamental Art consisted of making images as well as designs with grain, making a variety of flower garlands and the placing of flowers in pots, decorations of doors and gates, the proper and tasteful arrangements of offerings to gods. Beds were sprinkled with flowers in a particular arrangement with colours to correspond with moods.

The *Vetalapanchavimsati* has a story of two people, one fastidious about his food and the other fastidious about his bed. Their fame spread and reached the ears of the king. He invited both in order to test them and reward the better of the two. He tested the first by ordering an excellent meal with strict instructions regarding its quality. When the meal arrived, the king was gratified by its taste and appearance. He was surprised to see however that his guest was not eating the rice. On being questioned he complained that the rice was smelling of corpse. A thorough enquiry revealed that the paddy field where the rice was produced was next to a cremation ground! The king was struck by the man's keen sense of discrimination and rewarded the man. Next he ordered that the bed should be prepared with the greatest care. The bed was prepared, soft and smooth. But the guest got up complaining that there must be a hair or something in it which was pricking him and preventing his sleep. A careful search of the bed revealed a fine hair under the seventh mattress. The second man's reward was greater.[7]

These stories are absurd and amusing but they get the message across that to achieve-excellence a person must strive to be a perfectionist.

Cooking also was a great art. Vatsyayana divides cooking into two parts, (1) Art of cooking and (2) Art of preparing uncooked food. Apparently both Draupadi and Bhima were excellent cooks, while King Nala was an expert in preparing uncooked food. Food is classified as soft-solid, hard-solid, semi-liquid and liquid. Curry prepared mainly from vegetables are classified into ten groups. These are from root, leaf, young shoot, tip, fruit, stalk, sprout, skin, flower and thorn.

Drinks are divided into fermented and unfermented. Alcoholic drinks were produced by fermentation as well as distillation etc. and divided into strong, moderate and light liquor. Drinks consisted of appetizers as well. Knowledge of cooking was considered as essential for good health.

There is a story of a youth by the name of Shantikumar who finds himself the right wife by going as a guest and then judging by the attention he receives. The girl proves herself to be not only gracious and hospitable but also thrifty, clean, considerate, organized, a good cook, serving a well-served and well-placed dinner and having excellent manners.[8]

The art of inlay is a very ancient one. It was called *Mani bhumika karma*. It was the custom to pave the floors and walls of rooms and temples with glass pieces or semiprecious gems like Marakata, Padmaraja, etc. to keep the place cool in summer. These were usually designed to resemble leaves and creepers. Hindu temples were bedecked with this inlay jewel work which were plundered by barbarian invaders.

Engineering arts were known as Vastu Vidya. Vastu means a thing. This could include house, ground, land, garden, building, bridge, lake, etc. Even towns, temples and palaces were called Vastu. Vastu Vidya meant designing something with skill. Visvakarma is the traditional propagator of this art. He founded the nine classes of artisans. These are the goldsmith, blacksmith, brazier, carpenter, weaver, painter, gardener, potter and conch-shell artisan.

We find that Hindu artisans excelled not only in the finest of worksmanship on wood and ivory but also conceived and executed grand temples on a massive scale.

Dressmaking, darning, quilting, embroidery, knitting, cane-weaving of baskets, mats, cots and boxes as well as spinning, chiselling, polishing and lathe-work as well as carpentry and making of children's toys were not overlooked.

Gardens were an indispensable feature in house and town planning in ancient India. Horticulture was known as *Vriksayurvedayoga* as well as *Vanaspatividya*. This included the art of laying out orchards and gardens. It also dealt with planting, growing, curing of plant diseases, the making of hybrid varieties, growing seedless fruits, grafting etc. The natural look was preferred in the garden, and flowers with scent preferred to the colourful flowers. In the *Matsya Purana* (Chap.270.28-29) there are instructions regarding what should be planted. To the east of the *mandapa* of a temple fruit-bearing trees should be planted in the temple grounds. The trees planted to the south should be those having milky sap, to the west should be a reservoir of water with lotuses therein while to the north should be a flower garden and 'sarala' and 'tala' trees.

Yantramatrika deals with machines for use. These machines are divided into *sanjeeva* (animate) run by living beings like horse, bullock, buffalo, camel etc., and *nirjeeva* (inanimate) run by means of water, wind, steam etc. Anil Baran Ganguly in his *Fine Arts in Ancient India* states that there is evidence to establish that ancient India had invented warships, aeroplanes, guns and chariots of different kinds. He mentions an old manuscript discovered in the Deccan which describes aeroplanes run on mercury steam.[9] Some understand this art to include the making of images that move and speak. Art meant not only skill but also the amusing, wonderful and useful.

The magical arts can be traced to the *Atharva Veda*. Kusumachara was an Ekdesin Acharya of the *Kamasastra* of ancient times. Author of *Upanishadika Adhikarana* he describes in detail the intrinsic worth of articles. He shows how the ugly can be made to appear beautiful, the old into young, magical acts like exorcism and what should be done for good fortune. The amusing arts consisted of games, puzzles requiring wit, humour, knowledge of words, rhymes and literature. They were a test of memory as well as a source of amusement and relaxation. Some puzzles and games were played by priests engaged in the ceremony of the sacrificial ritual, in order to break the monotony.

Aksaramustikakathana means 'concealing idea in fist'. Here communication was done by using the fingers. This was employed for conveying secret messages in times of war.

Sabhasa was a covered language which conveyed the meaning through fingers. This method was employed by the deaf and dumb, and traders and moneylenders. *Mlecchitavikalpa* consisted of speaking in foreign jargon, word scrambling etc.

Desabhasyavijnyana was the knowledge of linguistics, a thorough knowledge of the history, customs and literature of a country and its people. *Dharanamatrika* made possible the memorising of a piece by hearing or reading it once (unfortunately there is no extant book on it). *Vijayamiki* dealt with physical culture which included walking, ju-jutsu, gymnastics, games, sports, exercises with and without instruments, yogic breathing exercises, wrestling etc.

Vaijayaki was the art of victory. It was divided into the supernatural (*daivi*) means which employed tantric formulas, and human (*manusi*) means which concerned the proper use of weapons.

Vainayiki is the social art of courtsey, politeness and modesty in behaviour which teaches etiquette and harmonious social relations helping to make a success of life.

Sanatana Goswami in his *Brihadvaisnavatosini* mentions the three smaller branches of thought — reading (*parachittajnyana*), clairvoyance (*durasravanadarsvcinta*) and telepathy (*ratnamartavisesanirman*). Medieval alchemy was used for making tonics or the Elixir of life or for imitation jewellery etc.

Some of the books containing the above knowledge are given by Anil Baran Ganguly in his *Fine Arts in Ancient India*. India is a vast treasure-house of knowledge. Useful information can be gleaned from old Sanskrit and Pali texts. Much work needs to be done on ancient works.

There should be enough indication even from the brief information given here as to the extent of knowledge existing in every field of human activity in ancient times. It is a testimony of what we have lost or allowed to be lost. The loss of knowledge is no credit to any civilization and strenuous efforts should be made to repair the damage done.

Ganguly points out that Thyagaraja, the great saint-musician from South India, who lived barely a hundred years ago had composed no less than 24000 *kritis*.[10] Only seven or eight hundred are known today.

No country or people can afford to lose their priceless heritage. Civilization comes through the aim for excellence in all fields. Not only must knowledge be preserved, but it must be added to, because knowledge is limitless.

It is a modern-day myth to believe that science, rational thought and the pursuit of knowledge belong only to modern times. Knowledge cannot come to minds that are narrowed to accepted beliefs or conventional moralistic attitudes. Truth is beyond these definitions. It defies description and hence an open mind alone can do justice to it.

Vatsyayana's *Kamasutra* is over fifteen hundred years old. The subject itself has an earlier tradition in literature. There were no doubt learned men in India even then who objected to any study on *kama*. But as we can see this holds equally true for the 'enlightened' Europe of the nineteenth century, when England was at the peak of imperial power.

The *Kamasutra* was first translated into English by Sir Richard Burton and F.F. Arbuthnot in AD 1883. So afraid were they of the violent reaction it may cause in England wallowing in Victorian prudery where the very word sex was a moral offence, that they severely restricted the number of copies, gave it an aspect of 'research' by a 'society' which actually consisted of just the two of them. Not only did they withhold their names but even reversed their initials! This is not surprising because even the earlier translation of the *Arabian Nights* by Paine had evoked a storm of protest.[11]

Western moralist attitudes have been largely responsible for regarding the *Kamasutra* as pornography. The *Kamasutra* has also been compared with either *De Sade* or *Ovid*. It does not bear comparison with either. It is far more comprehensive and also fulfills a higher purpose than either. Vatsyayana is both scientific and sociological.

The first step to acquiring knowledge is the recognition that Truth is not the monopoly of any place, person or age. It has to do with complete honesty, understanding and integrity. Man has progressed through the ages because both scientific and rational thought have been there from man's earliest days. Man has relapsed every now and then into ignorance by giving greater importance to "image" than to knowledge.

References

1. *Fine Arts in Ancient India* by Anil Baran Ganguly (Abhinav Publ., N. Delhi, 1979), p.58.
2. ibid., p.84.
3. ibid., p.83.
4. ibid., p.31.
5. ibid., p.105.
6. *A New History of Sanskrit Literature* by Krishna Chaitanya, chap.I (III).
7. *Fine Arts in Ancient India* by Anil Baran Ganguly, p.114.
8. ibid., p.123.
9. ibid., p.131.
10. ibid., p.63.
11. *The Kamasutra of Vatsyayana* translated by Sir Richard Burton and F.F. Arbuthnot (1963). This edition is based on an earlier translation of 1883.

12

Karma

The doctrine of *Karma* and *punarjanma* (re-birth) has been accepted not only by all the six philosophical systems in India but also by the Jains and the Buddhists. Sikhism which emerged much later, also accepts this doctrine. It is significant that while each philosophical and religious system may have differed on other matters, the one doctrine they all agreed on and did not even consider as a matter of dispute was the law or doctrine of *Karma* and *punarjanma*.[1]

Very simply, this doctrine states that the attainment of liberation or another birth is determined by man's acts in this phenomenal world. These acts consist, of thought, word and deed. Moral acts alone can lead to liberation while others lead to another birth and bondage. This doctrine is the greatest compulsion to morality, a morality that is self-imposed, having nothing to do with an external law.

Metempsychosis was not a new thought. It has been shared by other civilizations as well. Metempsychosis means the transmigration of a soul from one body to another after the death of the body. Heredotus says that some Greeks used these doctrines as their own, but that the Egyptians were the first to teach that the human soul was immortal and at the time of death it entered another body.

Pythagoras seems to have believed in this doctrine, and some western opinion is of the view that he got his ideas from India. Alexandria in Egypt was known for its intellectual activity. Not only did the thoughts and teachings of many lands come to Alexandria but were also dispersed from there to other lands. Many achievements in the different fields of human activity in other lands entered Greece via Alexandria and presumably Greek knowledge went to other lands in the ancient world the same way. Empidocles and Plato also believed in the pre- and post-existence of the soul and that the several births would bear relation to the lives they had lead. Those who practiced the social and civic virtues called temperance and justice, disengaging themselves from the life of the senses only could release the soul and achieve happiness.[2]

The undeniable fact however is that nowhere else in the world does there exist the theory of *Karma* and transmigration in so detailed, so influential and so thorough a manner as in Sanskrit literature.[3]

We can trace the progressive development of this doctrine from the most ancient Rig Vedic times, till we come to the *Upanishads* where we find the first clear statement of this doctrine.

Karma in the *Rig Veda* means exploits or valiant deeds or religious works like gifts and sacrifices. The germ of the idea of transmigration is seen in the reference to Vasishta's many births. Later, the *Brahmanas* refer several times to (casting off *punarmrtyu*) (renewed death) and *Satapatha Brahmana* had also arrived at the idea that man's will and corresponding deed will govern the world he will reach after death. It also indicates that each fashions his own birth and that he who sacrifices to the gods does not win such a place as he who does so to the *atma* (soul).[4]

It is in one of the oldest *Upanishads*, the *Brihadharanyaka*, that we find the first clear statement on the doctrine of transmigration. "To whatever a man's mind or subtle body is attached to that he goes together with the fruits of his deeds and after having obtained the end (the last result of) of whatever deeds he does in this world, he returns again from that world (where he temporarily went by way of reward) to this world of action; so much with regard to him who is consumed with desires. . . . . when all hankering that found an abode in a man's heart vanish, then he who was liable to death becomes immortal here (in this body itself) he attains to Brahma.

So truly according as he works and according as he behaves so will he be, a man of good deeds will become (be born) good, a man of evil deeds will become (be born) evil. He becomes holy by holy deeds and evil by evil deeds. Here they say a person only consists of desires (or is fashioned out of) desires and as his desire is, so will be his (determination or) will and as his will, so his deed, and whatever deeds he does that he will become (reap)."[5]

The above passage shows the sequence of Desire, Will and Act. While all phenomenal universe is Brahma, all these forms are impermanent leaving the subtlest Truth alone as the indestructible Eternal Value that is the base of the whole physical universe in all its myriad forms. While the whole physical universe is guided by certain laws, the Truth being beyond the physical universe as well as beyond Cause is ever-free. It is the ignorance of the ego self that identifies the form or body with truth and does not recognize its true Self as the soul of the whole world, eternal, all-pervading and incorruptible. Ignorance belongs to the unreal while knowledge is from the Real. To identify what is Real and vital with matter, is ignorance, and those who do so keep on getting reborn as they keep on desiring objects that belong to the world phenomena. It is only when Truth of the real Self is realised that man realises that he is already free and the bonds he has identified himself with are only imaginary. Once having realised this he uses his judgement freely and fearlessly with love for all. While the animal is ignorant, not having the capacity to discriminate and choose, man has this capacity. What he becomes is thus entirely in his own hands.

The Law of *Karma* and transmigration pre-supposes certain beliefs: (1) that the Soul is eternal and separate from the physical body, (2) that other organisms like animals, plants as well as inanimate objects also possess souls and (3) that the soul is both doer and sufferer, (it is not the real Soul but the ego-self).

The doctrine of *Karma* is based on the principle that every act in manifest universe produces a certain result which cannot be avoided. The universal Law of Causation rules in the physical universe. The doctrine of *Karma* extends this to the mental and moral sphere. The *Karma* doctrine is not just a mechanical law but also a moral and spiritual necessity. The doctrine emphasises, (a) that the present existence is a sort of expiation of doings in the previous existences, (b) that an evil deed cannot be expiated by works of merit and that its fruits must be borne and (c) that the punishment for wrong is automatic and personal.[6] The errors of one person are not passed on to anyone else but the one who commits it. All good or bad acts reap the fruits of the actions.

The doctrine of *Karma* leads logically to the doctrine of transmigration. Man's actions in past births fashion the nature of his present existence and the present existence together with the balance of actions in the past would determine the future existence.

The *Karma* theory is neither fatalistic nor pessimistic but emphasises all-out human effort in the present life. It accepts both pre-destination as well as free will. Desire is not in our hands but rising above it is.

The word *Karma* is synonymous with the world process. There can be no manifestation without *Karma* and no *Karma* without manifestation.[8] *Karma* therefore belongs to the physical universe. It means deeds, action and energy. Manifestation itself is an act. *Karma* or act is of thought, word and deed.

Nothing in the world is destroyed, according to the Laws of Persistence of Force, Indestructibility of Matter and Conservation of Energy. Just as a body takes only another form so also man's desires, emotions and feelings do not die and take re-birth in an environment that fits them.[9]

Desire is the root of all manifestation. It is only when all desires cease, when man is content with just a being, that re-birth ceases. The ultimate state of equanimity is the state of desirelessness.[10]

The doctrine of *punarjanma* which states that a man's actions in his previous births determine his future birth serves to explain both heredity as well as talents and inclinations.

Man thus becomes the sole architect of his own future.[11] If, for example, a man wishes to satisfy only his animal passions, has no interest in knowledge, morality or cultural pursuits, he quite obviously has no need of learned, civilized and educated parents. He could just as well be born a hog where he could uninterruptedly gratify his animal desires. Again, if a man pretends a certain disability in order to gratify his material desire then he could be born with the disability. It will be a wish he has brought on himself.[12]

According to the Law of Evolution, nobody can stagnate. Each evolves in his own time. Hence one should not look down on anyone. All desires are born out of love and love is nothing but God. Unselfish love is a part of one's godly nature while selfish love is of the lower animal nature. All desires bear fruit faster when they spring from unselfish love.

According to the Law of Evolution, only the fittest survive. Those desires that have the greater strength carry the day. Strength comes from Truth and truth alone. Those desires that have greater truth in them, more righteousness, justice, godliness or purity carry the day.[13]

A question may legitimately be asked as to why anyone should desire to be poor. Vedanta answers that not all wish to be millionaires. If one has Rs.4, another may be content with Rs.10 and so on. Again, not all are consistent in their desires.

It could also be asked why there are disparities between man and man, since all must have started on the same footing in the beginning of the world. To this Vedanta answers there is no beginning and no end. Cause-and-Effect are inseparable. It is the mind that thinks in terms of beginning and end. Actually the Soul Brahma is eternal. All manifest phenomena issues from Brahma and dissolves back into Brahma. Brahma evolves and involves. This cyclical motion is Brahma in manifestation and Brahma Unmanifest.

The three Sutras of the *Vedanta Sutra* II.I.34-36 are of great importance.[14] They are a reply to charges such as God being unjust to cause all inequalities. Says the *Vedanta Sutra*, that were God to create ineqalities of his sweet will the charge would be justified. But God is like the rain which falls on all. Each variety of seed, however, sprouts according to its potentiality. So we have rice, wheat, barley and so on. *Atma* or *Brahma* is the common cause of the evolution of all things, but inequalities are due to the specific potentiality of each. The Absolute *atma* is neither exalted by good work nor degraded by evil work, being unaffected by either. But the *atma* inspires to good acts those who are to be raised over the worlds and to evil acts those who are to go down. Higher or lower life depends on the quality of the deeds. *Samsara* is without beginning and without end. This is supported by reason as well as Sruti texts.

The discussion on *Karma* also explains that the Supreme *atma* is one and free. In the empirical state however the faculties of intellect and mind see the soul as individual and separate. In this state it is controlled by Isvara, not according to the will of Isvara, but based on conduct. Isvara thus becomes the Law of Cause and Effect in the physical or finite world.[15]

All *Karmas* in life are concerned with the three goals, *dharma*, *artha* and *kama*. Hindu thought commands life as worth living provided all actions are based on morality (*dharma*). Summed up it comes to "Do your duty; do not fall into temptation; perform duties for their own sake." (*Bhagavadgita* II.47, III.19).

Dharma therefore was most important for man. This is also why the Dharmasastras are so important, as they give the guidelines for moral behaviour. They state that the four sources of knowing *dharma* are the Vedas, the Smritis, the conduct of the good, and last but not the least, doing that which is good for one's Soul. Man's conscience must be supreme.[16] All Dharmasastras place moral qualities as the most important. *Ahimsa* (non-violence), non-stealing, purity and restraint of the senses are recommended to all. *Gautama Dharmasutra* lays down eight qualities of the soul. These are compassion towards all beings, forbearance, freedom from jealousy, freedom from excessive harm (to oneself), doing auspicious acts, absence of abjectness, of miserliness and absence of discontent, *sauca* (cleanliness) was both of the body and mind. *Manu* (V.106) expressly provides that he who is pure as to money matters is really pure and not he who washes himself with sand or water.

Satya (truth) we are told, appears in thirteen aspects, *thyaga* (renunciation of attachment to pleasures), *samata* (impartiality), *dama* (self-restraint), *ksama* (forbearance), *hri* (being ashamed to boast of one's good deeds), *anaruyya* (freedom from jealousy), *daya* (compassion) and so on, the last being *ahimsa* (non-violence).

It is worth noting that although non-violence is a virtue it is only in Jainism that absolute *ahimsa* is preached. The Buddha had no objection to eating meat provided the animal was not specially killed for feeding or honouring him.

The Vedanta accepts the law that all creation and destruction are a part of manifest universe. It accepts that all life feeds on another. Man has to live off animals even when he does not eat them. Animals are used as conveyance or for their milk etc. Vedanta is even not against eating the flesh of animals when necessary but is against doing so for self-indulgence. *Kshatriyas* who are expected to fight, eat meat. The man of religion avoids meat because the chemical reaction in the body by so doing is not considered conducive to a religious life.

Man is constantly confusing truth with a set belief or a mode of thought. This has to be constantly clarified because truth is a living need and not an inert form. There are many anecdotes to bring this point home.

There is a story in the *Charaka Samhita* of Svetaketu suffering from a skin disease. The Asvins recommended *madhu* (either honey or wine) and meat as a cure. When asked how a Brahmachari could have these, they replied that a man must save himself from disease and death in all ways, as a man can perform meritorious acts only if he lives.[17]

Some western writers have suggested that vegetarianism among Hindus and others has to do with the doctrine of transmigration. They have obviously given the matter very little study. The doctrine of re-birth had nothing to do with vegetarianism. The reasons could have been the philosophy of the One-in-all; or that every act brings its own retribution; or that with greater cultivation the need for meat was less, or the reasons could be all the three. Jainism also influenced thought. But although a large section gave up meat, an equally large number did not. Even when the doctrines of *Karma* and Transmigration were in full swing, meat was allowed to be eaten as well as offered in sacrifice in all the ancient Dharmasastras. We find from the *Grhya* and Dharmasutras that even the cow was killed at times. There are four sacrifices where Manu allows the eating of meat.[18]

The Hindus stressed on the sanctity of the cow as her value in the agricultural economy was fully appreciated. The cow nourished the land and the people, just as Mother Earth did.

Thoughtless *Karmas* are obviously *Karmas* that bind to worldly existence as they are done in ignorance. *Karma* performed with impure motives without any discrimination and understanding are also karmic *Karmas*, and hence also bind one to this world.

The 'poor' are as much an issue today as they were in all times and climes. There is vast literature on *daana* (charity) in the Dharmasastras. Gifts were given as a part of sacrifice even in the most ancient times. But then as now, there must have been those more keen on the 'image' of doing something for 'the poor' and those who saw it as a human need and duty.

It is the reason for an act that determines its merit and not the act itself. Two acts may be exactly similar externally but the motives differ in each. While one may be meritorious the other may not.

Gifts were to be given not only to one fit to receive it but also to be given without any expectation of return. Similarly when gifts were given to *Brahmins* they were not to be given to the unfit, who were mean, covetous, hypocritical and without Vedic knowledge.

Vishnudharmattora directs that in gifts of food and clothes the only consideration must be the need for these and not the caste or quality of the recipient. Manu says that he who gifts with honour and he who accepts with honour both go to heaven.

The merit of a gift does not depend on its amount or size but the purity of the act. A gift depends on the mental attitude of the giver, the capacity of the giver as well as the way the donor acquired wealth. A gift made without real conviction, or even if the whole world is given when it has been acquired unfairly, or given to an unworthy person, acquires no merit. On the other hand even a handful of vegetables given with a full heart to a worthy person brings merit. Those who give according to their ability get equal rewards regardless of the individual amounts of each.

Yajnavalkya says the reward of making gifts secretly, possessing knowledge without being conceited, and engaging in *japa* (prayer) secretly without others seeing it is infinite.[19]

All these guidelines are for those who live with their worldly responsibilities to discharge. Manu says that there are two kinds of activity, *pravrutta* and *nivrutta* (active and passive). While the latter retires from worldly duties, the former does not, but neither can escape activity. It is just that each engages in a different kind of activity, both of which are required in the world. The rules set down for each were different. While it was not desirable for the sanyasi who had taken the path of *nivrutta*, to become angry, unless the man of the world felt righteous anger at injustice he would not be effective. He had to ensure that his reasons were not selfish and that they were in the highest interest and free from a vindictive spirit.

Certain practical guidelines were laid down for a man with worldly responsibilities. He was to make gifts, perform rites and sacrifices. Wealth was to be sought in a righteous way. It was recommended that one-third of the wealth be spent on *dharma* and *artha* and another third on *kama*, while the last third was to be increased.[20] This ensured productivity in a balanced manner.

It is not the act but the appropriateness of the act that determines the right and wrong of the act. According to the Vedanta the merit or otherwise of an act depends on the source from which it springs i.e. the reason for the act. If it is based on the spiritual value the act is right, if it is based on the material value the act is wrong, no matter what material returns may issue out of it. All hypocricy comes from the worship of 'image', which is material.

Thus *Raja Yoga* is recommended for concentration and development of character, which can only come from a respect for Truth. The best method of spreading the message of the Vedanta (highest knowledge) is by example. Truth has to be lived. It is not the external that reflects truth. Truth is the seed within. To pity oneself is no better or worse than pitying another. The world is God. God cannot be pitied. It is the height of ignorance to do so. Sun is pointed out as the true Vedantin which gives without expectation of return. Life is to be lived not for anyone, but because it is one's function. Vedanta says be not a lover but Love itself. No man gets anything by begging and praying. Creation is helped by renunciation. Clinging attachments are due to lower nature. The true Self is without desire because it is energy itself.[21]

Religion is concerned with improving the discrimin- atory faculties of man. Foolishness is not a part of religion.

All foolishness and hypocricy belong to those who believe in the material as truth and reality, who falsely identify truth with number, quality, quantity, time and place and all other forms. Truth is beyond all these. Even suffering in this world helps man to remember God and so helps in attainment of the final goal of liberation.

The ordinary human being's exasperation with events that overtake him and for which he can find no rational answer is echoed by Draupadi in the *Mahabharata*. When the Pandavas were living in the forest facing great hardships after Yudhishtira lost his kingdom, Draupadi one day wonders aloud how God can be called benign like a parent, when all indicates that he is more irascible than anything else. How else, says she, could such a fine, just and righteous person like Yudhishtira be allowed to suffer such punishment when he has done no one any harm. Yudhishtira warns her that she is talking like an atheist, and that he has never acted with the expectation of any return, having performed his duty as he saw it for the sake of the duty alone and without the expectation of any reward. He bids her therefore, not to disrespect God. Draupadi acknowledges that she meant no disrespect but perhaps spoke like an atheist under the pressure of her distress. She then enters into a discussion of what people mean by *dista* (fate), *hatha* (chance) or *svabhava* (nature), and comes to the conclusion that whatever a person gains is all the result of deeds in past lives.[22]

There is perhaps no greater compulsion to morality than the law of *Karma* and re-birth. This theory is as logical as others that are propounded. It could be said to be more satisfactory than the theory of absolute annihilation after physical death which is the view held by atheists, or the view of an eternal reward or retribution in heaven or hell just after one life.

Yet *Karma* has been described by some western

commentators as 'fatalism', which sapped the will to strive. Whereas some of these views can be attributed to ignorance of this philosophy, it would be foolish to ignore the fact that some of these views were also necessary to create the image of the idle 'lotus-eating' easterner who preferred to sit and 'contemplate his navel' rather than bestir himself into healthy and helpful activity. This was in unfavourable contrast to bustling 'Christian charity'. This image helped to present both the white man and his proselytising religion in a favourable light. This is not to deny that there were, among those who subscribed to the doctrine of *Karma* and *punarjanma*, some who, due to laziness and ignorance, regarded *Karma* as destiny against which it was pointless to strive. This easy-going attitude is however due to an individual's own lethargic inclinations and not the doctrine of *Karma* as explained in the religious texts of the eastern philosophies. Inertia (tamas) is intrinsic to nature. Used wisely and well, it can give stability, when not used wisely it can lead to sloth and ignorance. This is true not only of the east but also the west. The three properties in nature, Harmony, Activity and Inertia are universal. The ignorant Hindu or other easterner who looked upon the Law of *Karma* as a passport to a lazy existence which saved him from the necessity to strive, was actually no different to the ignorant and lazy Westerner who made out that the mere act of being baptised into a religion, the change of a religious label, automatically made the proselytised into the 'God's Chosen' or that by a mere act of confession all sins would be washed away.

Shantiparva, says (205.2) 'Not to sit and mope over misery, is the best medicine'.

The doctrine of *Karma* and *punarjanma* has been found to be of solace not only to easterners who subscribe to the philosophy but also to others. Sir William Jones in a letter to Earl Spencer wrote, "I am no Hindu, but I hold the doctrine of the Hindus concerning a future state to be incomparably more rational, more pious, and more likely to deter men from vice than the horrid opinion by Christians of punishments without end."[23]

In *Religion and Immortality*, Lowes Dickinson observes, "It is really a consoling idea that our present capacities are determined by our previous actions and that our present actions again will determine our future character."

In *The Scales of Karma*, Owen Rutter says that Christianity has failed to solve the intellectual and moral problems which beset those who live in the complexities of the modern world, that he began to study the doctrine of *Karma* and re-incarnation seven years before writing his book which is a personal statement rather than an essay on *Karma*. 'Many who have written against this doctrine while conceding that the Upanishadic doctrine is an ancient and serious attempt to solve the problem of injustice and evil in the world, call it weak and beset with difficulties. One should like to ask, what religious systems are not beset with difficulties. To all non-Christians (and to several Christians also in modern times) its doctrine of Original Sin, its damnation of unbaptised infants, of pre-destination deduced from the belief that God is an omniscient and omnipotent Creator of heaven and earth appear strange and unjustified."

The German philosopher Emmanuel Kant felt that it was only by pre-supposing an Eternal Existence that phenomenal existence could be explained.

But the greatest gift of this doctrine is what the *Upanishads* and the *Gita* observed several hundred years ago, that a man of good deeds is nearest to God because of his goodness, while the man of evil deeds cannot secure divine grace no matter what book or prophet he might follow. It respects man's true worth, irrespective of caste, creed and community.[24]

References

1. *History of Dharmasastra* by P.V. Kane, vol.V, pt.2, chap.XXXV, sec.IX, p.1532.
   Religion of the Hindus by Prof. Wilson (London, ed.1862. vol.II, p.112).
2. ibid., vol.V, pt.2, chap.XXXV, sec.IX, p.1530, 1531.
3. ibid., vol.V, pt.2, p.1531.
4. ibid., vol.V, pt.2, chap.XXXV, sec.IX, p.1533, 1534, 1536.
5. ibid., vol.V, pt.2, chap.XXXV, p.1546, 1547.
6. ibid., vol.V, pt.2, chap.XXXV, p.1561.
7. ibid., vol.V, pt.2, chap.XXXV, p.1561, 1562.
8. ibid., vol.V, pt.2, chap.XXXV, p.1567, 1568.
9. ibid., vol.V, pt.2, chap.XXXV, p.1561, 1562.
   In the Woods of God-realisation by Swami Ram Tirtha, vol.II.
10. ibid., vol.V, pt.2, chap.XXXV, sec.IX, p.1548.
    ibid., vol.V, pt.2, chap.XXXV, sec.IX, p.1573.
11. ibid., vol.V, pt.2, chap.XXXV, sec.IX, p.1573.
12. *In the Woods of God-realisation* by Swami Ram Tirtha, vol.II.
13. ibid., vol.II.
14. *History of Dharmasastra* by P.V. Kane, vol.V, pt.2, chap.XXXV, sec.IX, p.1558, 1559.
15. ibid., vol.V, pt.2, chap.XXXV, sec.IX, p.1159.
16. ibid., vol.II, pt.1, p.7, 8.
17. ibid., vol.II, pt.2, chap.XXII, p.796.
18. ibid., vol.II, pt.2, chap.XXII, p.776.
19. ibid., vol.II, pt.2, chap.XXV, p.849.
20. ibid., vol.V, pt.2, chap.XXXV, p.1630.
21. *In the Woods of God-realisation* by Swami Ram Tirtha, vol.I.
22. *History of Dharmasastra* by P.V. Kane, vol.V, pt.2, chap.XXXV sec.IX, p.1569, 1570.
23. ibid., vol.V, pt.2, chap.XXXV, sec.IX, p.1594.
24. ibid., vol.V, pt.2, chap.XXXV, sec.IX, p.1562.

13

Chaturvarna

The *Chaturvarna* system is the four-tiered scheme of social order which was a practical expression of Hindu philosophical thought. It demonstrates that thought was not confined to the ivory tower but was meant for practical application.

The *Chaturvarna* system has invited much comment, both admiring and derisive. Within the Hindu fold itself it has been condemned as well as upheld. As regards the comments on the *Chaturvarna* from outside the Hindu fold (mainly the west) it must be understood that it is more due to its novelty and uniqueness than any other reason. This has not been appreciated by many Hindus, who are at times even irritated by the constant harping on the caste system, which *Chaturvarna* is called.

The *Chaturvarna* system happens to be the only such system in the world. Although a sort of caste system based on birth and occupation prevailed in ancient Persia, Rome and Japan, these dwindled and disappeared in course of time.[1] They were also not as complex nor as rigorous as the caste system in India. There were also the thinkers in both the ancient and modern world who have considered the need of having a class or caste system with certain functions in order to preserve civilization. Plato thought of it as also some French and English thinkers of the twentieth century. But these thoughts were not followed up. The only place where it was not only devised but also put into execution, and which has survived through the centuries, is India.

India's civilization is acknowledged as the oldest continuing civilization. Toynbee in "Reconsiderations" Vol.XII in his *Study of History* observes, "..... the maintenance of the *Brahmin's* monopoly of the religious ministry gives Indian history a continuity throughout the period running from the Aryan invasion to the impact of the West." It would however be impossible to appreciate the structure without understanding the basic philosophy on which it was based. One would then perhaps be able to appreciate that the Hindu civilization was not due just to the efforts of the *Brahmins*, though they undoubtedly played a very important part, but on its constant stress that the moral conduct is the unselfish conduct. While all form is but an expression of the Spirit, it is the unselfish conduct alone that nourishes all form. Like all creation, man also is a form, and so is society.

Dharma, artha, and *kama* are the legitimate aims of the soul, in creation. *Artha* and *kama* based on morality alone lead to final liberation, (*moksa*). Economic, vital and cultural pursuits are therefore not only legitimate but also necessary in creation. Productivity is essential for the world. By being productive, man is helping all creation. Productivity cannot be unthinking and uncontrolled but must be thoughtfully carried out in a disciplined manner. Man's physical, emotional and mental capacities must be fully utilized to make the best of life. Those who do so are helping all creation. This also served man's spiritual need. Thus man's life also was sought to be divided into four stages so that while he may develop himself to the full in life he also did not forget the final goal of all life. Truth is not death but Life Eternal. But just phasing an individual's life was not enough. Just as the individual had needs so did society. These needs of society had to be met. Knowledge is essential for any civilization. We have to have the know-how to understand how to make best use of the things around us in this world that we live in. This expertise must be used to help society as well as to maintain the individual. This ensured service as well as payment as appreciation for service. Morality is concerned not only with giving of one's best but also appreciation of services rendered. Only those who themselves work well can understand and appreciate good work. The recognition of merit is essential for every civilization. But Hindu thinkers recognized that whereas it was in the hands of each to do his or her best, it was not in the hands of the individual to change others. So, work to be done for its own sake and without expectations of reward was put before each and all as the highest worship. This was the "work ethics" taught.

The individual found self-expression, self-confidence and self-discipline through work which was of value for all. Hindu thought considers that just as creation evolves from desire, need, function to organ, so also society's needs must be met in order to preserve civilization. The needs of society are knowledge, not only scientific and secular, but spiritual as well, as the latter knowledge alone can influence moral acts. A political or ruling class is also needed so that government can be effectively run; the needs of society are also production, which means the agriculturist and industrialist as well as labour. These four needs of a stable society were sought to be met by the *Chaturvarna* structure with *Brahmins*, *Kshatriyas*, *Vaisyas* and *Sudras* meeting the respective needs.

The law-givers, however, were not content merely with this structure. While explaining the divine source of all form in creation of which the *Chaturvarna* also was one, they were realistic enough to be aware that there had to be something higher for all to abide by. A Law had to ensure justice for all. Indian political treatises often refer to the Law of the Fishes. In the *Mahabharata*, Bhishma explains how this law acts as a restraint for all who otherwise in the absence of such a law would be exploited and suffer injustice. "The child, the old, the sick, the ascetic, the priest, the woman and the widow would be preyed upon according to the logic of the fish."

This "logic" consists of exploitation of the weak by the strong. Hindu mythological stories abound with the misuse of power by the arrogance of the strong, the learned, the wealthy etc., and shows how, when *dharma* is kicked in this fashion *dharma* always destroys those responsible. *Dharma* (law) was the highest of all and all had to abide by it.

Society's needs were thus sought to be met by naming the functions that were needed to meet the needs and then creating the organs required for those functions.

In the earliest portion of the *Rig Veda* there is reference only to the *Brahmin* and *Kshatriya*. *Brahmin* represented prayer and *Kshatriya*, valour.[2] They thus functioned as activity based on knowledge and faith. There was change of function as well, as we see references to an individual moving from one function to another. A *Kshatriya* could become a *Brahmin*. The presumption is that it was so because of inclination, as no reasons are given. It is only in the later *Rig Veda* portion that we see *Vaisyas* and *Sudras* mentioned. Earlier, chariot-makers etc. are referred to according to professions,[3] while later they belonged to the *varna* of *Sudras*. The inference is that as society became more complex its needs also increased and diversified. A larger number of those with the necessary skills were required and so had to be accommodated into the caste structure. The *Chaturvarna* system had taken deep roots by the time of the *Brahmanas* (about 2500 BC) Even when the *Chaturvarna* system was well established and the professions were more or less according to heredity, there was a change of caste when four, five or six generations had been following the same professions or marrying into the same caste. It appears that in the days of the *Manusmriti* (X.45) there were mixed castes who spoke *mleccha* tongues as well as Arya languages who were treated as *dasas* (*Sudras*). Most castes and sub-castes arose from *varna-samskara* (inter-caste marriages.).[4] *Yajnavalkya Smriti* differed from the previous Smritis and prohibited one belonging to the three upper castes from marrying a *Sudra* woman.[5] There is nothing to show that inter-marriage and inter-dining were prohibited in the Vedic age.

Changes in the laws are accepted by Smritis as laws are meant for the good of society and to meet its needs. The changing laws of the Smritis in different ages are indications of the changing needs of the times.[6] *Shantiparva* points out that what was *adharma* (an immoral custom) in one age may become *dharma* (moral) in another and that *dharma* and *adharma* are both subject to the limitations of country and time.[7]

This shows that thinkers were aware of the fact that man often acts unwisely when he clings to the form of custom or law thinking it to be truth, while not understanding that truth is not an inert form but that which is a living need. Brihaspati also warns that 'the decision (in a cause) should not be given by merely relying on sastras, for in the case of a decision devoid of reasoning, loss of *dharma* results."[8] Sastras are only meant as an aid. They are not a substitute for our reasoning and not meant to be followed blindly or literally, even when seen to cause injustice or unhappiness. The law in other words, is meant for man and not man for the laws.

In the earliest times the 'out-castes' were the *chandalas*. Others were added later. The *chandalas* were either the offspring of the union of a *Sudra* man and a *Brahmin* woman, or the child of illicit relations, or the children caused by the union of two belonging to the same *gotra*, prohibited by the Smritis.[9] Dharmasastras only referred to the *chandalas* as outcastes. But there is no sanction of the Smritis for the kind of untouchability practiced in some parts of India where even the shadow of an outcaste was considered impure and the untouchable had to leave the road to make way by loudly announcing his presence so as not to pollute others.

But even the *chandalas* although outcastes, (they lived outside the village) had to be fed. This was a social duty.

The old caste system was based on quality with corresponding duties and not privilege. The later *jatis* tended to become hide-bound, clinging to privileges while ignoring the duties. The common characteristics of this *jati* system are: heredity, by which a man was assigned to a caste by birth in that caste; restrictions of food as to what may or may not be taken and by whom; rigidity of occupation by which members of one caste followed only that occupation assigned to that caste; endogamy and exogamy which restricted marriage to only those within that caste and not marrying relatives and others in the same caste; gradations of caste which put some at the top of the scale while others so low as to be untouchable. Not much is left of most of these today, except perhaps endogamy to some extent and the theory of birth.[11]

The *varna* system was looked upon as a necessary order needed to manage a civilized society. The codes of Manu spell out the duties of each *varna*. But this information was not a secret document meant to be misused. This was for the information of all so as to ensure that they knew when it was being carried out in the spirit meant and when not. The Puranas and the two epics were meant for all *varnas*. The duties of the *varna* are clearly expressed in them. The Puranas give the personal and social obligations of the Hindus as, "The *Brahmins* should make gifts, should worship God with sacrifices, should be assiduous in studying the Vedas, should perform ablutions and libations with water and should preserve the sacred flame. For the sake of subsistence he may offer sacrifices on behalf of others and may instruct them in the sastras; and he may accept presents of a liberal description in a becoming manner (or from a respectable person and at an appropriate season). He must ever seek, to promote the good of others and do evil to none; for the best riches of a *Brahmin* are universal benevolence. He should look upon the jewels of another person as if they were pebbles and should, at proper periods, procreate off-spring by his wife. These are the duties of a *Brahmin*.

The *Kshatriyas* should cheerfully give presents to *Brahmins*, perform various sacrifices and study the scriptures. His special sources of maintenance are arms and protection of the earth. The guardianship of the earth is indeed his special province, by the discharge of which duty a king attains his objects and realises a share of the merit of all sacrificial rites. By intimidating the bad and cherishing the good, the monarch who maintains the discipline of the different castes secures whatever regions he desires.

Brahma the great parent of creation gave to the *Vaisyas* the occupation of commerce and agriculture and the feeding of flocks and herds for his means of livelihood; and sacred study, sacrifice and donation are also his duties as is the observance of fixed and occasional rites. Attendance upon the three generate castes is the province of the *Sudras* and by that he is to subsist, or by profits of trade or the earnings of mechanical labour. He is also to make gifts;

and he may offer the sacrifices in which food is presented as well as obsequial offerings. (These imply the worship of *Visvadevas*, the rites of hospitality, occasional oblations on building a house, birth of a child or any occasion of rejoicing; when mantras were chanted they had to have the *Brahmins* for it.)

Apart from their respective duties, they all have the common obligations applicable to humanity. These for all were the acquisition of property, supporting their families, having progeny, tenderness towards all creatures, patience, humility, truth, purity; contentment, decency of decoration, gentleness of speech, friendliness, and freedom from envy, avarice and detraction.

"The theory of *varnas* as conceived by Manu and other Smritikars was based on the idea of division of labour, the idea of balancing the rival claims of the different sections of the community laying greater emphasis on the duties of the *varnas* than on the rights and privileges. It raised the *Brahmin* to the highest pinnacle of reverence but at the same time placed before him the ideal of not going after temporal power, leading a life of comparative poverty and making his knowledge available to other classes for a scanty and precarious return. It made the military classes feel they were not all in all but had to look up to some other class as superior to themselves. The *Brahmins* had to bring up their own families and their pupils and also make gifts to others, without a regular fat salary or belonging to a monastery. They never arrogated to themselves the authority to depose kings or hand vast territories to whomsoever they liked as did Pope Alexander VI by his Bill of 1493 making over the New World to Ferdinand and Isabella."[12]

Rajadharma, the duty of the King was considered most important since the peoples' good depended on the king. National good was the king's only duty. The coronation oath runs thus, "I shall always regard the country (*bhauma*) as the highest God (Brahma). And whatever is to be prescribed by law on the basis of statecraft I shall follow without hesitation, never my own inclination."[13]

The concept of a king was that of a royal sage. Although hereditary rights were normally assumed, there were exceptions. Even when kingship was traced to the god there was nothing like the western concept of the Divine right of Kings. The king was held accountable to the people. Banishing a bad king and even his death was sanctioned, no matter what his pedigree was. There was great emphasis on the king's duties and little on his rights and privileges. Although the people were asked to look on the king as a god and revere him, it equally obviously meant that the king had to deserve it.[14]

Kautilya refers to the soldiers and the different sources from which they were drawn for the army. He states that those to be preferred are those who are the professionals. This refers to the *Kshatriyas* who are the professional soldiers with fighting as their profession.

The Greeks testify that during Chandragupta's reign the best armies they fought against in Asia were the Indian armies.[15] But the army was quite obviously not restricted to a caste, because Kautilya's *Arthasastra* refers very clearly to *Brahmin* armies as well. So all castes and classes must have been there.

While heredity may have been the ideal, and quality an even higher one, life does not always confirm to the ideal, and the pressure of needs recognizes no laws. Destiny which is seen as the force of circumstance might suddenly reduce one from the luxury of wealth to the most abject poverty. It might throw whole communities out of employment due to changing needs and discoveries and so on. The Smritis recognize this fact. In times of distress interchange of caste functions was allowed. The *Brahmin* could follow the occupation of a *Kshatriya* or *Vaisya*, or a *Kshatriya* that of a *Vaisya* as well as the *Vaisya* of a *Kshatriya*. The last two were exhorted never to descend to the functions of the *Sudra* and as far as possible to avoid them. Manu permits *Vaisyas* in times of distress to perform the work of the *Sudra*. Where this was not possible they were at least to try and shun the work of the *chandalas*.

This must be understood in the context of the philosophy on which the whole system was based. Faith, knowledge and intelligent activity are needed for any civilization. The three higher classes were the educated. Constant striving alone can keep knowledge and excellence alive if society is not to descend to ignorance and superstition. To be content with less is to give way to the inertia ever-present in nature, but harmful to any civilization. When the educated classes were initiated by a rite as student, it was meant to impress upon them their new role and duties to society.

It was recognized that the system demanded sacrifice from each *varna* as there will always be the individuals who aspire for another profession. There may be the *Brahmin* who would rather take up another profession, the *Kshatriya*, *Vaisya* and *Sudra* who are not wanting their hereditary profession and feel they are better suited for another. This was apparently recognized by the Smritikars who often refer to the *Chaturvarna* as *Chaturyajna* (sacrifice)[16]. Each sacrificed for the good of all. The four *varnas* *Brahmin*, *Kshatriya*, *Vaisya* and *Sudra* are also described (in the *Purusa Sukta*, portion of the *Rig Veda*) as issuing from the mouth, arms, thigh and feet of Brahma, respectively.[17]

Usually the *Brahmin* was the teacher though it did happen at times that the roles were reversed and the *Kshatriya* more wise, taught a *Brahmin*. But these were exceptions rather than the rule.[18] The *Vaisyas* were more numerous than the *Brahmins* or *Kshatriyas*. Being the most prosperous they also bore the brunt of taxation. There were strict rules on violating rules of associations and conventions. There were village and local association as well. There were various professional guilds of potters, weavers, bamboo weavers, betel sellers, oilmen etc. They were both prosperous and dependable, and would have large sums of money deposited with them on which a regular interest would be paid. Large temples were built by them. Many *Sudras* came up socially because of their prosperity.[19] Coomaraswamy points out the necessity of restoring the status and prosperity of the skilled artisan and village craftsman. "Trade guilds received support from Indian kings, these were withdrawn by the British."[20] Kings were meant to preserve and extend knowledge, culture and skills. From even the mythologies we get an idea of the courts of the king and his duties towards his subjects. The Court of Rama contains intellectuals in philosophy, religion and law, but besides them, those who were proficient in music, dance, architecture, sculpture and painting. The king would hold assemblies of the learned and give rewards. Samudragupta was proficient in music and so was the Pallava King Mahendravarma, who was proficient in painting, sculpture, literature and engineering as well. Harshavardhana was also supposed to be proficient in these arts. Bhoja of Dhara was known for his proficiency in art, engineering, medical science, philosophy, literature etc. He is known for the many irrigation tanks he built. The list is long.[21]

The *Manusmriti* lays down that the king should engage different fields of craftsmen throughout the year and encourage their art. Megasthenes notes that the State was responsible for the protection of crafts. Artisans were exempted from paying taxes and even received maintenance from the Royal Exchequer. He who caused an artisan to lose his eye or hand was put to death.

There seems to have been the appreciation of good work from the bad which is the hall-mark of a cultured society. *Dindin* was the word used to describe that artist who while repairing works in palaces or temple, superimposed inferior work over the original!

The most exacting standards were kept before the *Brahmin*. Living a life of simplicity and study he had to serve society by preserving, propagating and augmenting the ancient literature and culture. A learned *Brahmin* had to memorize at least one Veda, the *Brahmana* texts, the six *Vedangas*, the *Kalpasutra*, *Grammar of Panini* of about 4000 sutras, twelve chapters of *Nirukta*, Metrics, Phonetics and *Jyotish*. These extensive texts were generally committed to memory.[22] It is understandable therefore that it should be said that it was a bad omen for any kingdom where a *Brahmin* dies of hunger. Quite obviously this had no reference to those *Brahmins* who were engaged in other activities that were outside the *Brahmin*'s real profession. It reflected ill on any kingdom where a *Brahmin* whose profession was to keep knowledge alive and who had no other means of livelihood had to die of starvation. It implied that the state and the citizens were not interested in the spiritual needs and avoided the rites and ceremonies where the *Brahmin* was needed and also they were not appreciative of knowledge and learning. A state that has no regard for merit will ultimately destroy itself.[23]

It should not be supposed that the educated could get away from their responsibilities by taking refuge under 'privilege' of caste. Parasara (I.60) calls upon kings to fine that village where persons of the higher castes wander about begging, though they are not observers of vows (like *brahmacharya*) and are not studying the Veda.

Indiscriminate begging was never allowed by the Smritis even for *Brahmins*,[24] leave alone others. *Manu* (VIII.338) prescribes that the *Brahmin* who knowingly is guilty of theft should be levied a fine 64 or 100 or 128 times as much as a *Sudra* guilty of the same unknowingly while the latter is eight times as much if knowingly committed.

Nobody was allowed to be unproductively idle or take refuge behind caste.

All received representation. There is great divergence as to the number of ministers the king may have. They probably differed according to age and place. Manu says seven or eight ministers should be taken by the king to advise him on matters of state. These should be brave, well tested and of good family. (Shivaji's was similar). *Shantiparva* says there should be 34 of whom there should be 4 learned and bold *Brahmins*, 8 valiant *Kshatriyas*, 21 prosperous *Vaisyas* and 3 *Sudras*, and one *Suta* well-versed in the Puranas, but verse 11 adds that the king should settle matters of policy among 8 ministers and not less than 3.[25]

Quite obviously too many advisers were not considered a help. Very few *Brahmins* became kings. Kings have mostly been from the *Kshatriya* caste or the *Sudra*.[26]

It is reassuring to see that whenever 'authority' threatened to become rigid and unyielding, voices were raised. When the *Smartha dharma* of the Smritis which worked out a regular order for society as well as the individual in which he may develop himself, did not suit a larger number, it brought about the rise of the *Bhagawat dharma*. Even at a time when *Sudras* and women were not allowed to take part in sacrifices (a later development) the sage Badari (P.M.S.VI.1.27) advocates that *Sudras* should perform the sacrifices as well as study the Vedas.[27] Also, the Puranas and the two epics were meant for all.

They were expressly meant for *Sudras* and women for "If they could not go to the Vedas the Vedas would go to them". Education was not denied to anyone.[28] They were more realistic perhaps in acknowledging the fact that the women and *Sudras* finding less time from their other activities could not be expected to spend time learning what they may not need. Religious teachers, social reformers and saints all fought caste when it was practised as discrimination and not a function for the common good.

The saints did not denounce caste, but pride of caste which was thoughtless and went against the reason for caste. This created the feeling of superiority and inferiority. It also promoted the foolish ideas that some professions were better than others. All functions are necessary for society. This is what they tried to explain. But what they singled out for special mention was not the four *varnas* but the fifth caste of untouchables. They were the ones who were really deprived. They were the outcastes of society. Every enlightened Hindu, be he saint or social reformer has sought to eradicate this injustice. In recent times not only M.K. Gandhi the great son of India, but also Savarkar the great revolutionary asked Hindus to remove untouchability from their midst. He hammered on what he described as the seven fetters to be broken to free Hindu society. These included untouchability, prohibitions of several kinds such as sea travel, mutual dining among the various castes and sub-castes, the prohibitions against following certain occupations, prohibition against re-admission into Hinduism of the people who were converted to other religions by force, fraud or ignorance.[29]

Without condoning the untouchability practised which goes against humanity, we must first understand what untouchability meant to the Hindu. Untouchability was practised even in one's own house with family members. Untouchability was practised for reasons of hygiene, medical reasons, religious reasons and as ex-communication for crimes. *Mlecchas* and other sects were also untouchable. A woman became 'untouchable' during a certain period of the month. She became 'untouchable' for a certain period after child-birth. This not only ensured rest but also was protection against infection. Members of a family in which a death had taken place as well as those who carried the bier were 'untouchable' for a certain period.[30] This would no doubt be more acceptable today if wrapped with the label of 'quarantine period'. The mid-day meal which was the main meal was offered to God first. This had to be cooked in scrupulous cleanliness. The cook was 'untouchable' at this time. Woe betide if anyone touched, because it meant another bath for the cook! Similarly a *pujari* performing the devotional rite of *puja* also was 'untouchable'. Those performing unclean occupations were also 'untouchable' albeit for different reasons.

In course of time the real reasons for untouchability must have disappeared and what remained was a mindless performance of a rite which had been reduced to a fetish. However, the baby cannot be thrown out along with the bath-water. While we may dispense with the rite, we cannot discard cleanliness which is essential for health. Dharmasastra's laid down certain rules of purity and impurity to develop civic and social consciousness as well, e.g., "One's own bed, garment, wife, child, waterpot — these are free from taint to oneself, but these are impure to others."[31]

The untouchable while being considered as beyond the *dharma* of ceremonies nevertheless still abided by the moral code and could worship Vishnu. The Smritis allowed touch in temples, religious processions, marriages, sacrifices, in all festivals, or when a whole village was involved in a calamity, during wars, fire or invasion. The untouchable could draw water from large tanks along with others but not from small reservoirs. Public roads were considered to be purified with the sun's rays, moon and wind, even when trodden on by the untouchables.[32]

A glance at the Smritis gives one a rough idea of how *dharma*, the law, worked. It must be remembered that the *Brahmin* referred to for respect is not one who has the virtue of mere birth but of learning and other virtues.[33] *Brahmins* were not to be taxed. Others who were not taxed were women of all the four *varnas*, boys before attaining majority, students engaged in austerities, a *Sudra* who washed the feet of the three *varnas*, the blind and dumb, diseased and those forbidden (like ascetics) to possess wealth.[34]

Rules of the road gave the *Brahmin* the right over the king. In a crowd or obstruction, precedence was given to a cartman, very old men, the diseased, women, 'snatakas' and then the king. Men carrying burdens were given precedence, and 'all those desiring own welfare' were to give precedence to fools, sinners, drunkards, lunatics, and the lower *varnas* to the higher *varnas*.

The law-givers seemed to have blended humour with common-sense! That they also had their hearts in the right place is obvious from the tradition that the bride being taken to the groom had precedence over all![35]

Rules and regulations are meant for the good of society and so must be followed with discrimination, intelligence and honesty. However, inertia and sloth are also a part of nature and it is easy to take the unquestioning way out. A genuine function becomes a parody when function is forgotten and only form retained. This is image-worship, worship of the inert form forgetting its purpose. But this will be seen as the problem in the world in all ages and in every place. The only difference is that at a certain time there are more honest, intelligent and knowledgeable people in a place and fewer of the others or the other way round!

It would be unrealistic to imagine that all did their tasks as prescribed. One has to make allowances for individual nature and its weaknesses. It would be equally unrealistic to imagine that the *Brahmin* by being the highest caste was in some ways a superman. He was a human being like anyone else.

Atri sarcastically refers to the various kinds of *Brahmins* thus: *Deva Brahmin* is one who daily performs his bath, *sandhya japa*, *homa*, worship, honouring of guests and *vaisvadeva*.

Muni Brahmin is one who has relinquished worldly life, stays in the forest, subsists on roots and fruits and vegetables and performs daily *shraddhas*.

Dvija Brahmin is one who studies the Vedanta, gives up all attachments and is engaged in reflecting over Sankhya and Yoga.

Ksatriya Brahmin is he who fights.

Vaisya Brahmin is engaged in agriculture and trade and rears cattle.

Sudra Brahmin is one who sells prohibited things like lac, salt, dyes, like kusumbha, milk, ghee, honey and meat.

Nisada Brahmin is a thief, a robber, a back-biter and always fond of fish and meat.

Pasu Brahmin is one who knows nothing about Brahma and is only proud of wearing his sacred thread.

Mleccha Brahmin obstructs or destroys wells, tanks, gardens, without any qualm.

Chandala Brahmin is one who is a fool, devoid of prescribed rites, beyond the pale of all *dharma*, and cruel.[36]

Atri also is unsparing of the so-called poser god-men (of all classes) and caustically describes them thus; "Those who are devoid of Vedic lore, study sastras, (like grammar, logic, etc.); those who are devoid of *sastric* lore, study the Puranas (and earn money by reciting them); those who are devoid of even Puranas reading become agriculturists, and those who are devoid of even that become *bhagavataars* (pose as great devotees of Siva and Vishnu).[37]

And now it might be worth while to have an outsider's views on the caste system. They are widely divergent. But before proceeding to give the views of writers and scholars it would be better to give the opinion recorded by an experienced British military officer who was for some time the Surveyor General of India and had to travel widely all over India. His views are reproduced by Sir William Monier in *Modern India and Indians* (5th Ed.1891). His views were formed in the course of a minute survey of the country. At that time the villagers of every caste were found by him and his assistants to be 'simple and temperate' in their habits, 'quiet and peaceful' in disposition, 'obedient and faithful in the fulfilment of duty'. 'It was believed that 'they had the advantage of Europeans of the same class, not only in propriety of manners, but in the practice of moral virtues.' They had no conspicuous vices. 'The affection and tenderness of parents were returned by the habitual dutifulness of the children'. Hospitality towards strangers was carefully observed. Everywhere throughout the country 'there was charity without ostentation'. No beggars were to be seen 'except those who were religious mendicants by profession'. 'Though there was no law, the indigent and diseased were always provided for by the internal village arrangements. 'There was everywhere such mutual confidence that no written documents in transactions of money payments were required. The cultivators paid their share and took no receipts. Money and valuables were deposited 'without any other securities than the account of the parties'. On a particular occasion at an immense fair on the banks of the Narmada 200,000 people were collected, yet there was no rioting, no quarrelling, no drunkardness or disorder of any kind. "All were intent on their religious duties. The officer employed on the survey had no other guard but the village watchman, 'yet no robbery was committed nor the smallest article ever pilfered from the tents".

"In every village there is a close intertwining of communal relations so that the separate existence and independence of any individual of the country were barely recognized." (p.40)

"And I may here remark that the Hinduism of the present day is by no means a system that exists for the *Brahmins* alone. It is no rigid system of hard and fast lines. On the contrary it possesses great elasticity and delights in compromises and compensations. If strict on some points, it is lax in others. If it gives power to one caste it gives power of a different kind or at least some complementary advantage to another." This officer's views bear relevance as he was intimately able to study the behaviour of the country people.

While much of western views (particularly those against) may be dismissed as motivated particularly because the Europeans had tried to make themselves into a higher caste in India still it is worthwhile noting the different views expressed.

Sydney Low in his *Vision of India* (1907) reflects: "There is no doubt that it is the main cause of the fundamental stability and contentment by which Indian society has been braced up for centuries against the shocks of politics and the cataclysms of nature. It provides every man with his place, his career, his occupation, his circle of friends. It makes him at the outset a member of a corporate body, it protects him through life from the canker of social jealousy and unfulfilled aspirations. It ensures him companionship and a sense of community with others in like case with himself. The caste organisation is to the Hindu his club, his trade union, his benefit society, his philanthrophic society. There are no work hours in India and none are as yet needed."

Abbe Dubois wrote about 200 years ago: "I consider the institution of caste among the Hindu nations as the happiest efforts of their legislation; and I am well convinced that if the people of India never sunk into a state of barbarism and if, when all of Europe was plunged in that dreary gulf, India kept up her head, preserved and extended the sciences and arts and civilization, it is wholly to the distinction of castes that she is indebted for that high celebrity." He goes on to justify his opinions.

Maine in his *Ancient Law* calls, it, 'The most disastrous and blighting of all human institutions'; while Sherring in *Hindu Tribes and Castes* states, 'It is the most hateful, hardhearted and cruel social system that could possibly be invented for damning the human race."

Meredith Townsend on the other hand in *Europe and Asia* says, "I firmly believe caste to be a marvellous discovery, a form of socialism which through the ages protected Hindu society from anarchy and from the worst evils of industrial and competitive life. It is an automatic poor law to begin with and the strongest form known of trade unionism."

In rare cases it has even been attributed to 'crafty *Brahmins*'.[38] Mahatma Gandhi (who was not a *Brahmin*) was asked, "You talk of releasing the energies for spiritual pursuits. Today those who follow their father's profession have no spiritual culture at all — their very *varna* unfits them for it." Gandhi's reply was: "We are talking with crooked notions about *varna*. When *varna* was really practised, we had enough leisure for spiritual training. Even now you go to distant villages and see what spiritual culture villagers have as compared to town dwellers. These know no self-control. But you have spotted the mischief of the age. Let us not try to be what others cannot be. I would not even learn the Gita, if every one who wished could not do it. That is why my whole soul rises against learning English for making money. We have to re-arrange our lives so that we can ensure to the millions the leisure that a fraction of us have today and we cannot do it unless we follow the law of *varna*."[39]

India's poverty was often attributed by Europeans (who themselves were largely responsible for it) to her Hindu 'caste system'. Even now one hears such statements. India was not poor when the British came to India. India became poor during British rule because India 'had to be bled to make England richer'. The zamindari system was enforced by the British government. This deprived the villagers of the village common lands which acted as a cushion in times of need, and made the villagers poorer and entirely dependent.[40]

The extreme poverty of England under the Pope is amply recorded. Ireland was known for its extreme poverty. Even if the Irish were not responsible and put the blame on England then England was a Christian country too if not Catholic. The French revolution was caused by the crushing poverty of the people under the Church and State. So was the Russian Revolution. The Catholic country of Venezuela is known for the imbalances in the population. Therefore we are forced to conclude the reason for India's poverty cannot be the caste system. We would have to look elsewhere.

The answer is in the Vedanta itself. Let us not look anywhere else or blame this or that. Vedanta assures that no effort is ever wasted. Let us do our work in honesty and dedication. The material will look after itself. The undeniable fact is that no civilization can survive unless knowledge and expertise are kept alive. No knowledge can survive unless it is firmly based on wisdom. If Hindu civilization exists even today it is due to all those who faithfully and fearlessly carried out their tasks as they honestly saw them. There can be honest differences. It is not the difference that is important but the honesty. No two people need to see a thing the same way. It is perhaps even necessary that they do not. But it is important that the views are honestly held.

References

1. *History of Dharmasastra* by P.V. Kane, vol.V, pt.2, chap.XXXV, sec.X, p.1633.
2. ibid., vol.II, pt.1, chap.II, p.27, 28, 32.
3. ibid., vol.V, pt.2, chap.XXXV, sec.X, p.1632.
4. ibid., vol.V, pt.2, chap.XXXV, sec.X, p.1634, 1635.
5. ibid., vol.V, pt.2, chap.XXXV, sec.X, p.1632.
6. ibid., vol.V, pt.2, chap.XXIX, sec.VII, p.1267.
7. ibid., vol.V, pt.2, chap.XXXV, sec.X, p.1630.
8. ibid., vol.V, pt.2, chap.XVIII, sec.VII, p.1469, 1470, vol.III, chap.XXXIII, p.867.
9. ibid., vol.II, pt.1, chap.III.
10. ibid., vol.II, pt.1, chap.IV, p.175.
11. ibid., vol.II, pt.1, p.23, 24.
12. ibid., vol.II, pt.1, chap.III, p.137.
13. *A New History of Sanskrit Literature* by K. Chaitanya (III, Political order).
14. *History of Dharmasastra* by P.V. Kane, vol.III, chap.II, p.36; chap.III, p.58.
15. *Poverty and un-British Rule in British India* by Dadabhai Naoroji.
16. *Gita Rahasya* by B.G. Tilak (Marathi), chap.III.
17. *History of Dharmasastra* by P.V. Kane, vol.II, pt.1, chap.II, p.33.
18. ibid., vol.V, pt.2, chap.XXXV, sec.X, p.1639.
19. ibid., vol.II, pt.1, chap.II, p.66, 67, 68.
20. *Art and Swadeshi* by A. Coomaraswamy.
21. *History of Dharmasastra* by P.V. Kane, vol.III, chap.III, p.59, 60, vol.III, chap.XV, p.404.
    The Painter in Ancient India by C. Sivaramurti.
    Art and Swadeshi by A. Coomaraswamy.

22. ibid., vol.V, pt.2, chap.XXXV, sec.X, p.1636, 1637.
23. ibid., vol.III, chap.III, p.56, *Shantiparva* (23.15) quotes a gatha of Brihaspati, "As a snake swallows mice lying in holes, so the earth swallows these two viz, a king who does not fight (an invader) and a *Brahmin* who does not go on a journey for acquiring knowledge from famous teachers", p.57, King's duty to restrain *brahmanas* from engaging in unworthy acts is specially emphasised.
Mahabharata, Udyog Parva (H.D. vol.III, chap.V, p.170) "Man should always press forward (make efforts) should never bend; striving is manliness; one may even break at a point which is not the joint, but should never bend".
24. ibid., vol.II, pt.1, chap.III, p.133.
25. ibid., vol.III, chap.IV, p.106, 107.
26. ibid., vol.III, chap.II, p.38.
    ibid., vol.V, pt.2, chap.XXXV, sec.X, p.1639.
27. ibid., vol.II, pt.1, chap.II.
    ibid., vol.V, pt.2, chap.XXXV, sec.X, p.1641, 1642.
28. ibid., vol.V, pt.2, chap.XXIV, sec.V.
    ibid., vol.V, pt.2, chap.XXXV, sec.X, p.1641, 1642.
29. ibid., vol.V, pt.2, chap.XXXVI, sec.X, p.1621, 1622.
30. ibid., vol.IV, chap.VIII.
31. ibid., vol.IV, chap.VIII.
32. ibid., vol.II, pt.1, chap.IV.
33. ibid., vol.II, pt.1, chap.III, p.108, 10.
34. ibid., vol.II, pt.1, chap.III, p.142, 143.
35. ibid., vol.II, pt.1, chap.III, p.146.
36. ibid., vol.II, pt.1, chap.III.
37. ibid., vol.II, pt.1, chap.III.
38. ibid., vol.II, pt.1, chap.II, p.19, 20, 21, 22.
39. *The Teaching of the Gita* by M.K. Gandhi, edited & published by Anand T. Hingorani (Bharatiya Vidya Bhavan) p.87.
40. *Poverty and un-British Rule in British India* by Dadabhai Naoroji.

14

The Six Philosophical Systems

The etymological meaning of the word 'philosophy' is love of learning. There is a natural desire and urge in human beings to know and understand the world they live in and their own place in it. Obviously only the balanced and rational intellect can acquire any worthwhile knowledge. The choice, as Aldous Huxley observes, is not between metaphysics and no metaphysics but between good metaphysics and bad metaphysics.

There are six systems of philosophy which form a part of Smriti literature of the Hindus. They contribute to man's knowledge of the universe. We find nature identified as matter with its properties acting in various combinations, creating the whole manifest universe. The evolutionary as well as cyclical movement in nature is observed and inferred. The structure of matter is also studied, and the theory of atomism developed. Nature by itself is incapable of intelligence and is stimulated into creation by the Spirit. This all-pervading unmanifest Spirit exists in manifest creation. It is the Soul of the universe and present in all forms in creation. This Soul is the Reality. While all matter perishes, the Soul alone is imperishable. This Reality or Soul is the source of all knowledge and hence deserving of all enquiry. This Reality is Truth. Truth alone is the true value of the universe.

The Spirit is the source, the sustainer, and into which all nature dissolves. The cause is present in the effect, and so the soul is present in nature. Nature must be studied but the Soul must be realised, because the former is dependent on the latter. The Soul is the guiding principle of nature and also of man. Knowledge of the Soul, the highest knowledge, invests all actions with value.

In India, the philosophical systems are called *darsanas*. 'See the Self' is the keynote of all schools of Indian philosophy. *Darsana* means both 'vision' and also 'instrument of truth'. They are more than a mere intellectual enquiry into truth. These philosophies are also religious sects because they emphasize the practical realisation of Truth.

Philosophy however was not restricted only to the religious. It was recognized as a need for all people in every class of life. This philosophy which seeks to make man realise his own true Self and his own true worth, advises him to throw away the crutches of dependence. This message reached society at many levels of intellectual disparity in a way possible for them to comprehend. This was conveyed through literature; art, song and drama, and by the saints who lived among the people and practised what they preached.

The importance of philosophy was acknowledged by the sharpest intellects in India. Kautilya, known for his *Arthasastra*, as well as numerous other works on a variety of subjects, considered philosophy as the foundation of all other sciences 'for it sharpens the mind, and makes it fit for thinking, speaking and acting properly in all conditions of life both in adversity and in good luck.

It can hardly be ignored that in India men of religion well-versed in their philosophies have contributed, as no other group has, to every branch of human knowledge, secular or religious. This is equally true of the Jains and the

Buddhists. We must conclude that philosophy gave them the foundation, the intellectual clarity, commitment and devotion to their enquiry in the spirit of truth, which alone can serve the goals of any enquiry. The Jains and Buddhists were considered as heterodox only because they did not acknowledge the authority of the Vedas and Smritis. There are many common beliefs among all the philosophical systems in India. While some are theistic and others not, the one doctrine not disputed and which is accepted by every (except Charvaka's) philosophical system in India, including the Jains and Buddhists, is the doctrine of *Karma* and *Punarjanma*. *Karma* is action, and this doctrine states that man's future birth is dictated by his actions in this life according to the Law of *Karma* that prevails as the Law of Cause and Effect in the universe. The physical law is carried to the moral sphere as well. It is significant that while a Hindu may deny God, he may not deny the moral law.

The philosophy of materialism existed in ancient times as well. The founder of this system is acknowledged as Brihaspati though the system is identified by giving it the name of the best-known exponent of this system, Charvaka. They were also known as *lokayatikas*. Not much is known of their thoughts today. They did not believe in the existence of the soul, nor in a moral code. They were however unable to build a connected system of thought because while they acknowledged perception they did not acknowledge inference. While the *Lokayatikas* must no doubt have served as a corrective counter-balance to excessive religiosity and hypocrisy, materialism has within itself the seeds of superficial thinking and hypocrisy, since all the material itself is 'image'. It is not surprising therefore that they invited the scorn of every other philosophy.

The six orthodox philosophical systems are usually

clubbed together in pairs as they share common themes. The *Poorva* and *Uttar Mimamsa* deal with the underlying philosophies of the *Karma Kanda* and *Jnana Kanda* of the Vedas. The *Sankhya* and 'Yoga' deal with the theoretical aspect and the practical achievement of discrimination between Spirit and matter. The *Vaisheshikha* and *Nyaya* elaborate on the structure of matter involving the smallest particle called *Paramanu*, and evolve a system of logical reasoning.

Of all the philosophies the *Uttar Mimamsa*, the philosophy of the Vedanta based on the *Upanishads*, is acknowledgedly the most perfect. It resolves the lacunae in the other systems.

The philosophical systems accepted that freedom from pain is a desire of all. Pain is inherent in nature. There are three kinds of pain. Bodily pain comes from sicknesses of the body, emotions and mind. Pain is caused by external factors as well, i.e. animals etc.; while the third kind of pain comes from elemental and supernatural forces. Freedom from pain also results in supreme happiness. This is achieved through *shravana* (hearing the truth), *manana* (reflection and intellectual conviction after critical analysis) and *nidhidhyasan* (practical realisation).

The Vedanta accepts Brahma as the only Reality. Brahma is Being (Existence). The manifest universe is created from Brahma, and as such is Brahma. Created universe is bound by time, space and causation. It is the world of form, which is in constant motion. The essence of this world of form is the formless. This is unmanifest and beyond time, space and causation. It is eternal, all-pervading and motionless. The world of form is merely the outward expression of the essence (Spirit). Brahma bursts forth spontaneously as both nature and soul. Brahma and nature are the "Being and the becoming" of Vedantic thought. Brahma, unmanifest and beyond nature is the Eternal Witness. Problems of morality in life normally arise because of the pulls between the negation of form and the assertion of form. Universality can come only by the sacrifice of personality.

Individuals renounced worldly life, family and friends and worldly transactions in order to become one with the Universal. On the other hand the demand of the world is for productivity. Mankind has to survive, civilization has to survive; *artha* (economic needs) and *kama* (vital and cultural needs) are necessary in the world.

Vedanta points out that nothing can escape action in this world. Action is necessary for all. What helps creation is the Moral act. The unselfish act is the moral act. All form is an expression of the spirit. Spirit acts through form. Those who act with their thoughts centred on the spirit within, achieve liberation. If a person's inclination is towards a life of seclusion and meditation then he should certainly engage himself in the same. The *sanyasi*'s life is not one of laziness. It is an active life. He has to discipline himself physically, emotionally and intellectually. His selflessness helps creation. It is interesting to note that Shankaracharya the great *Advaita* philosopher was active in every way and few have managed to achieve what he did when he died at the early age of 32.

Those who accept the worldly life have to go by worldly conduct. They have to serve the community by doing their duty. Moral commitment is necessary in worldly affairs as well. They must therefore also understand their duties in life. This involves duty to family, community, country and world. By bearing their burdens honestly in life they also are helping all creation.

Vedanta shows that creation, the active world of form, is dependent on the uncreated inactive formless. It is Brahma, the value, that gives meaning, relevance and glory to all creation. Brahma is eternal and everpresent. Brahma is knowledge.

Brahma is Reality. Brahma is Truth. The *Atma* (soul) is Brahma. Thus Truth is a value present in all. The one who truly realises it becomes Brahma. The Vedantic view is that parts (the material world) are dependent on the whole (the Spirit). While the parts are transitory, the Whole is Eternal. Man is not only the physical, emotional and intellectual but also the spiritual. What is good for the spirit is good for the whole man. This is so for the universe as well.

False values come from worship of the material. This, according to Vedanta, is image-worship. Those who believe in the reality of the material are image-worshippers.

It is worth clarifying here, the wrong interpretations made of the world being an 'illusion'. The Shankaracharya emphasises that from the phenomenal point of view the world is real. It is not an illusion but a practical reality. But when man acquires true knowledge and understands the transitoriness of the material then he sees it as the illusion it is.

The whole world is Brahma. It is there only because of Brahma. We do not recognize it for Brahma because nature intervenes. We see what is really a rope as a snake because of the illusion created in our own minds.

We need to understand nature itself that creates these illusions in our minds and binds us. Once these illusions are removed by understanding nature then we become free, or rather, realise that we are not bound at all but have always been free. This freedom comes, through knowledge. When we understand nature and the relationship of nature with Brahma then we learn to use nature wisely and well. Nature by itself is neither 'good' nor 'bad'. Hence the understanding of nature is essential and also it's relationship to the Eternal Reality or Truth.

It is understanding of the relationship between action and knowledge.

It is because of this that we find that no aspect of man's knowledge was neglected. Among all forms in nature man is the most highly evolved. While he shares his lower and baser nature with the animals where the mind serves as instinct or a reflexive action, man also has an intellect by which he can discriminate and decide. This is meant to enable him to be more rational. It also gives him the power to choose.

Nature consists of the three *gunas* (properties) *sattwa*, *rajas* and *tamas*. *Tamas* is inertia and associated with denseness and heaviness. *Rajas* is activity while *sattwa* is harmony and associated with lightness and buoyancy. Brahma is the Principle of Pure Intelligence that guides all nature. Nature by itself is unintelligent.

Man is capable, by striving to overcome his lower nature and attaining his higher nature (*sattwa*), of attaining the highest state of non-duality, the State of Existence, Knowledge and Bliss Absolute.

Brahma, the highest goal is beyond all attributes and can only be described as *Neti, Neti* (not this, not this). Brahma the Infinite, cannot be identified with anything in finite creation.

From *sat* or pure Being, evolves truth or moral integrity, *satya*. This lends value to all activities in life, and man reaches his highest state of creativity.

Patanjali describes the grammarian as a *yogi* whose inward vision enables him to look within and see the eternal flow of pure consciousness. This consciousness manifests as sound and meaning which we call speech, the instrument of communication and which is nothing but the spirit active within. To Patanjali the alphabets are not just a phonetic type but the sparks of Brahma lighting all existence.[1]

All form can only be understood by understanding the Spirit. The word or letter by itself has no meaning unless we understand the spirit it seeks to express.

An adherence to form alone to the exclusion of the spirit results in rigidity in thought and defeats the very purpose of form. The commitment to form may lead to superstitious beliefs or false conceits. Intellectual debates will consist in assertion of form, all quoting from one authority or another, to the exclusion of the spirit.

It needs a deeper perception and honesty to understand the spirit within. It is hardly surprising that all great religious teachers have had to question the interpretations of texts by the learned priests, because while they have been aware of the form, they have overlooked the true meaning. This is equally true of ideologies. It is evident in other spheres as well. Scientists have also had to face severe condemnation from their own scientific community who felt the 'authorities' they had been brought up on, were being questioned. The Vedanta helps us to understand why this takes place. It also gives the strength to stand up for what we believe to be right.

The Vedanta has influenced many schools of thought in the world. There is a strong body of opinion that Pythagoras derived some of his ideas from India. Pythagoras, Plato and Empedocles believed in the pre- and post-existence of the soul. Upanishadic ideas also seem to have influenced Persian Sufism, the Neo-Platonists the Alexandrian Christians and the doctrines of Eckhart. Hindu philosophy influenced the thoughts of Kant, Schopenhaur and Fitche. These philosophers in turn influenced Carlyle and Ruskin. Thoreau, the source of the new thought of modern America, in his *Walden Letters*, refers frequently to Vedanta. Emerson was influenced by Thoreau. When Emerson was seen off in England by

Carlyle the latter presented him with a copy of the *Bhagwad Gita* by Edwin Jones.[2]

Knowledge has to do not only with those who contribute, but those with the discrimination to appreciate. A civilized society needs both.

Some of the opinions of the modern day western authors on the Vedanta are worth repeating because by understanding and appreciating this philosophy they bring credit to themselves.

Schopenhaur in his book *World is Will and Idea* says, "In the whole world there is no religion or philosophy so sublime, so elevating, as the Vedanta (*Upanishads*). The Vedanta has been the solace of my life and it will be the solace of my death."

The French historian of philosophy Victor Cousin says. 'There can be no denying that the ancient Hindus possessed the knowledge of the true god. Their philosophy, their thought is so sublime, so elevating, so accurate and true, that any comparison with the writings of the Europeans appears like a Promethean fire stolen from heaven in the presence of the full glow of the noon-day sun" And again he says, "When we read with attention the poetical and philosophical monuments of the east, above all, those of India which are beginning to spread in Europe, we discover there many a truth and truths so profound and which make such a contrast with the meanness of the result at which the European genius has sometimes stopped that we are constrained to bend the knee before the philosophy of the east, and to see in this cradle of human race the native land of the highest philosophy."

Schlegel says that in comparison with Hindu thought, the highest stretches of human philosophy appear like dwarfish pygmies in the presence of grand majestic titan. In his works on Indian language, literature and philosophy he says, "It cannot be denied that the early Indians possessed a knowledge of the true God; all their writings are replete with sentiments and expressions, noble, clear and severely grand, as deeply conceived and reverentially expressed as in any human language in which men have spoken of God." Speaking of the Vedanta he says, "The divine origin of man is continuously inculcated to stimulate his effort to return, to animate him in the struggle and incite him to consider a re-union and re-corporation with Divinity as the one primary object of every action and exertion."[3]

Hindu influence and Hindu thought reached South-east Asia up to east Borneo. The *Ramayana* and *Mahabharata* express Hindu philosophy but many other works, both secular and religious travelled to South-east Asia.[4]

The Vedanta does not deny form. It explains how form is invested with the spirit. The world of form is order out of chaos. It is created by a process of evolution, beginning with desire and graduating to need, function and organ successively.

So long as we recognize the form as dependent on the Spirit we make the form worthwhile and purposeful. When we treat form as an end in itself we distort the form through our own ignorance. Man's life was divided into different stages to enable him to develop fully in accordance with the four aims of man, *dharma*, *artha*, *kama* and *moksa*; and the orders of caste were forms constructed to benefit man and society. The professions were based on the needs and functions required by a civilized society. They were based on duty and not privilege.

Similarly all the rites and ceremonies were intended to

keep man active mentally, emotionally and physically. It was meant to discipline as well as purify. Thus the philosophy was sought to be practically applied.

Rationalism and authority are both aids to our knowledge and understanding. But the understanding of Truth requires a purity of mind which can only come through one's own efforts. This is what Hindu philosophy points out. Whenever the Hindus have understood their teachings well, they have contributed to every field of human activity that few have surpassed. Whenever they have not understood the teachings and have relied on the form (material alone) they have descended to ignorance and superstition.

One hopes the time never comes that Hindus stop even appreciating and trying to understand the sublime teachings of the great Ancients. They will then have wilfully and unthinkingly lost their most precious possession.

POORVA MIMAMSA

Hindu philosophical thought can be traced to the Vedas. Although gods are mentioned in the *Samhitas* and *Brahmanas* (the *Karma Kanda*) there is an awareness of the Eternal One.

"The One Real, the wise declare as many." (*Rig Veda* I.164-46) "*Purusha* is all this, all that was, and all that shall be." (*Rig Veda* X.90)

"He is the Custodian of *Rta* (Truth), the binding Soul of the universe the unity-in-difference in the cosmic and the moral order." (*Rig Veda* 190.1)

"Desireless, self-possessed, immortal, self-proved, ever full of Bliss, inferior to none, ever young and everlasting is He, the Soul of this universe; through His Knowledge alone can one spurn death." (*Atharva Veda* X.8.44)

The *Karma Kanda* was associated with the rites of sacrifice, as it was a period when action and performance, both were necessary. But faith must inspire all actions because faith alone gives sincerity to all actions. 'Brahman' meant prayer.

The word *mimamsa* is of great antiquity. It means discussion, investigation and consideration. 'Man' means desire to know, which involves investigation and final conclusion. Long before the *Upanishads*, *mimamsa* had come to mean 'investigation into a topic of discussion and coming to a conclusion thereon.'

The same word acquired a restricted sense to mean investigation into *dharma* and arriving at conclusions on doubtful matters by interpretation and reasoning.[5]

There are four indispensable elements to every *sastra* (discipline): *Visaya, Prayojana, Sambhandha* and *Adhikarin* which mean the subject to be treated, the purpose or object, the relation of the discipline to the purpose, and the person entitled to or competent to study the *sastra*. *Slakavartika* remarks that so long as the purpose of the *sastra* is not declared, it will not merit study.

The *Poorva (Purva) Mimamsa Sutra* is the most extensive of the *darsanas*. It contains 2700 Sutras and over 900 *Adhikaranas*. The massive size of the *Poorva Mimamsa* is due to it being overlaid by commentaries upon commentaries.

Jaimini is recognized as the author of *Poorva Mimamsa*. (Incidentally Jaimini, Badari and Badarayana are *gotra* names).

The *Poorva Mimamsa* is the recognized authority on the *Karma Kanda*. Jaimini holds that except for *Sabda* (i.e. The *Veda*) there is no means of knowledge about *dharma*. It is not possible to perceive directly what *dharma* is. All other disciplines except *Sabda* are based on the perceivable and they cannot define or explain what *dharma* is.

Some of the fundamental doctrines of the *Poorva Mimamsa* are:

(a)   The *Veda* is eternal, self-existent, not composed by any author, human or divine, and is infallible.

(b)   The connection between word and sense is eternal.

(c)   Although there is no reference to individual soul in any sutra, there is an implicit acceptance of it. The reward for Vedic rites was *Swarga* (Heaven), and this reward went to the performer of this rite.

(d)   The offering was considered as more important than the gods.

(e)   It held that there is no real creation and dissolution of the World. The world as a whole has no beginning and no end, even though some of its parts may come and go. The description of creation and dissolution was only to demonstrate the futile vanity of human effort before the power of destiny, and to encourage men to perform the duties recommended by the *Veda*. The world is eternal and whatever takes place is not due to human effort.

(f)   It upholds the Doctrine of *Apurva*. The various acts of sacrifice create a potency and capacity for *Swarga*. It was the creation of this capacity that differentiated between doing and not doing. This potency or capacity resides in the performer or arises from the act of sacrifice and is called *Apurva*.

(g)   *Snatah-pramanya* (six)

The ideas of heaven as given by Jaimini, Sabara or Kumarilla are different from the Vedas and Puranas. *Swarga* was to be enjoyed in another life. The views on *moksa* (liberation) are dealt with only by Kumarilla and Prakaranepanika who say that liberation is not having to assume a body again. Neither the *Poorva Mimamsa Sutra*, nor Sabara nor Prabhakar dealt with it. The doctrines of the early and principal writers of *Poorva Mimamsa*, their arguments about the eternity and self-existence of the Vedas were fallacious and were not accepted even by the other systems.[6]

UTTAR MIMAMSA (VEDANTA)

Just as the underlying philosophy of the *Karma Kanda* is dealt with in the *Poorva Mimamsa*, the *Uttar Mimamsa* explains the philosophy of the *Jnana Kanda*. The *Jnana Kanda* (*Upanishads*) are called the Vedanta, the end and culmination of the Vedas.

The *Vedanta Sutra*, also known as *Brahma Sutra*, explain the philosophy of the *Upanishads*. The *Vedanta Sutra* is attributed to Badarayanacharya. As a philosophical system it evolved after the other systems, which enabled it to resolve the difficulties in the earlier systems. There are many *Upanishads*. Some are attached to the Vedas while others are independent works. They also span an extensive period of time. It was necessary to give a connected and systematic explanation of the philosophy. This has been done in the *Vedanta Sutra*.

The Vedanta, while investigating, and rejecting or accepting the various theories regarding the creative process, concerns itself with Brahma, the source of all manifest creation, and leads the individual on to the knowledge of this soul within himself. Step by step it shows, by using reason, where reason itself fails due to its own inherent incapacity. It shows how, by purity and peace of mind, the soul can be intuitively perceived. In this field, the field of *adhyatma*, the Vedanta excels. Here, 'the lion of the Vedanta brooks no rivals.' There are many schools of Vedanta, but the universally accepted is that of Shankaracharya who preached *Advaita* Vedanta. *Advaita* means one without a second. *Advaita* is monistic. All manifest creation is from the one unmanifest. This is Brahma, the Soul of the universe. It is all-pervading. The soul in man and in all else, is Brahma.

Three sentences may sum up the philosophy of *Advaita* Vedanta.

Brahma is real
Jagat (nature) is false
Atma is Brahma

Vedanta examines step by step the various 'layers' in man. It examines the three states of consciousness and establishes that the soul is beyond these three states. It shows how, when the individual consciousness merges into the general consciousness alone the realization of "I am Brahma" comes.

There are seven steps which lead to self-realization. First step is to aspire. The next stage is of enquiry, hearing and reflecting. The third stage is meditation. The fourth stage is when the mind is illumined by *sattwa* the higher nature, which prepares the mind for self-realization. The fifth stage is removal of ego or "my" ness. The sixth stage is when all things do not appear as separate objects. The seventh and last stage is beyond the world of duality and multiplicity. This Oneness is Supreme Bliss. This corresponds to the fourth psychological state of *Turiya*.

The three levels of consciousness are called the Waking state, the Dream state, the Deep Sleep state and the fourth and the highest state of *Turiya*.

The waking state is at a subconscious level. Man is ruled by the subconscious and does things by instinct or as a reflex action. This sub-conscious state is also found in animals.

The Dream state is unconscious. Here man is controlled by racial memory. It is a higher state than the former but still within the world of duality. Where the earlier subjective fear for self is not so pronounced, here the fear will be for race or community. It can illuminate and inspire to sacrifice. It can be stirred by religious gatherings or historical personages etc. However, it still reacts and though higher than the former, is still within worldly dualities.

The third is the Deep Sleep state. Here man comes to the threshold of the final state. Here, he observes, but does not judge. He is free of past and present. He is at peace. This opens the door to the fourth and final state of *Turiya* where man becomes one with the Infinite.

The evolutionary process begins with ether and successively, generation of air, fire, water and earth. Each has its own properties as well as the property of the former element. The subtle properties of each are generated before the heavy element.

The doctrine of the five sheaths also shows the evolutionary process of creation. The lowest level is of matter, called the *Annamaya*. The next stage is the development of the organic from the inorganic. Life enters. This stage is *Pranamaya*. This corresponds with vegetable matter. The next to evolve is the mind, *Manomaya*. This is shared by man with the animals. It is ruled by instinct rather than rational thought. The next higher state is the self-conscious or rational state. This is the intellectual state called *Vijnanamaya*. This distinguishes man from the lower animals. This is the metaphysical plane, but still a prey to worldly dualities. The state of non-duality is achieved only at the fifth plane called *Anandamaya*. This is Bliss Absolute where all is one. Here the Spirit is one.

The Vedanta accepts many of the theories of *Sankhya*, but where *Sankhya* recognizes the Spirit as separate from nature (*Prakriti*), Vedanta recognizes only one, the Spirit from which all things arise. Nature (*Prakriti*) is inherent in the Spirit.

Again whereas *Sankhya* says that in its primary state *Prakriti* (Nature) is one and homogenous, the spirit remains as innumerable individual souls, Vedanta disagrees. Vedanta points out that it makes no sense to say that while *Prakriti* can resolve to a homogenous state, the spirit cannot do the same. Again, what separates the innumerable spirits? The Vedanta answers this poser, Vedanta says that the spirit Is. Reality is the Spirit. The world (*Prakriti*) issues from the spirit and resolves back into it. The world is unreal because it evolves and resolves back.

The individual souls (the *Purusas*) of *Sankhya* become the *Jiva* of Vedanta; the *Prakriti* of *Sankhya* becomes the *Jagat* of Vedanta while the *Purusa* of *Sankhya* is elevated into the Brahma of Vedanta. Vedanta says that it is *Maya*, the world process, that generates the illusion that the world is reality. It is only a superimposition. Reality is the substratum Brahma.

There are other schools of Vedanta. While they differ with each other on the relationship of Nature, individual soul and Universal Soul (Spirit), they all share the Vedantic view of all issuing from the One Brahma.

These schools are the *Visishtadvaita* (qualified monism) of Ramanujacharya (AD 11th century), *Dvaitadvaita* (Dual-non-dual) of Nimbarka (AD 12th century), 'Madhva' (13th century) who broke from monism, considering God, soul and world as separate entities and Vallabha (15th century) whose system was claimed as pure monism.

Some stressed on the devotional aspect, others on the knowledge aspect while still others on the meditational. All sects have quoted from the *Bhagavad Gita* to suit their persuasions. There can be no doubt that each fulfilled a need of the people of their time.

Just as we have pure mathematics and applied mathematics, Vedanta also has a practical Vedanta.

Practical Vedanta instils optimism. It shows how the

Vedantic ideals can be followed in life. It points out how "Work is rest". Just as all manifest universe is in constant motion while the soul is motionless and at rest, so must we be, the body subject to the law of dynamics and the self always at statistical rest. Work should be performed for its own sake. This means that the means and the ends must be brought together. It is selfishness that spoils work. This kind of work is not restful but restless. We achieve true performance when we renounce ego and small-mindedness. When we rise above selfish considerations with our self at peace then we do not feel a work as hard. An example is that of an oil lamp. If it tries to spare it's wick it will remain dark and be a failure. By denying its ego and not sparing its wick and oil, the light shines brightly. So must, the Vedanta teaches, the body and muscles be cremated in the fire of use.

Unselfish sacrifice is the foundation of all morality. We corrupt our work when we do it with a selfish motive. It is like a selfish pond advising the river not to waste its water on the ocean. The river says happily, "I must work because I love to work for its own sake. To work is my aim, to keep in activity is my life, my soul is energy itself, I must work." Pouring its water into the ocean the river stays fresh. Silently the water from the surface of the ocean gets taken up and keeps on replenishing the river. The monsoon and trade winds bring fresh water back to the river. The selfish pond however, wishing to keep whatever it has to itself, becomes dry, stagnant and full of festering filth.

Love comes with the realisation of the One in all. This love shines on all. There is no selective attachment and favouritism in such love. We love all things because of the Self. Discord arises when we go against this essential truth.

Cheerfulness is an essential quality of the true Vedantin. Those who rest in the one Self are above the dualities in matter. They are above pleasure and pain. Not identifying themselves with the body or ego, they do not suffer or feel the pangs of mental or bodily pain. Just as it would be foolish for an actor to mistake a character in a play and think it as real, so it is foolish for us to mistake the wordly phenomena for reality. So long as we keep running after the shadow, it will keep on eluding us. But when we stop doing so, turn our back on it and face the sun instead, the shadow will run after us. Similarly so long as we run after the material it will elude us. When we concentrate on the light within us the material follows by itself.

Fearlessness comes from faith in the One. Dread comes to those who believe in the many. When we rise above the body, self and have faith in the One Self we are free from fear. Vedanta and fearlessness are inseparable.

Self-reliance comes with faith in the inner Self. Self-trust is a fundamental principle of Bliss. As we think so we become. A living faith in Truth and the right knowledge of things around shows everything in its true worth. When the Spirit is realised to such a degree then the world becomes unreal, this earth, name, fame, popularity or unpopularity, worldly honour or disgrace, criticism or flattery, relations, all become meaningless. The saving principle is not material. This subtle principle, Truth, is very fine. This is worth more than any material object.

The pure person is the successful person. What a man thinks so he becomes. The law of *Karma* retaliates and baffles when it is abused and misused for selfish ends. Let the intellect rest in the Self. Let not the thought of doing good to humanity worry you. The world is not so poor as to be begging for your attention. Cast out desire. Banish all worldly motives from work. Work minus desire is the highest worship. Do the work nearest to your hand. There is no high work and no low work. It is no self-respect to shun that not sanctioned by fashion. True self-respect is respect for the real Self. Body respect is the opposite pole of virtue. All bondage is of the mind. The real Self is free. Fear belongs to the body-self and not the real Self. No sword can cut unless you think it cuts.[7]

Vedanta does not subscribe to blind faith. This faith has to be a conviction that comes from knowledge. Blind faith is superstition born out of ignorance. Faith in the Unmanifest is not blind faith. The Vedanta is against ignorance and superstition of any kind. Belief in the material alone as the reality results in ignorance and superstitions. Truth is beyond the material. But the material depends on Truth.

SANKHYA PHILOSOPHY

Sankhya in Sanskrit means 'right knowledge' as well as 'numbers'. The founder of the *Sankhya* philosophy was Kapila who lived before the Buddha. Many of the *Sankhya* thoughts also correspond with some of the major *Upanishads*. Buddha too, seems to have accepted many *Sankhya* doctrines. *Sankhya* discriminates between spirit (*Purusa*) and matter (*prakriti*). It holds that *Prakriti* evolves because of the *Purusa* and for the *Purusa* without the *Purusa* being involved or affected by the process. It holds that liberation can be achieved when *Prakriti* realises and discriminates between nature (matter) and spirit (*Purusa*). When this happens *Prakriti* stops evolving around the individual *Purusa*. *Sankhya* thus puts the effort for securing liberation on *prakriti*. Because of the view that the individual must seek his own salvation through his own efforts by discrimination between soul and matter, *Sankhya* is also associated with renunciation and asceticism.

Sankhya propounds an evolutionary process of creation which adds up to twenty-five. *Asura* and Pancha-sikha were two pupils of Kapila who are also well known. Panchasikha's work was called *Sastitantra* because it expounded on sixty topics.[8]

It would not be incorrect to say that what Darwin and Lamarck did for the world in the nineteenth century was done by Kapila for his and the succeeding centuries.

Kapila's contribution has been recognized and rich tributes paid. In the *Gita*, Sri Krishna says, "Of the *Siddhas*, I am Kapilamuni". Bhishma (*Shanti*, 301-309) observes that *Sankhya* findings regarding the universe have been repeated in the Puranas, History, diplomacy (*Arthasastra*) etc. and in fact 'all the world's knowledge is derived from *Sankhya*'.

Sankhya exerted great influence in its day. The Puranas dissert on *Sankhya* doctrines. Great poets like Bana and Kalidasa were fond of using *Sankhya* doctrines and terminologies. Even Tantra was influenced by *Sankhya*.[9] In AD 540 *Sankhya* was translated into Chinese and Chinese sources say that at one time there were eighteen schools of *Sankhya*.[10]

There is also the view expressed by scholars that the *Sankhya* philosophy of numbers influenced Pythagoras.[11]

Sankhya was the first to systematically work out the evolutionary nature of manifestation from the subtlest to the gross.

Sankhya believes that the effect pre-exists in the material cause. This is known as *satkaryavad*. That which pre-exists is *sat* and *karya* is effect. *Purusa* is the principle of pure consciousness. It is the soul, self, spirit, subject, knower, while the body senses, mind, ego and intellect all belong to *prakriti* (nature or matter).

While the *Purusa* is detached and actionless it is *Prakriti* that creates. Since it is *prakriti* that binds the *Purusa* it is *prakriti* alone that can set free the *Purusa*.

The *Sankhya*'s evolutionary table can be describes as "The Primeval matter (*prakriti*) was at first homogenous. It resolved (*buddhi*) to unfold itself, and by the principle of differentiation (*ahamkara*) became heterogenous. It then branched off into two sections, one organic (*Sendriya*) and the other inorganic (*Maindriya*). There are eleven of the organic and five of inorganic creation. From the five subtle elements (*Tanmatras*) of sound, touch, form, tastes, and smell come the five gross or heavy elements (*Mahabhutas*) of ether, air, fire, water and earth."

***Sankhya* Table of Creation**

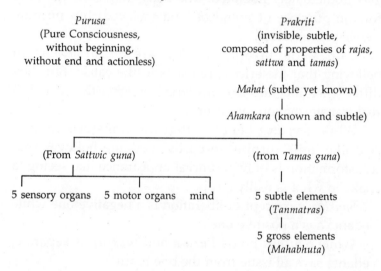

All together add up to twenty-five. Just as evolution takes place so does dissolution. The earth loses its property of smell and dissolves to water. Water loses the property of taste and becomes fire, fire loses its properties of heat and light and dissolves into air which loses its property of touch relapsing into ether. The property of sound belongs to ether which losing this property dissolves into *ahamkara* which in turn dissolves into *buddhi* and finally into *prakriti*, which in its primary state is homogenous.

According to *Sankhya*, freedom and liberation are the complete cessation from all suffering. This is the highest end in life. *Purusa* is pure and always liberated. It is *prakriti*'s ignorance in identifying *prakriti* with *Purusa* that results in the feeling of bondage. Bondage is therefore due to ignorance and non-discrimination. *Karmas* good or bad, lead to bondage and not liberation. Right knowledge by discriminating between spirit and matter, leads to liberation. The moment right knowledge dawns the person gets immediately liberated. The body may continue only for the purpose of *prarabdha* (past *karmas*) but no new *Karmas* accumulate.

Both Vedanta and *Sankhya* are *Satkaryavadis* in believing that the effect pre-exists in the cause. But they differ when it comes to considering whether the effect is a real transformation, or an unreal one.

While *Sankhya* believes that the transformation is real like 'milk turning to curds' Vedanta believes that transformation is only an unreal appearance like seeing 'a snake in what is really a rope'.

Sankhya's concept of liberation is a negative one while Vedanta's is a positive one.

While *Sankhya* holds *Purusa* and *prakriti* as separate, Vedanta says all issue from the one Spirit.

Vedanta and *Sankhya* agree, apart from these differences. Vedanta picks up the thread of creation where *Sankhya* leaves off. But *Sankhya* made a great contribution to scientific thinking in its day. The assertion in *Santiparva* that "Whatever knowledge is found in the Vedas, in Sankhya Yoga, in the various Puranas, in the extensive Itihasas, in the *Arthasastra* and whatever knowledge exists in the world, all that is derived from *Sankhya*"[13] was not an exaggeration.

PATANJALI YOGA

The Patanjali Yoga system seeks to put into practical application the philosophy of *Sankhya*. The aim of this discipline is to discriminate between spirit and matter and by this realise the true Self.

"Yoga" is used to mean different things. The word Yoga is derived from the root *Yug* to unite. Yoga means union. It also means to yolk. It is also used to mean skill, the best way, or best method. It is used in each of these senses in the *Bhagavad Gita* and other works.

In Patanjali Yoga, the word is used to mean the effort or the endeavour to attain.[14]

However, Patanjali was not the first propounder of Yoga. This practice dates back to the most ancient times.

Patanjali probably systematised and improved on previous practices. Patanjali Yoga is sometimes referred to as theistic Yoga, as *Om* was used by Patanjali for the purpose of concentration.[15]

Patanjali's *Yoga Sutra* is brief, comprising 195 *sutras* divided into four parts. The first part deals with *Samadhi* (Concentration), the second deals with *Sadhana* (the means of attaining God), the third *Vibhuti*, describes the supra-normal powers acquired through Yoga, while the last part, *Kaivalya*, describes the reality of liberation.

Patanjali Yoga is also referred to as *Raja Yoga* (Royal Path). It stresses on individual effort and prescribes a vigorous discipline for realisation of God. Yoga believes in God as the highest Self. With a firm belief in *Karma* and re-birth, it emphasises chastity in thought, word and deed. The *Yogasutra* doctrine is that by a scientific control of *Prana* (vital energy), whose most perceptible movement in the body is the movement of the lungs, it is possible to obtain control of the deep-seated (and ordinarily imperceptible) force in human consciousness as well as in the external world. Yoga stresses meditation, self-discipline and control of the mind. The aim is to attain *Samadhi* where the knower and the known become one. The mind is no longer a separate entity. It enters the noumena, liberated from all phenomena.

There are eight steps in Yoga. These are *Yama, Niyama, Asana Pranayama, Pratihara, Dharana, Dhyana* and *Samadhi.*

Yama is the controller of desire, adoption of celibacy and non-violence, and the giving up of all selfish desires.

Niyama is the observance of certain rules dealing with study, piety, and cleanliness.

Asana is the best posture for meditation.

Pranayama is to promote rhythmic breathing to keep the vital functions working while the mind begins its ascent. *Pratyahara* is for controlling the senses and their withdrawal from sense objects, thus insulating the mind from restless external stimulation. *Dharana* fixes the mind steadily on an object. *Dhyana* is the next step. It means meditation, an intense concentration into one's very being. In due course the mind begins to enter into the object of thought.

Samadhi is the final stage

Patanjali is the traditional founder of this Yoga system. It is not explicitly clear but also not improbable, that the grammarian Patanjali and the Patanjali of the *Yogasutra* are one and the same. The grammarian Patanjali states that "The taints that affect the body, speech and intellect are purified by the sciences of medicine, grammar and metaphysics."[16]

It will not be out of place here to give a brief outline of Yoga, a practical method of Self-realisation.

Yoga as a discipline may broadly be divided into three stages. In the Vedic age we find references to *munis* practising *tapas*, not caring for the world and seeking to merge themselves into the Infinite. The *Upanishads* use the word *yati* to describe one who has detached himself from worldly affairs, practises Yoga and is the seeker and realiser of Brahma. "The wise man reflecting on God by means of Yoga, by concentrating the mind on the Inner Spirit becomes free from joy and grief."

The Yoga practised during this period consisted mostly of *Pranayama*. We are given the name of Sanatkumara as the founder of Yoga and Hiranyagarbha is mentioned as the propounder of the *Yoga Samhitas*.

Patanjali Yoga is a further development on the earlier *Yogic* practices. There is often a confusion between *Hatha Yoga* and *Raja Yoga*. But they are not contradictory. *Hatha yogis* claim that they lead to Raja Yoga. They aim to preserve a healthy body, the attainment of *siddhis* and are the path to *Raja Yoga* and ultimate *Kaivalya*. The numerous *asanas* provided in *Hatha* Yoga are neither recommended nor considered necessary in Raja Yoga.

The third and later development in Yoga was that of *Tantra*. *Tantra* is a Sanskrit word derived from *tan* to expand. It is meant to be a systematic and scientific effort, expand man's consciousness and thus attain Self-realisation. It expands from the individual consciousness (which is limited) to the unlimited Universal Consciousness. Meditation seems to have been practised from the earliest times in India. Yoga is an integral part of Vedanta as well. *Yajnavalkya Smriti* says that the realisation of the Self is the highest *dharma*."'

Of the *yogi*, Jaijisavya observes: "*Yogins* do not talk much by way of censure or praise of others, and their minds are never affected by the praise or censure of them indulged in by others."[18]

Yoga helps a mind to attain equanimity. Yoga helps all.

All cannot be mystics. But with Yoga, a person does his work better. Yoga is a practical method which builds character. Through Buddhism, *Dhyana* entered China and Japan. It is practised as Cha'an in China and as Zen in Japan.[19]

A *siddhi* is one who has acquired supra-normal powers. There are eight *siddhis* from Yoga. These are *Animan* (becoming small like an atom), *Mahiman* (becoming magnified like a mountain or sky), *Laghiman* (Levitation), *Prapti* (getting close to objects-like touching the moon with one's fingers), *Prakamya* (non-obstruction to desire — like coming up from the ground as if it were water), *Vasitva* (mastery over the five elements), *Isitva* (full control over the production, absorption of arrangements and their products), *Yatra* — *Kamavasajitva* (the power to determine things as per ones wish i.e. like turning poison into nectar).[20]

The *Gita* describes the sage Kapila as a great *siddhi*. The *Yogasutras* describe the five kinds of *siddhis* that a person may possess viz., those proceeding from birth, from drugs, from *mantras*, from *tapas* (austerities) and lastly from concentration (meditation), the last being the best.

The *Yoga Sutra* states that some *siddhis* are obstacles to *Samadhi* and that they are *siddhis* only to those awakened from trance, (i.e. those who achieve Self-realisation).

Yajnavalkya states that the power to disappear, enter another body, temporarily abandon one's body, create objects at will etc. are characteristic signs of *siddhis* attained through Yoga.

All *Yogasutra* writers are very careful to point out that the mere attainment of *siddhi* powers is not the end goal of Yoga. The end goal is spiritual union while *siddhis* are merely an off-shoot of the Yoga discipline and these powers belong to the world process and are not spiritual.

Real *yogis* even warn that these sometimes deflect a *yogi* from the right path. Some possessors of *siddhi* powers may even be evil.

One great saint refers to the facility of walking on waters that an ascetic may achieve after much austerity. He says if that is all he has been able to achieve after so much effort then he might as well have paid a boatman to take him across.

There were many saints in India who are said to have possessed these powers. However, they themselves scoffed at these as having nothing to do with the spiritual.

Neither *siddhi* powers, nor a great intellect, nor even high moral qualities can define a person as a mystic.

Matsyendranath, the great Nath saint tells his equally illustrious pupil Gorakhnath that "until a man is able to see his own Form by the grace of his spiritual teacher, he may not be regarded as having attained to the highest mystical experience."

Yoga is open to all castes and creeds and requires a *guru*. It is very important that the *guru* is not fake, who dupes the foolish.

It may not be out of place to put before the reader the moral, physiological and mystical qualities of a true *guru*.

The true *guru* is joyful and fearless. There is no weariness, lassitude, neglect and dissatisfaction in him. Physiologically he does not need to control his breath or shut his senses. He is always Self-poised in the midst of all his activities. He sees God in all things, and there is in him perfect equanimity of mind and body. The *guru*'s function is to define spirit from matter, (i.e. Truth from falsehood), sharpen the intellect of his disciple, helping him to get rid of dirt and passion of desires and to round off all angularities as a potter does a clay pot. The function of the true spiritual teacher is not just the chanting of a *mantra* into the ear, but revealing God to the vision. He helps the disciple to reach the final destination.[21] The *guru* in other words, prepares the mind to receive the Spirit.

Discrimination is necessary in life to make out the genuine from the spurious. All systems of yoga warn against false *gurus*.

Tantra was a later development of Yoga. *Tantra* reached its zenith between AD 700 and 1300. It spread to Nepal, Tibet, China, Japan and South-east Asia. It's influence was also felt in the Mediterranean culture and Crete.

Criticisms of *tantra* have been from the uninformed as well as others, the former because of their own narrow views and ignorance and the latter because *tantra* was misused by imposters posing as *tantrics*.

Actually *tantra* must be seen as another intellectual movement, like all others, to clear the dross of form in the shape of tradition and fixed beliefs that accumulate in the human mind out of habit and not from rational thought. Fresh ideas can only be allowed to surface by clearing pre-conceived notions that clog the human mind.

During it's zenith *tantra* contributed much to man's knowledge in the field of sciences, art and psychology. *Tantra* influenced Hinduism, Buddhism and Jainism.

Some of the outstanding saints of India practised *Tantra Yoga*.

Tantra prescribes three ways. These are the *Dakshina Marg*, which they allege is the way prescribed by the Vedas, Smritis and Puranas. The *Varna Marg* is stated to be from the Vedas and Agamas, while the *Uttara Marg* is according to the words of the Vedas and a *guru* who is *Jeevan mukta* (liberated). A person may take whichever way he is best suited for.

While *tantra* subscribed to the philosophy of the

Upanishads, it also drew on its own unconventional sources. It also utilizes the findings of the *Nyaya-Vaiseshikha* and the *Sankhya-Yoga* systems.

Tantra lays stress on *mantra* and is also called *mantra Yoga.* It also uses *yantras* (symbols in geometric or other shapes). The *mantra* and *yantra* used in *tantra* are based on the structure of sound and matter.

The purpose of all Yoga is to raise the *Kundalini Shakti* (energy) which lies coiled at the base of the spine, and raise it through the *chakras* (nerve centres) to unite with Shiva in the *Sahasra* (thousand-petalled) *chakra.* This is achieved through meditation.

Although Patanjali Yoga does not specifically refer to the *Kundalini Shakti,* it is through this *Shakti* (in all forms of Yoga) that union is achieved. Ancient *Upanishads* that deal with Yoga refer to this *Shakti* as *Devi Shakti.*

The Principal *tantric* sects follow Shiva, Vishnu and Shakti. Their texts are called *Agama, Nigama* and *Yamala* respectively. There is much spurious literature described as *tantric.* Among these may be mentioned the *Rakshashi Tantra* which is not part of authoritative tantric literature.

What *tantra* tried to show, as have religious teachers earlier, is that social orders, conventions, and customs have nothing to do with spiritual realisation. Only a mind free of ego, prejudice, preconceived notions, passion and partiality has the capacity to perceive Truth, which is Knowledge Absolute. This is the only way that a mind can be receptive to knowledge.

However, *tantra's* very unconventionalism was in a sense its undoing. It attracted the base and provided them with a 'scientific' pretext for following their baser inclinations.

One of the ways was *Vamachara* (the name suggests that *tantrics* themselves considered this an unorthodox way). It used the five *makaras*, wine, flesh, fish, *mudra*, and *maithuna*. It was based on the principle that "Spiritual fulfilment was through the material."

That *tantric* literature itself warns against its misuse is uncontestable. The *Kularnava* says: "If by merely drinking wine a man were to attain *siddhi*, then all wretched drunkards may obtain *siddhi*. If, by merely eating meat a holy goal were to be secured, then all meat eaters in the world would be holy men. If, by intercourse with a woman (called *Shakti*) *moksa* was to result, then all men in the world would attain liberation. To follow the path of *Kula* is indeed more unattainable than walking on the edge of the sword, than clinging to a tiger's neck and than holding a serpent. Many who are devoid of traditional knowledge imagine that the *Kaulika* doctrine is this and that, relying on their (poor) intellect .

It is always the ignorant, the material-minded, the base, who are unable to understand a teaching. The form is more important to them, and so in due course the form is misused.

Tantra itself in due course became too formalised. We see it's effect on art, which suffered from the strict specifications that were laid down which only curbed the free and flowing movement of earlier art. Thus *tantra* which tried to do away with form, itself became another stultified form.

The base are not only in *tantra*. They are the ignorant in life who chase after the material. Their narrow and short-sighted minds are incapable of being receptive to knowledge. Every contribution is judged by what use they can make of it for themselves.

These two value systems have prevailed in the world from the earliest times. There is Knowledge and an open discriminating mind on the one side and the closed selfish and foolish mind on the other, seeing only the material.

Hence Charaka, one of the best-known names in ancient Ayurveda says, "Not for money nor any earthly objects should one treat his patients. In this the physician's work excels all vocations. Those who sell treatment as a merchandise neglect the true treasure of gold in search of mere dust."[23]

While *Sankhya* is forgotten, Yoga continues to flourish even today.

How relevant is Yoga to modern times? Those who know the purpose of Yoga would not ask this question. If knowledge is important for all times and for civilization itself, then Yoga is a practical necessity for all times. Character is the need of every age. The greatest poverty for anyone is poverty of the spirit.

Geraldine Coster in *Yoga and Western Psychology* (Oxford University Press 1934) observes, "I am convinced that the ideas on which Yoga is based are universally true for mankind and that we have in the *Yogasutras* a body of material which we could investigate and use with infinite advantage. . . . My plea is then that Yoga as followed in the East is a practical method of mind development, quite as practical as analytical therapy and far more practical and closely related to real life than the average university course. I am convinced that the *Yogasutras* of Patanjali do really contain information that some of the most advanced psychotherapists of the present day are ardently seeking". M. Charles Baudouin in *Suggestion and Auto-suggestion* (Allen and Unwin 1922) says, "As one of the curiosities of History and further a lesson in humility we must point out that the state just described under the names of collectedness, contention and auto-hypnosis are described with considerable psychological acumen (though not in modern psychological terminology) in the precepts by which for centuries past, the *yogis* of Hindustan have been accustomed to attain self-mastery". He refers to *Pratyahara* and *Dharana* and (on p.151) remarks that auto-hypnosis is encountered in Yoga but it is tinged with mysticism because the sacred word *Om* is repeated hundreds of times.

Dr. P.A. Sorokin of Harvard University (one of the greatest sociologists) in the Bharatiya Vidya Bhawan Journal (Nov.1958) in a paper submitted opens with, "The methods and techniques of the Yoga, particularly those of *Raja Yoga* contain in themselves nearly all the sound techniques of modern psychoanalysis psychotherapy, psycho-drama, moral education and education of character."[24]

NYAYA-VAISESHIKHA PHILOSOPHIES

The *Nyaya-Vaiseshikha* are complementary systems. *Vaiseshikha* is the older of the two probably of the 7th century BC. It was a well developed system by the sixth century BC.

The founder of *Vaiseshikha* was Kanada, also known as Kanabhuka, Uluka or Kashyapa. The name Kanada could have been derived from the fact that Kanada was an ascetic who lived off the grains he picked from the fields. Kanada also means particular and describes one expounding on particularity. Atomism is fundamental to Vaiseshikha thought. All matter is composed from the smallest indivisible atoms called *paramanus*. These *paramanus* were each of the four elements (actually only four basic elements since ether was the containing element that they combined in).

Vaiseshikha was so called because it tried to analyse the specificity by which categories could be distinguished according to substance, quality, action, generality, particularity and inherence.

Each atom is different by virtue of its particular (*visesha*) quality. Substance means the primordial elements, time and space. Quality includes number, measure, colour, taste and smell. Action includes the various forms of motion.

Of the four basic *paramanus* of the four elements, air had the quality of touch, fire the quality of form and colour, water the quality of taste and earth the quality of smell.

All knowledge and phenomenal elements are categorized in terms of these four elements.

The *Vaiseshikha Sutra* consists of ten chapters.

Nyaya not only developed the Vaiseshikha theory of atomism further, but also systemized logical thought. In fact it is recognized by many scholars today that the *Nyaya* syllogism, by giving due place to inherence, is a more perfected system of logic and therefore superior to the Aristotelian syllogism.[25]

The founder of the *Nyaya* system was Gotama.

The concept of *Dravya* (substance) is important in the history of science. The *Nyaya-Vaiseshikha* conceives it in terms of the four elements, space, time, mind and self.

The theory of atomism served to explain the basic stuff of the gross world. The *Nyaya-Vaiseshikha* describes logically and in detail the formation of gross bodies from atoms through dyads (*dvijamukhi*) and triads (*tryanukh* or trasarenu).

The conceptual scheme is explained on the basis of causality. Every event must have a cause and each event is a new event. The effect however cannot exist apart from the cause. It inheres in the latter. Atoms are the material cause in the formation of a dyad which is an effect. Three dyads are the cause of producing a triad, an effect. The cause thus brings about an effect but is absorbed in the latter, which again becomes the cause of another effect and so on.

The *Nyaya-Vaiseshikha* holds that two like *paramanus* unite only in the presence of another type of atom, the latter functioning as an accessory cause. This explains the different qualities of a single substance.

The concept regarding the structural arrangements (*Vyuha*) of the dyads in a triad and that the quality of a substance owes it's arrangement to the spacial placement of the constituents, can bear scrutiny even from the modern chemical point of view.

This is not so of Greek atomism.

Another Indian concept relevant to the history of science is the theory of impetus developed by the *Nyaya-Vaiseshikha* school. It deals in a rational way with the motion of bodies like the arrow, javelin, pestle etc., describing the relationship between the extent of motion and the effort brought into play. This was discussed in India in the AD 5th century. The West came to the theory of impetus in the AD 14th century.

The great contribution of the *Nyaya-Vaiseshikha* was to logic and physical concepts concerning substance, the five elements, motion, attributes, space, time and atomism.

All scientific study and calculations were to find the truth of the universe. Beginning as an atheist philosophy (one *Nyayika* is even reported to have called out *Pillava, pillava paramanu, paramanu* on his death-bed)[26] the later *Nyayikas* were theistic.

There were difficulties that the system faced. The problem of sentience was sought to be explained by positing a soul, as distinct from body, senses and mind. Consciousness was an attribute of the soul. There was thus a dualism of matter and mind and pluralism of souls.

The second problem was what was it that compelled

the atoms to behave in the way they did? Kanada proposed that the atoms moved under the action of an impersonal force or law which was Adrishta (Invisible).

Udayana in his *Nyaya Kusumanjali* outlines a blind but intelligent God as giving a plan to the cosmos.

Consciousness although an attribute of the soul, was not an inherent property of it. For consciousness soul had to link with body, senses and mind. What then was the condition of this soul when freed from the bonds of the body?

The *Nyaya-Vaiseshikha* concept of liberation seemed more a state of petrification of the soul, calling forth the comment from a Vaisnavite that 'it would be preferable to be a jackal in the gardens of Vrindavan than have the liberation of *Nyaya-Vaiseshikha*!'

And Sriharsa scathingly refers to the Vaiseshikha philosophy as *Auluka Darsana* 'Owlish philosophy',[27] and says that Gotama the founder of *Nyaya* justifies his name 'Gotama, an excellent bull!'[28]

Nevertheless as we can see, all the systems added greatly to man's knowledge of the universe as well as man himself.

It is interesting to see how from the *Nyaya-Vaiseshikha*, to *Sankhya* to Vedanta there is a progressive reduction of difference and an increase in identity between cause and effect.

The theory of atoms stimulated the interest of Indian scholars and was a subject of discussion and debate for over two thousand years. Not only did the Hindus contribute to the theory but also the Buddhist and Jain schools.

The Indian theory of atomism is historically earlier than the Greek schools, and also more developed.

What perhaps these pages will suffice to show is that 'scientific temper' does not belong to any particular age or place. It belongs to those men and women who have the desire to learn and take the trouble to make themselves receptive to knowledge from every source and pursue it with discrimination integrity and devotion. Those who offer work without expectations of the fruit thereof are performing the highest worship and thereby serving all creation.

References

1. *A New History of Sanskrit Literature* by K. Chaitanya, chap.III.
2. *Some Problems of Indian Literature* by M. Winternitz.
   In the Woods of God-realisation by Swami Ram Tirtha, vol.III.
   Indian Religions and the West: Historical Perspectives by B.M. Pande, in India's Contributions to World Thought and Culture (Vivekananda Rock Memorial Committee, 1970).
3. *In the Woods of God-realisation* by Swami Ram.Tirtha, vol.III.
4. India's Contribution to World Thought and Culture (V.R.M.C., 1970).
5. *History of Dharmasastra* by P.V. Kane, vol.V, pt.2, p.1152, 1153, 1154.
6. ibid., vol.V, pt.2, chap.XXIX, sec.VII, p.1217.
7. *Practical Vedanta as explained In the Woods of God-realization* by Swami Rama Tirtha, vol.I.
8. *History of Dharmasastra* by P.V. Kane, vol.V, pt.2, chap.XXXI, sec.VIII.
9. ibid., vol.V, pt.2, chap.XXXI, sec.VIII, p.1382, 1383.
10. ibid., vol.V, pt.2, chap.XXXI, sec.VIII, p.1353.
11. *A Critical Study of Indian Philosophy* by Chandradhar Sharma (Rider & Co., London), p.150.
12. *Gita Rahasya* (Marathi) by B.G. Tilak, chap.VIII.
13. *History of Dharmasastra* by P.V. Kane, vol.V, pt.2, chap.XXXI, sec.VIII, p.1383.
14. ibid., vol.V, pt.2, chap.XXXI, sec.VIII, p.1403, 1412.
15. ibid., vol.V, pt.2, chap.XXXI, sec.VIII, p.1402.
    A Critical Survey of Indian Philosophy by Chandradhar Sharma, p.169.
16. ibid., vol.V, pt.2, chap.XXXII, sec.VIII, p.1396.
17. ibid., vol.V, pt.2, chap.XXXII, sec.VIII, p.1459.
18. ibid., vol.V, pt.2, chap.XXXII, sec.VIII, p.1392.
19. *Hinduism and Buddhism* by A. Coomaraswamy, p.49.
20. *History of Dharmasastra* by P.V. Kane, vol.V, pt.2, sec.VI. p.1113.
21. *Pathway to God* in Hindi Literature by R.D. Ranade (1954) p.138.

22. *History of Dharmasastra* by P.V. Kane, vol.V, pt.2, sec.VI, p.1064.
23. *A New History of Sanskrit Literature* by K. Chaitanya, chap.I.
24. *History of Dharmasastra* by P.V. Kane, vol.V, pt.2, chap.XXXII, sec.VIII, p.1447, 1455, 1456.
25. *A Critical Survey of Indian Philosophy* by Chandradhar Sharma, p.199, 200.
26. *Gita Rahasya* by B.G. Tilak (Marathi), chap.VII.
27. *A Critical Survey of Indian Philosophy* by Chandradhar Sharma, p.190.
28. ibid., p.210.

15

Saints

The three traditional sources of *dharma* are the Vedas, Smritis and the standards set by the Self-realised individuals. The influence of these saints cannot be underestimated. It is in recognition of this fact that all religions advocate the company of the good.

The word *sat* means truth. *Sadhu* is derived from *sat*. If there has been a history of tolerance in India, this is due not only to the *Upanishadic Mahakavya* of *Tat Twam Asi* and the belief in the law of *Karma* and *Punarjanma*, or the Smritis making it one of the king's duties to protect differing sects and customs, but the example set by the good.

Those who contributed greatly to tolerance were the great saints and religious teachers. They won the reverence of the people because of their virtues, who saw that in their case there was no gap between practice and precept. They sought to sharpen the discriminating faculty of the people so that they would be able to see beneath the external. Minds which are led by the visible exterior are quite often superficial minds. They tried to make people aware of the truth of the all-pervading Reality, the Source of all.

Great saints were born in India in every age. They

came from every region and from all castes. Some have left a precious heritage of spiritual literature.

Tulsidas, Surdas, Kabir, Nanak, Mirabai, Matsyendranath, Gorakhnath, Jnaneshwar, Tukaram, Namdeo, Chaitanya are just a few of these great names to whom the people owe so much. If all the names were to be given from the most ancient times, they would probably fill more than just one book. In more recent times the names of Ramana Maharshi and Ramakrishna Paramahamsa are well-known.

There is no official organization in Hinduism that confers sainthood on any person. These persons attract the title by virtue of their own remarkable spiritual qualities. True saints, of all ages and countries, have always spoken the same language. It would not occur to anyone that the saint be given a 'prize' for his sainthood, nor would it occur to the genuine saint! The true saint is not after advertisement and publicity, in fact that is exactly what he asks people to beware of.

The image-worshipping mind is a mind which believes in the external image. This mind is fair game for those busy in creating images. The discriminating mind looks beneath the surface, in order to sift the genuine from the spurious. Good and bad actions are dependent on their source, i.e. on whether the source or reason for the action is genuine or spurious. In the realms of the spiritual there can be no racial, national or communal prejudice.

Mysticism involves a direct, immediate, and intuitive apprehension of God. Great mystics have not only intuition but intellectual power and absolute clarity of thought. The mystic is not only highly moral but leads a life of general good to the world. They have sentiment without being sentimental. This is the difference between the genuine and the spurious.

Tulsidas is known for his *Ramayana* which enriched Hindi spiritual literature. He compares *jnana* to a lighted lamp and Bhakti to a jewel that illumines. He explains name and form as attributes of God, and gives a remarkable exposition of relation between fundamental concepts of Name, Form, *Saguna*, *Nirguna* and *Dhyana*.

Surdas demonstrates with analogies the question of illusionism. Ramananda was a great thinker. Nanak who founded Sikhism, would exhort that no time should be wasted away from the spiritual. He also advocated the company of the good.

Matsyendranath, founder of the Nath School of Yogis examines ritualism, mere practice of Yoga, intellectualism and moralism and determines their proper place in the meditative process. Saint Jnaneshwar known, best for his *Jnaneshwari*, his commentary on the *Gita*, and for his high spiritual qualities, belonged to this school. God-devotion was recognized as superior to mere intellect and morality. Conventional morality is sometimes at odds with Truth. Tulsidas on God-love shows how Bharata gave up his mother, Prahlad left his father, Gopis left their husbands, Bibhishana left his brother, because of a higher call.

Inspite of writing no formal treatises on the science of ethics, their contribution to this science is remarkable from the analytical point of view. They espoused the individual virtues of activism, non-attachment, discrimination, self-control, courage, patience, sufferance and equanimity.

They stressed on social virtues such as keeping the company of the good, sympathy, benevolence and sacrifice.

They deplored the vices such as braggartism, pollution of mind, greed, hypocrisy, arrogance and voluptuousness.[1]

The spiritual virtues were celibacy, penance,

introversion, study of philosophy, reverence for master, meditation on God, divine optimism and seeing God in all things and everywhere.

We find some virtues receiving more prominence in a particular age depending on the prevailing need of the age.

God-love is the central virtue and all virtues are expressions of this. All vices are aberrations due to dereliction. Sympathy and compassion are sources of *dharma*. Self-surrender is Mukti.

Among the great religious literature left by the saints, some of the best-known and most popular are the *dohas* in Hindi, the *abhangas* in Marathi and *vachanas* in Kanarese. They are highly ethical, spiritual and even worldly-wise bon-mots. We see in them a combination of epigram, wit, humour, sarcasm, love, devotion, service and general advice to humanity. Some are rich in sentiment while others express a spiritual experience.

We have also the poet-saints like Narsingh Mehta.

There is much to be learnt from the saints. They teach to differentiate between the material and the spiritual, the development of character, how every art or science can be used for moral or immoral purposes.[2] They teach of charity and work, of the love of God being the Supreme virtue and the removal of ego being the only way to God Realization. Surdas says: "There is no use covering the body of an ass with saffron and sandal paste." "One should never try to please an ungodly man."[3] Surdas shows how an art can be double-edged. A dancer may help the moral and the spiritual but may also use dance to excite sexual passion. Charandas describes the valuelessness of speech without action: "A good man should act as he speaks. Words without action is like night without the moon."[4]

Charandas describes a Brahmin as one who has realised Brahma. This would apply to all castes.

Dadu explains 'kafir' as being the embodiment of vices like untruth, deceit and disbelief in God.

Charandas describes a virtuous and dedicated life as the only true way of worshipping God.

"All desires come to an end".

Maun, the highest state of equanimity being silence, is similar to 'epoche', also considered so by the ancient Greek philosophers, the Stoics, Epicureans and the sceptics.[5]

There is much to be learnt not only from the literature of the saints but from their lives. If the Hindus never lost hope or courage in the darkest days and retained their balance in the face of the gravest provocations and attacks on their freedom, religion and territory, it was because of the Inner Light of faith held high by the saints.

Man learns more by example than he does by precept. The high standards set by the saints showed that the high ideals were not impossible but possible to achieve by any man or woman who strove to do so. Facing pain, misery and contumely in the spirit of equanimity, humility and purity, unswerving in their devotion to truth, they were a living example of the power of Truth, the spirit of discrimination, devotion, and activism and self-surrender that it inspired.

Some of the great saints became founders of religions. The Buddha, Mahavira and Nanak are regarded as the founders of Buddhism, Modern Jainism and Sikkhism. But these saints were highly venerated by other Hindus too. Sainthood recognizes no barriers. Common myths and legends are found in all the religions of India. The message of the saints can also be seen as being responsive to the times.

During a time of turmoil and religious demarcation between the Hindu defenders and the Muslim invaders, when every irreligious act against the indigenous religion was depicted as a blow for Islam, Nanak pointed out that there was no Hindu God or Muslim God. Truth belongs to all. However, minds intent on achieving their own selfish material aims are more keen on asserting their superiority seeing it as a necessity to maintain their supremacy and if truth comes in the way then it is truth that needs to be discarded.

In due course this very reasonable message of Nanak came to be regarded with more and more suspicion. Some of the later Sikh gurus were tortured and killed.

To submit to religious intolerance was to allow ignorance to have its way. When submitting to indignities is due to a weak spirit then indignities and intolerance must be met with sword in hand, if necessary. Sikkhism which started as a peaceful religion, started veering to arms in self-defence. The last Guru, Gobind Singh marked the culmination of this change from the peaceful to the warlike. It was a response to the changing needs.

There were saints who travelled the length and breadth of the land. They gave their message in the language of the common people using motifs that the people understood.

Just as Buddha, Mahavira and Nanak used the common idiom of the people and thus helped to spread their message far and wide, so also did the other saints.

Sant Jnaneshwar, among his many other literary achievements, gave the people his priceless *Jnaneshwari*, a beautiful commentary on the *Gita* in Marathi, the language of the common man.

Sant Eknath who lived several centuries later again revised this work as language and idiom had changed with the passage of time. Eknath wrote not only in Marathi but also in Hindi.

Sant Namdeo who was a contemporary of Sant Jnaneshwar wrote innumerable *abhangas* in the language of the people. He also lived in Punjab for fifteen years.

About sixty of his *abhangas* are found in the Sikh Guru Granth.

All saints gave their message in the common man's language. Man is often found to forget that Truth is not an object. Image or object worship often comes in the way of recognizing the truth, by not understanding that the object is merely a symbol. Saints have come from all castes and religions. Sant Namdeo belonged to the caste of tailors. In need of spiritual instruction, Namdeo was sent by his guru to Gora Kumbhar known to attain Self-realisation. Kumbhar means potter. An incident is related of Namdeo's first meeting with Gora Kumbhar. Here the potter-saint teaches Namdeo that truth is not the image.

Arriving, Namdeo sees with consternation that Gora Kumbhar is sleeping with his feet on a Shiva Linga. Sure that Gora Kumbhar is unaware of this sacrilege, Namdeo wakes him and shows him where his feet are resting. On hearing Namdeo Gora Kumbhar tells him to put his feet where there is no Shiva Linga. Wherever Namdeo puts the feet of Gora Kumbhar there is a Shiva Linga. It then dawns on him that God is everywhere, and in all things.

There are many stories connected with the saints and how they were able to convey their message.

Each saint taught according to his genius and the understanding of the people. The intellectually inclined taught the way of Knowledge, others the way of Devotion while still others the way through Work. All showed the need for self-surrender.

Some saints insisted on earning their own keep by their labour. They were a living example that liberation could be achieved through work. All stressed the need for meditation. Many well-known saints were weavers. One of the best known examples is Kabir who uses many of the idioms of weaving in his *dohas*.

There were also saints like Ramdas Swami and

Madhava, who, like Guru Gobind Singh showed that spirituality was a concern for Truth and not violence or non-violence. Cowardice and submission are not Truth. Neither of them wielded the sword but it is said that Ramdas known for his *Dasbodh* which teaches the way of truth in life, was the spiritual mentor of Chhatrapati Shivaji.

It is said that Shivaji went to Sant Tukaram. But Tukaram recognized that Shivaji was meant for other things and sent him to Ramdas. Shivaji perhaps did not meet Ramdas Swami more than once or twice, but the latter was able to inspire him. The spirit of renunciation was seen in all these great saints who kept nothing for themselves.

Similarly Madhava is credited with being the spiritual preceptor of the Kings of the great Vijayanagar Empire. He guided the administration of the Empire from Sringeri. The accounts left by foreigners show that great tolerance prevailed and no discrimination was made on grounds of religion. This was said of Shivaji as well.

There was quite obviously a clear understanding of religion and its real purpose with opposition to its misuse like forced proselytising and subversion.

The Bhakti movement which started in the South inspired many saints like Chaitanya and Ramananda in other parts of India. The Bhakti cult spread from South India, northwards and to the whole of India.

The Vaishnavite saints of the Bhakti cult in the south were known as Alwars — devotees of Vishnu. The Tiruvaimizi is a compilation consisting of over four thousand stanzas by various Alwars. It is regarded as sacred as the Vedas. Shaivite saints were the Nayanaars. Ramanuja is regarded as the originator of the Bhakti cult in the south. As devotion requires two, he developed the philosophy of *Vishishtadvaita* where the individual soul is seen as separate from the universal soul. However, he also acknowledges the philosophy of the One in all.

The Bhakti movement helped understanding through love and devotion. Nature was seen as an expression and fulfillment of love. What was natural must be understood. Krishna's many incarnations made the many forms of man and animal better understood. This God seen from childhood till death in the many stages helped better understanding of what was natural behaviour to a child, a boy, a youth, a friend, a king and guide.

The new love and understanding found lyrical expression in art and literature. Jayadeva's *Gita Govinda* is the lyrical expression of Bhakti in verse. Mira's songs show complete absorption in Krishna to the exclusion of all else. The beautiful Rajput and Pahari paintings are mostly on Krishna themes. The fine eye for detail, the love for flora and fauna which come alive in these paintings is indicative of the great understanding and love of all nature.

Sainthood is not the exclusive privilege of anybody. Even those engaged in evil acts can change their whole life and attitude by God's grace. But true mystics, which saints are, are very few. The most sublime concepts can be misunderstood by narrow and literal interpretations. At one time South India saw some ugly manifestations of sharp religious differences between the Shaivites and the Vaishnavites, quite overlooking the fact that Shiva and Vishnu are but two names or attributes of the same God. The worship of Shiva is the worship of Vishnu. What is important is that we worship with faith and devotion. Faith in Truth must reflect in one's own conduct as well. It means being truthful oneself. Those who "know Brahma become Brahma".

There are many *tirthasthanas*, some of Devi, others of Vishnu and others of Shiva. A *tirthasthana* common to both the Shaivities and Vaishnavites was and still is Pandharpur. Almost all the saints of India have visited Pandharpur. It is said that the images of Vithoba and Rakhmai were secreted from place to place when temples and idols were being destroyed, so as to protect them.

No one who visits the shrine of Vithoba at Pandharpur leaves without visiting the shrine of the devotee Pundalik. Through his devotion to Pandurang (Vithoba) Pundalik realised that devotion to God also meant devotion to those around him. He served and tended his aging parents till their last days.

The message of the saints through the example of their own lives was that respect for truth alone makes man and his life worthwhile. He acts in the highest interest. Religion is not divorced from life but concerns life itself. Truth gives value to all actions and to all professions. Free of selfish ego man performs his duties in life with discrimination and devotion.

It is to these great men and women that Indians owe so much, for visibly putting into practice what would, without them, have only remained a precept.

References

1. *Pathway to God* in Hindi Literature by R.D. Ranade, p.89.
2. ibid., p.51.
3. ibid., p.50.
4. ibid., p.52.
5. ibid., chap.V.
6. *History of Dharmasastra* by P.V. Kane, vol.IV, chap.XV.

16

Women in Hinduism

Just as social laws changed at different times, so did the
position of women. Making allowances for the fact that
local customs (which were not anti-social or immoral)
were not interfered with, the Smritis provided the rules
generally for all Hindus to follow. Customs like a girl
marrying the mother's brother or the son of the mother's
brother etc. were allowed by the Smritis as a local custom
even if the Smritis did not generally allow marriage among
relations at least up to seven generations.[1]

Whether the felt needs of a particular age are justified
or not would depend upon the enlightened approach of
those who people that age. But it is obvious that Hindu
thought is against ignorance, because ignorance leads
to stupidity and superstition and means the end of
civilization. A woman's position would be indicative of
whether a particular age was enlightened or not and
also perhaps indicate the general level of enlightenment.
The ignorant may have followed the external form of
Hinduism but without understanding its teachings.

Religion considers man and woman as equal. This
finds expression in the symbolization of Shiva and *Shakti*
identified with *Purusa* and *prakriti*, the duality of spirit
and nature from which originates all creation. Shiva and
Shakti merged into One, as half man and half woman is the

Ardhanareshwar, the One source of all created universe. Woman is not considered as inferior to man, on the contrary her's is the creative force which the spirit inspires. Man and woman are mutually dependent and looked upon as equal partners. A man cannot function without a woman just as a woman cannot function without a man.

The Smritis considered human needs as legitimate so long as they did not violate *dharma.* The *Bhagavata Purana* observes (II.5-11) that in this world no one needs to be persuaded to indulge in sex, eat meat or drink wine. It is in man's nature to want these. It is in order to keep these wants under proper restraint that provision has been made for marriage, and *yajnas* like the *sautramani* (where meat was eaten and wine was drunk), and rules provided as general, guidelines to prevent unleashed self-indulgence. This seems a wise and balanced approach.[2]

However, problems usually arise when people wrongly interpret texts according to their (often limited) comprehension. If self-indulgence is one extreme, puritanism is the other. Wherever women have been criticised in religious or other literature we may presume two reasons as being responsible for these. One reason is obvious from Sabara, who says "The purpose of a text censuring anything is not censure pure and simple, but the purpose is to enjoin the performance of the opposite of what is censured and to praise such performance."[3] Since women were not the only ones criticised this observation must be taken in the spirit in which these were made. The other reason for women being regarded as something to be avoided must be put down to the literal interpretation made by the puritanical of the purely abstract concept of *Purusa* and *prakriti* being identified physically with man and woman. At a period when it appeared that salvation could only be achieved by sexual abstinence as one of the virtues practised, women must have been tempting indeed. The antagonism to woman was thus really a fear of themselves. These men were afraid of losing their own self-control.

Not all men agreed with these sentiments, but then not all are of the same understanding. And we must also remember that no matter what books and laws might say, they cannot go against nature. Even at times when man was considered as the head of the house, a more forceful wife did dictate. There is an amusing anecdote in the *Vishnu Purana* of a valiant king who could not stand up to his wife at home. He was hen-pecked!

The woman's status from the most ancient times can be discussed under three headings, educational, economic and social.

There seems no doubt that the educational level of women was far higher in the Vedic times than in the later medieval times, though they were better off economically in the latter period.

Among those who composed the Vedic hymns several were women. For example, *Rig Veda* (V.28) is ascribed to Visvavara of the *Atri* family, *Rig Veda* (VIII.91) is ascribed to Apata of the same family, *Rig Veda* (X.39) to Ghosa Kakrivati, Maitreyi the wife of Sage Yajnavalkya was a seeker, and Gargi Vacaknavi has a prominent place.

In the daily offerings of water to the rishis, three are women teachers. These are Gargi Vacaknavi, Vadana Pratitheyi and Sulabha Maitreyi.[4] Ancient grammarians like Panini and the later Patanjali were familiar with women teachers. There is also evidence to show that women could recite Vedic *mantras* during the Vedic period. It is not so well known that the *mantra* chanted at a Hindu wedding is taken from the *Rig Veda* and it has been composed by a woman.

There was a rite prescribed for those wanting a learned

daughter. The Upanayana ceremony was earlier meant for girls as well. Later, it was discontinued with marriage becoming the most important *samskara* for a girl.

There were poetesses like Vajja and Sita. Shakuntala could read and write. Vatsyayana the author of *Kamasutra* recommends that a woman should study the *Kamasutra* and the sixty-four complementary *kalas* before marriage, and with the permission of her husband after marriage. At that time women seemed to have married at a much later age. Child marriage was introduced much later. It was later that women were denied, along with the *Sudras* the right to study the Vedas. It is heartening to know that not all have agreed with these views. Even in the minority they are none the less significant. *Varaha-Mihira* raises his voice in the defence of women in the *Brhat Samhita* (AD 6th century)[5] "On woman depends *dharma* and *artha* and from man derives pleasure of the senses and benefit of sons and that they are the *Lakshmi* of the house and should always be given honour and wealth." He condemns those who, following the path of asceticism and other-worldliness, proclaim the demerit of women and are silent on their virtues. Says he, "Tell me truly what faults attributed to women have not also been practised by men? Men in their audacity treat women with contempt but they really possess more virtues than men". He cites a verse from *Manu* (7-10) 'One's mother or one's wife is a woman; men owe their birth to women'; O ungrateful wretches how can happiness be your lot when you condemn them? The *sastras* declare that both husband and wife are equally sinful if they prove faithless to their marriage vow; men care very little for that *sastra* (though women do care) women are superior to men" . . . He was supported by poets like Bana, Kalidas and Bhavabhuti.

Although the woman's economic status property-wise, improved in medieval times, 'nowhere were the property rights of a woman recognized so early as in India'.[6] The idea of *stridhan* can be traced to Vedic literature. In very few ancient systems of law have these rights been so largely conceded as in India. The Smritis describe in detail what constitutes *stridhan*, the woman's dominion over it and its inheritance. The husband has no right over the wife's *stridhan*.

About marriage, we are told in the *Mahabharata* (Anu.122), that earlier there was no marriage and women were free to marry. This however led to irresponsible behaviour and so Svetaketu enforced the restriction of marriage. We can see how historically, certain laws pertaining to marriage have been done away with or others introduced as they were more congenial. The earlier law of a man marrying the issueless widow of his deceased brother was later abolished, as it was no longer acceptable.

Marriage became the most important *samskara* for a woman. Earlier, till the *Yajnavalkya Smriti*, intercaste marriage took place between all castes. Later the Smritis prohibited the three varnas of *dvijas* from marrying a *Sudra* woman. The later restriction of marrying within one's caste came only in the AD 10th century.[7] This may have been to face the Muslim invasions.

Smritis laid down guidelines regarding the kind of wife or husband to be chosen. It is worth remembering though what the authorities in the Smritis themselves say i.e. that those Smriti rules that are based on the seen or worldly considerations, even when they are disregarded, do not violate any Vedic injunction. Here they quote Manu's advice on not marrying a girl with certain hereditary diseases in the family. These have been given for medical reasons with a view to the offspring as well. But they are not binding.

Those who belonged to the same *gotra* were not allowed marriage. This is no longer so, *gotra* means cow-stable or herd of cows. A *gotra* could mean having a common patriarchal ancestor or a group of people inter-connected.[8]

Though monogamy seems to have been the rule, in Vedic literature there are references to polygamy as well.[9] In the Sutra period one wife was recommended, and a second was allowed only if the two, *dharma* and progeny, were found wanting in the first. There was also punishment for a man abandoning a faultless wife. Before taking another wife a man had to wait eight years for progeny from the first, and twelve years if she gave birth to a daughter only, although immediate permission was possible if the wife was harsh of tongue! Regarding polyandry, there is not a single Vedic passage referring to polyandry. The most glaring example is of Draupadi. In the *Mahabharata* we are told that all are shocked when Yudhishtira makes Draupadi the wife of all five. Yudhishtira also tries to justify it by referring to tradition, but can ferret out only two cases![10]

In the Dharmasastra works there seems some aware-ness of polyandry, and this must have been a local custom or usage in some areas.

Adultery was not considered a sufficient justification for casting a woman out of the house. The rule was that women should never be killed or abandoned not even when guilty of adultery.[11]

Manu holds that the first duty of males in the family is to keep the women dependent and under their control, if they became attached to a life of pleasure; and Narada states that even women from good families come to ruin by independence.

Manu recommends that a wife should be guarded against even trifling attachments, because if they go astray they bring sorrow to two families, her husband's and her father's.

Manu, Harita and Sankha-Likhila all enjoin that the husband guards his wife from other men to ensure purity of issue. By guarding her the husband guards his reputation, his family, soul and *dharma*, since a woman gives birth similar to the male with whom she consorts or on whom she sets her heart during the days after the monthly illness.

But *Manu.* (IX.10) also accepts that a woman cannot be completely guarded and he recommends that she be kept occupied in family work and also that the husband try to deserve her affection and regard and show her honour.[12] It cannot be said that the Smriti writers were against women. *Manu.* (III.56) says, "where women are honoured there the gods love to reside; where they are not honoured, there all religious acts come to nought."[13]

Although we find sarcastic references to women in the *Rig Veda* we also find such about men. These references are to those who marry not for the person but for the wealth.[14]

The *Rig Veda* (III.563-64) describes a woman as "A haven of rest."

The Smritis with their penchant for classification describe the eight different types of marriages, and disapprove of the last four. The last four have to be rectified by undergoing a marriage ceremony. The eight forms are:

(1) *Brahma*, the gift of a daughter after decking and adorning her in fine garments and jewellery to a man of good conduct, learned in the Vedas, whom the father of the bride himself invites.

(2) *Daiva*, when the father gives away his daughter after decking her (with ornaments etc.) to a priest who duly officiates at a sacrifice, in the course of its performance.

(3) *Arsa*, is when daughter is gifted after taking a pair or two of cattle, only as a matter of fulfilling the law and not as sale of the girl.

(4) *Prajapatiya*, is when daughter is gifted and father addresses both 'may both of you perform your religious duties together', after he has honoured the bridegroom.

(5) *Asura*, is when father gives the girl to bridegroom after taking as much as the bridegroom can afford to the girl and her relatives.

(6) *Gandharva*, is the union of the girl and bridegroom springing from carnal love and passion and mutual consent.

(7) *Raksasa*, the forcible abduction of a girl amidst her cries, from the home of her slain relatives.

(8) *Paisacha*, the basest and most sinful, when man has intercourse with a girl while she is asleep, intoxicated or of disordered mind.[15]

The Smritis also condemn the sale of girls for marriage and say when a girl is bought by money she cannot act in rites performed as she is really a slave. One hears of money taken from the bridegroom rather than the other way round, as that seems to have been the custom prevailing then. But all the Dharmasastras condemn unequivocally making marriage a commercial transaction.

(*Baudhayana Dharamasutra* II.20, 21), "Those who blinded by greed give their daughters in marriage for a fee are sinners, sellers of their own selves, and perpetrators of great sin, and they fall into hell, etc."

Manu. (III.51, 54-55), "A father should not take even the smallest gratuity for his daughter; if he takes gratuity through greed, he becomes the seller of his child. When relations do not take for themselves the wealth given by the bridegroom as gratuity (but hand it over to the girl) the wealth so taken is for honouring the maiden and is only taken from the bridegroom out of loving concern for them. "Fathers, brothers, husbands and brothers-in-law desiring their own welfare should honour women and give them ornaments."

Manu. (IX.98) "Even a *Sudra* should not take gratuity when giving his daughter, since in taking gratuity he clandestinely sells his daughter."

Anu. (45.18-19) "Even a stranger cannot be sold, what of one's own children".[16] The great Shankaracharya laid down 54 *acharas*. Among these he prohibits *sati* and the sale of girls etc. *Atri* (V.389) also shares these views.[17]

(In AD 1425 *Brahmins* of Karnataka, Tamil, Telugu and South Gujarath signed an agreement giving up taking of gold for their daughters and to marry them in a simple *kanyadaan*, and agreeing to be punished otherwise. The Peshwas also forbade the taking of money by fathers for their daughters in marriage, and prescribed fines for those fathers as well as the intermediaries for not obeying the order).

Although a marriage was arranged by the elders, the girl's welfare was quite obviously also the concern of the *Smritikars* and the real reason for marriage was not forgotten. That a girl must be allowed to fulfill her role and function as a woman is quite obviously the reason why *Manu.* (IX.90) suggests that a girl should wait for three years after puberty. If her marriage is still unarranged then she may choose her own mate.[18]

An unchaste wife was to be confined by her husband in the same house and made to undergo the same *prayaschitta* that a man guilty of adultery had to undergo.

The texts say the widows guilty of adultery are purified by penance and may be restored to all their social privileges.

If a man abandoned a blameless wife with a minor son, she was to get one-third of his property. If the man was poor he had to maintain her.

The Smritis did not favour husband and wife complaining against each other. Efforts were made to patch up the quarrels.

Women had to undergo only half the *prayaschitta* that men had to undergo. They paid no taxes. They received precedence on the roads.

Prostitutes did not incur sin but a married man visiting one did, because he was not supposed to be unfaithful to his wife.[19] Sexual relations were forbidden with a woman of a superior caste. Relations were permitted with wanton women not *Brahmin* by caste, a prostitute, a female slave, one not restrained by her master, and of a lower caste than oneself.

Concubines were recognized by society and Smritis, and received maintenance from the properties of their masters. Two kinds of concubines were recognized. In the first case she stayed in the home and was forbidden to have relations with any other man. In the other case she was kept at another place under the care of a person. Here also she belonged only to one man.

Sati was not practised in ancient times. Later it seems to have been confined only to the ladies of the nobility in *Kshatriya* families. This was perhaps so as to avoid being taken as slaves in times of defeat in war. Later, *Brahmin* women also underwent *sati*. The *Garudapurana* waxes eloquent over wives (of all castes), immolating themselves on the husband's death. However statistics show that *sati* was more prevalent in Bengal than anywhere else in India, and this seems not a little due to the *Dayabhag* law that was followed in Bengal.[20] According to this law, in a joint family, where a man died without issue, his share of property went to his wife.

The rest of India followed the Mitakshara law.

There is no reference to the tonsure of widows in the *Grhya*, Dharmasastras or in the important Smritis like *Manu* and *Yajnavalkya*. This practice must have started about the AD 10th or 11th, century. The *Skanda Purana* alone refers to it.[21] There was no veil worn in ancient times. Ladies of the nobility alone were not normally seen in public.

One of the brightest spots in the Smritis is their attitude to the mother. To a son a mother, even if she be an outcaste (*patita*), is never to be abandoned.[22]

The *Smritikars* have understood the precarious plight of a helpless woman without any support in a predatory world.

According to Kane "the Smriti writers show love and concern for a daughter. Society expected a higher standard of moral rectitude from women than from men. The parents felt concern for a daughter's well-being and she was thus a source of anxiety. The Smriti writers recommend that only she can inherit after a son and none else."[23]

The popular support for pre-puberty marriage for girls came after AD 200. One of the reasons may have been the moral laxity among Buddhist nuns. Marriage was only a sacrament, consummation being after puberty. From AD 6th and 7th century to modern times pre-puberty marriage seems to have been more among *Brahmins*.[24] It is well to remember however that customs were never uniform at any given time throughout India. Enough leeway was given for customs to evolve to suit the needs of a time and place.

In India, from the earliest times the women have provided both physical and moral support to the men. Women have played a valuable part in retaining tradition.

Even when not educated in schools they had an understanding of life by reading the Puranas and the epics. If not
literate they were certainly educated. They could think
originally and independently. In ancient times also neither
Draupadi nor Sita were dumb. They could argue and
overrule. The women have been as gallant as patriotic and
as steadfast as the men. In recent times when India was
fighting for independence from British rule women came
out in their thousands at the call of Mahatma Gandhi.
They were beaten, arrested and served jail sentences.
In the Vedas there are references to women going along
with their husbands to procure cattle. These raids were
carried out on horseback. There are also historic female
personalities able and wise who have ruled well and
fought unflinchingly on the battlefield.

And it would be churlish not to recognize the part
played by Hindu men in the last hundred years to improve
the lot of women who had lagged behind educationally
and socially, to bring them to their present state of
emancipation. Men of religion, social reformers, writers,
dramatists and educationists have all played a part in
highlighting the weakness of a social structure where one
half was denied education which made them unfit to face
a new age. These men had to suffer social ostracism
themselves, they also had to do without much themselves
and sacrifice for the cause they had taken up. They did so
quietly without drawing attention to themselves or their
sacrifices. It would be a slur on knowledge itself if those
who have the advantage of education are unable to
appreciate those who have done so much without seeking
publicity. Ultimately education is not reading or writing, it
is that which enables one to look beneath the surface and
judge where true worth lies.

References

1. *History of Dharmasastra* by P.V. Kane, vol.II, pt.1, p.24.
   ibid., vol.III, chap.XXXIII, p.857, 858, 860, 861, 881.
2. ibid., vol.II, pt.2, chap.XXII, p.780.
3. ibid., vol.II, pt.1, chap.XI, p.581.
4. ibid., vol.II, pt.1, chap.VII, p.365, 366.
5. ibid., vol.II, pt.1, chap.XI, p.577.
6. ibid., vol.III, chap.XXX, p.770.
7. ibid., vol.II, pt.1, chap.IX, p.427.
8. ibid., vol.II, pt.1, p.430, 431, 479.
9. ibid., vol.II, pt.1, chap.XI, p.550.
10. ibid., vol.II, pt.1, p.554.
11. ibid., vol.II, pt.1, p.571, 593.
12. ibid., vol.III, chap.XXV, p.536, 537.
13. ibid., vol.II, pt.1, chap.IX.
14. *A New History of Sanskrit Literature* by K. Chaitanya, chap.II.
15. *History of Dharmasastra* by P.V. Kane, vol.II, pt.1, chap.IX, p.516.
16. ibid., vol.II, pt.1, chap.IX, p.505, 506.
17. ibid., vol.II, pt.1, chap.IX, p.506.
18. ibid., vol.V, pt.2, chap.XXX, sec.VII, p.1338.
19. ibid., vol.II, pt.1, chap.XVI, sec.XII.
20. ibid., vol.II, pt.1, chap.XV, p.635.
21. ibid., vol.II, pt.1, chap.XII, p.587, 592.
22. ibid., vol.II, pt.1, chap.XI, p.550.
23. ibid., vol.II, pt.1, chap.IX, p.571.
24. ibid., vol.II, pt.1, p.443.

17

Meanings of Symbols in Hinduism

Since we live in a world of form we use form for all activity. All action is creation of form. Thus a word is something more than just a word. It has a meaning. A group of letters with their own properties make up a word. Unless we understand what they are supposed to represent we will not be able to express ourselves nor understand anything. But even a word, as we all know, has to be understood not only by its literal meaning but also its spirit. The context in which a word is used gives it its real meaning. Our understanding itself is of two kinds. One is on the superficial plane which understands the letter while the other is a deeper understanding that searches for the inner motive or meaning

The Hindu view is that understanding of the spirit is essential in understanding all forms. All attributes, since they belong to creation, are also form. Form is synonymous with activity (creation). Form is not contrary to the spirit but is the expression of the spirit. Man has the capacity, if he so chooses, to understand not only the manifest external but the subtle Unmanifest as well. To understand the subtle requires a greater sensibility and sensitivity. This is the difference between the cultured and the uncultured. Culture is not merely arts and crafts and literature, but a sensitivity and understanding of the deeper values. The whole of Hindu philosophy is designed to make man aware of his own higher nature. He is made aware of not only his body but the divine spirit within him. Spirit and nature are One. Nature is inherent in the Spirit. The spirit acts through nature, i.e., form.

Not all can understand abstract concepts. There are men and women of different levels of understanding. Each one's level of understanding depends on each one's inherent sensitivity and capacity. These are not dictated by class, caste or wealth. The Hindu view is that poverty of form results from poverty of the spirit. It is not the spirit that is poor but the form which is incapable of recognizing the Divinity of the spirit within all form.

Form has been used to educate all to make them understand the relationship between nature and Spirit. Symbols are form. Idols are form. Nature is form. The more abstract the form, the closer it is to the Spirit, which is formless.

The highest can only be explained by *neti, neti,* (not this, not this) as it cannot be identified by any phenomena. It is beyond all phenomena.

The positive description of Brahma is Existence Absolute, Knowledge Absolute and Bliss Absolute.

Ishwar is a God with attributes and so, lower in scale, but more comprehensible to man.

The symbol *Om* (ॐ) is the holiest of all symbols as it represents the unmanifest and the manifest. It represents the first sound of creation, the soundless sound. Yet even if closest to the Spirit, it is still a form.

In the case of idols, the more abstract the idol the closer it is to the Spirit. The more the hands containing various attributes the lower in scale the idol. Because of this we find Shiva worshipped in the form of a Shiva Linga. The

Bana Linga, an egg-shaped pebble is also used to represent, Shiva. Similarly Vishnu is also represented by a *saligrama* a river-worn flintified ammonite shell with spiral grooves on it to represent the discus of Vishnu. We all know and take part in certain religious festivals where idols made for the occasion are worshipped for a number of days, and later taken in procession to be immersed in river, sea, pond or lake. This immersion of the idol is to bring home the fact that what was being worshipped was not the idol but the Spirit it represented. While the form may be destroyed, the Spirit is eternal and indestructible. Two of these well known festivals are the Kali puja and Ganesh puja.

In the *Vishnu Purana* we find the explanation of the image of Vishnu. The Puranas were meant for the education of all. We see in the form of Vishnu both individual soul and nature (matter). The serpent on which Vishnu reclines is the Formless Infinite.

"The Kaustuba gem of Vishnu, pure, unblemished, undefiled and devoid of qualities represents the pure Unmanifest Brahma or *atma* of the world. The Srivatsa mark in the heart of the Eternal is the principle of *pradhana* (*prakriti* or nature). The Sri Vatsa mark also represents Laksmi, the consort of Vishnu. Vishnu's mace is the intellect. The conch-shell and bow represent *ahamkara* (discrimination) consisting of the elements as well as the sense organs. The *chakra* (discus) in Vishnu's hands is the mind whose thoughts fly swifter than the winds. *Vaijayanti* the God's necklace comprising the five gems represents the five subtle elements. The arrows are the faculties of both action and perception. The bright sword is holy wisdom which is concealed by the scabbard of ignorance. We thus see that the person of Hari (God) combines the soul (*purusha*), nature (*pradhana*), *mahat* (intellect), *ahamkara* (egotism or discrimination), the elements, the senses, mind, ignorance and wisdom. Hari is both Cause and Effect, and everything."

Ignorance also forms a part of the scheme as each form evolves in its own time.

Parasu is the battle-axe that symbolises Shiva's strength and power. *Kadga* is the sword that indicates valour. *Vahni*, the fire, is the power of destruction. Fire destroys the bonds of attachment making enlightenment possible. *Nagas* are the snakes indicating Shiva's fortitude and the inviolability of His Law and Commandments. The *pasa* or noose represents the three-fold bondage of *Karma*, *maya* and *mala* (deeds, delusion and impurity). The ghanta is the bell symbolising sound, the original cause of creation. It indicates Shiva's mystic personality. *Ankusa*, the elephant god, stands for the discriminating faculty in choosing what is good for the soul.

Kali, the destructive aspect of Parvati, symbolises the cosmic power of Eternal Time (*Kala*), with its power of destruction. Kali symbolises not only destruction but also creation and preservation. Black represents destruction. All names and forms disappear in black. The full breasts denote preservation and motherhood. Her dishevelled hair is the mystery of death that surrounds all life. The fifty human heads worn by her represent the fifty letters of the Sanskrit alphabet — symbolic of power and knowledge. The girdle of human hands signify deeds (*Karma*) since hands are the instruments of work. Liberation can only be achieved through one's own actions. The three eyes of Kali govern the forces of creation, preservation and destruction. Her white teeth represent the quality of Satwa in nature, restraining her red and lolling tongue representing *rajas* (activity) from *tamas* (inertia). The hand holding the severed head represents destruction while the sword in the other hand cuts the thread of bondage. The two right hands dispel fear and exhort spiritual strength. Kali is the primordial power awakening Shiva. The inseparable union of the two represents non-duality.

We find the principle of Soul and nature repeated in other gods and goddesses as well. Just as Shiva's consort is Parvati, so Vishnu's consort is Lakshmi and Brahma's consort is Saraswati.

Brahma is shown with four faces, seated on a swan with a *kamandalu* of water in his hand. Saraswati sits beside him with a veena, and book. The four faces are the four faces of Truth. Brahma is the God of Knowledge symbolised by the four Vedas. Saraswati is the Goddess of learning, letters and music. The lotus beside Brahma represents creation and life, while the swan shows the mind, the root of individual manifestation.

Brahma, Vishnu and Mahesh (Shiva) are the trinity representing creation, preservation and destruction, respectively.

No God or goddess has only one name. They have innumerable names depicting their attributes.

Ganapati is worshipped at the beginning of all ventures. His two wives Riddhi and Siddhi mean wisdom and achievement of desired ends. Ganapati is the God of Knowledge and wisdom. He is the God who puts obstacles as well as removes them.

Ga stands for wisdom, *Na* stands for *moksa* or salvation, *Pati* is the Lord of these.

Ganapati is also known as *Ekadanti*. *Eka* denotes the One and Only Supreme Being, while *danta* denotes strength. Ganapati is also described as *Herambha*. *He* denotes helplessness and weakness, *rambha* means protection afforded. He is the protector of the weak. We are told that when the sage Vyasa decided to put the *Mahabharata* down in writing he approached Ganapati and requested Him to write while he dictated. Ganapati agreed on the condition that once he put down his quill he would not take it up again. Vyasa agreed but on the condition that Ganapati was not to put down his quill if he did not understand the words. Ganapati agreed. They began with Vyasa dictating and Ganapati writing. Every time it appeared that Ganapati was about to put down the pen, Vyasa would recite a few verses which would make Ganapati ponder over them. By that time, Vyasa would 'have composed some more verses. So they went on till the *Mahabharata* was complete!

Thus we see that it was recognized by all that the word and its meaning are inseparable.

Vishnu is the Preserver. Garuda the Brahmany kite that is the vehicle of Vishnu, symbolises Sun or Time. Vishnu's *chakra* is the revolving wheel of Time. It is also the cosmos imagined as a bounded circle. Vishnu's three steps signify motion. While Vishnu represents imminent form, *ananta*, the serpent on which Vishnu rests represents the unmanifest substratum. Lakshmi (Shri) the consort of Vishnu, depicts the fullness and beauty of life.

All manifestation is an expression of fullness. Fullness is the seed of eternal pulsation. The disappearance of this is the disappearance of beauty, art and life. The *purna kumbha* or *purna kalas*, a full vase that graces all auspicious occasions, represents fullness, prosperity and a life endowed with all the gifts moral, material and spiritual. Wherever there is the life principle there Shri also resides.

The lotus, *chakra*, 'conch' and *swastika* are ancient symbols. The lotus symbolises creation representing order out of chaos. It is also a symbol of purity. The *chakra* is another Vedic symbol. It represents Time, the wheel of the sun's chariot, *dharma*. The conch suggests an aquatic origin. It also represents the Divine Law of the universe. The *swastika* is a dynamic pattern with its four arms rotating around a focal point which generates the life force. The relative truths cancel each other leaving only the Absolute Truth.

There are numerous symbols which cannot all be accommodated here. Tantra also introduced new symbols. These were yantras meant for meditation. The best known and the most beautiful of these is the *Sriyantra*.

Tantra uses point, line, circle, triangle, square and lotus (mainly) for their symbols. The *bindu* was the point of zero dimension and placed at the centre of the yantra. This was the point from which all things unfolded as well as into which all dissolved back. Such a point was the *mahabindu*. In terms of mind this point becomes the mono bindu, where subject and object meet.

(The red *tilak* that is applied on the forehead also has a similar meaning.)

A circle describes the planetary motion. The square within the circle, having four gates represents the earthly plane which one must transcend to identify the core or essence. The triangle represents the three *gunas: sattwa, rajas* and *tamas*. The triangle with apex downwards represents 'yoni', the seat of energy (*prakriti* or Shakti), the triangle with apex upwards represents *purusha*. When the two triangles penetrate each other, the five-pointed star represents the five elements of creation. When the two interlocking triangles produce a six-pointed star, it represents the kinetic energy of *rajas* from the point of view of genesis. When the two triangles are separated making a *damru* pattern, it represents dissolution.

Many are the symbols used, and many are the interpretations. What is important to remember is that all symbolise the concept of creation and are designed to bequeath us with that most precious commodity, understanding.

All nature is invested with sanctity. Thus plant, animal and mineral are associated with god and goddess.

No animal is too mean. The mouse for example is the vehicle of Ganapati. Nandi, the bull is Shiva's while the Garuda is Vishnu's.

The confluence of rivers and where river joins the sea, serves as a reminder of the individual soul uniting with the universal. The holiest rivers are the Ganga, Yamuna, Godavari, Saraswati, Narmada, Sindhu and Kaveri. The four holy lakes are Bindu, Pampa, Narayana and Manasa.

The seven holy places are Ayodhya, Mathura, *Maya* (Hardwar), Kasi, (Varanasi) Kanchi (Kanchipuram), Avantika (Ujjain) and Dvaravati (Dwarka). Forests have had a great attraction for the Hindus. Some of the greatest educational institutions and the highest philosophical speculations were pursued in the quiet retreat of the forest. The mountains also have influenced religious thought. The snow-clad Himalayas are the abode of Shiva and Parvati. The Himalayas have attracted ascetics and philosophers. Many places of pilgrimage are located in mountains. Apart from the Himalayas, the seven holy mountains, are Mahendra, Malaya, Sahya, Suktimat, Rksa, Vindhya and Pariyatra.

The spires of temples are named after the different crests of mountains. The different designs are called Kailasa, Mandara, Meru etc. Flora and fauna are used not only in religious symbolism but also in art and design.

Several goddesses are vegetation deities. In a predominantly agricultural country the cow assumes special importance.

We are all familiar with the *Raslila* where Krishna dances with all the *gopis*. Krishna signifies the Universal Soul and the *gopis* the individual souls, who, unaware of their true identity, yearn after the Universal Soul. Krishna is always shown with a flute. The flute is a hollow reed. It is only when our own minds are emptied of impurity and are like the reed that we hear the sweet strains of Truth or *atma*.

Many stories contain accounts of fights between the gods and *asuras*. Both god and *asura* are in man. It is a fight between the higher and lower nature. There is the mythological story which is allegorical. We are told how the god Indra lost his powers because of his haughtiness, with consequent disaster to the world. When the gods supplicated Vishnu, He told them that through hard and continuous effort alone would they succeed in alleviating the sufferings of the universe. A steadfast mind and hard work bring their results. It was work alone that gave gods and men long life, peace and contentment. He advises them to churn the ocean.

Using Mount Mandara as the churner and the snake Vasuki as rope, the gods prepared to churn the ocean. The *asuras* hearing of the elixir of immortality, *amrita*, that was to be found in the ocean, also came forward and offered their help so that they too could get the Elixir.

The churning began with the demons holding the head of the snake and the gods the tail. It seemed an eternity. On and on they churned until Mount Mandara got stuck at the bottom of the ocean, and could not be lifted.

Vishnu was appealed to for help. He took the form of a tortoise and detached the Mount Mandara from the bed of the ocean. Next came the turn of the snake. The constant churning made him belch out poisonous fumes. The air was thick with the dark poison. The gods once more appealed for help. Shiva came to their rescue. To leave the poison in the atmosphere would have spelt death to the gods and *asuras*. He decided to eat the poison. Before He could swallow it, Parvati caught it at the throat to prevent it reaching the heart. Shiva let it stay in the throat. His throat became blue with the poison. That is why He is called *Nilakantha*, blue-necked.

As the gods and *asuras* churned on endlessly they were rewarded by the ocean giving up its treasures one by one. The milky *Kamadhenu*, *Kalpataru*, the wish-fulfilling tree, the jewel Kaustuba and the goddess Lakshmi all came out of the churning of the ocean.

At last, held aloft by Dhanvantari the physician of the Gods, was the jar of *amrita*. Suddenly a most beautiful apparition filled the space. This beautiful damsel was none other than Vishnu appearing as Mohini. She took the jar from Dhanvantari and walked off with it. She asked all to sit in rows, the gods on one side and the demons on the other. With jar and ladle she began with the gods. The demons were hypnotised by her beauty and could not take their eyes off her. But it suddenly occurred to one of them that the *amrita* was taking too long to reach them. He slipped in between Surya and Soma and put out his tongue. Mohini cut him in two with her ladle, but not before a drop had fallen on it. These are Rahu and *Ketu*. By this time the *amrita* had finished and the *asuras* got nothing.

Endeavour pursued with steady dedication brought out the treasures. *Kalpataru* or Kalpavriksa is the wish-fulfilling tree representing the mind which gives us everything by the mere thought. Mind is the most powerful creator. It is thought converted into action that brings fulfilment. Similarly *Kamadhenu* the all-bestowing cow symbolises word or speech. Thus knowledge and activity are the key to the fulfilment of wishes.

Sometimes, however, things may not always work out as we want. That is in the hands of the destiny that we ourselves have created. While the past may not be in our hands, the present is. To strive is in our hands, not the rewards.

Divinity is not only in all nature but also in man's endeavours. All arts and crafts and knowledge are also divine and need to be pursued for their own sake. They bring peace, prosperity and beauty to life. Bhagwan Rudra is described as a chariot-maker, wood-carver, potter, metal craftsman etc. Shiva teaches dance to Tandu and Bharata. Vishnu teaches painting to Vishvakarma. Vishvakarma is the divine architect and sculptor of the gods, who builds the aerial cars and mansions for the gods and to whom they owe everything.

Self-realised sages do not engage in worship of idols. But others need to have something before them. Idols are made to strict specifications so that they cannot be mistaken for a human figure. The lowest in scale is the idol with a number of hands. Each hand contains an attribute. Attributes being limitations cannot really represent the Infinite, beyond all attributes. In all temples the idol is always in the darkest part, the inner sanctum sanctorum. One can see it only by the lighted lamp. The idol represents the unmanifest *atma* in the body which we can only see by the lamp of wisdom. The lamp signifies the light of Knowledge.

Great thought was given to the different kinds of images and their effect on the mind. Images were classified as pacific and terrifying. The terrifying ones breathing death and destruction (which is also a part of nature) were normally located where soldiers went. They were in forests, marshes and other inaccessible places. If such an *ugra* (terrifying) form was found to be near a village, either a pacific idol would be placed in front of it or a water tank. The Bhoga form of image was considered appropriate for all. It was meant to grant desires. Just as the idol represented the *atma* so the temple also acted as the spiritual centre for the people. It was the nerve centre of all activities. Much thought went into the locations of temples so that they would have a beneficial effect on the mind. Those marshy areas or fortresses were meant for soldiers, while others in secluded places or the confluence of rivers were meant for quiet meditation.

The Hindu view is that the stronger force is the unselfish force. Form is more purposeful when it equips itself well. Not only is it necessary to learn about all forms, but even more necessary to understand the inner meaning of all forms.

References

Books mainly referred to have been:
  Studies in Indian Art by V.S. Agrawala.
  Elements of Hindu Iconography by T.A. Gopinath Rao.
  Cultural Heritage of India (Ramakrishna Mission Publication).

18

Hindu Contribution to World Knowledge

In Hindu thought there is no 'sin' but ignorance. All sins are committed due to ignorance. Understånding comes through knowledge. Knowledge Absolute is the highest goal.

The base or essence of all is the Principle of Pure Intelligence. This intangible Principle is present in all nature. It is the Spirit or Knower in man. The world process is described in terms of Knower, Knowledge and Known.

The true seeker first studies all that he can. His studies give him lower knowledge which even if it does not provide him with the essential moral qualities, helps him to manage and get along in the world, by giving him knowledge of his environment.

Higher Knowledge is the highest goal, because this results in value-based actions free of selfish needs and desires and hence nourishes all. The teacher is respected for his knowledge, but the Self-realised sage is respected more for he has reached the highest stage. The highest stage cannot be reached without spiritual purity.

Very few achieve this state, but no effort is ever wasted. Hindu thought places spiritual strength (soul force) as greater than will power. Will belongs to material phenomena. Spirit is beyond all phenomena.

The Spirit in man can make mountains move if it so chooses.

The Hindus understood the meaning and necessity of Law. *Dharma* was law, duty, morality, which sustained and nourished. They understood the meaning of Order. They tried to regulate man's life to enable him to make the best of life. They structured society to enable each one to meet the needs of all. This professionalised and preserved different skills. But even more than this they were aware of the corruption that can be caused by selfish material desires at the expense of the moral. They gave a code of work ethics. They called for work as a worship. The work was offered in devotion, dedication, and surrender without expectation of reward. Man's function in life was to fulfill a need. Doing his function well was the highest aim. In serving all he served the Spirit, and himself.

All manifestation is form. Form means individuality. No one person can know everything about everything. It was necessary therefore to have an open mind and hear other views and ideas. This is why from the earliest times there has been open discussion and debate. It was recognized that two contrary views may be honestly held. What was important was the honesty. Selfish material interests are usually narrow and bigoted. Morality, knowledge and understanding come to the unselfish mind.

It was this attitude to knowledge that made the Hindus not only open to ideas and thoughts from other lands and peoples, but also enabled them to preserve as well as augment their own knowledge throughout history.

The high and low periods in Hindu civilization are when knowledge was pursued with a free and open mind and when a static stage was reached, image became more important than the substance. In Hindu thought image-worship is worship of the material. Truth, the goal of all knowledge, is beyond all form. In our Age of Science it may be labelled 'unscientific' to talk of the importance of morality but then our age is not free of the conceit and arrogance found in man in all ages. It may be worthwhile to ask ourselves why the great thinkers of the past, not only in India but also in other lands who discussed all aspects of life, stressed so much on the moral qualities. In many a tribal society too we find customs which are meant to show that selfless conduct in man alone can make him suitable to lead others.

Great religious upheavals have invariably resulted in great intellectual and material gain. This has been so because of the moral strength which in turn has provided the right and open attitude to knowledge. Religious fundamentalism in due course has narrowed the vision by encouraging the irrational worship of form. This is the way to ignorance. Ignorance is the death of civilization.

The moral is as much a part of man as is the material. There has to be a balance. Man has to work to sustain himself and his dependants. He gets paid for his work. Morality demands that he earns the function he is paid for, because function is meant to serve a need.

To take pay and not to work honestly and efficiently (as best as he can) violates a moral law and hurts all. Again, to use his job as a means to harrass others and get extra illegal profit is again the violation of a moral law. If a drug company sells lethal drugs as medicine in order to make profits, it is false to its function. It is selfish material profit that is responsible for the harm caused to others. Such instances can be multiplied. Those who serve the spirit through honest work serve the material universe.

Thus knowledge, whether of art or science is not enough without morality. Morality is not conventional morality (which is again a worship of form) but complete honesty. The two value systems, the material and the moral have been there from the earliest days of man.

There is a tale given in the *Samhitopanishad Brahmana* (Ch.III) where Saraswati the goddess of learning approaches the teacher and says, "Preserve me, I am verily thy treasure. Deliver me not to one who is full of envy and discontent, one who is not straight in his conduct, nor to one of uncontrolled passions. But deliver me to him whom thou shalt know to be pure, attentive, intelligent, firm in chastity."

As the Upanishadic teacher tells his students in his farewell message to them on completion of their studies, "If you should have a doubt about a duty or a conduct, conduct yourself as is done by such learned men who can deliberate well, are devoted to their duties on their own and other's behalf, are not severe and are desirous of righteousness. This is the inner teaching of the Veda". (*Taittiriya Upanishad*)

The 'inner teaching' is understood by those who understand the spirit and not just the letter.

The importance of morality for all knowledge can hardly be under-estimated. The ancient teachers never under-estimated it. Perhaps many will agree there is still a lot we have to learn from them.

Indian civilization goes back into the mists of antiquity. India is well situated midway between east and west. The Harappan civilization traded with Pheonicia and Mesopotamia, Egypt and Ethiopia in the third millennium BC. We also know from Chinese references that India had trade wi.h China and other south-east Asian countries, certainly in the Ist millennium BC if not earlier. Indian ideas and institutions flowed both eastwards and westwards. Similarly ideas from other lands were also welcomed and assimilated in India.

There is sufficient evidence that points to the building skills of the early Harappan civilization. We also know that the Harappan civilization introduced glazed pottery about 1500 years before it appeared in Mesopotamia.

There is also enough evidence to show that the later Aryans imbibed the Harappan culture as well. It became a common culture with its own distinctive characteristics.

It is generally believed that iron smelting was first introduced in the Caucasus and Asia Minor by the Hittites. India is believed to have started iron smelting between 1000 and 800 BC. It is however indisputable that Indians had mastered and perfected this technique within a span of four to five centuries, and their iron goods were in much demand. These goods were preferred as arms, and by the Romans, as cutlery and armour.[1]

Recorded history goes back to about 6th century BC. Between 500 BC and AD 500 there were trade contacts between China, India, Persia and Rome. Trade contacts led to the transmutation of ideas in the field of art, culture, sciences, philosophy and religion.

Much of the work on India in modern times associates India (erroneously) with religion, philosophy, passivity and renunciation, rather than as having been involved in the active and vital quest of the truths of the universe and gaining mastery over several branches of knowledge in the arts and sciences. The contribution of the ancient Hindus was not only in the field of metaphysics which has provided the world with some of the most sublime and inspiring thoughts, but also in the other branches of worldly knowledge so essential to man's understanding of the universe. India's contributions in all these fields have not only been impressive but very valuable.

It has also been alleged that Indians did not put much into writing. This is perhaps more due to the fact that often what is presented as 'research' is based on the ideas expressed in other books and not from any references to ancient literature or works. In *Life and Culture of the Indian People* K.A. Nilakanta Sastri and G. Srinivasachari (p.6) point out that the widespread notion that Indians have no historical sense is incorrect, instead India is richer in documents, monuments, archives etc. than any other country.

There was a continuous literary output from the most ancient Vedic times to the modern times. The Smritis show that they appreciated the value of the written word in documents and as proof in courts of law.[2]

It is undoubtedly true that many works have been lost or destroyed when India faced invasions and lost her independence to intolerant regimes intent on establishing their rule. Temples and universities were the main targets of destruction, because they were the intellectual and cultural centres.[3] Ancient works in many fields of knowledge were stored in these institutions. Not only were the buildings destroyed but also the scholars associated with these institutions. Much of ancient literature has been lost to the world because of such vandalism.

Whereas some of the loss of knowledge may be due to the negligence of the people themselves, a significant reason was historical. Perhaps the most effective argument for a country not losing its independence would be the loss of knowledge, which reduces a people to the condition of a subject people and nothing better than hewers of wood and drawers of water.

As regards Indian cartography which is said to be practically non-existent, Wilson, in the notes to his English translation of the *Vishnu Purana*, observes that the few ancient maps he was able to get, showed all places correctly. Where he found difficulty was where the words of places had been distorted by the western penchant for mis-pronunication!

In any case it does seem extremely unlikely that a people who had colonised the eastern coast of Borneo as early as AD 1st century, had been able to do so without a clear understanding of cartography.

One 'modern' researcher tells us that the ancient Indian sailors were not too sure of their sailing. He draws his inference from a reference made to Indian sailors by the Pheonicians who observed that the Indians always said it was due to God's grace that they had been successful in their venture.

Had the 'researcher' been more conversant with Hindu philosophy he would have been conversant with this Hindu version of the Muslim "Inshe Allah". It does not mean that man ceases to strive. It only means that he is not so conceited as to think that he alone is responsible for all things that happen. All are but instruments of a Higher Will. But such type of research which does not seek to understand a people's basic philosophy can hardly be depended upon, as all inferences can only be fallacious to say the least.

Between the decline of the ancient civilizations and the rise of modern Europe, the Muslim civilization of the Arabs became the conduit in the transmission of knowledge. Islamic learning was deeply influenced by Syria, Mesopotamia, Persia, India and Greece.

India's greatest contribution to the Arab civilization was the introduction of technical knowledge and scientific ideas to the countries of West Asia. It was largely due to the liberal and broad-minded attitude to knowledge displayed by the Abbasid Caliphate that the Arab civilization could achieve what it did. It was during this time that the real scientific age of the Arabs began. It began with the Caliph al Mamun (AD 813-833). The great 'Translation Bureau' had already been established under *Harun ar-Rashid* where scholars and translators of all nationalities were employed for rendering books of scientific subjects into Arabic. Among the translators were also Indians.

With the help of Indian scientists astronomical observatories were established in AD 803 at Baghdad and Damascus.

The Arabs designed new instruments and showed more practical activity than the Greeks.

The Baghdad school represented the Indian scientific approach and spirit. After the decline of Baghdad in the AD 10th century, the mantle fell on the Buhaimid court.

The second half of the eleventh century again was a period of great intellectual renaissance in Arabia and Persia.

Al-Biruni (AD 973-1048) was one of the greatest scientists of Islam. Being well-versed in Sanskrit, he exploited the best sources of Indian sciences including mathematics, astronomy, and chronology. His theory of the earth's movement was borrowed from Aryabhatta (AD 5th century) His *Qanunal-Masudi* (AD 1030) is the most important work on astronomy based largely on Indian ideas. He also utilized the Indian knowledge in geology and mineralogy. He translated Varaha Mihira's *Surya Siddhanta*.

The Arabs certainly at a given period of history played a great part in retaining the precious heritage of world knowledge. That they were able to do so can be explained by their refreshingly open attitude to knowledge. *El Ghazzali* (AD 1111), the famous theologian and philosopher at Baghdad expounding on the duties of true believers quoted two 'hadiths' (traditions of the Prophet). One of these makes it the bounden duty of every Muslim to seek knowledge. The other bids man to seek knowledge even if it be in China. Al Biruni's own approach was similar. He wrote, "I do not scorn to accept truth from whatever source I can find."

Would the men all over understand their religious teachings as well as these two! One can hardly doubt that the great rishis would have applauded them. Religion is meant to give us an open and discriminating mind to be better able to perceive truth. Truth does not come to the bigoted and closed mind.

We can perceive the Buddhist influence also on the Abbasids. Their minister was a Barmak. The last Barmak was brought up in India and received his education in Kashmir, noted for its university. He was appointed minister in the court of Baghdad. Baghdad became the centre of Hindu learning.

History plays strange tricks. The Barmaks were the head priests of the Buddhist monastery at Balkh. When it was conquered by the Muslims, the mother was taken prisoner and converted to Islam, and her son later became minister at the court of Baghdad.

The decline of the Abbasids saw the rise of the Samanids of Transaxonia, who had a similar open attitude to knowledge. Their capital at Bukhara rivalled and almost eclipsed Baghdad. Finally, with the fall of Arab power the leadership of Islam went to the Turks who did not have the same receptivity as the Arabs. It was mainly due to the Abbasids and Samanids that the Arabs made their valuable contribution to the world.

It is significant that even as late as the AD 11th century the Arab Said-al-Andalusi, an astronomer and historian of science, in his work *Kitab Tabakat al-Umam* (the Categories of Nations) gives India the first place among the contemporary nations which had developed science by then.[4]

Perhaps of all the subjects the most favourite of the Indians and the Hindus was Mathematics. The Arabs named this discipline *Hindisa* (pertaining to India). Mathematics can be described as the base for all sciences.

Talking of *ganita* an old text says, "As the crests on the heads of peacocks, as the gems on the hoods of snakes, so is the *ganita* at the top of the Sciences known as the Vedanga."[5]

In that period *ganita* included Arithmetic, Algebra and Astronomy, while Geometry (Sulva) was counted along with a different group of sciences known as the Kalpa.

The Indian achievement in all these disciplines was considerable. One great contribution has been the decimal, the zero and place digits, by which each digit indicates its power by its place as a multiple of ten.

Severus Sebokht, A Syrian scholar of the AD 7th century, referred to the Hindu place value notation as a "computing that surpasses description." And Halstead remarks, "this giving to airy nothing, not merely a local habitation and a name, a picture, a symbol, but helpful power, is the characteristic of the Hindu race from whence it sprang."[6]

The Indian decimal place value notation spread to Indo-China, Indonesia, China and Japan probably around the AD 6th or 7th century. The Indian numerals (misnamed as Arab numerals) reached Arabia around the AD 7th or 8th century. *Al-Khwarizmi* was a well-known Arab exponent of this system. His works (AD 9th century) were translated in the twelfth century by Adelard of Bath into Latin. At the same period *John of Seville* and *Abraham Ibn Ezra* were propagating the system taken from Arab sources. This system was strongly opposed by the abacus users of Europe. In the 13th century the Italian Fibonacci expounded this system in his arithmetical work *Liber abaci*, which became extremely popular. By the AD 13th century the Hindu decimal place value notation had established itself in Europe and since then became universal.[7]

The Indian fascination for numbers goes back to very

ancient times. The *Yajur Veda Samhita* lists numbers up to (10^{12}). The highest terminology used by the Greeks around the 4th century BC (at least two thousand years later) was *myriad* (10^4) and for the Romans was *mille* which denoted (10^3). During the classical period the Indians developed a terminology to express numbers as large as (10^{24}) and (10^{53}).[8]

An idea of the great contribution of the Hindu place digit system may be got by placing the longest Roman numeral MDCCCLXXXVIII alongside the Indian equivalent 1888!

Reference to the decimal value and number 10 appears in the *Purusa Sukta* of the *Rig Veda*. While Europe was grappling with division as late as the fifteenth century, the Indians were conversant with it much before the AD 9th century.

In the classical period, India produced many great mathematicians. Many of these were astronomers as well. These were Aryabhatta I (AD 5th-6th century) Bhaskara I (AD 7th century) Brahmagupta (AD 7th century) Mahavira (AD 9th century) Aryabhatta II (AD 10th century), Sripati (AD 10th century), Sridhara (AD 11th century) and Bhaskara II (AD 12th century).

It is impossible in a few pages to sum up the achievements in the sciences, as these are considerable.

Aryabhatta I knew the rules for the extraction of square and cube roots, area of triangles, trapezium, circles, volumes of sphere and pyramid, arithmetical progression and summation of series, fractions etc. He also developed an alphabetical system for expressing numbers on the decimal place value model. He gave the value of Π correct to four places of decimal (3.1416) as an approximate. His greatest work was *Aryabhatiya* (consisting of four sections, one on Mathematics and three on Astronomy).

Bhaskara I shows a method for solving indeterminate equations of the first degree. Brahmagupta, recognized as an eminent mathematician of his time, gave the formula for the sum of 'n' terms of arithmetical progression of which the first term is Unity and the common difference is Unity. He stated clearly the rules regarding volumes of prisms and the area of cyclic quadrilaterals. His rules are in use to this day. His general solution in integers of the indeterminate equations of the first degree was given in the same form as found in modern text books on Algebra. He also dealt with indeterminate equations of the 2nd degree $Ny+I=X^2$. One of his results in indeterminate equations was re-discovered about a thousand years later by Euler (AD 1707–1783) which he refers to as the 'remarkable theorem'.

Mahavira in his *Ganitasarasangraha* deals with the use of zero and summation of 'n' terms of a geometrical progression. Aryabhatta II in his work *Mahasiddhanta* deals with a number of mathematical problems including zero. Sridhara is credited with a method of solving quadratic equations in his work *Ganitatilaka*. Bhaskara II in his famous work *Siddhanta Siromani* dealt with Arithmetic, Geometry and Algebra. He gives a correct assessment of a division of a finite number by zero. Letters are used to denote algebraical quantities. He deals with indeterminate equations of the first and second degree. The rules given by him in regard to these are in effect the same as rediscovered by European mathematicians like Fermat, Euler, and Lagrange in the 17th century. He also developed a cyclical method called Chakravala for rational integral solutions of the indeterminate equations ($Ny^2+I=X^2$). It is on record that "the glory of having invented the general methods in indeterminate analysis belongs to Indians. Bhaskara's cyclical method of solving the indeterminate quadratic equations constitutes the greatest in the theory of numbers before the time of Lagrange."

The *Sulva-sutras* (Rules of the Thread and Measuring line) which are a part of the Kalpa sutras deal with geometry. These are the earliest documents. Among these are the *Baudhayana, Vadhula, Apastamba, Hiranyakesin, Manava* and *Varaha*. The *Baudhayana* is the oldest (7th century BC) with 525 sutras and 3 chapters. Some of these sutras give specifications of measuring cord, gnomon etc. They deal with the construction of square and rectangles, relations of diagonal to sides, equivalent rectangles and squares, equivalent circles and squares, among many other things. Both *Apastamba* and *Baudhayana* describe a square to the sum of two different squares like $3^2+4^2=5^2$, $5^2+12^2=13^2$, $8^2+15^2=17^2$, $7^2+24^2=25^2$, $12^2+35^2=37^2$, $15^2+36^2=39^2$. Katyayana states to the effect that if the sides of a right angled triangle are A and $A\sqrt{2}$, then the hypotenuse is $A\sqrt{3}$.

Some western scholars also share the view that the origin of what is known as the Pythagoras theorem may be traced to the Hindu *Sulva sutras*.[9] G. Milhand considers the Pythagorian geometry to have been inspired to some extent by the Hindu model.

The binomial theorem discovered in Europe in the AD 16th century seems to have been known to Indians much earlier. The triangular array formed by the binomial coefficients (known in Europe as the Pascal Triangle) was known in India as the *Meru Prastara*, a pyramidical expansion of the number of combination 1, 2, etc. syllables formed of short (*laghu*) and long (*guru*) sound. This has been dealt with methodically by Pingala in his *Chandas sutra* (3rd century BC).[10]

Astronomy: We find a knowledge of astronomy even in

Rig Vedic times. During the Vedic period the moon became the measure of the month. Asterisms were called lunar mansions or *Naksatras*. *Naksatras* find no place in Greek astronomy. The *Naksatras* were used as fixed points to solve the problems of the length of time as to how many revolutions it would take the hands of a clock to meet again, etc.

The *Jyotisa Vedanga* is the earliest record of Hindu astronomical ideas. Some of the passages are enigmatical and need to be studied and understood properly.

Hindu astronomy is based on the concept of a cosmic cycle in terms of 10,800 or 432,000 years. This figure of 432,000 found favour in even later Siddhanta astronomy. It was accepted in Babylonia. The Greek thinker Heraclitus (5th century BC) conceived of a great year in terms of 10,800 years. It is known that the Greek and Babylonian thinkers were influenced by the Hindu concept.

There are 18 Indian astronomical works known as *Siddhantas*. Varahamihira (AD 6th century) in his *Panchasiddhantika* deals with only five viz., Saura, Vasishta, Paulisa, Romaka and Paitamiha. The *Surya Siddhanta* occupies the pride of place among the eighteen Siddhantas. This is of uncertain date and in its present form contains astronomical ideas which are very old and others comparatively recent. *Surya Siddhanta* deals with measurement of time, sine tables, and cosine functions, meridians, equinoxes, solstices, eclipses of the sun and moon, planetary motions, inclination of the *Naksatras* to the eliptic, heliacal risings and settings of stars, relative motion of the moon and sun, some astronomical instruments and calendar computations.

There seems to be a difference of opinion among scholars regarding foreign influence on Siddhantas.

"No Indian work admits of any Yavana knowledge nor do any ancient Sanskrit text works set out any large number of astronomical terms of Greek origin as Varaha does in astrology.

In *Panchasiddhantikas* . . . none of the subjects of words can be said to be originally Greek . . . .

Weber thinks that two of the five Siddhantas called *Romaka* and *Paulisa* suggest Greek origin. Even conceding for argument that Romaka referred to the Alexandrian school. . . no proof of Greek influence on Siddhantas. Varaha mentions Yavana views and frequently differs, but is generous towards Greek astrology saying, "Yavanas are indeed mlechas and this sastra is well cultivated among them; even they are honoured as if they were sages, what need it be said about a *Brahmana* well versed in astrology (he will be honoured all the more)." P.V. Kane points out that there is no reason to believe Pulisa as non-Indian when such ancient words *Pulayasta, Pulaka, Paulastya* etc. are found in Sanskrit.[11]

The inferences of foreign influence have been drawn from the names and mostly on pre-conceived ideas that such knowledge was not possible at that time in India. And Kane observes, "If ancient Indians were capable of analysing the elements of the Sanskrit language and raising such a system as Panini's and if they could plumb the depths of the human mind and create a mental discipline like Yoga, if they carefully noted centuries before Christ the parts of the glottis and other organs in the mouth in the production of the letters of their language and produced Pratasabhyas and Siksa works, if they could create a fable literature and invent the game of chess and make a gift of these two to the whole of mankind, if their knowledge of algebra was of a superior order (vide Colebrook's *Essays* vol.II p.446, and Cajori's *A History of*

Elementary Mathematics p.93-101), if they invented the decimal place value system for numbers and propagated it and the sign for a zero to Europe through the Arabs in the AD 12th century, there is hardly any compelling reason for saying that it would not have been possible to arrive at their own eccentric and epicycle system independently of any other people to explain the supposed motion of the sun, the moon and the planets round the Earth."[12]

The French Astronomer Laplace, commenting on epochs used by the Indians for purposes of calculation says, "nevertheless the ancient reputation of the Indians does not permit us to doubt that they have always cultivated astronomy and the remarkable exactness of the mean motion which they assign to the sun and the moon necessarily required very ancient observations."[13]

The Indian astronomical periods are regarded as successive parts of the great cosmic cycle.

Aryabhatta I developed the theory of the earth's rotation as well as that of epicycles. Brahmagupta who opposed Aryabhatta's rotation theory was well known for his two treatises *Brahma-Sphuta-Siddhanta* and *Khandakhyadaka*, which were translated into Arabic under the titles *Sindhhind* and *Arkhand*.[14] The Indian calculations of the annual rate of motion of the equinox as 54 seconds is a remarkable approximation to the modern value of about 50 seconds[15] a year (Mippaschus estimated it as about 30 seconds a year).

Ayurveda is considered as the Science of Life and Longevity. It can be traced to the *Atharvaveda*. It serves man, animal and plant. India's greatest contribution to science has been its humanism.

The most important classical texts on *Ayurveda* are the *Charaka Samhita* and the *Susruta Samhita*. Says Charaka, "Not for money, nor for any earthly objects should one treat his patients. In this the physican's work excels all vocations. Those who sell treatment as merchandise neglect the true treasure of gold in search of mere dust."[16]

Says the Hindu scientist, "When the perfection of Rasa (mercury) is achieved, I shall make humanity free from decay and death."[17]

Among the great civilizations of antiquity only three, India, China and Greece, had fully developed systems representative of physiology and pathology. Although Egypt and Mesopotamia did some rich medical work, it was more of the practical kind and not a systematic, rationally thought out attempt.[18] Some Greek and Indian theories are similar. There are also direct references in the Hippocrates Collection to the borrowing of Ayurvedic drugs from medical formulas. Also Plato's Timaeus is the only Greek treatise giving the Tridosa theory. Since no reference is given as to its origin, it seems to be the influence of Ayurvedic texts. Along with the other arts and sciences *Ayurveda* travelled to Central Asia, China, Indo-China, and Indonesia. China, Korea and Japan which had their own medical tradition, accepted Ayurvedic medicine, if not the theories. Both Tibet and Cambodia accepted *Ayurveda*, and later, Mongolia, Siberia also had a rich tradition of *Ayurveda*.

Roman Celsius (AD 1st century) describes in his medical works lithotomy practised in India earlier. Galen (AD 131–201) mentions borrowing Indian eye ointment and plaster.[19] Indian herbs were in much demand in Rome. Sanskrit texts in Pharmacology and Toxicology were translated into Arabic. Later *as-Razi's* comprehensive book *Kitab al-hawi* (AD 865-925) incorporating Indian medical knowledge was translated into Latin and known to medieval Europe as *Liber Continess*. This 13th century translation became a standard work in Europe.

Ayurveda based its doctrines on *Sankhya*, Yoga and *Vaisesikha*. It took its *Panchabhautic* theory from *Sankhya-Yoga* and its *Tridosa* and *Saptadhatus* from *Vaisesikha*. "In man", says *Ayurveda*, "life is the manifestation of body, sense, mind and the spirit."

The eight limbs of *Ayurveda* are *Salya* (surgery), *Salakya*, *Kaya-chikitsa* (internal medicine), *Bhuta vidya* (demonology), *Kaumara bhrty* (pediatrics), *Aganda* (toxicology), *Rasayana* (rejuvenation compositions) and *Vajikarana* (virilification).

While the *Charaka Samhita* concentrates on internal medicine, the *Susruta Samhita* concentrates on surgery.

Surgery was looked upon not as just a science but also an art. Susruta describes surgery under the following heads: *Chedya* (excision), *Lekhya* (scarification), *Vedhya* (puncturing), *Esya* (exploration), *Aharya* (extraction), *Visravya* (evacuation) and *Sivya* (Suturing).

Details are given regarding the making of 101 varieties of blunt surgical instruments and twenty of sharp instruments such as forceps, tongs, scalpels, catheters, bougies, trocare, syringes, speculums, needles, saws, scissors, lances, hooks, and probes.

It seems that as early as the 6th or 7th century BC Indian surgeons were proficient in surgical procedures such as incising, excising, puncturing, scarifying etc. Susruta gives a clear account of cataract crouching which was unknown to Greece and Egypt. Indians were also proficient in cranatomy and anal fistula operations. Careful attention was provided during both pre- and post operative stages. Surgical operation for affection of eyelid was known to Indian surgeons.

Dr. Guthrie in his *History of Medicine* observes, "It was in surgery above all that the ancient Hindus excelled. Susruta described more than a hundred instruments. This was their greatest contribution to the art of healing and the work was bold and distinctive. . ." And Newberger in *History of Medicine* says, "The outstanding feats of ancient Indian surgery related to laparotomy, lithotomy, plastic surgery, and plastic operations."

Susruta Samhita is regarded as the earliest document to give an account of rhinoplasty.

Sometimes ants were also used to join the lips of wounds by using their mandibles as clamps. This method was later adopted by the Arabs.

Like all other branches of knowledge *Ayurveda* also has a divine origin, descending from Brahma. The patron of *Ayurveda* is Dhanvantari, the physician of the gods.

In ancient times alchemic practices were mostly for the purpose of turning baser metals into gold or to produce an elixir that would ensure immortality. In India it was more the latter than the former.

Alchemic practices may have begun around AD 6th or 7th century. Some presume they came from China.

The Sanskrit word for alchemy is *Rasavidya* and for alchemist it is *Rasasiddha*. The early Indian alchemy based on mercury was the fore-runner of the iatrochemical practices of the AD 11th and 12th century. A reputed chemist from Tamil Nadu refers to his visiting Arabia and teaching there under the name of Yakub. Tamil alchemy has for its central theme a union of three salts called *muppu* in the nature of a philosopher's stone. Mineral medicines using mercury, sulphur and salt were used in India in the AD 11th and 12th century.

Much work needs to be done on Indian alchemic practices. Besides metals, India possessed a high degree of knowledge about alkali, acids and salts, cosmetics, perfumes and pyrotechnics. They were looked upon as useful arts rather than a developing branch of knowledge.

Physical concepts: Physical concepts form an integral part of the Indian religions and philosophies. Knowledge of the different sciences was pursued as an aid to the understanding of Absolute Truth. All physical truths are relative truths.

One of the pitfalls in any study was not unknown to the ancient seekers. "Not seeing the wood for the trees", is a common enough problem in any study. Says this *Rig Veda* verse (X.158-4), "Give sight to our eyes, sight to our bodies, so that they can see; may we see the world as a whole, may we see it in detail."

It is perhaps because of this awareness that they were not only able to go into the minutest detail, but also think in terms of the broadest of concepts.

For the study of any living science it is important that there should be an awareness of a universal natural law governing all natural phenomena. In India, all natural phenomena were explained in terms of this natural law, *Rta*.

In the history of the evolution of physical ideas, the *Sankhya* and *Nyaya-Vaisasikha* deserve special mention. The *Vaisesikha* system had assumed a definite shape by the 6th century BC. It deals with a number of physical concepts concerning substance, the five elements, motion, attributes, space, time and atomism.

At this time the pre-Socrates Greek thinkers were only gradually generating their views on the physical world. There is a considerable resemblance between the ideas contained in the *Vaisesikha sutras* (consisting of ten chapters) and those of the Greek thinkers, including Aristotle. It is more than likely that the well-formulated and systematic *Vaisesikha* theory may have attracted and stimulated thinkers in these lands.

The concept of substance is important in the history of science. Substance (*dravya*) is conceived in terms of the five elements, space, time, mind and self in the *Vaisesikha*.

The theory of atomism was propounded by the *Nyaya-*

Vaisesikha and some Buddhist and Jain schools giving a rational explanation of the basic stuff of the gross world.

The atomic view of matter stated by *Nyaya-Vaisesikha* is historically earlier than Greek atomism. Surprisingly, the atomism of Leucippus and Democritus which was neither so developed nor so sustained and systematic, has found its way into the history of sciences, and not Indian atomism which was a theme of discussion and debate by the Indian scientists for over two thousand years, covering both the ancient and medieval periods!

The *Nyaya-Vaisesikha* explains the difference in quality of substance by observing that the different qualities in a single substance are due to the fact that two like atoms can only unite in the presence of another type of atom which becomes the accessory cause. This is how a single substance has different qualities. It also holds that the quality of a substance owes its arrangement to the spatial placement of the constituents. These views that can bear scrutiny even from the modern chemical point of view, are not to be found in Greek atomism.[20]

There are also other differences between Greek and Indian atomism. While Greeks postulate void as a necessary concomitance of postulation of discrete minute units of matter, the *Vaisesikha* postulates Akasa, a *dravya* or substance of unlimited magnitude, in which all finite substances are in direct contact.

The theory of impetus is also important in the history of science, and this was developed by the *Nyaya-Vaisesikha*. This theory was expressed by the AD 5th century. The West came to this theory in the AD 14th century.[21]

While in India the theory of atomism held the field for over two thousand years drawing adherents as well as opponents, in the west the atomic views of the pre-Socrates thinkers were ably expounded by Lucretius in the 1st century BC, to be later revived with modifications and in a speculative way only in the 17th century by Gassendi, Boyle, Newton, Huygens and Voltaire.[22]

The *Sankhya* theory of creation propounding an evolutionary process from the subtle to the gross was as revolutionary in its day as the later conclusions of Darwin and Lamarck. The *Sankhya* is closer to the Lamarckian view in considering that the need or desire produces the function and the function produces the organ. *Sankhya* theories were discussed in China which had many *Sankhya* schools of thought.[23] There is a view held by some scholars that these views influenced Pythagorian theories as well. Both *Sankhya* and the *Nyaya-Vaisesikha* theories have been given in an earlier chapter of this book.

Religion: Among the Indian religions to have left the shore of their native land the best known is Buddhism. Emperor Ashoka who embraced Buddhism, sent emissaries to the courts of Syria and west Asia, Egypt, Cyrene, Macedonia, Epirus and Corinth. He also sent monks to Srilanka. Buddhism was propagated in South and South-east Asia by monks of intellect, understanding and dynamism. Indian Buddhist missionaries reached China about 65 BC. though Buddhist texts had reached there earlier in about the 2nd century BC. Buddhist texts were translated into Chinese in the AD 1st century. Dharma-raksha and Kasyapa Matanga were the pioneers. The largest number of Buddhist missionaries went to China between the third and sixth centuries. The greatest of these was *dharmadeva* who died there. Buddhism reached China through Central Asia.

Chinese records have it that Buddhism prevailed till the borderland of Persia and had a stronghold in Parthia. *Al Biruni* states that in former times Buddhism held sway in Khorasan, Persia, Iraq, Mosul and the country up to the borders of Syria.[24]

Buddhism was the first great missionary religion.

It is also necessary to record that a great factor which contributed in making Buddhism acceptable to the people was its complete identification with the people of each land. It clashed with no other religion. This is largely due to the proper understanding of *dharma* that Buddhist missionaries displayed. Their message was *dharma* for all men. *Dharma* comes through knowledge and understanding.

Hindu Upanishadic thought is very similar and there is thus no conflict with Buddhist thought. Hinduism though not a missionary religion also spread to other lands of South-east Asia, where its influence was both strong and lasting. The culture and philosophy of India went to other lands through saints, traders, ambassadors and religious teachers.

The South-east Asian countries which included Malaysia, Indonesia, Indo-China, Siam, and Cambodia were collectively known as Dvipantaras. They were regarded as being culturally integral parts of Bharatvarsha where the specific Hindu ceremony of sacrifice could be performed.

The Hindu kingdoms of South and South-east Asia lasted over a thousand years before the advent of Islam. Their eclipse in about AD 1400 came about not as a result of a military defeat but through conversion.

The liberal traditions of Hinduism remain in many countries of South-east Asia.

Hinduism was not an aggressive movement, but the result of a continuous flow of stimulating ideas and institutions of a vital people. The rise of Hindu influence and culture in South-east Asia corresponds to the Hindu revival in India which was a period of great literary and intellectual activity.

The earliest Hindu colony was in East Borneo which must have attracted trade due to its mineral wealth. This was as early as the AD 1st century. The kingdom of Cambodia was established by a local princess marrying a *Brahmin* called Kaundeya. It became a thriving and powerful kingdom. In Cambodia Buddha and Shiva were depicted identically. Laos became a great centre of intellectual and religious activity. Their most important script is *Tham* (*dharma*). The kingdoms of Funan and Sri Vijaya were strong and powerful in their day.

Indian thought blended with local culture. The Hindu epics, and Puranas blended with their own cults and beliefs. Sanskrit was a powerful medium. There are a number of Sanskrit words pertaining to religion, philosophy, art, law, commerce, government and administration. Indian treatises on *Arthasastra*, maxims of Kautilya, Manu and Kamandaka are known in many South-east Asian countries.

The first notable ambassador of Indian culture was the sage Agastya, who is also known as the first compiler of the Tamil grammar. He is said to have gone to Sri Lanka and to the Southeast Asian countries where he is highly venerated.[25]

Indonesia still has a large minority of practising indigenous Hindus. There are three million Balinese Hindus and two and a half million in eastern Java and thousands more in other parts of Java and the Celebes. Today we can find in almost all parts of the world Hindus who have migrated from India.

As regards the influence of Hindu religious thought in the west, it is commonly assumed that the contact between east and west came with Alexander. The contact had been established much earlier, though this contact was established in the period preceding the Persian wars. Persia was the link between the two. Indian soldiers in the Persian army had fought on Greek soil.

The Indian view of metempsychosis influenced Plato.[26]

For centuries before and after the Christian era the Hindu and Buddhist philosophical and religious influences flowed through the middle-east to the Greco-Christian civilization. Apart from the indirect influence of Hinduism through Buddhism, the *Brahmanas* were also known.

Indian philosophy was acquiring a growing reputation in the Hellenistic schools of Egypt and Asia Minor. The city of Alexandria played a major role in the cross-pollination of ideas.

We learn from Lamblichus, the biographer of Pythagoras that after studying the esoteric teachings of Egyptians and Assyrians and even the *Brahmanas*, Pythagoras propounded the theory of transmigration of souls from body to body. It is more likely that Pythagorian theories were influenced more by India than Egypt as all the theories of Pythagoras were known in India before his time.

Clement of Alexandria (AD 150-218) in his *Stromateis* refers to the Buddhists and the *Brahmanas* and the doctrine of transmigration. Bardisenes (AD 155-233) a well-known gnostic wrote a book on Indian religions. Appolonius of Tyana (AD 50) is stated to have gone to Taxila to study under a *Brahmin* teacher, and Plotinus (AD 205-270) who is credited with being the founder of neo-Platonism, went with Emperor Gordion against Persia so as to have the opportunity to study the wisdom of the east. According to Elliot, "In Plotinus the procedure preparatory to ecstasy is remarkably similar to those of Buddhist and Brahmanic systems."

King Menander (Milinda) was the greatest of the Indo Greek kings who was converted to Buddhism by the erudite Buddhist monk Nagasena. Menander was known for his many pious acts and when he died people vied for his ashes. Another Greek ruler was Agathocles who used only Buddhist emblems on his coins and took pride in calling himself a 'hinduja', an Indian by birth. In India itself we have Heliodorus, a native of Taxilla and a convert to Vaisnavism who came as the ambassador of King Antialcidas to the court of the Sunga ruler and who commemorated the visit by building a shrine at Vidisa.

In the development of Gnosticism which has been described as *Orientalism in a Hellenized mask*, *Sankhya-Yoga* played an important part. As Rawlinson states, apart from other resemblances the fundamental idea of the Gnostics, the knowledge of God or, Gnossis, is clearly similar to the Jnanakanda of the Hindus."

The remarkable similarities between the stories relating to the life of the Buddha and Christ can hardly be ignored. At least two orders of pre-Christian Judaism seemed to have been influenced by Indian religion. These were the Essenes and the Theraputae, whose precepts and modes of life have been recognized by scholars as the influence of Buddhism.

There are many common legends and myths, cults and rituals between India and the Semitic world, like the flood legends, cosmogenic myths, and earth and corn myths. Many legends of the Talmud and Midrash are directly or indirectly taken from Indian sources, e.g. the seven firmaments and the seven underworlds. Islamic literature has drawn largely from Jewish sources. The Jewish myth of Shemhazai and Azael becomes the tale of Harut and Marut in Islamic literature and has a striking resemblance to the story of Sunda and Upasunda in the *Mahabharata*.

Certain scholars point out that the name of Buddha also finds mention in the Koran along with prophets, Moses, Abraham and Christ. He appears as *Fil-Kifl* (belonging to Kapilavastu).[27] According to Islamic tradition, the first man and prophet descended on Indian soil from heaven and received the first divine message from God. The Muslim belief also is that Adam's eldest son Shith is lying buried at Ayodhya.[28] The prostration and circumambulation of the *Ka'aba* bears a close resemblance to Buddhist practice. The Prophet said, "From India comes the divine fragrance to me."[29]

In Iran under Shapur I (AD 241-272) the Magian Zoroastrian revival was taking place. "The King of Kings Shapur, son of Ardeshir, further collected those writings of the Religion that were dispersed throughout India, the Byzantine empire and other lands, and which treated of medicine, astronomy, movement, time, space, substance, creation, becoming, passing away, qualitative change, logic and other arts and sciences."

India contributed greatly to Muslim mysticism. Vedantic literature as well as wandering sadhus played a great part. Sufism came into existence in Persia in the latter half of the AD 8th century. The work of Jahiz was influenced by Hindu thinkers and Yogis. The Aizudiya form of Sufi thought according to which the Supreme Being is manifest in everything (*Hama-Osat*), the individual and universal soul existing in undifferentiated relation, resembles the *Advaita* Vedanta, while the Suhudwa school resembles Ramanuja's *Visistadvaita Vedanta*. Titus points out that "here the contribution seems to be made in thought, religious imagery and expression and pious practices, which came from both Buddhist and Vedantic sources."[30]

Perhaps one of the most interesting examples of the transmutation of a story is the Christian legend of Barlaam and Josaphat.[31] Taken from the original Sanskrit it was a modified and Christianised account of the Buddha's Great Renunciation. "It was utilized for Christian edification and adapted for the purpose of Christian apologetic." It had over fifty versions in the principal languages of Europe, the Christian Orient and even Africa.

Both the eastern and western Church canonized St. Joseph or Josaphat (i.e. The young Buddha). Barlaam and Josaphat are venerated by the Roman Catholic Church on November 27th, the Greek Orthodox Church on August 26th, and the Georgians on May 19th!

Art and Literature: While Indian art is more in evidence in the north and east than the west, India's literature has influenced all parts of the world. Indians were known for their skill in not only carving objects of beauty in metals, wood and ivory, but also carving out temples out of solid rock. Examples of Hindu skill can be seen in Ellora. This includes Buddhist and Jain!

Architecture was also art and there was the awareness for the need of the aesthetic. There are many treatises on art and architecture which include planning of towns, villages, markets, ports, harbours, bridges, gateways, wells, tanks, drainage etc. All types of constructions, for civil, religious as well as military needs have been dealt with. Impressive scientific data has been provided on the significance of ground and atmospheric conditions, nature of the soil, terrain etc.

Some treatises discuss not only furniture but also dress and personal ornament. Of the several treatises, the *Manasara* is the most comprehensive.

An example of Indian carving can be had from the temple architecture which also contains some of the most beautiful sculptures.

Angkor Vat in Cambodia is an example of this art in other lands. The temple of Angkor Vat is dedicated to Shiva.

India's painting heritage is ancient. Some of the earliest extant can be seen on the walls of the Buddhist caves of Ajanta. Later came the palm leaf and manuscript illustrations. The six canons of Indian painting migrated to foreign lands. The most elaborate treatise on painting is the *Vishnudharmottara*. Artists and craftmen had great importance from the Rig Vedic times. Painting and sculpture were branches of Vijnana.

The state had the responsibility for the protection of crafts.

The divine source of arts and crafts is conveyed through symbolism. Bhagwan Rudra described in his many forms is called a chariot-maker, wood-carver, potter, metal craftsman, etc. Shiva teaches Natyasastra to Tandu and Bharata, while Vishnu is the master of one thousand arts and the patron of painting.

In the epics Visvakarma and *Maya* emerge as the famous architects of gods and demons respectively. Visvakarma is worshipped by men on earth as the divine architect to whom they owe everything.

Much more study is needed on the course of Indian art to other lands. Far more is known of literature.

In *Wisdom of China and India*, Lin Yutang with true old-world Chinese courtesy writes about India first. In his introduction he observes, "India has a rich culture, as creative an imagination and wit and humour as any China has to offer", and that "India was China's teacher in religion, imaginative literature and the world's teacher in trigonometry, quadratic equations, grammar, phonetics, Arabian Nights, animal fables, chess, as well as philosophy, and she inspired Boccaccio, Goethe, Herder, Schopenhauer, Emerson, and probably also Aesop." He mentions that he has naturally not included India's achievements in the field of the positive sciences, but gives an interesting story of Houston Chamberlain, the "English apostle of Aryanism" who wanting to prove Aryan superiority had to point out Panini as the world's first grammarian! He refers to the poetry and dramatic works of Kalidas, apart from the great epics. He goes on to say. "It may be a complete revelation to find that the fabulous

Hindu mind is responsible for the genre of animal fables and many stories of the Arabian Nights type in which the Buddhist and non-Buddhist literature abounds ... Numerous fairy stories to be found in Grimm or Hans Anderson, including the Magic Mirror, the Seven Leagued Boots, Jack and the Beanstalk, and the Purse of Fortunatus, have been traced to Indian sources." He quotes from A.G. Rawlinson's article 'India in European Literature and Thought' in the *Legacy of India*. "Many of them are to be found in the *Gesta Romana*, the *Decameron*, and Chaucer's *Canterbury Tales*."

We see that India's fable literature travelled to other lands. One of the fascinating studies is the spread of the *Panchatantra*. It has travelled all over the globe. Winternitz observes, "Not only have single Indian tales been spread to other peoples by travellers, merchants and itinerant monks, but even whole Indian books of stories have become the common property of many people." "When Theodos Benfry traced the history of the *Panchatantra* and its wanderings through world literature he laid the foundation of what has since been termed 'Comparative History of Literature', and has become a new branch of historical and literary research ... Already in AD 6th century its fame had reached Persia." Under orders of King Khosran Anosherwan it was translated into Persian. In AD 570 there were Syrian and Arabic translations, but the Pehlevi work consisted of not only the five books of *Panchatantra* but several more books in which were some tales of the *Mahabharata* and some Buddhist tales as well.

Traces of these works can be seen in the most popular works of western literature e.g. *Gesta Romana* and similar collection of monks' tales in Latin, in the French *Fabliaux*, in the works of famous story tellers Boccaccio and Straparola in Italy, of Chaucer in England and Lafontaine in France, and even in the German household Tales collected by the Brothers Grimm.

Other Indian tales that have contributed to the narrative literature of the world are the *Vetala-panchavimsatika*, part of which is included in the Mongolian story *Siddikus*; the *Vikrama-charita* was translated into Persian by Emperor Akbar in AD 1574, of which there is a Mongolian version titled *The Story of Ardshi Bordshi Khan*; the Sukasaptati the 70 stories of the Parrot' which in its Turkish translation is known as the *Tutinameh* (the Parrot Book). "It is even highly probable that the two famous books of world literature, the book of Sindbad and the Arabian Nights are at least partly of Indian origin. The book of Sindbad is known in Arabic, Persian, Syrian, Hebrew and Greek versions ... The Arabian writer Masudi (who died in AD 956) says that the *Kitab-es-Sindbad* was derived from the Indian book".

Similarly, the Judgement of Solomon is found in many countries. There are many tales from the Buddhist Jatakas in Greek, Arabic, Hebrew, Persian and Coptic.

In the eighteenth century there was again a revival of interest in the knowledge of other countries. These scholars were mostly from the west. *Bhagavad Gita* belongs to world literature. It was translated into English by Charles Wilkins in AD 1785. And Warren Hasting's letter to Nathaniel Smith printed in this translation says, "the *Bhagavad Gita* will survive when the British Dominion in India shall have long ceased to exist, and when the sources which it once yielded of wealth and power are lost to remembrance." In 1823 August Wilhelm Schlegel (the first Professor of Sanskrit in Germany) published the first critical edition of the text with a Latin translation. It attracted Wilhelm von Humboldt who called it "the profoundest and loftiest thing the world had ever seen".

The *Light of Asia* describing the life of Buddha by Edwin Arnold received enthusiastic acclaim. Buddhist stories and ideas influenced the west.

So also at this time tales from the *Mahabharata* of Nala and Damayanti, Savitri and Satyavaan were translated into European languages and appreciated in the west.

Similarly the story in the *Mahabharata* of the man in the well is also a part of world literature, not only for the Sanatani, Buddhist and Jain in India, but also Jews, Mohammedans and Christians.

Kalidas's great epic *Shakuntala* is also a part of world literature. It was first translated by Sir William Jones in AD 1789 and later into German. Many other Sanskrit works were also translated and dramas enacted in Germany.

The study of Indian Sanskrit literature in the late eighteenth and the nineteenth century laid the foundation of several sciences, such as the science of language, of comparative religion, of thought, and of mythology.

In the *History of Indian Literature* (1931) H.H. Gowen observes, "Indian literature has an intrinsic value which no remoteness avails to destroy. For sacredness, variety and continuity scarcely any others may compare with it, certainly none surpasses it. As for sacredness no other scripture, even our Bible, may compete with the Veda in its continuity or in the matter of general acceptance."

India's greatest contribution has been "to preserve for itself and for the world a vast treasure in the best part of which the principal theme is to ask men never to cease their efforts to control their senses and to reach higher and higher heights of morality and spirituality."[32]

References

1. *India's Contribution to the History of Science* by B.V. Subbarayappa in India's Contribution to World Thought and Culture (Vivekananda Rock Memorial Committee, First Ed., 1970), p.64.
2. *History of Dharmasastra* by P.V. Kane, vol.III, chap.XI, p.306, 307, 308.
3. ibid., vol.V, pt.2, p.1025.
   ibid., vol.II, pt.2, p.907, 909 on functions of temples and mathas.
   ibid., vol.IV, chap.XIII.
4. *India's Contribution to Arab Civilization* by W.H. Siddique in India's Contribution to World Thought and Culture (V.R.M.C., 1970), p.585.
5. *A New History of Sanskrit Literature* by K. Chaitanya, chap.I (II).
6. *India's Contribution to the History of Science* by B.V. Subbarayappa in India's Contribution to World Thought and Culture (V.R.M.C., 1970), p.48, 49.
7. ibid., p.49.
8. ibid., p.49.
9. ibid., p.50.
10. ibid., p.50.
11. *History of Dharmasastra* by P.V. Kane, vol.V, pt.1, p.519.
12. ibid., vol.V, pt.1, p.519.
13. *India's Contribution to the History of Science* by B.V. Subbarayappa in India's Contribution to World Thought and Culture (V.R.M.C., 1970), p.53.
14. ibid., p.53.
15. ibid., p.54.
16. *A New History of Sanskrit Literature* by K. Chaitanya, chap.I.
17. ibid.
18. *The Expansion of Indian Medicine Abroad* by Jean Filliozat in India's Contribution to World Thought and Culture (V.R.M.C., 1970), p.67.
19. *India's Contribution to the History of Science* by B.V. Subbarayappa in India's Contribution to World Thought and Culture (V.R.M.C., 1970), p.58. The Expansion of Indian Medicine Abroad, by *Jean Filliozat* (as above) p.67.
20. ibid., p.61.
21. ibid., p.62.
22. ibid., p.61.
23. *History of Dharmasastra* by P.V. Kane, vol.V, pt.2, chap.XXXI, sec.VIII, p.1353.
24. *India's Contribution to Islamic Thought and Culture* by N.N. Bhattacharya in India's Contribution to World Thought and Culture (V.R.M.C., 1970), 574.
25. *Indian Influence in Siam* by C.B. Pandey in India's Contribution to World Thought and Culture (V.R.M.C., 1970), p.456.

26. *Indian Religions and the West: Historical Perspectives* by B.M. Pande in India's Contribution to World Thought and Culture (V.R.M.C., 1970), p.616.
27. *India's Contribution to Arab Civilization* by W.H. Siddique in India's Contribution to World Thought and Culture (V.R.M.C., 1970), p.586.
28. ibid.
29. ibid., p.587.
30. ibid., p.576.
31. *Indian Religions and the West: Historical Perspectives* by B.M. Pande in India's Contribution to World Thought and Culture (V.R.M.C.), p.621.
32. *Some Problems of Indian Literature* by M. Winternitz, Calcutta, (1923), chap.IV.
33. *History of Dharmasastra* by P.V. Kane, vol.V, pt.2, p.1650.

Some Problems of Indology

In India religion never came into conflict with science as it did in the west. This was so with all the religions born in India. Knowledge was synonymous with Truth. All scientific knowledge was regarded as a step towards the Ultimate Truth.

It was realised by the serious seekers that knowledge comes only to those who are receptive to it — knowledge comes only from a commitment to truth, which necessarily requires an open, balanced and discriminating mind.

In India image-worship did not refer to idol worship but the worship of the material. Image worship is basically the suspension of one's own faculties of reason and blind acceptance of the authority of another, either in the form of book or person or from fear and self-interest.

Image-worship is as much a problem in other disciplines as it is in 'religion'. In fact in India if so many 'religions' co-existed it was because it was realised that 'religion' is essentially a path to Truth and not *the Truth*. Man's worth depended on his regard and commitment to truth and not the religion or customs he professed.

It was because of this understanding that Indians could appreciate individuals of character and talent even when they did not belong to their class or community.

Narrow as well as broad-minded people will be found

in all communities all over the world. Also all over the world we find those who have respect for truth and those who indulge in dishonesty, being ruled by material considerations.

It is not that this was so only in India. It will be seen, if read and understood correctly, that the great religious teachers of the world have all sought to strengthen man's knowledge and understanding by teaching him to discriminate between the true and the false. They have dealt with every aspect of a man's life and tried to show the value of truth and morality.

Knowledge and understanding, which form the purpose of all religions can therefore hardly be against science. Like every other discipline, science also requires a respect for truth and clarity of thought. Character is required for each and everything in life.

If the ancient civilizations had come to this realisation earlier, the western civilization also had many who were aware of the problems of image worship. And it will not be unreasonable to assume that that is indeed why the west was able to achieve so much after the 'renaissance'. The thoughts of the great philosophers of ancient pagan Greece had not a little to do with modern western scientific attitudes,[1] which was to bring about a technological revolution in the world. But so long as ignorance continues, so long will image-worship also continue to be part of the world phenomena.

A study would show that it has always been the genuine thinkers who have contributed the moral content as well as knowledge to society. There have at the best of times been only a few, but their influence has far exceeded their numbers.

It was not religion but an improper understanding of religion by narrow minds that brought about the collision between science and religion in the west.

Scholars as well as men of 'religion' are as susceptible as anyone else to material pressures and pulls. It would be 'image-worship' to believe otherwise.

We see the many attitudes among the modern scholars of Indology as well. Although we see the transmutation of ideas and philosophies in ancient times from one region to another between China, India, Persia and Greece, in recent times most of the work in Indology was done by scholars of the countries of the west. This was made possible by their establishment of empires around the globe which made them financially as well as materially better-off to undertake the otherwise unremunerative and time-consuming job of research.

Some western Indologists, being inspired by the spirit of pure intellectual enquiry, have done the most commendable work. If they have made mistakes this in no way detracts from their efforts as it is impossible for any one person to know everything. The fear of making mistakes would put a stop to all activity which would hardly be desirable. An honest mistake cannot be held against an honest researcher.

Among the many who pursued their self-appointed labour of love were scholars, poets, archaeologists and military officers. Inspite of some genuine mistakes their works will have a permanent value in Indian studies. The names of scholars like Sir Charles Wilkins, Sir William Jones, Sir Thomas Colebrooks, Fredrick Schegel, James Princep, August Wilhelm, Von Schegel, Franz Bopp, Wilhelm Humboldt, Frederick Ruckert, Eugene Burnouf, Sir Alexander Cunningham, Franz Keilhorn, Hermann Jacobi, Seymour Sewell and many others will be remembered for the earnestness and integrity with which they pursued their tasks.

It will not be untruthful to say that the effort put in by western scholars into the study of Indology brought a well-deserved and valuable return because Sanskrit is a treasure-house of knowledge. But the translations of ancient Indian works from the Sanskrit into English and other western languages served the purpose of bringing the Hindus face to face with a mirror. What had been accepted as a way of life for so long suddenly needed to be gone into deeper and the meanings found. Some of the best minds in India also took up the study of ancient Sanskrit and other works. They had the additional advantage of knowing both the language and religious philosophy which the western scholars did not have.

While one must admit and appreciate the interest and perseverance shown by western scholars in Indology inspite of a lack of knowledge in Sanskrit, it must also be admitted that some mistakes did creep in as a result. Again, while a large number of western scholars were pure scholars, there were also, regretably, others whose intentions were not purely scholarly, and who perhaps more than anyone else have been responsible for many of the misconceptions about Hinduism.

Nor was Hinduism the only religion to suffer thus. Many other religions in other parts of the world were also similarly misinterpreted.

One striking example of 'image-worship' in the field of Indology is regarding the date given to the Vedas.

Lord Acton warns "Guard against the prestige of great names. No trusting without testing".

Acton would be applauded by the ancient Hindus for his perceptivity. P.V. Kane in his *History of the Dharma-sastras* also warns against taking the conjectures of former scholars as valid conclusions by later writers.

But this is just what did happen in the case of the date given to the Vedas.

Winternitz[2] points out that "In his Gifford Lectures on Physical Religion (1840) Max Muller makes clear that his dates are tentative as 'whether the Vedic hymns were composed 1000, 1500, 2000, or 3000 BC no power on earth can ever determine', and although the foundation on which Max Muller's calculations were based were so arbitrary, it had become a habit among scholars for a long time to speak of 1200 or 1000 BC as 'the date of the *Rig Veda* which Max Muller was said to have established. And to many people it appeared as something of a heresy when in AD 1899 the Indian scholar Bal Gangadhar Tilak and the German scholar H. Jacobi (simultaneously though independently of each other) tried to prove a much higher age, for the Veda. "Both these scholars started from astronomical calculations. One's conclusions took the Vedas 6000 years back while the other's 4500 years back.

P.V. Kane points out how many misconceptions have occurred by the western scholars trying to make sense out of the Vedas "principally by reference to grammar, comparative philology and the comparison of several passages containing the same word or words."[3]

A word may have several meanings and the nuances can only be gauged from a reference to the context. A knowledge of the underlying philosophy would certainly help in understanding. These scholars lacked both. Most translations were done with the help of ordinary Sanskrit pandits and inferences were drawn on the basis of their own European backgrounds and culture.

The misconceptions arising from these methods would hold true for all scholars. Indeed we see a similar mistake made by Lin Yutang,[4] who though a Chinese is not a Buddhist, being of Christian parentage, and hence is perhaps not too well versed in the philosophy of Buddhism. He describes *Karma* as 'sin', saying this is the most distinctive concept in Buddhist teachings. He breaks up the Chinese word for *Karma* into 'Nieh' which he tells us means sin in Chinese, and 'Chang' which he tells us means an obstacle or screen which prevents us seeing the truth.

But as we know *Karma* does not mean 'sin'. There are good *Karmas* and bad *Karmas*, while there cannot be good sins and bad sins. *Karma* means deeds. *Karmas* done in ignorance are those that are inspired by material, selfish considerations and so lead to sinful acts. The Christian concept of sin is not quite the same in the eastern philosophies.

A. Coomaraswamy[5] points out how in ancient times before translating a religious work the philosophy was studied for ten or fifteen years and thoroughly mastered. Many scholars came from China and stayed on for years. Similarly many went from India to China.

There is a great difference between the understanding of the letter and the spirit. Scholars even with the best of intentions are not infallible and hence it is wise to be aware of this fact.[6] Lin Yutang is on firmer ground when he relates an amusing instance of what he calls 'cumbersome circumlocation which passes for translation'. He quotes from James Legge's translation of the Confucian classics incorporated in *The Sacred Books of the East* edited by Max Muller. "Legge" says Lin Yutang, "makes a fetish of literalness as if a certain air of foreign remoteness rather than clarity, were the mark of fidelity". He points out how Legge's translation of Mencius 'Opportunities of time, (vouchsafed by) Heaven are not equal to the advantage of the situation (afforded by) the Earth, and the advantage of the situation (afforded by) the Earth are not equal to (the union arising from) the accord of man' only means that 'the weather is less important than the terrain, the terrain less important than the army morale.'

A work of translation has many pitfalls, and literalness

is a major one. A similar amusing example of 'cumbersome circumlocation' can be found in Indian translations as well, for instance the mantras recited at a Hindu wedding.

These mantras are drawn from the 10th mandala of the 85th Sukta of the Rig Vedic Samhita (this Sukta incidentally is the work of a woman). This Sanskrit verse has been translated by Griffith as 'Soma obtained her first of all; next the Gandharva was her lord; *Agni* was her third husband; now, born of man, is thy fourth. The same again is translated by Wilson 'Soma first obtained the bride, the Gandharva obtained her next. *Agni* was thy third (husband); thy fourth (husband) is born of man'.

This verse actually describes the four stages of a woman's life, as a child, as a girl, a young maiden and woman-hood. She is first enjoyed by the moon, next by the gandharva, then by fire and lastly by man, her husband.

Poetic imagery can be reduced to an absurdity in translations. When the meanings of words are not correctly understood it naturally leads to faulty conclusions.

R.G. Bhandarkar,[7] for instance points out how the word 'Hidaraja' in the 13th Asokan Rock Edict which was taken by both M. Senart and Dr. Buhler as a proper name actually means 'here', the meaning being the 'the kings here'. Ashoka distinguishes between 'hida' and 'antesy' i.e. his own empire and the territories of his neighbours.

Acad Rinchen[8] in *Influence of Indian Philosophy on Mongolian Shamanism* also narrates how the incorrect understanding of the Mongolian word 'domur' led the Soviet academician Sergei Kosino to a faulty conclusion.

There are of course the outrageously factual errors. P.V. Kane[9] (Vol. II, Introduction) points out how Sherring gives a list of Brahmanical tribes saying "hundreds of these tribes if not at enmity with each other, cherish mutual distrust and antipathy to such a degree that they are socially separated from one another as far as it is possible for them to be — as much as *Brahmins* are from the lower outcastes — neither eating nor drinking together nor intermarrying." As Kane points out the list Sherring proceeds to give are no more than the surnames of *Chitpavan Brahmin* families who not only inter-dine but also intermarry. The only time intermarrying was not permissible was if the bride and groom belonged to the same 'gotra' or were related within the specified period allowed by the Smritis.

Indian scholars have pointed out how the western view of Hinduism as being renunciatory is largely due to the fact that most of the western translations of Hinduism are from the works of those who favoured renunciation.

The world is fairly familiar by now with half-baked observations regarding the caste system, vegetarianism as being due to the belief in transmigration, *Karma* as fatalism, Hinduism being without ethics, that Hindus were concerned only with their own salvation and not that of others, that there is no charity and compassion in Hinduism etc.

Mistakes pointed out by Indian scholars time and again have had no effect and continue to be repeated.

Pre-conceived notions are drawbacks in any work at the best of times. As Professor Sorokin observes[10], "The study of civilization can hardly become truly scientific or scholarly until it divests itself of emotional concern about crisis, decay, collapse, extinction and doom". These materials compartmentalised and time-bound attitudes in modern scholarship have been more a hindrance to knowledge than a help. Coomaraswamy[11] points out how "one of the strangest controversies in the history of orientalism turned upon the 'Origin of *Bhakti'* as if devotion had at some given moment been a new idea and thenceforth a fashionable one. It would have been simpler to observe that the word *Bhakti* means primarily a given share and also the devotion and love that all liberality presupposes, and so inasmuchas one gives God his share, one is his *Bhakta*."

Earlier Europeans had been deeply impressed with the translations of the *Bhagavadgita*, the *Upanishads*, Kalidas's play *Shakuntala* and the life of the Buddha. Wilhelm Von Humboldt ranked *Bhagavadgita* above the works of Lucretius, Parmenides and Empedokles describing this poem in the *Mahabharata* as 'the only truly philosophical poem that we can find in all the literature known to us'. Fr. Von Gentz observed that 'it is perhaps the deepest and loftiest thing the world has to show'.

The *Gita* and the *Upanishads* influenced some of the finest minds in Germany, France, England and the U.S.A. Liberal ideas and freedom of thought came to Europe and the U.S.A. as much from India as from Greece.

However, the exigencies of politics as well as smaller minds brought about a change in the work of western orientalists. It was noted by many scholars that western scholars were prone to favour the Greek, Babylonian or Egyptian civilizations in preference to others. They were reluctant to give antiquity to the Vedas.

Their dates for Panini or Chanakya were given, as well as changed, without explanation. The assumptions, unsupported by any facts, were mostly made on the consideration that at that age it was impossible for anyone to have as much knowledge. They had over-looked the fact that not only was there the capacity of contributing at that time but that both quote from even earlier works.

Indology has suffered from many wrong conclusions in many fields. A rather amusing one is the illusion nursed by some that the Aryans were fair haired and blue-eyed. There is no foundation for such beliefs.

The origin of the *Brahmi* script also exercised scholars.

Dr. Buhler tried to establish that both *Brahmi* and Kharoshti originated from the same source. Ojha, however, pointed out convincingly that two scripts drawn from one source could hardly become so dissimilar within 700 years.[12] He went on further to demonstrate how by a logical application of Buhler's method ancient *Brahmi* could equally well be derived from modern English!

Some of the moral strictures on the *Arthasastra* of Kautilya[13] or the *Kamasutra* of Vatsyayana[14] betray a mental or moral block more in the critic than the one criticised.

Winternitz seems to be shocked that Kautilya who shows himself to be a practising *Brahmin* should make suggestions so devoid of morality in his *Arthasastra*. The Hindu scholars recognized that Truth was knowledge and not conventional moralistic attitudes. Such attitudes must have prevailed in India then as well. It speaks highly of these scholars that they were able to dissociate themselves from the constrictions of conventional thought. The study of no discipline can be rewarding if 'image' in the form of conventional attitudes is allowed to interfere in one's enquiry.

The ones who brought science at logger-heads with 'religion' in the west were those who sought to impose their ill-understood mental image of 'religion' on those who were engaged in a free enquiry.

It is not the act but the reason for the act that justifies an act. A great drawback of modern scholarship has been to draw literal meanings. Many stories are allegorical and meant for moral edification. We see this attitude even among some Christian scholars of the west out to prove 'scientifically' whether a certain cloth was indeed used to wrap the body of Christ! One would think the importance of Christ was not in the cloth but in his teachings.

Winternitz seeks to draw very materialist conclusions

from the religious works and perhaps this has been the greatest obstacle to understanding the religious literature, which is concerned with Truth, which is not the material.

Coomaraswamy points out in his *Hinduism and Buddhism* how "it would hardly be an exaggeration to say that a faithful account of Hinduism might well be given in the form of a categorical denial of most of the statements that have been made about it, alike by European scholars and by Indians trained in our modern sceptical modes of thought."

Winternitz thus with an insufficient understanding of the underlying philosophy sees the work of crafty *Brahmins* when the *Upanishad* even when asking man to strive for higher knowledge on his own, nevertheless asks him to study the Veda as a first step.

If higher knowledge in man's own direct Self-realization was held in greater regard as providing the right direction to man's actions, lower knowledge was also considered essential for living and making the best of life.

Winternitz makes the mistake of regarding the Veda as some sort of Hindu Bible of myth and miracle, the preserve of jealous priests. The message of the Vedas is 'Rise above us'. The greatest stress is laid on man's effort, because nature is an instrument of the Spirit. In the story of the *Brahmin Kaushekiya* who is asked by a housewife to learn true non-violence from the meat-seller, Winternitz instead of seeing the moral lesson i.e. not to judge by appearances and profession, prefers instead to take it as an instance of the *Brahmin* being shown his place. Superficial attitudes are found among all peoples including scholars, and religious teachings are meant for all. Religious literature is replete with stories showing that Truth is not in the externals such as birth, wealth, power, learning etc. but in inner purity.

We see such conceits in some of our modern scholars as well. Rudolph Roth, one of the joint editors of the *Sanskrit-German Dictionary* of St. Petersburg gave as his considered opinion that a qualified European was in a better position to interpret the Veda than a *Brahmin* due to the latter's theological bias. He declared moreover that with the German science of comparative philology, he could interpret much better than Yaska, the hymns of the Veda!

Roth with his blind faith in his 'science' was supported by an equally self-opinionated American, William Dwight Whitney, whose knowledge of Sanskrit was questionable even if his conceit was not. Meanwhile the massive *Sanskrit-German Dictionary* of St. Petersburg prepared by Rudolph and Otto Bohtlingk invited severe strictures from Prof. Goldstucker[15] (Theodore Goldstucker: *Panini, His Place in Sanskrit Literature*, Allahabad 1914). In his rage A. Weber subjected Goldstucker to much abuse and Goldstucker exposed Bohtlingk, Roth, Weber and Kuhn thus, "It will of course be my duty to show," wrote Goldstucker, "at the earliest opportunity, that Dr. Bohtlingk is incapable of understanding even easy rules of Panini much less those of Katyayana and still less capable of making use of them in the understanding of classical texts. The errors in his contribution to dictionary are so numerous, that it will fill every serious Sanskritist with dismay, when he calculates the mischievous influence which they must exercise in the study of Sanskrit philology... Questions, which in my mind, ought to be decided with the utmost circumspection and which could not be decided without very laborious research have been trifled in his Worturbuch in the most unwarranted manner". Compelled by the motivated attacks on the Vedic tradition Goldstucker remonstrated, "When I see that the most distinguished and the most learned Hindu scholars and Divines — the most valuable and sometimes the only source of all our knowledge of ancient India are scorned in theory, mutilated in print, and as a consequence, set aside in the interpretations of Vaidic texts. . . . when a clique of Sanskritists of this description vapours about giving us the sense of the Vedas as it existed at the commencement of Hindu antiquity, and when I consider that this method of studying Sanskrit philology is pursued by those whose words apparently derive weight from the professional position they hold. . . . then I hold that it would be want of courage and a dereliction of duty if I did not make a stand against this saturnalia of Sanskrit philology."

While the *Brahmin* was not considered fit to translate the Veda because of 'theological bias', Christian missionary scholars with an acute theological bias were considered fit to do so. Some examples of Max Muller's theological bias are given below.

When Dr. Spiegel expressed an opinion that perhaps the Biblical account of creation was borrowed from Iranian sources, Max Muller, enraged, wrote, "a writer like Dr. Speigel should know that he can expect no mercy but invite the heaviest artillery against the floating battery which he has launched in the troubled waters of Biblical criticism."

Though Biblical criticism offended the feelings of Max Muller, he wasn't so considerate towards the feelings of others as regards their religious literature. He observes,[16] "A large number of Vedic hymns are childish in the extreme, low, commonplace." He was convinced that the Parsis had come nearer to Christian beliefs and that the Yasna, Venidad and Vispered would have a pre-eminent place as purely historical relics but 'as oracles of religious faith, they are defunct and a mere anachronism in the age in which we live."

He expresses his fervent if bigoted faith in Christianity thus: ". . . history seems to teach that the whole human race required gradual education before, in the fullness of time, it would be admitted to the truths of Christianity. The religion of the Buddha has spread far beyond the limits of the Aryan world, and, to our limited vision, it may have seem to have retarded the advent of Christianity among a large portion of the human race. But in the sight of Him with whom a thousand years are as but one day, that religion like the ancient religions of the world may have but served to prepare the way for Christ by helping through its very errors to strengthen and to deepen the ineradicable yearning of the human heart after the truth of God".

While earnestness and yearning are all very well in their proper place they might tend to give a rather lop-sided view. Hindu religious literature thus warns even the ascetic who is constantly yearning for *moksa*.

Max Muller wrote in a letter to the Duke of Argyl, the Under Secretary of State for India, "The ancient religion of India is doomed and if Christianity does not step in, whose fault will it be?"

Sir Monier William of the Boden Professorship also expressed the view that "Brahmanism therefore, must die out. In point of fact, false ideas on the ordinary scientific subjects are so mixed up with its doctrines that the commonest education, the simplest lessons in geography without the aid of Christianity must inevitably in the end sap its foundations." and, "when the walls of the mighty fortress of Brahmanism are encircled, undermined, and finally stormed by the soldiers of the Cross, the victory of Christianity must be signal and complete."

(The assault on *Brahminism* in India was similar to

that on the mandarins of China. Lin Yutang[17] relates how it was a Chinese mandarin who objected to the dumping of opium on China by the British by burning the bales. After the opium wars and China's defeat he was sent into exile. What was necessary to undermine was not the *Brahmin* or mandarin who could be bought for imperialistic or proselytising ends but those who could not. Authority interested in entrenching itself fears knowledge and integrity in others the most.)

Some scholarships had strings attached. This was so with the Boden professorship of Sanskrit at the University of Oxford. Its reasons as described by Sir Monier William that "its founder Col. Boden stated most explicitly in his will (dated 15-8-1811) that the special object of his munificent bequest was to promote the translations of scriptures into Sanskrit so as to enable his countrymen to proceed in the conversion of the natives of India to the Christian religion.

Horace Wilson, a nobler soul than many of his colleagues, a translator of the *Rig Veda* and the first Boden professor, was also bound by his terms of appointment, and admitted that he had written the book *Religion and Philosophical Systems of the Hindus* in order to help candidates for a prize of £ 200/- given by John Muir for the best refutation of the Hindu religious system.

While it was nobody's contention that such works should not be undertaken, those interested in genuine scholarship must view such work with scepticism and suspicion. To accept such motivated work without subjecting it to one's critical faculties or without comparing such work with the original texts would be the worst kind of 'image-worship.'

Will Durant commenting on a *Rig Vedic* hymn reflects "the loftiest of the poems is an astonishing Creation hymn, in which a subtle pantheism, even a pious scepticism appears in this oldest book of the most religious of people", 'Zenaide A. Ragozin observes, "one of the greatest beauties of this matchless piece is that while reaching the outermost bounds of philosophical abstraction, it is never obscure except to the uninitiated."

Bigoted minds can hardly be in a position to appreciate truth. LT. Hothouse[18] in *Morals in Evolution* (1916) points out how all systems with a personal god, particularly Christianity are beset with difficulties about God's Chosen people.

The rational view would be that a God who was partial, was no God. Prof. Toynbee in *Christianity among Religions of the World* (1958) says that Christians have begun to urge that Christianity must be purged of such beliefs.

If there were missionaries who were Indologists there were missionaries who were not Indologists but who nevertheless had their say.

A Rev. Lorrinser[19] on a comparison of the *Bhagavadgita* and the *New Testament* found many similarities, including some passages that were common. He then propounded his remarkable findings. His conclusion was that the *New Testament* was known to the composer of the *Bhagavadgita* and that the *Gita* was composed 500 years after Christ. Needless to say these surprising views were hastily disowned by all the reputed orientalists of the west.

Lorrinser's views were disposed off by K. Telang with facts and figures in his *Bhagavadgita*, translated into English in blank verse with notes. He showed conclusively that far from the *Bhagavadgita* being derived from the *New Testament*, there was enough evidence to show that the *New Testament* had benefited from the *Bhagavadgita* through Buddhism.

Dr. A. Schweitzer[20] says in his book that 'the *ahimsa*

commandment does not arise from a feeling of compassion but from a feeling of keeping a person undefiled.'

There must certainly have been Hindus for whom Dr. Schweitzer's observations held good, as there are Christians and others as well, but had the good doctor taken the trouble to study the Hindu religious works he would have found that there was no justification for his views.

Self-righteousness is an attitude of mind that is seen more among those engaged in 'good works,' religiosity or austerity.

Many are the books with scholastic pretensions which continue to be written where statements and observations are made without any supporting evidence.

An example of this can be seen in the Historic India Series of the Time-Life Books. While these books would not certainly go under the heading of serious scholarship, those who read them are greater in number than those who read more serious literature. In the Index on p.188 under 'J' there is the bold statement that 'Jesus regarded as an incarnation of Vishnu by some Hindus.' Page 88 referred to simply says 'Some Hindus credit the Buddha as an incarnation of Vishnu, some accept Jesus as one.' . . . No more details of any kind are given to substantiate these statements, the truth or untruth of which are capable of verification even today. Suffice it to say that no Hindu has thought of Christ as an incarnation of Vishnu. The Hindus would think no less of Christ, but perhaps it would matter to those who think of religion not in terms of Truth but numbers.

Similarly again under the *Hindu Pantheon* page 183 on Krishna one reads, "These aspects of Krishna had different origins, Aryan, Dravidian, perhaps Christian.'

The 'Christian' aspect of Krishna discovered by the

Time-Life Books, since they do not give their source, must be presumed to be based on the findings of Rev. Lorrinser!

There is such a thing as the 'superstition of facts', and no field is immune to it. The 'image-worshipper' would believe such claims merely because they have appeared in the Time-Life Books!

Those who believe in advertisement and publicity are basically image-worshippers. There are those who create images and those who believe them.

Some random selections from A.L. Basham's *The Wonder that was India* (Fontana Ancient History) are given below. The author claims in his preface that it has 'been widely used as a college text book not only in England, but also in India itself and in America'. It is a very readable book and undoubtedly much work has gone into it. However, it is not without errors apart from suffering from some of the drawbacks mentioned earlier that Indology has suffered from.

On page 503 the author observes 'a correct inference was established by syllogism of which the Indian form was somewhat more cumbrous than the Aristotelian'. He later observes that 'the three-membered syllogism was admitted by the Buddhists who rightly rejected the fourth and fifth members of the orthodox system as being tautological.'

Here Basham makes the point that the Indian syllogism was more 'cumbrous' than the Aristotelian. He seems to be under the impression that in a matter of reasoning a majority holding a view is justification enough to decide which is 'right'. Here it is necessary to ask the question as to what purpose a syllogism is meant to serve. Since presumably it is meant to give us as correct an answer as is humanly possible then we must reject what is inconsequential. Two syllogisms being equal one would certainly select the less 'cumbrous' method. Basham fails to inform us that a sizeable body of opinion holds the Indian syllogism to be more perfected than the Aristotelian. This is mainly because while the latter employs only the deductive, the Indian syllogism employs both the deductive and inductive. It thus acted as a double-check on answers attained by reasoning. Basham's use of the word 'rightly' is more an expression of his own view than anything else.

But the most important defect in Basham's book is that he tries to pad together a body without the skeletal framework — in other words he tries to piece together a society without knowing the basic philosophy on which it is built.

On page 251 he says, "the main purpose of the sacrifice was the gratification of the gods in order to obtain boons from them." The whole concept of sacrifice has already been explained in earlier chapters and hence it is not necessary to go into it here. The concept of sacrifice is common to all religions not excepting Christianity. It has to do with the spirit of selflessness, the essence of morality. In Vedic sacrifice the gods are less important than the act of sacrifice itself. Basham's interpretation would bring it down to the level of bribery for one's selfish material betterment.

The materialistic man would certainly behave thus, but then that is not the reason for the sacrifice, as given in religious texts.

He describes Surya, Savitr, Pusan as different gods whereas they are the same god in the different aspects. They are different names of the sun. On page 262 referring to Buddha, "Though according to legend his life was accompanied by many wonders, the earliest traditions record a few miracles performed by the Buddha himself. Once he is supposed to have performed feats of levitation and other miracles at Sravasti as a result of a challenge from rival teachers, but he sternly forbade the monks to imitate him and there is no record of his healing the sick by supernatural means. One touching story of the Buddha is interesting in this connection since it contrasts strikingly with the Gospel stories of the miracles of Jesus. He goes on to relate the story of how Buddha helped the weeping mother who had lost her child to understand that this is the inevitable end of all form and thus has to be accepted.

Surely miracles are the least important part of religious teachings? In Hindu thought miracles are physical feats that can be achieved through practice. They are not to be confused with Truth which is non-material. The person who believes in the reality of miracles will just as easily be led to believe in the magician as a miracle-man. The difference is only of degree. Buddha brought understanding to the mother which is the purpose of all teachings.

And surely Basham could not be unaware that Christian missionaries used to propagate Christianity in Northern Europe by telling them that the Christian god was stronger than theirs; that (falsely) there was a majority of Christians, and lastly, by spreading stories of miracles? (Bamber Gascoigne *The Christians*).

Neither Buddha nor Jesus claimed any divinity. The Gospels themselves were written much after the death of Christ.

Unfortunately the Christian fathers of the organized religion made much of miracles and Gibbons in *Decline and Fall of the Roman Empire* describes "the supernatural gifts, which even in this life were ascribed to the Christians above the rest of mankind, must have conduced to their own comfort, and very frequently to the conviction of infidels. Besides these occasional prodigies, which might sometimes be affected by the immediate intervention of the Deity when he suspends the Laws of nature for the service of religion, the Christian Church, from the time of the apostles and their first disciples, has claimed an uninterrupted succession of miraculous powers, the gift of tongues, of vision, of prophecy, the power of expelling demons, of healing the sick and of raising the dead. The knowledge of foreign languages was frequently communicated to the contemporaries of Irenaeus, though Irenaeus himself was left to struggle with the difficulties of a barbarous dialect whilst he preached the Gospel to the natives of Gaul. The divine inspiration, whether it was conveyed in the form of a waking or sleeping vision, is described as a favour very liberally bestowed on all ranks of the faithful, on women as on elders, on boys as well as upon bishops. When their devout minds were sufficiently prepared by a course of prayer, of fastings, and of vigils, to receive the extraordinary impulse, they were transported out of their senses, and delivered in esctacy what was inspired, being mere organs of the Holy Spirit, just as a pipe or a flute is of him who blows into it.

We may add that the design of these visions was, for the most part, either to disclose the future history, or to guide the present administration, of the church. The expulsions of the demons from the bodies of those unhappy persons whom they had been permitted to torment was considered as a signal though ordinary triumph of religion and is repeatedly alleged by the ancient apologists as the most convincing evidence of the truth of Christianity. The awful ceremony was usually performed in a public manner, and in the presence of a great number of spectators, the patient was relieved by the power or skill of the exorcist, and the vanquished demon was heard to confess that he was one of the fabled gods of antiquity, who had impiously usurped the adoration of mankind. . . At such a period when faith could boast of so many wonderful victories over death, it seems difficult to account for the scepticism of those philosophers who still rejected and derided the doctrine of resurrection. A noble Grecian had rested on this important ground the whole controversy, and promised Theolophilus, the Bishop of Antioch that, if he could be gratified with the sight of a single person who had actually been raised from the dead, he would immediately embrace the Christian religion. It is somewhat remarkable that the prelate of the first eastern church, however anxious for the conversion of his friend, thought proper to decline this fair and reasonable challenge."

Gibbons' descriptions of the doings of the church brought him strong condemnation from churchmen.

But it is nevertheless sad to see a scholar discussing not the philosophy but miracles of religion as Basham does.

On page 346 Basham while describing the Syrian Church in India writes, "But the Syrian Church was corrupt. There is no evidence that Indian Christians ever accepted the doctrine of transmigration, but many Hindu customs had been adopted, and the Kerala Christians like the Buddhists and the Jains before them were in the process of becoming a rather heterodox Hindu sect. Jesuit missionaries of the 16th and 17th centuries succeeded in preventing further decadence. One section of the Syrian Church accepted the authority of Rome, while the other, which remained true to its traditions reformed and purified itself."

All things material are prone to 'corruption', and hence it would not be surprising if the Syrian Church in India also got 'corrupted' like all other religious organizations. But Basham does not clarify what he really means by the word 'corrupt' in relation to the Kerala Christians. It would seem, to go by his views, that further decadence was prevented by the Jesuit missionaries of the 16th and 17th centuries.

Basham quite obviously regards the form as religion and not the spirit. He thus looks at religion in its most narrow sense which negates knowledge and understanding and promotes image-worship. It is precisely this attitude on the part of some western scholars that brought them into conflict with scientific thought in the west, because they felt scientific discoveries were going against Biblical beliefs.

It would be worthwhile to compare Basham's assertions with the state of things in Europe and other parts of the world including India at that time in which the Jesuit missionaries took a leading part.

The Inquisitions were started by the Dominicans and continued by the Jesuits. Cecil Roth's *A Short History of the Jewish People* describes them and Henry C. Lea in *Superstition and Force* describes the Inquisitions thus, "Thus the whole system of the Inquisitions was such as to render resort to torture inevitable. Its proceedings were secret; the prisoner was carefully kept ignorant of the exact charges against him and the evidence on which they were based. He was presumed guilty and the judges bent all their energies to force confession. To accomplish this no means were too base or too cruel."

The Inquisitions staged acts called Auto-da-fe where tortures became a public spectacle to entertain at the births and marriages of the nobility. During the three centuries that the Inquisitions were active it is recorded that 375,000 were condemned of whom one tenth were burnt.

The Syrian Christians who 'remained true to their traditions, must be admired for doing so because what they were against was the force and strong-armed tactics that were being used against them by the Jesuits who wished to impose their own Latin on them as well as their own Bishop.

To hunt down heretics, real or supposed, has been the

favourite business of some religions (Jeremiah 29, 8-9, Collossians II.8. Galatians I.7-9). It is hardly necessary to point out further the aberration of Christ's teachings. Clear reason is obstructed by blind prejudice resulting in the most inhuman acts. One can only be surprised at scholars incapable of seeing it. It is a fine example of 'missing the wood for the trees'.

Bamber Gascoigne writes in *The Christians* that Pope Boniface, founder of the 'Holy Years' and the 'Sale of Indulgences' termed the latter as 'happy commerce' in his *Papal Bull*. Many were granted the favour of selling the relics as Indulgences. Gascoigne records that "On All Saints Day when Frederick's Indulgences were on offer, the people were returning from the more persuasive Tetzel who had promised that 'they were so powerful that they could save even someone who had raped the Virgin Mary'".

One wonders whether Christ or his teachings mattered at all to those engaged in this 'happy commerce'.

The Sale of Indulgences saw the parting of ways (not surprisingly) between the Roman Catholic Church and the Protestants. In an entirely different context while explaining the similarities of literature all over the world Winternitz observes, "the conclusions must always be the same, that the human mind is same all over the world how else could it be possible that Indian ideas, Indian tales, Indian poetry appealed to so many countries, that foreign ideas could be infused into Indian literature and that there was this constant mutual exchange of ideas between peoples of the east and west ... The Vedanta teaches that he only can be saved who knows the Unity. Civilized mankind also can only hope to escape that ruin which is terribly near, by the Knowledge that all disunion is infatuation, is *Maya*, and that Union only is real and Truth. May India help the west in realising this truth."

The west also had those who were honest enquirers after Truth, just as in India and the rest of the world. There are those who believe in the form alone as reality, and they are incapable of seeing anything beyond their self-created narrow confines.

Those who have made a study might find themselves unable to share Basham's ideas on what is 'corrupt' and what is 'decadent'. But scholars who propagate their own views under the cover of scholarship are really no better than propagandists who are more keen on influencing the opinions of others and not increasing their knowledge. Basham's lack of understanding of the Hindu philosophy is demonstrated on page 307 on Krishna where he remarks "For all his divinity Krishna could do nothing to quell the fued, which involved the whole people." It sounds rather like "Physician, heal thyself", from those who taunted Christ.

Krishna is personified only to make man understand better how matters take their course and how man's acts influence his destiny. Activity as well as creation and destruction are a part of nature, while the Spirit is Eternal and beyond all. All mortals must die. That is a Law. There is no reason why God should suspend this natural law, if the intention is to educate. In fact the *Ramayana* gives the story of *Trishankhu* who wishes to flout this natural law by going up bodily to heaven. He succeeds only in hanging midway.

On page 154 on slavery Basham rightly avers that there was slavery in India. (Megasthenes, not a very dependable source according to scholars, was incorrect when he said there were no slaves). Basham admits that while there must certainly have been those who ill-treated slaves in India 'he was probably better off in India than in most parts of the ancient world.' One only wishes that there he had done more justice to all the ancient world in general, because there has been slavery in the modern world as well.

On black slavery when African slaves were pirated from Africa to the Americas, Westermarck in *Origins and Development of Moral Ideas*, Vol.I (1912) page 711 observes, "This system of slavery which at least in the British colonies and slave states surpassed in cruelty the slavery of any pagan country ancient and modern, was not only recognized by Christian governments but was supported by the large bulk of the clergy, Catholic and Protestant alike." (Slavery was abolished in the British dominion in 1832 and in British India in 1843).

Whether the 'modern man' is qualified to pass judgement on older systems is itself questionable.

It has unfortunately been the practice of many a modern commentator to compare ancient and modern practices only where they show the modern in a better light. Where it does not, they are silent. This is basically dishonest and in no way helps a proper evaluation, nor does it further one's understanding. On page 36 describing the four classes he says, "The Sanskrit word used for them *varna* means colour, and suggests their origin in the development of the old tribal class structure through contact with people of a different complexion and alien culture." On page 138, a connecting resemblance is sought to be drawn with the racialism in present day South Africa with a "dominant fair minority striving to maintain its purity and its supremacy over a darker majority."

Here we see a modern-day aberration being sought to be given legitimacy by referring to ancient practices. However, as those who have read Hindu religious texts will know, the *varna* system was not thought of in terms of colour but of inherent quality. The word *varna* has other meanings apart from colour. Even the much later *jatis* were based on birth, which could be logically justified, and not on colour.

Where a philosophy specifies that all form is unreal and hence false, it is hardly likely that a society would be structured on anything so superficial as colour. Had it been based on anything so flimsy it would certainly not have been able to withstand for thousands of years the forces of disintegration. There are references in the *Rig Veda* to the Aryas being fairer and the *Dasas* being darker. It is assumed by scholars that when the *varna* system was formed the Aryas were the *Brahmins* and *Kshatriyas* while the *Dasas* became the *Sudras* and *Vaisyas*. Even if we are to accept these inferences as being partly true, then the question would have to be asked as to what became of the chariot-makers and other professions who are referred to in the early *Rig Veda* and who took part in the various Vedic ceremonies? These also formed a part of the Aryan community. When society increased and diversified they quite obviously must have got absorbed into the class which included their profession.

We also know from the references in the *Mahabharata* that inter-caste marriages were common. It was only the *Yajnavalkya Smriti* which prohibited marriage between a *Brahmin* and a *Sudra* woman. By this time there must have been a proper mixture of all the *varnas*. There is enough indication that the concern was not for the preservation of racial purity but the preservation of expertise. If the Indian civilization has survived this long this is the one most important reason.

On page 168, one of the several probable reasons given by Basham for child marriage may be amusing to many Indians. He observes that, "the sexuality of the Indian character may have played a part in it." It is difficult to make out on what grounds we are to determine "the sexuality of the Indian character." Basham furnishes us with none. But it is possible to assume that Basham shares some of the attitudes of those brought up on stories of the Immaculate Conception, where truth needs to be garbed in the clothes of conventional morality. Puritanism is not new to the world. India has also had its share. But it is basically an inability to face facts, and this inevitably leads to wrong conclusions.

It is more than possible that works like the *Kamasutra* and objects of worship like Shiva Linga and the sculptures of Konarak and Khajuraho have given rise to the idea among Christian scholars about the 'sensuality' of the Indian character. But it does not seem to have occurred to them that the need for these were exactly to combat attitudes of puritanism the attitudes of those who identified truth with conventional morality.

Shiva Linga is not a sex totem. Rather it demonstrates that Truth is a vital power that creates the whole universe, and it cannot be confined to any known form. Man regards the form as truth, not realising that Truth is the spirit within. The form cannot be worshipped ignoring need and function. For those reaching out to knowledge it is always necessary to first free themselves from the bonds of form.

Those who avoid sex through knowledge and understanding are those who wish to concentrate on their spiritual progress, and hence see no point in transitory and frivolous things. Their approach to all things is balanced. Their decision is a considered decision. It is an individual decision which cannot be faulted.

There are those who avoid sex through ignorance. Their attitudes are not well thought out. They have been told sex is bad and so they look upon it with horror and revulsion. Some avoid sex, while others engage in it on the sly because 'appearances must be kept'. While two acts might outwardly look the same, there is a qualitative difference between the act done from knowledge and the one from ignorance.

Hindu thinkers were keen that people were educated so that their actions were inspired with knowledge and understanding. Knowledge is essential for all actions.

We see how scholarship is affected by pre-conceived notions, fallacious inferences and other weaknesses of the human character.

It is not that these authors should not be read. Banning books is not the way to knowledge and understanding. But reading must not be restricted to some authors, because thereby we are in danger of being misled. This defeats the very purpose of study. Inertia contributes the most to ignorant attitudes. This is why activity was always extolled by the Upanishadic teachers. The Upanishadic teacher in his farewell address to his departing students advises them even after they have left not to study less but study more.

This fervent plea from the great Indian poet Rabindranath Tagore will find an echo in the hearts of all who seek the Truth.

"Where the mind is without fear
And the head is held high,
Where knowledge is free;
Where the world has not been broken
Up into fragments by narrow domestic walls;
Where words come out from the
Depths of Truth;
Where tireless striving
Stretches its arms towards perfection!
Where the clear stream of reason
Has not lost its way into the
dreary desert of dead habit;
Where the mind is led forward
By thee into ever widening

Thought and action —
Into that heaven of freedom
My Father,
Let my country awake".

References

1. *The Christians* by Bamber Gascoigne.
2. *Some Problems of Indian Literature* by M. Winternitz (Readership lecture delivered at Calcutta University, Aug.1923), chap.I *Age of Veda*.
3. *History of Dharmasastra* by P.V. Kane, vol.II, pt.2, p.976.
4. *From Pagan to Christian* by Lin Yutang (Heinemann 1960), p.172.
5. *Hinduism and Buddhism* by Anand K. Coomaraswamy, p.49.
6. *From Pagan to Christian* by Lin Yutang, p.51.
7. *A Peep into the early History of India* by Sir R.G. Bhandarkar, p.13.
8. *Influence of Indian Philosophy on Monogolian Shamaanish* by Acad Rinchen in India's Contribution to World Thought and Culture (Vivekananda Rock Memorial Committee, 1970), p.409.
9. *History of Dharmasastra* by P.V. Kane, vol.II, pt.1, p.24.
10. ibid., vol.V, pt.2, p.1617.
11. *Hinduism and Buddhism* by Anand K. Coomaraswamy, p.20.
12. *Some Western Indologists and Indian Civilization* by Kailash Chandra Varma in India's Contribution to world Thought and Culture (V.R.M.C.), p.174-175.
13. *Some Problems of Indian Literature* by M. Winternitz (Calcutta, 1923), p.92.
14. *The Kamasutra of Vatsyanana* (translated by Sir Richard Burton and F.F. Arbuthnot, 1963, based on a translation that appeared in 1883).
15. *History of Dharmasastra* by P.V. Kane, vol.III, chap.XI, p.306, 307.
    Some Western Indologists and Indian Civilization by Kailash Chandra Varma, in India's Contribution to World Thought and Culture (V.R.M.C., 1970), p.169.
16. *Some Western Indologists and Indian Civilizastion* by Kailash Chandra Varma (V.R.M.C.), p.168.
17. *From Pagan to Christian* by Lin Yutang, p.36.
18. *Morals in Evolution* by L.T. Hothouse, pt.2 (1906).
19. *Gita Rahasya* by B.G. Tilak (Marathi) *Gita* and Bible, pt.7.
    Some Problems of Indian Literature by M. Winternitz, chap.IV.
20. *History of Dharmasastra* by P.V. Kane, vol.V, pt.2, chap.XXXV, sec.X, p.1646, 1647.

20

Conclusion

Understanding comes through knowledge and knowledge comes through enquiry.

The Hindu Seekers studied the material world of form to seek the meaning of form. Their study was scientific, and as behoves the scientific mind, impersonal. Their theory of evolution is a testament to it. But in the course of their investigation they made another discovery. Truth, the inner meaning or Soul of the universe, was so subtle that only a pure consciousness was capable of realising it. The Seeker of Truth became Truth. It resulted in a complete change of personality of the individual. Truth expresses itself as morality in man.

Their scientific enquiry into all forms (which is, nature), led them to a paradox. While one form disappeared another appeared. The seed surrendered to the plant, the flower to fruit, the fruit to seed and the seed to plant again. One form gave way to another. The abandonment of form preserved form. The Spirit was not form but the base of all form. There was a natural law by which all nature moved. This has to do with selflessness. The selfless individual is the moral individual. Man being a part of nature belongs to the world of form which is nature. While nature is subject to certain laws which keep changing according to the needs of nature, Truth beyond all form, unchanging, infinite, incorruptible and eternal, is present in all nature.

Man is constantly seeking to differentiate between the genuine and the false. The genuine is that which is considered to be of worth, while the false is not. The worldly-wise will recognize the value of gold as compared to gilt even if both shine. This is because they know that gold has an intrinsic value that the gilt does not have. But here they are judging by material values in terms of money.

The moral value since it rests on Truth which is beyond the material, does not depend on material values. Those who go by moral values have a different value system to those who go by material values. The understanding of the Soul or Spirit in ourself results in a better understanding of oneself and all else. It does not negate the form, but inspires form. By surrendering to the Spirit man acts for Truth alone. The Spirit is actionless while action belongs to form. The Spirit acts in the whole universe through form.

Truth is all-pervading, unchanging, indivisible, infinite, free and incorruptible, while form is constantly changing, is divisible into myriads of parts, is finite, bound and corruptible.

Those who go by the Eternal Value are at peace, content, unemotional, detached, dispassionate, impartial, discriminating, balanced, understanding, incorruptible, fearless, and steady. They have a goal, they have dedication, and their joy lies in their function which they do to the best of their ability. Like the sun which keeps on doing its function and benefits all without drawing attention to itself, these individuals help all the material world because of their selfless conduct in thought, word and deed.

Those who go by material values, i.e., for whom the

world of form is the reality, are ruled by the material. They are ruled by fear and self-interest, because they are constantly identifying all things in terms of quantity and numbers and size.

Their loyalties keep changing according to their self-interest. The material minded person is also the superficial person. Believing in the material he worships the material. He is attached to wealth, to power, to person. Since he goes by external values he is impressed by externals. He becomes an easy prey to superstition, propaganda and publicity since he is devoid of the discrimination to look beneath the surface. His ideas of personal freedom are to shrug off all unpleasant responsibilities and engage in self-indulgence. Indisciplined, he cowers under external discipline. The 'image' becomes important. Religion, ideology or virtues are meant to be used for public recognition. The label is more important than the content. While loudly castigating religious rites as humbug and a waste of time and money, or those who benefit others in other ways, he will unhesitatingly sacrifice others in his greed for material possessions at the altar of his self-interest. Acts done for the most material of reasons are presented as moral acts. Dishonesty is natural to those ruled by fear and self-interest.

Those who believe in the reality of the material are bound, and their actions, belonging to the material world come under the laws governing the material world of form, the law of cause and effect. Those who understand Truth as Reality are liberated individuals. They are liberated in this life itself. They see the Truth in all things. Very few attain this highest state, but nevertheless it is worth striving for. No effort is ever wasted and according to the law of evolution every individual will reach the highest stage some day.

Form is constantly impinging itself on man, who constantly identifies the form with truth. Truth is beyond all form. This understanding ensures an open, receptive and understanding mind.

While Truth is present in all form, it is not the form. While form is basically an unintelligent matter, Truth is vital. While all form (matter) gets destroyed Truth alone is Eternal. It is Existence Eternal.

To understand Truth is to understand the meaning of all form. This leads in turn to the proper use of form.

Just as we learn the meaning of words and their use in constructing sentences in order to facilitate proper communication, so our understanding of the meaning of form helps us to use it wisely and well. Truth is absolute purity.

Man learns to use his limbs, emotions and mind for the functions they are meant.

Hindu thinkers realised that two acts may differ and yet both may be inspired by truth. They also realised that two acts may be similar and yet one may be inspired by truth while another by dishonest selfish reasons.

Rig Veda (VII.104-12) says, "True speech and false speech run a race against each other. Soma protects of the two what is true and straight-forward and strikes down what is false."

The *Brihadharanyaka Upanishad* remarks that in practical life truth and *dharma* are identical.

Historical existence means form and form means individuality. Each individual has characteristics. Some are inherent while others are produced by environment and experience. There are many facets to each and every personality. While there may be points of difference there are points of similarity.

The selfless open-minded approach strives for harmony. But harmony is not truth and neither is disharmony. Truth beyond all, is that which keeps the balance.

Dharma was a code of conduct drawn from the natural law that prevailed in the universe. It was duty, law, and morality. But it was realised that to some, *dharma*, the form, is the truth. It is in order to show that truth is not the form, that the teacher of the *Taittiriya Upanishad* points out to his students that truth is first and *dharma* next.

Brihaspati carries this point further and warns, "the decision (in a cause) should not be given by merely relying on the sastras (text), for in the case of a decision devoid of reasoning loss of *dharma* results."

That injustice may result by hard and fast enforcement of rules and thus go against the very purpose of the laws and rules was fully realised. The *Mahabharata* says that no custom or practice can be said to be beneficial to all alike (and hence variations in practices were to be tolerated by the king).

For those who identify rituals (form) with truth the *Chandogya Upanishad* points out that truth is not ritual and nothing can be achieved through blind observation of ritual. It compares the priests and the sacrificer to dogs in procession.

The dialogue between Visvamitra and the *Chandala*, the latter is horrified to see Visvamitra eat a dog's tail during a famine and quotes against doing so by repeating the scriptures, shows that texts are general guidelines but cannot replace truth. Visvamitra points out that 'therefore a learned man whose soul is pure should act after relying on his intelligence in the matter of deciding what is *dharma* and a*dharma*'.

It is in order to avoid injustices caused by blind adherence to laws and rules that are no longer relevant to another age and which violate truth thereby that *Manu*,

Yajnavalkya, *Vishnudharma-sutra* and Puranas expressly provide that "one should not observe but give up what was once *dharma*, if it came to be hateful to the people and it would end in unhappiness.'

Dharma is not for unhappiness, but as the nourisher and sustainer of all beings. *Taittriya*, *Aranyaka* avers that "*Dharma* is the support of the whole world."

Hindu thought was entirely rational and also humanistic. But it points out that truth is both and beyond both. Self-restraint, charity and compassion are recommended to all.

Man is meant to use his head, heart and hands in all honesty and integrity. If he is guided by truth alone he will not be wrong. Man judges by externals and is impressed by them. He takes his values from these. The Dharmasastras point out that "wealth, kindred, age, (performance of) religious rites and sacred knowledge confer title to respect, but each succeeding one is superior to the preceding one."

Hindu thought seeks to impress each and all with their own true worth so that they can also see the true worth of others. Stories, legends, myths and mythology are used to make us understand the meaning of Truth. Man is not meant to suspend his reason. Man's head, heart and limbs are meant to be used. Where the intentions are pure and honest the act is a virtuous act, and where dishonest that act is devoid of virtue.

The right thing is doing the appropriate thing at the appropriate time when we know it to be right. All forms are needed and are necessary in life. To make the best use of form we have to be able to use it wisely and well. Water for example is 'good' for a thirsty man but 'not good' for a drowning man. Similarly fire can be used well or misused. Knowledge is not good or bad. It has to be used wisely and well.

Thus while anger was not recommended nor desirable

for the *sanyasi*, the *Karmayogi* must feel righteous anger if he is to stand up against injustice. If we go by the principle of not hurting others, others also are expected to abide by the same principles because these are for the benefit of all. This is why in the *Mahabharata* even forgiveness is hedged with certain conditions for the sensible man. Even charity is to be practised taking into consideration the time, place and whether the recipient is deserving of charity or not. It is not in the interest of truth to give to the undeserving because it would only encourage them to continue their ways.

The sastras recommend contentment, but this cannot be misconstrued to mean that one should be content with what one has studied. Bhartrahari (*Nitisataka* 63) points out, "Liking and urge (ambition) must be there — but for good; and greed also must be there — but for gaining knowledge, then these are not wrong". And again he says, "In danger, courage; in power, mercy; in public, eloquence; in war, bravery. These are virtues. The deed performed at the appropriate time is the virtuous deed."

All religions commend nonviolence, forgiveness, peace, mercy etc. but to follow these precepts without understanding is not truth or *dharma*. Unthinking acts, a blind following of precept or authority, may not lead to *dharma* but to *adharma*. That is why Manu points out that the four sources of *dharma* are the Vedas, Smritis, the doings of the good and last but not the least doing that which is good for the Soul. Man has to decide for himself as to what is right, in the spirit of Truth. Others are guides, but the decision is for each individual to make according to his perception and in honesty and selflessness.

We may have two acts which seem contradictory and yet may reflect truth. We have the story of Visvamitra telling the *Chandala* not to quote the scriptures. He tells him that where there is no life there can be no *dharma*.

As opposed to this we have the story of Dadhichi Rishi, who, on being requested by the gods to give his bones for the good of the world, gladly gives up his life.

Great men have given their lives for truth. They have given up their lives for truth, a promise, country, religion etc.

Dilip offers his body to save Guru Vasishta from a lion. Jeemootvahana offers his body to the garuda to save a snake, while Shibi Raja offers his own flesh to the hawk who comes after the dove that seeks his protection.

Karna, despite being warned not to give up his protection, the *kavachkundala*, nevertheless gives it up to the disguised Indra because he says he would prefer to lose his life rather than his honour. King Ramachandra spent fourteen years in the forest in order that the promise of a king, his father, be kept.

But what happens when a son becomes a king and his father's wrong-doings are brought to his notice?

Manu says, "He who does not act according to *dharma*, whether he be a father, acharya, friend, mother, wife, son or anyone else, must be punished by the king accordingly."

It was on this same principle that the great Surya-vanshi Raja Sagara, finding his wayward son causing misery to his subjects, expelled him from the kingdom.

We are given the story of Angiras Rishi who at a young age was advanced in knowledge and many of his elders came to him for instruction. Once accidentally he addressed them as children. They were indignant at this and went to the gods with their complaints. They said Angiras was going against scriptural injunctions of giving reverence to elders by addressing them thus. The gods gave their judgement saying, "Angiras is right. White hair does not make a man older (wiser). A wise man even if young is considered old by the gods."

This is acknowledged not only by Manu and Vyasa but by Buddha too. The story of Prahlad shows how a mighty and arrogant king wishes to be acknowledged as the mightiest in the world. Prahlad his son not only does not succumb to his wishes by telling him what he would like to hear, but also reproves his gurus for succumbing.

Bhishma tells Yudhishthira that the guru is greater than even father or mother, yet when the guru of King Marut sacrifices him out of greed, King Marut says there can be no question but that a guru who does wrong for his own ends must be punished.

Wealth and desire by themselves are not against *dharma*. It is only wealth and desire that transgress *dharma* (morality) that should be avoided.

In the *Gita* (VII.11) Krishna identifies himself with *kama* that is not in conflict with *dharma*.

Anusasanaparva (Chap.III.18-19) states that *dharma*, *artha* and *kama*, are the three prizes (fruits) of human life, these three should be striven for but in such a way as not to conflict with *dharma*.

In the Upanishadic story of Satyakama, we see how truth is not conventional morality'. The mother tells her son the truth, the son does not hesitate to tell the truth about his parentage to the teacher and the teacher appreciated the real worth of Satyakama. Those who really understand truth are not afraid nor do they seek to dress it up.

Truth is not the preserve of the rich or poor, the high or low. King Janashruti goes to the cartman Raikwa to seek knowledge. The *Brahmin* learns from the *Kshatriya* when he is found to know more. The house-wife tells the *Brahmin* ascetic Kaushikeya who has lost his temper, that if he really wishes to be non-violent, then he must learn from the meat-seller.

It shows how a man's profession is no indication of his quality. If one were to go by mere externals it would be natural to infer that the man leading a religious life would be in control of his passions and hence be non-violent, but the wife points out that the meat-seller who would normally be expected to be violent because of his profession is really in this case the gentler person.

A gift given with devotion is of far greater worth than the monetary worth or appearance of a gift. Old Shabari offers Ramchandra the berries. Because of her great love she makes sure that they are sweet by tasting them first. To those who go by external judgements the berries are contaminated apart from being hardly fit to be eaten by a guest as they are common jungle berries. But Ramchandra appreciates her gesture and eats the berries given with love and devotion.

The *Aswamedha Yajna* (horse sacrifice) was considered to be very meritorious but religious texts say that if a hundred *Aswamedha Yajnas* and Truth were weighed Truth would be heavier.

It is inner purity that is of real worth and not the mere external act. It is not the act but the reason for the act, that makes it moral or otherwise.

There is a difference in approach among those who follow custom, convention or tradition. All these are forms. Those who follow these with knowledge, understanding and sincerity because they find truth in them are right in following them. Those who perceive these as going against truth are right in not abiding by them. The one thing that really unites the two apparently contradictory acts is the truth in both. Those who act when they do-not believe are dishonest, and violate morality. Equally foolish are those who do so because of superstition or imitation. They are worshipping form or image. There are people who worship idols in the spirit of truth and devotion. They are really worshipping not the image itself but what it represents. If they find this helps them then they are right in doing so. Not all can think in terms of the abstract. Most people understand by identifying with various things in their experience. When something is understood in terms of that which is recognizable then it is possible to advance to the next stage having become familiar with the first stage.

Thus stories and parables help to explain the abstract by concrete parallel examples in life.

Truth or Reality cannot be defined in any term known to man. Yet it can only be explained in terms of attributes known to man, so that he may understand its various aspects in life.

Examples abound of how truth acts through form.

The same Arjuna, the redoubtable, invincible warrior of the *Mahabharata* war found his strength gone once the task was over. He could not even save some women given in his protection from robbers, no matter how much he tried.

Hiranyakasipu who could not be vanquished by man or beast meets his death at the hands of a man-beast.

When certain things have to happen, events work towards that end. Man's perception also is affected. The *Panchatantra* points out that inspite of the fact that Ramchandra knew that there could he no such thing as a golden deer, he went after it. This was so because of what had to happen.

With the best will and effort in the world it may be impossible to realise the consequences of certain actions. They may not be that which we envisage. This is beyond one's control. What is important is that we act with the purest motives.

No one in this world can escape action. All forms are instruments of a Higher Power. The Spirit is in all form. We have to strive to make ourselves the proper instruments.

Those aware of the Spirit within, reach the highest heights, and serve as an inspiration to all.

The seemingly materially invincible are not so invincible as they seem. This truth is portrayed in various fables and other stories as well. The lion, king of the forest is freed by a mouse. Birds caught in a net outwit the bird-catcher by flying off in unison.

Knowledge and understanding are important so that we make the best use of what we have. But it is even more important to know how to use our knowledge and talents for the best use of all, because that is our function. Forms may change but Truth is eternal. This value is constant at all times and needed for all times. Truth is purity. It is integrity and honesty in thought, word and deed.

While it may be true that a greater number of people of a certain place may possess greater moral qualities than others at a given time, this is not true for all people at all times. Truth is essentially that which pertains to the individual. And this is why it was said over two thousand years ago that every person attains salvation through his own efforts and not by following any religion, book or prophet.

A person may or may not believe in God. Morality is a necessity for all. Morality comes from an understanding of truth, and it has to do with selflessness. Udayana the great logician (AD 984) who composed the *Lakshnavali* breathes this spirit, 'May Hari, Lord of the three worlds, bestow on you the desired reward, whom the *Saivas* worship as Shiva, *Vedantins* as Brahma, the *Bauddhas* as Buddha, the Naiyyayikas proficient in the means of knowledge as the Creator, those devoted to Jain teachings as *Arhat* and Mimamsakas as *Yajna*."

There is the constant awareness and acceptance that Truth is not the form. No hard and fast form can contain truth. To enforce it may go against Truth.

Thus even if there was a structure of varna and *asrama*, those who wished could opt out. A life of ascetism was open to all, but begging as an occupation was not looked upon with favour. Inactivity was not favoured either. Inertia leads to ignorance and superstition leading to worship not of truth but of form. Miracles were not miracles but due to physical phenomena and not the spiritual. Both reason and authority are given their due, not as an end, but only the means to an end.

The word Veda is drawn from the Sanskrit root Vid meaning 'to know'. Apart from the four Vedas concerned with religious literature, there were in all fourteen other branches of knowledge in the different sciences and arts also known as Vedas. These consisted of the six *angas*, subsidiary portions of the Vedas viz., *siksa* (rules of reciting); *kalpa* (ritual); *vyakarana* (grammar); *nirukta* (glossarial comment); *chhandas* (metre); *jyotish* (astronomy); *mimamsa* (theology); *nyaya* (logic); *Dharma* (institutes of law); Puranas; *Ayurveda* (medical science); *Dhanurveda* (science of arms); *Gandharvaveda* (drama and other arts) and *Arthasastra* (science of government).

Knowledge of science and art was necessary for one's functions in life, but the Higher Knowledge of the Self was even more needed. The message of the Hindu sages throughout history has been the message of rationalism, humanism and activism. Knowledge helps one's understanding to achieve a proper balance between these. Balance is essential to harmony. Imbalances are created again and again when a society becomes too materialistic and interprets religion and laws by the letter instead of the spirit. This inevitably results in actions which deform creation rather than ennobling it.

Every religious movement in India (as also the world over) will be seen to be not a denial of religion but only a correction to existing imbalances in society due to narrow views and narrow interpretations. Every religious wave has really been a moral wave to sweep aside existing rigid beliefs or image-worship that only comes in the way of receptivity to Knowledge.

Thus when the acts of sacrifice and charity as recommended in the Vedic *Karma Kanda* came to be parodied by an increasingly materialistic society, by being performed either as a blind and superstitious belief or with an eye to improving one's own image in the eyes of others rather than as an act of self-surrender and sharing what one has with others, the *Upanishads* condemn such acts. The *Upanishads* stress the purity of mind and thereby the purity of intention. They stress the need for self-purification i.e. a moral rejuvenation.

We must assume that the *Upanishads* applied a much-needed corrective at that age.

Most of the *Upanishads* however, barring a few, stress on the act of renunciation as essential to self-purification. It is not unlikely that this also in due course led, after its initial spiritual upliftment, to a desire to relinquish productive life and the cares and responsibilities that go with it.

The *chaturvarna* system too, for those engaged in productive worldly pursuits may have seemed to be getting too rigid with the castes taking pride more in the professions of the castes than their function to serve the needs of society. Certain sections like *Sudras* and women were denied Vedic knowledge.

These attitudes that created an imbalance in society and retarded the development are corrected by the *Bhagavat dharma*. It shows that God (Truth) belongs to all and is no one's monopoly. It points out that all forms are only a means to an end. The end is liberation, which is open to all. Knowledge is open to all who seek it. It explains that the *chaturvarna* caste system is only a law which is required to serve the needs of both man and society. Those who misuse it and see it as a privilege are not fulfilling their role. A profession, whatever it is, is meant to perform certain functions. These functions are meant to serve the needs of all. While man works, as he must, to maintain himself and his dependents, he also has a higher responsibility to creation itself. This can best be achieved by the integrity and devotion he invests in his professional duties.

All religious movements are also meant to give us a better understanding of life. Where the caste system had formalised itself to a matter of strict and austere duty, sometimes going against nature instead of harmonising, the Bhagavat *dharma* served admirably to demonstrate that all forms have their inherent nature. It is this that we must strive to understand. Love and devotion beautify and elevate all creation. The hungry baby is God, the little mischievous child is God, the pranks played by a boy, valour of youth, are also God and so is creation and destruction. . . In an age which was against the taking of any life, it was pointed out that destruction was as- much a part of the world process as was creation. The issue is not therefore one between violence and non-violence but the reason for being violent or nonviolent. The deed performed with pure intention at the appropriate time for the appropriate reason is the moral deed. To quietly accept injustice and intolerance because we are afraid of the consequences is not 'tolerance' but cowardice and submission.

Work, play, rest, creation and destruction are all aspects of Existence.

Buddhism and Jainism were not different from Vedic Hinduism except in that they rejected the authority of the Vedas. They really rejected the assumed authority of some to interpret the Vedas. In this they helped correct a society sought to be led by 'authority' of texts. Buddha stressed on moral action and refrained from dwelling too much on the metaphysical which was too obtuse for the common man. Jainism also played its part in softening man's attitude towards the taking of life.

But all things over-emphasised or literally interpreted led eventually to distortions. Tantra also in its way helped focus man's mind on the need for scientific thinking and the need for achieving knowledge which can only come from an expansion of the mind and not to the narrow mind.

No religious movement is ever new. It is only a much needed clarification of the true values already expressed from the most ancient times.

Without honesty and integrity creation suffers. Religion points this out and exhorts all to strive to attain this Truth which is inherent in all, but unperceivable to those who are not purified.

The man of renunciation and meditation, free of worldly duties and free of material needs, to a large extent is a living example that man can live in peace and contentment even without material comforts.

The *Karmayogi* also is needed in life. Productivity is essential and worldly responsibilities also have to be discharged. It is possible for man to discharge his duties and also not be attached to the material.

It is selfish needs and desires that interfere and leads to imbalances. Selfishness is the outcome of the desire for the material. Materialism is synonymous with ignorance while knowledge is the understanding of Truth as the Eternal Spirit. In this world, forms are constantly changing. Forms are related to needs and functions. Changing needs give rise to different functions and different forms.

This understanding is reflected in the religious laws, which reflect the changing needs of each age and society. As the *Mahabharata* points out "The age determines the Law". A law is only a corrective to enable a society to function well. Foolishness and image worship are in the worship of form. Knowledge is in understanding that truth is not finite material form but the infinite spirit inherent in all forms. This realization is the highest knowledge.

Truth is with us and all around us. We have but to realise it. Understanding of Truth comes by freeing our minds of the mental barriers that we ourselves impose. This realisation leads to liberation because Truth is ever-free. Paradoxically, liberation does not promote self-indulgence, but self-restraint, not selfishness but selflessness.

Knowledge is infinite. The understanding of the spirit of the Vedas is to go "Onwards with the Vedas".

Chronological Table of Important Works

This chronological table is given by P.V. Kane in his *History of the Dharmasastra* as those referred to by him in his work. But this also serves to show us perhaps better than anything else, the continuous literary tradition that has come down to us from the most ancient times, which gives India the first place among nations of being the oldest continuous civilization.

Knowledge has not only to be retained but also augmented. Activity is essential in life. Activity alone can keep knowledge alive. Inertia which is a property of nature intervenes all too often. The easier way is often the lazier way. This results in due course in the obliteration of knowledge. With the passage of time we also see changes in language and meanings of words. It becomes necessary to bring earlier works up to date in order that they be fully understood. This has been done continuously in each successive age.

4000–1000 BC: Period of Vedic Samhitas, Brahmanas, and Upanishads.

Some hymns of the Rig Veda, Taittiriya Samhita, Brahmanas and the Atharvaveda may possibly go back to an even earlier period than 4000 BC and some Upanishads (even those regarded, as the earliest ones) may be later than 1000 BC.

800–500 BC:	The Nirukta.

The Nirukta of Yaska which is one of six *Angas* of the Vedanga is an extensive work and deals with the derivation of words semantics, explanations of several hundred Vedic verses in whole or in part. It claims that without its help one cannot understand the meaning of the Veda, that it has a purpose of its own and is a complement of grammar, and it contraverts at great length the view of Kautsa that Vedic mantras have no meaning (or purpose) and emphatically asserts that Vedic mantras have a meaning (and a purpose) because the words they contain are the same as those employed in popular speech and that a Brahmana passage states that Sacrifice has a perfect form when a Rk verse or Yajur formula refers to the rite that is being performed (H.D. by P.Y. Kane, Vol.V, pt.2, chap.XXIX, Sec.VII, p.1275).

800–400 BC:	The principle Srauta Sutras (of Apastamba, Asvalayana, Baudhayana, Katyayana, Sankhyayana, Latyayana, Drahyayana, Satyasadha) and some of the grhyasutras (Asvalayana, Apastamba etc.) and Vedanga Jyotisa.
600–300 BC:	The Dharmasutras of Gautama, Apastamba, Baudhayana, Vasishta and the Grhyasutras of Paraskara, Baudhayana, and some others.
600–300 BC:	Panini.
500–200 BC:	Jaimini's Purvamimamsasutra.
500–200 BC:	The Bhagavadgita.
300 BC:	The Vartikas of Vararuci, Katyayana on Panini's grammar.
300 BC–AD 100:	(closer to former date) Kautilya's Arthasastra.
200 BC–AD 100:	The Manusmriti.
150 BC–AD 100:	(closer to former) Mahabhasya of Patanjali.
100BC–AD 100:	Upavarsa, author of commentary on Purvamimamsasutra and Vedantasutra.
100 BC–AD 300:	Patanjali, author of Yogasutra.

AD 100–300:   Yajnavalkyasmriti.

AD 100–300:   Vishnudharmasutra.

AD 100–400:   Naradasmriti.

AD 200–400:   (closer to former) Sabara, author of Bhasya on Purvamimamsasutra.

AD 200–500:   Vaikhanasa-Smartasutra.

AD 250–325:   Sankhyakarika of Isvarakrsna.

AD 300–500:   Brhaspatismriti on Vyavahara and other topics (not yet found).

AD 300–600:   Some of the extant Puranas, such as Vayu, Brahmanda, Vishnu, Markandeya, Kurma, Matsya.

AD 400–600:   Katyayanasmrti on Vyavahara (not yet found).

AD 400–600:   Kamandakanitisara.

AD 400–500:   Matharavrti on Sankhyakarika.

AD 400–500:   Yogasutrabhasya of Vyasa.

AD 476:   Birth of Aryabhatta, author of Aryabhattiya.

AD 505–587:   Varahamihira, author of Brihtsamhita Brihajjataka, Pancasiddhanta etc.

AD 550–700:   Yuktidipika, commentary on Sankhyakarika.

AD 600–650:   Bana, author of Kadambari and Harshacharita.

AD 650–660:   Karika of Vamana and Jayaditya, commentary on Panini's grammar.

AD 650–750:   Kumarilabhatta, author of Slokavartika, Tantravartika and Tuptika.

AD 600–900:   Most of the Smritis and some of the Puranas.

AD 680–725:   Mandana.

AD 700–750:   Gaudapada, author of commentary on Sankhyakarika and Paramaguru of Sankaracharya.

AD 788–900:   Shankaracharya, the great Advaita philosopher, author of Bhasyas on the Gita, Principal Upanishads and the Vedantasutras.

AD 800–850:   Visvarupa, com. of Yajnavalkyasmrti.

AD 900:   Medhatithi, commentary on Manu.

AD 900–1100:   Parthasarathimisra, author of Sastradipika, Tantraratna, Nyayaratnakar.

AD 966:   Utpala, commentator of Brihat-Samhita, Brihj-
                jataka.
AD 1000–1055:   Dharesvara (Bhoja), author of numerous works
                such as Yuktikalpataru, Rajamartanda (a comment-
                ary on Yogasutra).
AD 1070–1100:   Vijnaneshwara, author of the Mitaksara,
                commentary on Yajnavalkya.
AD 1050–1150:   Bhavanatha, author of Nayaviveka.
AD 1080–1140:   Govindaraja, author of commentary on Manu-
                smrti.
AD 1100–1150:   Lakshmidhar, author of a large digest called Krtya-
                kalpataru.
AD 1100–1130:   Apararka, A Silahara king, author of an extensive
                comm. on Yajnavalkya.
AD 1100–1150:   Jimutavahana, author of Dayabhaga, Kalaviveka,
                and Vyavaharamatrika.
AD 1127–1138:   Manasollasa of Someswaradeva.
AD 1114–1183:   Bhaskaracharya, author of Siddhanta-siromani of
                which Lilavati is a part.
AD 1150–1160:   Rajatarangini of Kalhana.
AD 1150–1180:   Aniruddhabhatta, author of Haralata and Pitra-
                dayita and Guru of Balalasena, king of Bengal.
AD 1150–1200:   Smrtyarthasastra of Sridhara.
AD 1150–1300:   Haradatta, commentator on Dharmasutras of
                Gautama and Apastamba and some Grhyasutras.
AD 1200–1225:   Smritichandrika of Devanabhatta.
AD 1150–1200:   Kulluka, author of *Manvartha Muktavali*, comment-
                ary on Manusmrti.
AD 1200–1300:   Vyavaharanirnaya of Varadaraja.
AD 1260–1270:   Hemadri's Caturvargacintamani.
AD 1279–1310:   Sridatta, author of Pitrbhakti, Samaya-pradipa,
                and other works.
AD 1290–1370:   Candeswara, author of the Grhastha-ratnakara
                and other Ratnakaras.
AD 1300–1380:   Madhavacharya, author of Jaiminiyanyayamala-
                vistara, Parasara-Madhaviya etc.

AD 1300–1386: Sayana, author of Bhasyas of Vedic Samhitas and Brahmanas.

AD 1360–1390: Madanaparijata compiled under King Madanapala.

AD 1360–1448: dates of birth and death of Vidyapathi, author of Gangavakyavali and other works, patronised by several kings of Mithila.

AD 1375–1460: Sulapani, author of Dipakalika, Tithiviveka, Ekadasiviveka and several works on Dharmasastras called Vivekas.

AD 1425–1450: King Madansimha completed a large digest called Madanaratna.

AD 1375–1500: Digest composed by Prithvichandra, son of Nagamala called Dharmattavasudhanidhi.

AD 1400–1450: Nyayasudha of Someswar, a commentary on Tantravartika.

AD 1425–1460: Rudradhara, author of Varsakrtya, Suddhiviveka, etc.

AD 1425–1490: Vacaspati, author of Krtyacintamani and other works called Cintamani and some called Nirnaya.

AD 1440–1500: Vardhamana, author of Dandaviveka, Gangakrtyaviveka etc.

AD 1490–1512: The Vyavaharasara of Dalapati a part of the Nrsimhaprasada.

AD 1500–1525: The Sarasvativilasa compiled under King Prataprudradeva.

AD 1512–1570: Raghunandana, author of many works called Tattavas.

AD 1554–1626: Appayadiksita, author of Vidhirasayana and numerous works on different sastras and topics.

AD 1560–1620: Shankarabhatta, son of Narayanabhatta and author of Dvaitanirnaya, Mimamsabalaprakasa and other works.

AD 1590–1630: Nandapandita, author of Dvaitanirnaya, Vaijayanti (commentary on Vishnudharmasutra).

AD 1600–1665: Khandadeva, author of Bhattakaustuba and Bhattadipika.

AD 1610–1640: Time of literary activity of Kamlakara-bhatta, a author of Nirnayasindhu, Sudrakamalakara and many other works.

AD 1610–1640: Mitramisra, author of a huge digest called Viramitrodaya on Tirtha, Puja, Samaya and many other topics.

AD 1615–1645: Nilakanthabhatta, son of Shankarabhatta and author of digests on topics on Achara, Samskara, Vyavahara etc.

AD 1620–1690: Visvesvara alias Gagabhatta author of Bhatta-cintamani and other works.

AD 1645–1675: Probable period of literary activity of Ananta-deva, author of a large digest called Smrti-kaustubha.

AD 1670–1750: Nagesha or Nagijibhatta, an encyclopaedic writer on Grammar, Poetics, Dharmasastra, Yoga and other sastras.

AD 1700–1740: Smrtimuktaphala of Vaidyanatha.

AD 1790:   Date of the composition of the Dharmasindhu-sara by Kashinatha Upadhay.

AD 1750–1820: Balambhatta, author of Balambhatti, a comment-ary on Mitaksara.

(A sutra (aphorism) should be concise, containing a few letters, but clear in its meaning, substantial, of wide application, should be without pauses and interjected letters and should be faultless.

A Bhasya is that which sets out the meaning of the sutras in sentences that follow the words of the sutras and that makes its own contribution to the elucidation of the subject of the sutra.

A Vartika considers what is stated in the sutra and what is omitted or not well stated).

Pronounication of words rendered from
English to Devanagari

Aayamatma	अयमात्मा	Arsa	आर्ष
Abhimanyu	अभिमन्यु	Artha	अर्थ
Adhikarana	अधिकरण	Arthasastra	अर्थशास्त्र
Adhyatma	अध्यात्म	Aryabhatta	आर्यभट्ट
Advaita	अद्वैत	Asana	आसन
Aganda	अगंद	Asrama	आश्रम
Agastya	अगस्त्य	Asura	असुर
Agni	अग्नि	Asuri	आसुरी
Agnicurna	अग्निचूर्ण	Asvamedha	अश्वमेघ
Ahamkara	अहंकार	Asvini	अश्विनी
Aharya	आहार्य	Atharva	अथर्व
Ahimsa	अहिंसा	Atri	अत्रि
Aitareya	एतरेय	Ayas	अयस्
Ajagana	अजागण	Ayodhya	अयोध्या
Akakathana	अकाकथन		
Aksaramusti	अक्षरमुष्टि	Badarayanacharya	बादरायणाचार्य
Aksauhini	अक्षौहिणी	Badari	बदरि
Alekhya	आलेख्य	Bana	बाण
Amba	अम्बा	Baudhayana	बौधयन
Ambalika	अम्बालिका	Bhagavadgita	भगवद्गीता
Ambika	अम्बिका	Bhagawan	भगवान्
Amrita	अमृत	Bhagwat	भागवत
Anandamaya	आनन्दमय	Bhanga	भंग
Anasuya	अनसूया	Bharata	भरत
Angaraga	अजगराज	Bharatvarsha	भारतवर्ष
Animan	अणिमन	Bhargava	भार्गव
Ankusa	अंकुश	Bhasa	भास
Annamaya	अन्नमय	Bhaskara	भास्कर
Anusasana	अनुशासन	Bhasya	भाष्य
Apala	अपाला	Bhaume	भौम
Apastamba	आपस्तम्ब	Bhava	भाव
Apurva	अपूर्व	Bhavabhuti	भवभूति
Aranyaka	आरण्यक	Bhavati	भवति
Aranyakanda	अरण्यकाण्ड	Bhavisya	भविष्य
Arjuna	अर्जुन	Bhima	भीम

Bhishma	भीष्म	Dadu	दादू
Bhutta Vidya	भूतविद्या	Daiva	दैव
Bhoja	भोज	Daksa	दक्ष
Brahmagupta	बह्मगुप्त	Damayanti	दमयन्ती
Brahmana	ब्राह्मण	Damyata	दम्यत
Brahma Sphuta Sidhanta	ब्राह्मस्फुट सिद्धान्त	Dasaratha	दशरथ
Brahmavaivarta	ब्रह्मवैवर्त	Dasbodh	दासबोध
Brahmavid- Brahmiva	ब्राह्मविद् ब्रह्मैव	Dassera	दसेरा
		Datta	दत्त
		Daya	दया
Brahmi	ब्राह्मी	Dayabhaga	दायभाग
Brhat Samhita	बृहत संहिता	Dayadhwam	दयध्वम्
Brihadharanyaka	बृहदारण्यक	Desabhasya- vignana	देशभाषाविज्ञान
Brihadvaisnava- tosini	बृहद्वैष्णव– तोषिणि		
Brihaspati	बृहस्पति	Deva	देव
Buddha	बुद्ध	Devala	देवल
Buddhi	बुद्धि	Dhanvantari	धन्वन्तरि
		Dharana	धारण
		Dharanamatrika	धारणमातृका
Chaitanya	चैतन्य	Dharini	धारिणी
Chakra	चक्र	Dharma	धर्म
Chakravala	चक्रवाल	Dharmaraja	धर्मराज
Chanakya	चाणक्य	Dharmasastra	धर्मशास्त्र
Chandala	चाण्डाल	Dhritarashtra	धृतराष्ट्र
Chandogya	छान्दोग्य	Dhruva	ध्रुव
Chandrakanti	चन्द्रकान्ति	Dhyana	ध्यान
Chandragupta	चन्द्रगुप्त	Dista	दिष्ट
Charaka-Sakha	चरकशाखा	Divali	दिवाली
Charaka Samhita	चरक संहिता	Dnyaneswar or Jhaneswar	ज्ञानेश्वर
Charandas	चरणदास		
Charvaka	चार्वाक	Draupadi	द्रौपदी
Chaturvarna	चतुर्वर्ण	Drupad	द्रुपद
Chedi	चेदि	Drona	द्रोण
Chedya	छेद्य	Durasravana- drsanacinta	दूरश्रवणदर्शन– चिन्ता
Chhandas-sutra	छन्दस्सूत्र		
Chokhamela	चोखामेला	Durmukha	दुर्मुख
		Duryodhana	दुर्योधन
Daan	दान	Dushyanta	दुष्यन्त

Dusshasana	दुश्शासन	Isitva	ईशित्व
Duta	दूत	Isvara	ईश्वर
Dvapara	द्वापर		
Dvija	द्विज	Jabala	जाबाल
		Jabali	जाबालि
Ekadanti	एकदन्ती	Jagat	जगत्
Esya	एष्य	Jambudveepa	जम्बूद्वीप
		Janaka	जनक
Gandhari	गान्धारी	Janardana	जनार्दन
Ganga	गंगा	Janasruti	जनश्रुति
Ganitsahastra-	गणितसहस्र-	Jarjara	जर्जर
Sangraha	संग्रह	Jatayu	जटायु
Ganitatalika	गणिततालिका	Jati	जाति
Gargi Vacaknavi	वाचक्नवी	Jayadratha	जयद्रथ
Garuda	गरूड	Jayamangala	जयमङ्गला
Gautama	गौतम	Jiva	जीव
Ghatasphota	घटस्फोट	Joytisi Vedanga	ज्योतिषि वेदाङ्ग
Ghosa Kakrivati	घोषा काकृवती		
Gita Govinda	गीत गोविन्द	Kabir	कबीर
Gorakhnath	गोरखनाथ	Kaikeyi	कैकेयी
Goswami	गोस्वामी	Kaivalya	कैवल्य
Govadha	गोवध	Kalasa	कलश
Grhya	गृह्य	Kali	कलि
Guna	गुण	Kalidasa	कालिदास
		Kalivarjya	कलिवर्ज्य
Hanuman	हनुमान	Kalpa	कल्प
Hardrumatta-	हर्दुमत्त गौतम	Kalpataru	कल्पतरू
Gautama		Kama	काम
Hastinapur	हस्तिनापुर	Kamadhenu	कामधेनु
Hatha	हठ	Kamala	कमला
Hiranyaksa	हिरण्याक्ष	Kamandaka	कामन्दक
Hiranyakasipu	हिरण्यकशिपु	Kamasutra	कामसूत्र
Hemadri	हेमाद्रि	Kanada	कणाद
Hinayana	हीनयान	Kandu	कण्डू
Hri	ह्री	Kapila	कपिल
		Kapilavastu	कपिलवस्तु
Indra	इन्द्र	Karma	कर्म
Isavakya	ईशावाक्य	Karna	कर्ण

Karttavirya	कार्तवीर्य	Licchavi	लिच्छवि
Katha	कठ	Linga	लिङ्ग
Katyayana	कात्यायन	Lokayatika	लोकायतिक
Kaumara bhrty	कौमार भृत्य	Ludhra-renu	लोध्ररेणु
Kausalya	कौसल्या		
Kaustaba	कौस्तुभ	Madhusudan	मधुसूदन
Kautilya	कौटिल्य	Madhu vidya	मधुविद्या
Kaya chikitsa	काया चिकित्सा	Madhwa	माध्व
Kena	केन	Madri	माद्री
Ketu	केतु	Mahabharata	महाभारत
Khamboja	कम्बोज	Maharishi	महर्षि
Khandakhyadaka	खण्डनखाद्य	Mahasiddhanta	महासिद्धान्त
Khandikeya	खाडिण्केंय	Mahavira	महावीर
Kosala-Videha	कोसलविदेह	Mahayana	महायान
Krama	क्रम	Mahendravarma	महेन्द्रवर्मन्
Krishna	कृष्ण	Mahiman	महिमन
Krita	कृत	Maindreya	मैन्द्रेय
Krytyakalpataru	कृत्यकल्पतरू	Maitreya	मैत्रेय
Ksama	क्षमा	Maitreyi	मैत्रेयी
Kshatriya	क्षत्रिय	Malla	मल्ल
Kumarilla	कुमारिल्ल	Manana	मनन
Kuru-Panchala	कुरुपांचाल	Manasara	मानसार
Kusinara	कुशीनारा	Manasottara	मानसोत्तर
Kularnava	कुलर्णव	Manava	मानव
Kulluka	कुल्लूक	Mandala	मण्डल
Kumbha	कुम्भ	Mandukya	माण्डुक्य
Kumbhakarna	कुम्भकर्ण	Mani-bhoomika-karma	मणि भूमिका-कर्म
Kunti	कुन्ती		
Kurma	कूर्म	Manomaya	मनोमय
Kurupada	कुरूपाद	Manthara	मन्थरा
Kusumaracharya	कुसुमाराचार्य	Mantra nukta	मंत्र नुक्ता
		Manusmirti	मनुस्मृति
Laghuman	लघुमान	Manvantara	मन्वन्तर
Lakshmana	लक्ष्मण	Marisha	मारिष
Lakshanavali	लक्षणावलि	Markandeya	मार्कण्डेय
Lalitavistara	ललितविस्तर	Mathura	मथुरा
Lavanya	लावण्य	Matsya	मत्स्य
Lekhya	लेख्य	Matsyendranath	मत्स्येन्द्रनाथ

Maurya	मौर्य	Panchala	पाञ्चाल
Maya	माया	Panchasikha	पाञ्चशिख
Meru Prastara	मेरु प्रस्तर	Panchavati	पञ्चवटी
Mimamsa	मीमांसा	Pandu	पाण्डु
Mirabai	मीराबाई	Panini	पाणिनि
Mitaksara	मिताक्षरा	Parachittajnyana	परचित्तज्ञान
Mithila	मिथिला	Parasnath	पारसनाथ
Mleccha	म्लेंच्छ	Parasara	पराशर
Mohini	मोहिनी	Parasu	परशु
Munduka	मुण्डुक	Parikshit	परिक्षित
Muni Asita	मुनि असित	Parsurama	परशुराम
		Patanjali	पतञ्जलि
Nachiketas	नचिकेतस्	Paulisa	पौलिष
Nagarjuna	नागार्जुन	Phenaka	फेणक
Naimittika	नैमित्तिक	Pinda	पिण्ड
Naksatra	नक्षत्र	Pingala	पिङ्गल
Nakula	नकुल	Poonarjanma	पुनर्जन्म
Nala	नल	Prabhakara	प्रभाकर
Nalanda	नालन्दा	Prachinaverhis	प्राचीनवर्हिस्
Namdeo	नामदेव	Pradhana	प्रधान
Nanak	नानक	Prahlad	प्रह्लाद
Narada	नारद	Prajapatya	प्रजापत्य
Naradiya	नारदीय	Prakamya	प्राक्मय
Narsingh Mehta	नरसिंह मेहता	Prakriti	प्रकृति
Natya-nrtya	नाट्यनृत्य	Prakrit	प्राकृत
Nisada	निषाद	Pramanam	प्रमाणम्
Niyama	नियम	Pramlocha	प्रम्लोचा
Niyoga	नियोग	Prana	प्राण
Nyaya	न्याय	Pranamaya	प्राणमय
		Prapti	प्राप्ति
Om	ॐ	Prarabdha	प्रारब्ध
		Prasna	प्रश्न
Padapatha	पदपाठ	Prayaschitta	प्रायश्चित्त
Padma	पद्मा	Preta	प्रेत
Paitamiha	पितामह	Pritha	पृथा
Pana	पाना	Prithu	पृथु
Panchabhautic	पञ्चभौतिक	Purana	पुराण

Purta	पूर्त	Salya	शल्य
Purusa	पुरुष	Sama	साम
Purusartha	पुरुषार्थ	Samadhi	समाधि
Purusasukta	पुरुषसूक्त	Samata	समता
Purushottama	पुरुषोत्तम	Samdhan	संधान्
Purvamimamsa-sutra	पूर्वीमीमांसासूत्र	Samhitopanisad-Brahmana	सम्हितोपनिषद्-ब्राह्मण
		Samskara	संस्कार
Rahu	राहू	Sanatana	सनातन
Raikwa	रैक्व	Sanat Kumar	सनतकुमार
Rajas	रजस्	Sanjaya	संजय
Ramananda	रामानन्द	Sankha-likhila	शंखलिखित
Ramayana	रामायण	Sankhya	सांख्य
Ramdas	रामदास	Sanskara	संस्कार
Rasa Siddha	रससिद्ध	Sanskrit	संस्कृत
Rasa Vidya	रसविद्या	Santanu	शन्तनु
Rasayana	रसायन	Saptadhatu	सप्तधातु
Ras lila	रास लीला	Sastitantra	शष्टितन्त्र
Ratnamrta-Visesanirman	रत्नामृतविशेष-निर्माण	Sastra	शास्त्र
		Satagni	शताग्नि
Rk	ऋच्	Satanika	शतनीक
Romaka	रोमाक	Satapatha-Brahmana	शतपथब्राह्मण
Rukmini	रुक्मिणी		
Rupa-Bheda	रूपभेद	Satkaryavad	सत्कार्यवाद
		Satwa	सत्व
Sabara	शबर	Satya	सत्य
Sabda	शब्द	Satyakama	सत्यकाम
Sabhasa	सभाषा	Satyavana	सत्यवान्
Sadachara	सदाचार	Saundriya	सेन्द्रिय
Sadhana	साधन	Saura	सौर
Sadharana	साधारण	Sauria	सौर्या
Sadhu	साधु	Sautramani	सौत्रामणि
Sadrisya	सादृश्य	Savitri	सावित्री
Sahadeva	सहदेव	Shakuntala	शकुन्तला
Sajeeva	सजीव	Shamasastri	शमाशास्त्रि
Sakya	साक्य	Shankaracharya	शंकराचार्य
Salakya	शालाक्य	Shanti parva	शान्ति पर्व

Shraddha	श्राद्ध	Swarga	स्वर्ग
Shravana	श्रवण	Swastika	स्वस्तिक
Shuddhi	शुद्धि	Swayambhu	स्वयम्भु
Siddha	सिद्ध	Sweta	श्वेत
Siddhanta- Siromani	सिद्धान्त- शिरोमणि	Taittiriya	तैत्तिरीय
Siddhi	सिद्धि	Takshasila	तक्षशीला
Siksa Valli	शिक्षावली	Tamas	तमस्
Sita	सीता	Tandu	तण्डु
Sivya	सीव्य	Tanmatra	तन्मात्र
Skanda	स्कन्द	Tantra	तन्त्र
Slokavartika	श्लोकवार्तिक	Tantravarlika	तन्त्रवार्लिक
Smartha	स्मार्थ	Taranath	तारानाथ
Smirti	स्मृति	Tattwamasi	तत्वमसि
Snatah-pramanya	स्नत:प्रामाण्य	Thyaga	त्याग
Soma	सोम	Thyagaraja	त्यागराज
Srauta	श्रौत	Tirthasthana	तीर्थस्थान
Sri	श्री	Treta	त्रेता
Sridhara	श्रीधर	Tukaram	तुकाराम
Sri Krishna	श्री कृष्ण	Tulsidas	तुलसीदास
Sripati	श्रीपति		
Subhadra	सुभद्रा	Uddalaka Aruni	उदालक आरुणि
Sudra	शूद्र	Udvartana	उध्वर्तन
Sukaspati	शेकस्पति	Udyog Parva	उद्योग पर्व
Sukra	शुक्र	Upanayana	उपनयन
Sukracharya	शुक्राचार्य	Upanishad	उपनिषद
Sulabha Maitreyi	सुलभा मैत्रेयी	Upanishadika	उपनिषदिक
Suniti	सुनीति	Uttanapada	उत्तानपाद
Surdas	सूरदास		
Suruchi	सुरुची	Vadana Pratitheyi	वदना प्रातिथेयी
Surya	सूर्य	Vadhula	वाधूल
Surya Siddhanta	सूर्यसिद्धान्त	Vaijaiyaki	वैजयिकी
Susruta Samhita	सुश्रुत संहिता	Vainaijiki	वैनेयिकी
Suvarna	सुवर्ण	Vairajya	वैराज्य
Svabhava	स्वभाव	Vaisheshika	वैशेषिक
Svetaketu	श्वेतकेतु	Vaisya	वैश्य
Svetasvetara	श्वेताश्वतर	Vajja	विज्जा

Vaji Karan	वाजीकरण	Vigyana Brahma	विज्ञान ब्रह्म
Vajra	वज्र	Vijnanamaya	विज्ञानमय
Valmiki	वाल्मिकी	Vikramacharita	विक्रमचरित
Vamana	वामन	Vikramaditya	विक्रमादित्य
Vanaspati Vidya	वनस्पतिविद्या	Vikramasila	विक्रमशीला
Vande Mataram	वन्दे मातरम्	Viraj	विराज
Varaha	वराह	Virata	विराट
Varaha Mihira	वराहमिहिर	Vishnugupta	विष्णुगुप्त
Varna	वर्ण	Vishnu Puran	विष्णुपुराण
Varnika	वर्णिका	Vishnuvyasa	विष्णुव्यास
Vashishta	वसिष्ठ	Visravya	विश्राव्य
Vasitva	वशित्व	Visvakarma	विश्वकर्मा
Vasnika	वासनिक	Visvamitra	विश्वामित्र
Vastu Vidya	वस्तुविद्या	Visvavara	विश्ववारा
Vasudeva	वासुदेव	Visvesvara	विश्वेश्वर
Vayu	वायु	Vrksayurvedayoga	वृक्षायुर्वेदयोग
Veda	वेद	Vyakta	व्यक्त
Vedhya	वेध्य	Vyasa	व्यास
Vedanta	वेदान्त	Vyayamiki	व्यायामिकी
Vena	वेण		
Vesali	वेसाली	Yajnavalkya	याज्ञवल्क्य
Vetalapanca-	वेतालपंचविशती	Yama	यम
vimsati		Yajur	यजूर:
Vibhishana	बिभिषण	Yatrakamana-	यत्रकामान–
Vibhuti	विभूति	sayitva	सार्जित्व
Videha	विदेह	Yoga	योग
Vidura	विदुर	Yudhishtira	युधिष्ठिर

Bibliography

Acton, *Lectures on Modern History.*
Agrawala, V.S., *Studies in Indian Art*, Varanasi, 1968.
Al-Biruni, *Qanun al-Masudi.*
Anil de Silva, *The Spice and the Silk Road.*
Arnold, Edwin, *The Light of Asia.*
Aryabhatta I, *Aryabhatiya.*
Aryabhatta II, *Mahasiddhanta.*
as-Razi's, *Kitab al-hawi* (AD 865-925).

Bankim Chandra, *Ananda Math.*
Banerjee, P., *Hindu Scriptures in Ancient Afghanistan.*
Basham, A.L., *The Wonder That Was India*, 1975.
Baudouin, M. Charles, *Suggestion and Auto-suggestion*, Allen and Unwin, 1922.
Barth, A., *Religions of India.*
Bhandarkar, R.G., *A Peep into the Early History of India*, Bombay, 1930.
Bhaskara II, *Siddhanta Shiromani.*
Burton, Richard (Tr.), *The Kamasutra of Vatsyayana*, Bombay, 1974.

Cajori, *A History of Elementary Mathematics.*
Cambridge History of India, Vol.3.
Chaitanya, K., *Profile of Indian Culture*
Chaitanya, K., *A New History of Sanskrit Literature*, New Delhi, 1977.
Chidbhavananda, Swami, *Commentary on the Bhagavadgita*, Sri Ramakrishna
    Tapovam, 1984.
Ching Ping Mei (A Chinese Classic).
Coomaraswamy, A.K., *Art and Swadeshi.*
Coomaraswamy, A.K., *Hinduism and Buddhism.*
Coster, Geraldine, *Yoga and Western Psychology*, OUP, 1934.
Cultural Heritage of India, 4 Vols., Calcutta, 1970.

Davids, Rhys, *Journal of the Pali Text Society* for 1896.
Dickinson, Lowes, *Religion and Immortality*.
Dutt, Romesh, *Economic History of India*.
Dutt, Romesh, *The Great Epics of Ancient India*, New Delhi, 1976.

Elliot & Dowson, *History of India*, 8 Vols.
Elphinstone, M., *History of India*, 2 Vols.

Gandhi, M.K., *The Teachings of the Gita*, Bombay.
Ganguli, A.B., *Fine Arts in Ancient India*, New Delhi, 1979.
Gasoigne, Bamber, *The Christians*.
Gibbon, *Decline and Fall of Roman Empire*.
Gopinath Rao, T.A., *Elements of Hindu Iconography*, 4 Vols.
Gowen, H.H., *History of Indian Literature*, 1931.
Guthrie, *History of Medicine*.

Hibbert, *Great Mutiny*.
Hothouse, L.T., *Moral in Evolution*, 1916.

India's Contribution to World Thought and Culture, Madras, 1970.

Jayadeva, *Gita Govinda*.
Jehangir, *Memoirs*.

Kamasutra of Vatsyayana.
Kane, P.V., *History of Dharamshastra*, 5 Vols. in 8 parts, Pune.
Kautilya's *Arthasastra*.
Kriplani, J.B., *Gandhi: His Life and Thought*, New Delhi, 1970.

Lea, Henry C., *Superstition and Force*.
Low, Sydney, *Vision of India*, 1907.

Maine, H.S., *Ancient Law*, Agra, 1970.
Mahavira, *Ganitasarasangraha*.
Mehta, Rohit, *The Call of the Upanishad*, Bombay, 1970.
Minakshi, C., *Administration and Social Life under the Pallavas*, Madras, 1938.
Mitra, R.C., *Decline of Buddhism in India*, Shantiniketan, 1954.

Naoroji, Dadabhai, *Poverty and un-British Rule in India*, Delhi, 1969.
Nehru, Jawaharlal, *Discovery of India*.

Panchatantra.
Patanjali, *Mahabhasya*.
The Perfumed Garden (An Arabic Classic).

Ram Tirtha, Swami, *In the Woods of God Realisation*, 3 Vols.
Ranade, R.D., *Pathway to God in Hindu Literature*, Bombay, 1954.
Rolland, Romaine, *M.K. Gandhi*, New Delhi, 1976.
Roth, Cecil, *A Short History of the Jewish People*.
Rutter, Owen, *The Scales of Karma*.

Said al-Andalusi, *Kitab al-Uman*.
Said al-Andalusi, *Kitab Tabakat al-Uman* (The Categories of Nations).
Schopenhaur, *World is Will and Idea*.
Sharma, Chandradhar, *A Critical Study of Indian Philosophy*, London.
Shastri, K.A.N. & G. Srinivasachari, *Life and Culture of Indian People*, New Delhi, 1975.
Sherring, M.A., *Hindu Tribes and Castes*, 3 Vols.
Sridhara, *Ganitatilaka*.
Sivaramamurti, S., *The Painter in Ancient India*, Delhi, 1978.

Thapar, Romilla, *History of India*, Pelican, 1976.
Tilak, B.G., *The Gita Rahasya* (Marathi ed.).
Townsend, Meridith, *Europe and Asia*.
Toynbee, A., *Christianity among the Religions of the World*, 1958.
Toynbee, A., *Study of History*, OUP, 1973.

Udyana, *Nyaya Kusumanjali*.

Varahamihira, *Pancasiddhantatika*.
Varahamihira, *Surya Siddhanta*.

Westermack, *Origins and Development of Moral Ideas*, Vol.1, 1912.
William, Monier, *Modern India and Indians*, 5th ed., 1891.
Wilson, H.H., *Religion of the Hindus*, London, 1862.
Wilson, H.H., *Religion and Philosophical Systems of the Hindus*.
Winternitz, M., *Some Problems of Indian Literature*, Calcutta, 1925.

Yutan, Lin, *From Pagan to Christian*, Heinemann, 1960.
Yutang, Lin, *Wisdom of China and India*.

Index

Arjuna, excellent archer, 164; help
from Krishna, 165; wants
Krishna, 166; given Pasupat
by Shiva, 170; doubles his
attacks on Karna, 177;
surveying the opposing
forces, 183; faced with
conflicting loyalties, 184; not
easy to be convinced, 185;
flings himself into the battle,
190
army, consisted of people from all
varnas, 202, 25
Arsa, type of marriage, 326
Artha, for attainment of worldly
needs, 64
Arthasastra, rule of the
accomplishment of a visible
worldly purpose as a goal,
31; does not recommend
blind trust in worldly affairs,
51; deals with science of
government, 195; contents
of, 203; 1st published in 1909,
208; deals in all aspects
dealing with man's economic
well-being, 211; meant to
teach worldly wisdom, 215
Aryabhatta I, greatest work was
Aryabhatiya, 355; theory of
earth's rotation, 360
Aryan culture, earliest centre, 4
Aryans, vital and active people, 1;
origins of, 2; belong to Indo-
European group, 3; pure, 4
Aryavarta, in the *manusmriti*, 5
Asana, best posture for
meditation, 296
Ashoka, Emperor, his enlightened
rule, 11
Asrama Dharma, rules such as
begging etc., 101
Asramas, four stages of man's life,
64; three rivers, 136

Astronomy, from Rig Vedic
times, 358
Asura, type of marriage, 327; and
gods, 341
Aswamedha yajna, horse sacrifice,
72
Atma, realized only by an
illuminated intelligence, 85;
realized by meditating on it,
92; common cause of
evolution of all things, 239;
inspires good and bad acts,
240
atomism, theory of, 307;
propounded by Nyaya-
Vaisesikha, 365
Atri, refers various kinds of
Brahmins, 265
Aurangazeb changed the name of
Benares to Mohammedabad,
18; imposed jazzya tax on all
non-belivers, 23
Ayodhya, capital of Kosalas, 146;
a constitutional monarchy,
149
Ayurveda, the science of
medicine, 74; science of life,
360; spread to many places,
361; 8 limbs, 362; has divine
origin, 362

Barmaks, head priests of Buddhist
monastery, 353
Basham, A.L., on syllogism, 396-
397; on Syrian Church, 400;
on child marriages in India,
405-406
begging, by higher castes, 260;
not allowed by Smritis, 261;
as an occupation not
favoured, 421
Benares, has a hoary past, 18;
famous for cloth, 19
Besant, Annie, a Britisher also a
member of Congress, 36

abroad also, 219; provided
sex education to men and
women, 220; over fifteen
hundred years old, 232;
regarded as pornography by
western attitude, 233

Kamdhenu, all-bestowing cow,
342

Kanada, founder of Vaiseshikha,
304

Kane, P.V., on Brahmanical tribes,
387

Kapila, founder of Sankhya
philosophy, 291

Karma Kand, the Mantras and
Brahmanas together are
known as, 69; demanded acts
of valour and performances
of sacrifices, 79; rites of
sacrifice, 283

Karma, the doctrine of, 6, 237; all
action leads to some result,
66; means deeds, 69; law of,
187, 245, 246; in Rig Veda
means exploits, 235; belong
to physical universe, 238;
binds one to this world, 242;
is action, 274; does not mean
sin, 384

karmic acts, inspired by worldly
motives, 187

Karna, son of Kunti, 163;
challenges Arjuna, 164; vow
to kill Arjuna, 165; calls to
Arjuna, 177; killed in battle,
178; man of great virtues, 179

Katha Upanishad, deals with death,
82

Katyayana Smriti, on human
means of proof and divine
proof, 105

Kausalya, Rama's mother, 152

Kautilya, uses Vairajya for foreign
rule, 31; known as Chanakya,
195; stresses importance of

character in every profession,
196; a believer in the theory
of Mandala, 199; cites the
causes that lead to
improverishment, 201; no
time for world-renouncing
ascetism, 202; lived in the
AD 3rd or 4th century, 208;
good administration itself
was religion, 209; discusses
the enemy's army, 211-213

Kena Upanishad, points out that
function determines the
organ, 81

Khilji, Allauddin, destroyed 1000
temples, 17; destroyed
monks, 20.

King(s), duties of, 9; not
considered as having any
divine right, 11; cannot be
like sanyasi, 93; to safeguard
the special usages of guilds
etc., 111; divinity in human
form, 112; in kali age, 132;
good of the subjects, 146; in
India have been of all varnas,
197; qualities, 197, is state,
198; concern was justice, 199;
the ultimate court of appeal,
200; disciplining of, 203-204;
consider his country as God,
209; duty, 256-257, gave
rewards, 259

knowledge, is search for Truth,
53; one of the greatest gifts,
55; is eternal, 56; dispels
ignorance, 63; two types, 85;
not an end in itself, 85; of the
void gives value to things, 89;
2 kinds, 122; is that Spirit
which is one and in all, 186;
learn renunciation through,
188; not good or bad, 218; is
limitless, 232; essential for
any civilization, 251; highest